ALSO BY ABIGAIL KIRSCH

The Bride and Groom's First Cookbook

INVITATION TO DINNER

Abigail Kirsch's

Guide to

Elegant Entertaining

and Delicious

Dinners at Home

INVITATION TO DINNER

Abigail Kirsch
WITH DAVID NUSSBAUM

DOUBLEDAY

New York   London   Toronto

Sydney   Auckland

PUBLISHED BY DOUBLEDAY
a division of Bantam Doubleday Dell Publishing Group, Inc.
1540 Broadway, New York, New York 10036

DOUBLEDAY and the portrayal of an anchor
with a dolphin are trademarks of Doubleday, a division of
Bantam Doubleday Dell Publishing Group, Inc.

Book design by Marysarah Quinn
Illustrations by John Burgoyne

Library of Congress Cataloging-in-Publication Data
Kirsch, Abigail.
Invitation to dinner: Abigail Kirsch's guide to elegant
entertaining and delicious dinners at home / Abigail Kirsch
with David Nussbaum.
p.   cm.
Includes index.
1.   Entertaining.   2. Dinners and dining.   3. Menus.
I. Nussbaum, David.   II. Title.
TX731.K53   1998
642′.4—dc21   98-15169
CIP

ISBN 0-385-48817-3
Printed in the United States of America
November 1998
1   3   5   7   9   10   8   6   4   2
First Edition

FOR BOB

My Husband and Best Friend

Thank you for always being there for me.

ACKNOWLEDGMENTS

I am fortunate to have had the support of many extraordinary people whose tremendous skills have made this book a reality.

To my friend and personal editor, David Nussbaum, thank you for being the perfectionist you are and pushing me to reach the culinary pinnacles vital to this book. To Gayle Kirsch, my multitalented daughter-in-law, thank you for planting the seeds that made *Invitation to Dinner* a reality. To Alison Awerbuch, my friend, partner, and talented corporate executive chef, thank you for your steadfast support. An enormous thank you to Chefs Megan Neisser, Geraldine LaSala, and Laura Baldassarri and the entire kitchen staff at Abigail Kirsch, for being patient and listening to my culinary chatter in the middle of the "busy season." To photographer Mark Thomas and food stylist Rori Spinelli for understanding my concepts and their attention to detail. A special thank you to Stephanie Haims, who spent many hours with me in the kitchen testing the recipes, we had fun. To my editor at Doubleday, Judy Kern, thank you for having faith in me. Thank you to my agent, Pam Bernstein, who counseled me when I reached out. To Jim Kirsch, my son and partner, thank you for letting me vent my thoughts when the going got rough. To Margaret Happel, my good friend, thank you for all the priceless advice. To Fran Kelly, my invaluable assistant, thank you for your precision and dedication to this project.

CONTENTS

INVITATION TO DINNER

PART I

I Love Planning Parties!

AN INTRODUCTION TO THIS BOOK

I love planning parties, and it's a good thing I do: In a typical week, my banquet rooms are filled with guests for eight weddings, a couple of confirmation and bar mitzvah celebrations, a half dozen luncheons or brunch buffets for business clients, and maybe a wine tasting or two for community organizations. In addition, there are a dozen or more parties that my staff and I bring to museums, department stores, art galleries, private apartments, and country estates all over the New York area: cocktail and hors d'oeuvre parties, buffet suppers, and formal dinners for two to two thousand guests!

Catering parties has been my work for more than twenty-five years, whether in my turn-of-the-century mansion above the Hudson River, our Terrace Ballroom at The New York Botanical Garden, Pier Sixty on the Hudson in Manhattan, or in thousands of off-premise locations. All in all, my staff and I plan, prepare, and serve fabulous food to over 125,000 hungry guests every year. It's a lot to think about, a lot of food to cook, a lot of cleaning up to do—and I love it.

Yet it often seems that I have less and less time for the very parties I love the most: entertaining my friends and loved ones in my own home, cooking great new dishes that thrill my guests and wonderful feasts that bring the family together for special occasions. Like millions of Americans, my busy days at work just seem to lead to busy evenings and weekends. There are cooking classes to prepare for, culinary meetings to attend, new cookbook recipes to test—and a house and family to keep up with. There's the garage to clean out, the grandchildren to take to the zoo, a new computer to master. When the weekend's coming or holidays approach—when a special anniversary or milestone appears on the horizon—I hear myself asking the question I never thought would come out of my mouth: "Who's got time to plan a party?"

WHO'S GOT TIME TO FOLD NAPKINS, ANYWAY?

Of course, I am not the only person asking that question. I hear similar concerns from friends, students in my classes, and clients. Sociologists and food-service-industry reports tell us that fewer people are cooking and entertaining at home every year. And if you are one of these way-too-busy people, I am sure you are wondering how to fit entertaining—and all it entails—into your life:

How can you possibly pay back all the people who have invited you to dinner in the past—without sacrificing a year's worth of weekends in the process?

How can you possibly do a formal dinner when you don't have china or silver—and wouldn't have time to polish the silver if you did?

What can you possibly cook for a dinner to impress the boss—without having to call in sick in order to prepare it?

How can you possibly host an engagement party for your daughter's ninety "best friends"—when the dining table seats only six?

And then there's the most common question of all: How can you possibly do all the things a party needs and still manage to be the charming, gracious, witty, unflappable, and perfectly-at-ease host you have always wanted to be . . . even when the soufflé falls, the ice-cube maker breaks, or it rains on the day of your cookout?

I've written *Invitation to Dinner* to help you find answers to these and many other questions, to help you have fun rather than a headache when you invite people over. I can assure you that you *do* have the time for a party—one you will be proud of and that will please your guests. In the coming chapters, I will show you that by figuring out just what you want your party to be—knowing the things that you can really do and accepting the things you can't—you can have an event that will fit into your schedule, your home, your budget, and your taste.

Whether it's a spur-of-the-moment dinner for a few friends from work or an elaborate buffet with more dishes than you have ever cooked—and for more people than you have ever invited—I will show you how to do it without quitting your job or losing your cool. I will share with you menus, recipes, and cooking plans for a wide range of parties, each filled with choices to suit your taste, timing, and cooking ability. And I will give you hundreds of simple ways to create a party setting in your home, decorative and atmospheric touches that will let your guests know they are part of a special occasion.

In short, I wrote this book to help you rediscover—or experience for the first time—the special pleasure that comes from entertaining in your home. With the confidence that comes from thorough planning, and the acclaim that comes from serving your own delicious creations, you will find that being a host is no cause for alarm but rather an exhilarating, challenging, and uniquely rewarding activity.

CATERERS CREATE A GAME PLAN, AND YOU CAN, TOO

There's one thing this book won't do, however, and that is kid you about the basic facts: Entertaining at home does entail work. It demands time for planning and preparation, and it means that you can't sit around at your own party—at least not all the time. But I will be sharing with you my best party-planning strategies, tips, and shortcuts to help you limit the work, manage it wisely, and avoid disasters.

The most important strategy I will be teaching you—the key to an easy, efficient, and problem-free party—is to ask the right questions from the outset. As a professional, I help my clients figure out *exactly* what they want their parties to be and then figure out *exactly* what we must do to achieve it (our Party Game Plan) by answering a comprehensive set of questions. In this book, you will learn to think like a caterer about your own event: to consider everything that will happen, from sending out invitations until everything is cleaned up and put away. In the process, you will determine what you need to do at every stage, according to a schedule that works for you. In short, you will have created your own Party Game Plan.

HOW TO USE THIS BOOK

Entertaining at home is an art, not a science. Every party—even one planned and cooked exactly as I suggest—will have a unique character. That, of course, is just as it should be. I want your parties to reflect your personality, not mine. They will be expressions of what you like: your home, your food, and the special treatment you choose to give your guests.

There are no "rules" in my approach to party giving. Indeed, one of the great reasons to enjoy entertaining these days is that we are free to create our own party style. You don't have to be "formal" or "proper" to impress and please your guests. In fact, informality, spontaneity, and surprise are elements that can make a party truly fabulous.

What do *I* think is a fabulous party? What is *my* style of entertaining? In the next chapter I share with you my philosophy of being a host, the principles of party giving that I follow in my home. You may choose to do things differently, of course, and my purpose is to get you to think about these possibilities.

In Chapter 3, you will find an introduction to my basic categories of home entertainment. Each of these eight party formats—casual dinners, formal dinners, buffet dinners, outdoor grilling parties, family dinners, brunches, hors d'oeuvre parties, and dessert parties—has a distinct character, offers particular advantages, and places certain demands on the host. In Chapter 4, I will guide you through the essential questions to figure out

which party type is the best one for your special occasion and your home.

Once you have figured out what kind of event you want to have, it is time to create your game plan, as explained in Chapter 5. This is where I take you through the comprehensive planning that professionals do: asking all the right questions, making the decisions and schedules that will help you fit your party into your life—without having a fit. Making a game plan doesn't mean giving up what you want to do. Rather, it will help you to envision new possibilities. In fact, you might well discover that you can do more with your time, your home, and your cooking than you ever thought possible.

A TREASURY OF GREAT OCCASIONS AND MENUS

Part II of this book is where you will find the delicious details of planning and cooking each of the eight basic party formats. Each format is explored in several imaginatively conceived events, with different themes, menus, recipes, kitchen schedules, beverage suggestions, and decorating ideas. While the events I write about are somewhat fanciful, all the menus, recipes, schedules, and decorating information are absolutely real and suitable for *real* occasions.

You will notice that each menu has a main course ("The Main Event"), a dessert ("The Grand Finale"), and *two* sets of side dishes that are designated with the following symbols using a chef's toque: ♟ ; ♟ ♟ . The one-toque dishes are simpler to prepare and will allow you to complete your cooking in a shorter time. The two-toque dishes are somewhat more complicated, best suited for occasions when you have more time or kitchen help. *Both* sets of dishes are perfect accompaniments to the Main Event for that menu; both are delicious, and you should try them all!

These recipes are tremendously versatile, and I suggest various ways you can enjoy them in a feature called "The Inventive Chef." Each menu is designed to taste great as a whole and work perfectly for its particular party format, but you can certainly prepare the dishes for another party—or just try them for dinner one night (you'll have great leftovers!). Also, feel free to bring your own favorite recipes to the party menus. Dishes you love, and love to cook, are the ones that will be most appreciated by your guests.

Finally, the kitchen schedules that accompany each menu are an important part of your overall party game plan. These schedules outline an efficient way to prepare as much of your meal as possible *before* the party begins, and they will remind you of what must be done to complete and serve the meal smoothly *during* your party. You will find other helpful information throughout the book, in sidebars and in the appendixes on increasing your guest capacity, beverage service, food presentation, and other important topics. Remember, good planning ensures happy guests *and* a happy host. Enjoy!

Lessons from a Lifetime of Entertaining

MY PRINCIPLES OF PARTY GIVING

I will never forget the first time I cooked and served a meal to a visiting guest of honor. I was fourteen years old; the guest was my favorite uncle (visiting our Brooklyn home from far-away Boston); and the main dish was scrambled eggs.

I just adored my uncle and I can still feel the thrill I got from bringing a smile to his face with my cooking. Now, literally thousands of parties later, I have come to understand that this is what entertaining is really all about: making people I care for feel special through my efforts. Of course, throwing a hit party isn't always as easy as scrambling eggs (and I don't always love my guests as much as I did my uncle), but I want all my entertaining to have some of the unforgettable flavor of that day.

I have learned many lessons like this during my many years of professional observation—about what makes guests happy, what makes hosts satisfied, and what makes parties fun to give and to attend. These have made me a better caterer, but even more, they have helped me gain greater pleasure from being a host at home, especially when the hours spent preparing a party seem many times longer than the event itself.

It may sound corny, but I truly believe in the importance of entertaining well. Following are some of the most important lessons that guide me: *my* personal principles of party giving. I hope they get you thinking about the kind of host you want to be, what you want to share with your guests, and how to make entertaining an exciting and creative part of your life.

LESSON 1:
IT'S NOT ABOUT FOOD . . . IT'S ABOUT WELCOME!

Sometimes a friend will tell me about a party he or she has been to and say, "It was the most terrific party . . ."

Of course, I immediately ask, "What food did they serve?"

"You know," comes the surprised reply, "I don't even remember, I was having such a good time!"

Though I hope my guests don't ever forget the food *completely*, this is how a party should be. What makes any social gathering truly wonderful is the spirit and the atmosphere a host creates at home. It is providing an ambience that says to every guest, we welcome you to our home and we care about you. You are special to us, and with your presence, this occasion is special.

Certainly that spirit of welcome is not expressed in words alone, or in food alone, but in your total effort as a host, in every thoughtful gesture you make from the moment you open the door. Great food, beautiful decor, a relaxed and gracious attention to guests' needs: These are all the means by which you show guests your regard and affection.

LESSON 2:
ENTERTAINING IS ACCLAIM AND EXCITEMENT FOR THE HOST, TOO!

No one likes to admit it openly, but inside, we always want our parties to be a big hit. Clients for my catered parties will say they just want their guests to have a great time. But what they *really* want is for all their friends to call them up the next day and *really mean it* when they say, "That was the best party I ever attended!"

To desire acclamation for your entertaining efforts is natural, especially when you have done a party all by yourself. In fact, I think it's very important for a host to have pride and a bit of self-interest mixed in with the generous spirit of giving. Wanting to impress people is a perfectly acceptable motivation for giving great parties.

But the pleasure for a host goes much deeper than showing off. Long before I started catering, I loved to plan my dinner parties weeks ahead. I enjoyed the challenge of bringing all the elements together: creating new dishes, cooking for days, making a lovely stage setting for my feast and for stimulating conversation. Entertain-

ment is theater, of course, and the excitement of giving a great party is really like putting on a show.

Certainly for me—and I hope for you—as a host, the fun isn't just in the few hours the guests are in the house (though that has to be a pleasure too) but in all the time spent creating a magical space where people and food and drink and atmosphere all mesh perfectly. When it's over you can feel great for *days* about what you accomplished. The bigger the challenge, the greater the glory: I think hosts deserve it!

LESSON 3:
"FLOW" IS MORE IMPORTANT THAN "FANCY"

When I go to a party, I am ready to have a good time—*if* the host is ready for me. I am not a snob: I can have a great time sitting on the staircase or be perfectly happy with a good peanut-butter sandwich—*if* there is an atmosphere of ease and comfort in everything that is offered and everything that happens.

I call this the "flow" of a party, and it is one of my most important entertaining principles. I always want to be physically prepared and mentally in the mood to greet my guests and take care of their every need. From the moment they come through my door, I want them to experience a sense of welcome and readiness. And as my event progresses, I want that feeling to continue: to ensure that the party is without frenzy, that I don't get frazzled, and that everything flows easily and graciously.

Providing this smooth rhythm is, to me, the host's essential task. And there is only one way to achieve it: to think through all the stages of the party in advance and to anticipate what will make your guests, and you, happy and comfortable at all times. (That's your Party Game Plan—and that's what this book is all about!)

LESSON 4:
GUESTS ARE LIKE
KINDERGARTNERS: LET THEM
KNOW WHAT TO EXPECT

It doesn't matter how old, how sophisticated, or how dressed up they are—when they walk into a party, people are *always* a bit insecure. To me, they're just like kids on the first day of kindergarten: They don't know exactly what to expect, or what they are supposed to do—or who's going to take care of them.

If you are prepared, as a host should be, you will dispel this anxiety immediately. All it takes is for you—or perhaps your partner—to take their coats, direct them to the food and drinks, which you have all ready and waiting, and introduce them to someone with a mutual interest. Your mission is accomplished: You are taking care of them, and they feel fine. You have given them something to do ("Go fix yourself a drink" is a fine way to put a guest at ease) and have let them know what's coming.

The more you have told people about your party, the less will be their insecurity—and the quicker they will get into the flow of your event. Be certain that your invitation has communicated to them what to expect: what to wear and what you will be serving (see more about invitations in Chapter 5). To alleviate another point of high anxiety—sitting down at the dinner table in a group of strangers—consider using place cards (see more about this on page 80).

LESSON 5:
ENTERTAINING WELL MEANS
NEVER HAVING TO SAY
YOU'RE SORRY

Here's one of my least favorite party conversations:

Host: "What can I get you to drink?"

Guest: "I would love a vodka with a slice of lemon."

Host: "Oh, I'm sorry, I forgot to buy lemons. Maybe I can find one in the fridge. Hold on!"

Guest: "No, don't bother. It doesn't really matter . . ."

Dialogue like this makes me wish I had stayed home. The host feels embarrassed because he forgot something, the guest feels defensive because she appears fussy—and she *still* doesn't get the drink she wants. I *never* want to have to say "I'm sorry" to any of my guests' requests—and I truly hope this book will make it unnecessary for you to have to say it either. Make a game plan, think everything through before your party—and buy the lemons!

LESSON 6:
ENTERTAINING AT HOME IS A
"SERVICE BUSINESS," TOO

Catering is the ultimate service business. When I am catering in someone's home I have to be a perfect reflection of the host, down to her most detailed instructions. Are water glasses to be filled with ice or not? Will everyone's filet mignon be cooked medium-rare, or will they be cooked to order? But as the "expert," I have to go even further: Because my staff and I know all the things a party (and guests) demand, because we know all the things that can go wrong, we have to take all the extra steps. We have to be prepared for the guest who wants not just ice, but *only* bottled water. We have to be prepared for the guest who doesn't want any filet mignon—only vegetables.

It's helpful to me to think of entertaining at home as a "service business," too. Every time I invite people into my home I am undertaking a responsibility to do something special for them—to take the extra step. Even if it is just a spur-of-the-moment supper—or a friend coming over for tea—I am going to give it special attention. What vegetable can I serve with the lamb chops that will make our simple dinner seem special? What teacup will lend a lovely touch to our brief get-together? Even if it's my very closest friends whom I see all the time, I want to make it special: After all, it's most rewarding to take that extra step for people you truly care about.

LESSON 7:
"WHAT WORKS FOR ME?"
DEPENDS ON WHO YOU ARE

Where did my entertaining style come from? My mother had strict standards for proper dinner service, and, I admit, I grew up deeply influenced by her "of course" opinions: *Of course* you put linens on your table!

Of course you serve only your best wine! *Of course* you light the table with elegant tapers! *Of course* you always have beautiful flowers as a centerpiece. You even have fresh flowers in the bathroom!

Sometimes I feel old-fashioned in a world of casual and on-the-run entertaining. I have friends who can throw together a dinner party in the time I take to set my table (which I often do the night before the party). But I have to do things in my style because that's what works for me. It makes me happy, and it makes my guests happy, too.

But my (and my mother's) "of course" rules are not for everybody—of course. As the host and creator of a party, you must ask yourself, "What works for me?" "What will make me happy?" Is it okay with you if people sit anywhere they want in your house? Is it okay with you to serve simple dishes, so you can spend less time in the kitchen and more with your guests?

Discovering what truly works for you is the key to having parties that *you* will actually enjoy. As you use this book—choosing among the party formats, creating a realistic Party Game Plan that makes sense, picking a menu you will have fun cooking—make the choices that will make *you* happy, and will fit into *your* life and style. If they work for you, I believe, your decisions will make your guests happy and comfortable, too.

CHAPTER 3

Eight Great Events

MY FAVORITE FORMATS

FOR ENTERTAINING

WANT·TO·HAVE AND HAVE·TO· HAVE PARTIES

When I plan a party just to please myself, there are only a few things I absolutely need: a roaring fire; close friends to cook for; and to hear that it was the best meal they ever had! That's what I call a real "want·to·have" party. I want to have that party again and again.

But, for better or worse, life is filled with occasions for "have·to·have" parties, too: times when we have to have certain people to our house, must create a certain impression, or need to recognize an important family occasion. Perhaps the holiday season rolls around and there's a crowd of people we haven't seen in ages; or business calls for bringing VIPs to our home for an evening of formal dining; or one of our parents has reached a milestone year. This spurs me to think about all the different kinds of events we can do in our home, and pick the one that works best for the occasion.

No doubt, there are plenty of "want·to·haves" and no shortage of "have·to·haves" in your life, too. Use these occasions to try a new style of entertaining. If you need to take care of a crowd, consider a buffet or an hors d'oeuvre party. If you just want to see a few of your dearest friends but your schedules never seem to coincide, consider a brunch—and visit with them while you are cooking in the kitchen.

In this chapter I introduce a range of event possibilities, organized in eight different party formats (for which you will find detailed plans and menus in Part II of the book). In the next chapter, I will give you a professional's method for evaluating what's possible in your home. When you put together what you *can* do, with what you *want* or *have* to do, you will be well on your way to formulating a successful Party Game Plan. And when you are confident that the event you are planning is really going to work, even a "have·to·have" party can be a pleasure to produce.

1: CASUAL DINNERS

As we head into the twenty-first century, this is the standard for contemporary entertaining: casual dinners are special occasions with a relaxed attitude. This is the category into which I put my favorite kind of "drinks·

◆ 1 3

by-the-fire and soul-satisfying dinner party," but you don't need a fireplace to enjoy it. A few decorative touches and a welcoming spirit will give your home the classy but comfortable atmosphere you want. (And that—classy yet comfortable—is how everyone will be dressed as well.)

I plan casual dinners for small groups of friends and acquaintances who will enjoy one another's intimate company. I think eight is a wise maximum, but if you can seat only six at your dining table, that's your limit. The flow of this party is smooth and easy. Welcome your guests to fix drinks for themselves and enjoy canapés in the living room, which will be arranged for conversation. The dining table will be all ready to go with a charming seasonal centerpiece and colorful place mats—and mismatched dinnerware is okay! The food will be flavorful and plentiful; the wine unpretentious. I don't usually serve a first course at casual dinners, and I prefer family-style service—using lovely bowls and plat- ters, of course.

You can limit your labor by choosing your menu carefully, and control your budget similarly. This is cer- tainly a party you can do all by yourself (with a good Party Game Plan), and it is perfectly acceptable—indeed, it's part of the welcoming spirit—to allow your guests to help out. Ask them to open a bottle of wine, to slice the French bread, or scoop the ice cream.

2 : FORMAL DINNERS

This is the ultimate dinner theater: Your dining table is the stage set, your food and wine are the stars of the evening. Your guests are the royal audience—and you are the hardworking set designer, the director, the master of ceremonies, and the cook!

Dim the lights, light the tapers, and create a bit of elegant magic: sparkling crystal, gleaming silver, and all that.

Once the norm for entertaining, formal dinners are something of a delightful rarity these days. If you haven't done one recently (or ever), you will love it. This is the format for an occasion of importance: for special celebration; for creating the biggest impression; or for enjoying the sheer fun of extravagance. Reserve this treatment for small, carefully selected groups of guests (maximum of eight). Remember, the smaller the group, the more wonderful the conversation.

The house will be aglow with candlelight, and from the moment they walk in, you will be taking care of your guests' every need. The table setting will be elab- orate: flatware for each course; wineglasses for each wine you intend to pour; underliners for soup bowls; bread- and-butter and salad plates; and, yes, even fancy folded napkins. (For more information on table settings, see page 363.) The food—starting with a formal first course—will be individually plated and gorgeously pre- sented.

If it seems you will be busy, you are right; yet you will need to be the epitome of ease. The greatest gift to your guests will be your presence at the dining table and, later, in the living room, where you will repair for after-dinner drinks, a sweet, and more conversation. Thus, you may want to consider hiring a kitchen helper for service and clean-up. And your choice of food and wine can definitely have a budgetary impact in this style of entertaining.

3 : BUFFET DINNERS

Don't think you are cutting corners: A home-cooked buffet is a gracious and generous form of entertaining. You are giving your guests two marvelous gifts: a *feast* of great food and the *freedom* to enjoy it however they want. They can choose to eat what they want—and however much they want—with no self-consciousness. That's a real party favor!

A buffet is also a *feast for the eyes.* It is the one meal where all the food (except dessert) is displayed at once. Your buffet table is the centerpiece of the event, a living menu from which your guests can "taste" all the choices with their eyes before deciding what they will put on their plates. Creating the visual presentation is part of your pleasure, as you utilize your most beautiful platters, bowls, and baskets and lay them out in a gorgeous tableau of shapes and colors, arranged on many levels.

More reasons for a buffet? Adaptable for all occasions, this basic entertaining format can be as fancy and formal or as relaxed as the purpose or guest list demands. It is really the best way to host and feed more than the small number of people who can fit around your dining table. After guests serve themselves from your beautiful buffet (walking around it for efficient flow), they can casually sit anywhere in your house that's comfortable (you'll accommodate the most this way), or find a place at one or more tables to eat together in a more formal manner. You will want to consider a buffet whenever your guest list is more than twelve.

Are there any disadvantages? Contrary to most people's expectations, a buffet really requires more work for you, the host—and often costs more than anticipated. Though it's all done ahead, you have to prepare considerably more food than for a seated dinner, and there's plenty to do during the party—directing and assisting at the buffet itself, clearing, and replenishing. You will also need to rearrange the table for your dessert and beverage course. The larger the crowd, the more back-up help you will need; and you may have to rent specialty equipment such as chafing dishes or a large coffeepot.

4 : OUTDOOR GRILLING PARTIES

People love to be outside by the grill so much that I think if you merely lit the coals (and didn't throw any food on it), they'd have a great time hanging out and helping themselves to drinks and snacks. The pleasure of grilling parties definitely comes from just being near the fire, savoring the smoke and the smells, and the simple fascination of seeing food cook. These events have been so popular in recent years that they've become their own distinct kind of party. (By the way, if there are Southerners around, don't call it a "barbecue" unless you are smoking food in a pit for hours at low temperature.)

Grilling and eating outside naturally makes everyone as relaxed as possible. You can set out the food in a casual buffet style for guests to serve themselves and eat at picnic tables (I believe in tables for grilling parties because it's no fun trying to cut a steak while holding a plate on your lap!). Or you can sit people down and bring them their food, plated, right from the grill—which will provide an elegant touch with hardly any effort at all (see my "Midsummer Night's Dream" menu, page 196). Nature, even on an urban terrace, will provide a lovely atmosphere; and simple touches like flowers from your garden, bowls of seasonal produce, and outdoor candles will seem fabulously decorative.

Cooking at a grilling party is always fun and easy. You can prepare things well in advance: side dishes can be ready in the fridge; meats, vegetables (and fruits) can be marinating on skewers. In the spirit of the party, guests *always* want to help, and you, as chef, don't have to miss the action while you make the main course; in fact, you will *be* the main action. Best of all, after watching and smelling the food as it goes on the grill, guests will love *everything* you prepare. This is especially useful if you are a bit timid about your cooking: Guests are very forgiving at a grilling party. It's also fun to do some culinary exploration in the cooking. Try spicy new flavors from Asian, Latin, and other exotic cuisines in your grilled dishes.

Planning is essential. You add several variables to your Party Game Plan when you move your party outside (see "What Can I Do in the Great Outdoors?", page 21), including the chance that you might have to move it back *inside* if the weather's bad. But you offset the added work by the casualness of the format. You can use top-quality paper plates and napkins, and clean-up will be a breeze. And watching day fade into night (light citronella candles only after dinner is over, please) is a pleasant postprandial activity that everyone will be happy to share, including the host.

5 : FAMILY DINNERS

Once upon a time (really just a generation or two ago), families ate supper together every night. And every week or so, there would be a festive meal prepared with a special kind of love. Times change fast. Today, when take-out food eaten on the run is normal and American families are more dispersed than ever—my four children all live in different states—having the extended family together for a big meal is, indeed, a special occasion. I am happy to plan this as a party because my creating a spirit of specialness is genuinely appreciated by the "guests" I care about most in the world.

My family-dinner format is really a variation of the casual dinner. It's a sit-down meal served (naturally) family-style. But the emphasis here is on fun and visiting, so I keep all the decor and setting-up chores as simple as possible without losing the festive atmosphere. Fruit in a bowl is a fine centerpiece; everyday china works well on mismatched place mats.

The feeling is inclusion. I love to include children in the cooking, and it is part of the meal to have them help set the table. I don't necessarily choose "kid" food, but by including them in preparing one or more of the dishes, and as part of setting-up, they feel that the meal is partly their creation and are willing to try new things.

Family dinner menus are easy to plan and worry-free. First of all, you are cooking for people you know well, so you can make things you know they love. Second, your guests love you, so you don't have to worry about mistakes; they will forgive you. If there's something I want to make but know someone else doesn't like it, I might make two dishes. I have a sister-in-law who hates chocolate (can you believe it?) so I make two desserts, one to please me and one to please her. Because the occasions for family dinners often coincide with holidays such as Thanksgiving and Christmas, the traditional themes, activities, and foods also influence my planning and menu decisions.

Taking care of family—as I do all dinner guests—not only shows them my love, but also transforms ordinary mealtimes into more dignified occasions. As much as possible these days, I encourage dressing neatly for dinner, especially among the younger crowd. (In my mind, I can hear my mother saying, "Ripped jeans? That's a way to sit down to dinner?") As for any other dinner, there will be a smooth flow, with a relaxing time for hors d'oeuvres and beverages before the meal, graciousness during the meal, and a few relaxed moments after. If you are like me and don't have the opportunity to enjoy the company of close family as much as you would like, make the most of it whenever you get your loved ones together.

6 : BRUNCHES

A calm, casual brunch—coffee steaming in mugs and newspapers spread out in the breakfast nook—can be a soothing "morning-after-the-night-before" with close friends who are visiting for the weekend. Or brunch can be hosting a bustling house full of neighbors or relatives alive with morning energy and good humor, heaping their plates with fruits, freshly baked muffins, and frittata from a colorful buffet spread. Or brunch can be a quietly impressive repast for new acquaintances, with separate first and main courses, formally served at the table in a sun-filled dining room.

A smart way to entertain four or 40, brunch is a versatile party format that can fall anywhere on the spectrum of casual to formal. It can be a sit-down meal or a buffet with plates on laps; or a serve-yourself (sometimes even a cook-it-yourself) gathering right in the kitchen. The advantages to the host are many: everybody's hungry in the morning and even simple, fresh foods will be greeted with relish; cooked dishes will be met with ravenous excitement. Spirits are naturally high—alcoholic stimulants are consumed modestly, if at all—and it's a great time to bring the family together. And (not the only consideration but an important one, nevertheless) hosting a brunch means that you will be done with all your work by early afternoon!

Of course, different brunches call for different game plans, settings, and kitchen schedules. But for many occasions, especially when evenings are not suitable, this is a delightful and practical entertainment format.

7 : HORS D'OEUVRE PARTIES

These are not cocktail parties: I hate cocktail parties! The chatter and the frenetic flow of a typical cocktail party just do not satisfy my need for substantial conversation, and these gatherings never satisfy my need for good food.

However, a stand-up social event is often the only realistic way to bring a large number of people together. My hors d'oeuvre party format (in my business we call it "dinner by the bite") does this in smashing fashion, and is one of my favorite creations. Everyone has copied this party!

I take the emphasis off drinking and focus it on a grand variety of delicious finger foods, which fuels all the lively interaction of the party. And, since most guests don't need to sit down to enjoy their bite-size dinner, you can fit in as many people as your rooms allow (see "What Can I Really Do in My House?" in the next chapter). Furthermore, when there's a balanced choice of savory dishes, guests can eat as much or as little as they like. No one should have to eat fifty cheese crackers to ease their hunger, or find a place for supper after they leave the party.

This is also a party that really has no beginning or end: Guests can come and go, stay as long or as briefly as they want. This freedom has great appeal for guests, and makes the hors d'oeuvre party a fine format for all kinds of business and social affairs, such as engagement parties, where you want to introduce people to one another for the first time. Your invitation will clearly state the duration of your affair: 5:00 P.M. to 7:00 P.M. is perfect timing, I believe.

The setup for this format is essentially simple: tables for the food and beverages are all you really need. You will need to prepare a lovely and well-balanced assortment of both fresh and cooked foods that will taste wonderful at room temperature. People are hungry in the early evening hours and will be clamoring for your irresistible creations.

The nonstop nature of this party also demands the

host's constant attention. You won't have to serve separate courses—the coffee and small pastries that serve as dessert will be available throughout the party—but you will have to replenish the food frequently. At least one full-time kitchen helper is probably essential, and you might want two, if you need to mingle with the guests. There are some things to look forward to: Cleanup is simplified, as there are no plates and very little silverware to deal with, and the event itself will end pleasantly early, allowing you the rest of the evening to relax and enjoy what you've achieved.

8: DESSERT PARTIES

A delectably different party that will guarantee a happy crowd for a wedding shower, a bon voyage party, or a "come-and-meet-the-new-baby" gathering—anytime there's someone to be feted or something to be celebrated. In practical terms, this is a type of buffet, offering the multitude of choices and beautiful presentation that every buffet has, but with an infectious spirit of indulgence that makes everyone a bit giddy.

Of course, a dessert party must be right for you and your guests. The timing must be correct (midafternoon is my recommendation) and the guest of honor should definitely have a sweet tooth. While you might feel apprehensive if you haven't made lots of desserts before, don't be discouraged: There are wonderful, simple recipes to try (see Chapter 13) and you can augment your creations with natural sweets such as fresh and dried fruits.

One memorable feature of a dessert party can be the hedonistic diversion of such "do-it-yourself" activities as a dessert fondue or a make-your-own ice cream bar. The kid in each and every one of us gets excited by the notion of building the greatest ice cream concoction ever— it feels like a children's party for grown-ups. As a host, you will love it for its ease—almost everything is prepared ahead of time—and the magical effect it has on the crowd.

What Works?

CHOOSING THE PERFECT PARTY

FOR YOU AND YOUR HOME

WHAT CAN I REALLY DO IN MY HOUSE?

I hope you will have an opportunity to host all the types of parties I've described in the preceding chapter. But before you decide just what you are going to do next—say, putting on an ice-cream-bar dessert party for your daughter's middle-school graduating class—you will have to evaluate objectively what can work in your home.

Professionals assess the functional capacity of your house (inside and out) to accommodate guests according to the three basic styles of food service, which encompass all our party formats:

1. Your capacity for a sit-down dinner: This formula is for any event at which you bring food to guests sitting at your dining table, and applies to my casual dinners, formal dinners, and family dinners. Your maximum sit-down dinner party capacity is defined simply by the number of people who can sit around your dining table. Do you need to fit more guests around the table? Can you add a table? (See "The More the Merrier," page 20, for tips on gaining space.)

2. Your capacity for a buffet meal: There are actually two formulas used here, and they correspond to the two kinds of buffets I mentioned in Chapter 3. (Note that these apply also to dessert parties, brunch buffets, and, heaven forbid, outdoor grilling parties, if everyone has to come in out of the rain.)

• A lap-service buffet is when your guests pick up food from the buffet (usually set up on the dining table), sit wherever they want, and hold their plates in their laps. Your capacity is determined by *all* the places people can sit comfortably. Count *every* usable seat in your living and dining rooms: Remember that somebody at your party will be happy to sit on the piano bench, at the bottom of your carpeted staircase, on the cushioned armrests of the couch. Don't forget: Your dining table is taken up with the buffet and you need to allow people to walk all around it to serve themselves. Some other space will be occupied by the bar.

Tips for Increasing Your Home's Party Capacity

• **Use skinnier chairs:** For any kind of sit-down dinner, you can increase the number of guests at your table by renting "party chairs," which are narrower than normal dining-room chairs. These are inexpensive, attractive (often lacquered wood), and usually only seventeen to eighteen inches wide.

• **Add a table:** Rent or borrow a folding table that is the same height as your dining table to accommodate more guests. (Rent extra tablecloths to cover the extension.)

• **Consider moving furniture:** If your rooms are crowded with furniture, clear out easily movable pieces. You can increase sit-down capacity by making space for cocktail or extra dinner tables, chairs for lap-service, or standing-room space for an hors d'oeuvre party.

• **Make your own "bar room":** You can increase space in the main party rooms by setting up your bar in an office or other auxiliary room. If you have several small rooms, you can clear space in them and set up cocktail tables for quiet conversation areas.

• **Have your party in shifts:** "Back-to-back parties" are a smart way to entertain a lot of people in a weekend, to have a wonderful small-party atmosphere, and to save time, effort, and money in the process.

You can give casual or formal dinner parties on Friday and Saturday nights or Sunday night. You shop only once, for both parties. You set up the house only once, for both parties. You do your preliminary cooking only once, for both parties. You clean up twice, but that's the easy part!

• Your maximum lap-service buffet-party size is thus defined by the number of places people can sit, in all the areas of your house where you want the party to take place, including extra rooms you may have opened up.

• The seated buffet—when your guests sit and eat at designated tables after filling their plates—is also called a formal buffet. Usually, this format has a much smaller capacity than a lap-service buffet. If you arrange your buffet in the dining room, you will have to set up tables in the living room and other areas. Your maximum seated-buffet party size is defined by the number of people you can seat at the tables you set up. (See the tips on expanding capacity, at left.)

3. Capacity for an hors d'oeuvre party: If your food doesn't require plates, lots of people will be happy to stand. As in a buffet, your dining table will be set with trays of food and the space around it must be clear of chairs. You can make an estimate by counting (as for a lap-service buffet) all the comfortable seating in all the party rooms. Then double that number. Your estimated hors d'oeuvre party capacity will be twice the number of all the places guests can sit. If you can count fifteen seating spots, you can safely serve thirty people at a time: Remember that people are coming and going in this kind of party. In many homes, you can easily accommodate more than double the number of seating spots.

A NOTE OF CAUTION: As you evaluate the seating and standing-room capacity of your home, remember that you may be losing some existing space when you set up your bar area. This can be a significant factor, especially at a large party. (For more on setting up a bar, see Chapter 14.)

WHAT CAN I DO IN THE GREAT OUTDOORS?

A party in the warm season can utilize the increased capacity of the outdoor areas of your home. Whether you stage your event entirely outside or use outside areas as additional space, you can use the same formulas as for the inside: Count the table capacities for sit-down meals, count overall seating capacity for lap-service meals, and estimate standing room, remembering that one third to one half of your guests will want someplace to sit. You will have to ask some further questions, however, about the functionality of your outdoor space:

• Is it level enough to accommodate dining tables in all areas?

• Are grassy areas firm and dry enough for people to stand comfortably?

• Does your outside space give you convenient access to the kitchen?

• Does the space give your guests convenient access to the house and its facilities?

• Does your outdoor area provide protection from the sun, and if not, can you provide a shaded area?

• Can you erect a tent in your outdoor area to accommodate guests in the event of rain? If so, how large can it be?

Your game plan for an outdoor party must address what you will do in the event of rain—don't even *think* of an outdoor party without considering this possibility. You can postpone the party if inclement weather threatens, or plan to move the party inside and under cover. Your capacity, then, is defined by your table and seating space inside *plus* any covered areas you provide outside.

FACTORING IN THE BUDGET

Before you commit yourself to a particular type of party, especially any large party, it's wise to first make a rough estimate of your expenses—and decide if your preferred format is a realistic choice. This process will also get you going on your game plan, as you evaluate whether you need to hire help, rent large equipment such as a tent, tables, or chairs, or rent or buy utensils for food service. Also consider how much you can afford to spend on food and beverages. If your budget is limited, consider a format with modest food costs, or scale back your guest list.

WHAT DO YOU WANT TO ACCOMPLISH? GETTING A GRASP ON THE INTANGIBLES

It is a big part of my business to help people figure out what kind of party they want. After we evaluate what kind of party they are *capable* of having, I pose the subjective questions that only they can answer. Ask yourself these questions before deciding what format is best for your occasion:

• What's the purpose of my party? Is there a social purpose, such as a particular celebration?

• Is there a business purpose, such as introducing people to one another?

• Is this a party just to entertain good friends or family?

• Who am I inviting and what kind of party would they like?

• What level of casualness or formality would be most comfortable for my guests?

• How much time and energy do I have to plan and prepare for this party?

• How busy do I want to be at my party?

• Do I need to be with the guests throughout the party?

And be sure to ask yourself the most important question of all:

• What kind of a party would make *me* happy?

Now you can put together what you *can* do in your home with what you *want* or *have* to do for your occasion, considering all the information I have given you about various party formats, and the planning guidelines in the next chapter. With all these possibilities, I am sure you will be able to design a party that will suit the purpose of your occasion *and* the style of entertaining that is best for you and your guests.

Game Plans for a
Winning Party

In 1972, I received a phone call that changed my life. "Would you like to provide lunch for five hundred guests of PepsiCo at our corporate headquarters?" a woman asked me. I took the job, and stayed up nights figuring out how I (with some high-school helpers) would prepare, pack, transport, and present five hundred exquisite lunch boxes with salade Niçoise, fruit and cheese, and a home-baked pastry. I had never catered a party before.

Though I didn't know it at the time (I ran a small cooking school and loved it), that big lunch was the launching of a new career. And my long nights started an education in big-party planning that continues to this day. For years, as my business has grown, I've made strategic lists of everything that needs to be done for every event, assigning every task involved in setting up, decorating, cooking, and cleaning up: from turning ovens on (and off), to arranging the garnish on each plate, to having the Dumpsters emptied when the party is over. It is this organized approach to entertaining—creating a comprehensive game plan—that I want to teach *you* in this chapter.

Why have a game plan? In business, it's obvious: If we don't figure out everything that needs to be done well ahead of time, and decide who's going to do it and when, we are going to forget something. That's just not acceptable in our profession.

And I believe the same principle applies to entertaining at home. When people come to your home, you should be prepared with everything that will make them feel comfortable and special—and *you* should be ready to have a good time.

How can you really welcome your guests—how can you be genuinely happy to see them—when you are still racing around frantically, doing a dozen different things at the last minute? How can you really enjoy precious time with your guests when you have to disappear from your party every couple of minutes to find the things you forgot, or didn't have time to bring out in the first place?

There is a different way to host a party—even a large, complicated event—and in this chapter I will show you how to do it. I will teach you to think like a professional. You will figure out in advance exactly what you have to do, what you need to provide, and you will create a game plan to take care of it all.

In the following pages, I have distilled the hundreds of questions we ask our clients, and the dozens of factors we consider in large-scale event-planning, into ten basic steps. These address all the issues and practical necessities a host has to face sooner or later—and surely, sooner is much better!

This is not just a matter of listing tasks, but a guide to the choices you will have to make. As you carefully consider each facet of your event, decide on the things that you *absolutely have to do*—such as renting equipment or shopping for groceries—and set a realistic time frame in which to do them.

At the same time, evaluate the elements that can vary, such as the menu and the decor: If you have extra time, you can choose to indulge in an extravagant meal, or you can streamline your plans to save time, money, and effort. There are no "wrong" answers to the questions you will ask yourself: Your choices will help you shape a party that expresses your entertaining style and fits into your lifestyle. And your game plan will guarantee that *you* will have a good time preparing, and attending, your own party.

READY TO START A GAME PLAN?

The time to start rigorously planning your event is *after* you have decided on the format. You know the purpose of your event, you know the feeling you want, and you probably have a guest list nearly complete. You should definitely know the capacity of your home to accommodate the planned number of guests (using the formulas in Chapter 4). If not, confirm that you have the table, seating, or standing room you will need. Now you are ready to consider the first practical question in your game plan.

STEP 1:
PICKING A DATE AND TIME
FOR YOUR EVENT

It's not just the calendar you must consult; you must also take into consideration your life and the lifestyles of the people you want to invite.

◆ What is a time and date for your event that gives *you* sufficient time to comfortably plan and graciously execute the party?

Don't rush to the first available opening in your date book. Be realistic about your life, your other obligations, and your schedule. The larger and more formal the occasion, the more planning and preparation time you will need. Don't start to plan a formal dinner for next weekend—unless you have a butler and a chef.

Should I Call My Guests to Help Set a Date?

The only time I call someone about an event *before* I have chosen a date is when there is some key player—an individual or a couple around whom I really want to build a party. Their availability is crucial to my event, and I don't like to leave that to chance. Otherwise, if I have selected a date and time that considers the calendar and people's normal activities—with sufficient advance notice—my chosen date almost always works for the people I want to have the most.

• Will seasonal—or, more likely, unseasonable—weather have any effect on the type of party you have planned?

Don't plan a grilling party in late spring—without rainy-day options. Think twice about winter parties for which out-of-town guests may encounter travel difficulties.

• Will your event date conflict with family holidays or school vacations that will occupy your guests?

• Will your party compete with many other events at Christmas holiday time, or June graduation and wedding time?

• Is the time for your party a natural one for the meal you have planned?

A multicourse dinner will be wasted on guests at a luncheon. Don't schedule a dessert party to start at 6:00 P.M.!

• Is the time for your party going to interfere with people's normal activities?

If many of your friends are weekend golfers, don't start the party at 4:00 P.M. on a Saturday in late May. But late afternoon might be a perfect time to gather for an early supper on a Sunday in January.

STEP 2:
ISSUING INVITATIONS

However you deliver them—by mail, phone, or (I am sure it is happening somewhere) E-mail or fax—your invitations have to communicate much more than the time and date of your party. Remember that people always want to know what to expect, and almost always worry about what to wear. Your invitation will tempt and *reassure* them by letting them know what kind of event you

---

Begin the Party Weeks Ahead of Time

You can set the mood and kick off the fun of your party in the instant your guests open their invitation. Tantalize them with the pleasure that lies in store with some charming hint:

• Having a summer clam-bake? Fold a lobster bib into the envelope with the invitation.

• Anticipate a swank dinner's splash of glamour and romance with a note card lettered in gold and red (with a few silver confetti hearts in the envelope).

• Write your invitation note on a colorful latex balloon. (Blow it up and pinch it closed while writing with a glittery felt-tipped pen. Deflate and mail.)

• Enclose a packet of flower or herb seeds for a springtime party.

---

will be having; indicating whether you will be serving a meal; and, in the cleverest way you can, telling them how to dress for the occasion.

• How are you going to make your invitations?

For a party of twelve or more, it is usually easier to send invitations by mail. A blank note card with an appropriate design (in which you handwrite the party information) is a simple alternative to printing. For a smaller party, extending an invitation over the phone is efficient and perfectly acceptable.

• How can you announce a formal dinner?

Even if it is a small affair, you can highlight the specialness—and the fun—of a formal dinner with a classy, mailed invitation. A handsome, handwritten invitation is, in my opinion, especially thoughtful, and demonstrates from this first moment the personal care you are putting into the event.

STEP 3:
DESIGNING THE MENU

Your menu is one of the most important factors in the game plan. Decide on it early, as it is the basis for planning your equipment, table and utensil arrangements, site preparation, beverage service, and shopping tasks. Also, cooking and serving your menu are often the main tasks of home entertaining. Of course, for some people (like me) cooking is the *best* part of giving a party, but whether you love it or fear it, it is *absolutely* critical that you think carefully about the time involved in preparing your menu—long before you start cooking (read about kitchen schedules below).

As you design your menu, consider:

• What is the flow of your party? What will you serve when guests arrive? Will you socialize for a long time before dinner is served? Will you serve fruit or sweets after the main meal is completed?

• Do you have the time to prepare these dishes before your party?

• How much time are you willing to spend dealing with food *during* your party and how much time do you want, or need, to be with your guests?

Look at the kitchen schedules that accompany each of the menus in this book to see how much time a typical menu demands. Consider choosing dishes with less preparation time or cutting the number of courses you will serve. Hiring a kitchen helper to do some of the cooking and/or serving is often a great idea if your budget permits.

• Does the food cost of your planned menu fit into your resources?

• Does your kitchen have the stove and oven capacity to cook the dishes in your planned menu?

Even the most ardent cook can't overcome the physical limitations of kitchen equipment. If your cooking facilities are limited, be cautious when planning extensive menus.

• Will this menu appeal to your guests? Does it give them enough to eat at the time of day when you will be entertaining?

• What beverages best accompany this menu, and can you afford them?

This is the time to consider if you want to serve mixed drinks at the beginning of your event; whether you want to serve a dinner that requires a full service of wines; whether sparkling wine is a necessity in your menu.

STEP 4:
THE BIG FOUR—ALL THE THINGS YOU NEED FOR FOOD SERVICE

With your menu set, you are ready to deal with "the big four" which is what caterers call the major categories of meal-service items: table linens, stemware (crystal or other glassware), flatware, and china. You will have to figure out your total needs, assess how much of each you have in your home, and decide if, where, and when you will get the items you don't have. If you don't want to rent or borrow extra items, you have two choices: You can entertain fewer people, or—with the exception of linens—you can wash glasses, silverware, or dishes between courses. It is your choice.

◆ What are my table linen needs?

Tablecloths and cloth napkins are essential at formal dinners and other elegant events, and you can choose to use them in many other formats as well. As major elements of setting and decor they introduce a range of colors, textures, and moods. If you have a naturally beautiful dining table, consider using place mats—casual or elegant—to show off the table. (One occasion where you can easily forgo linens is a casual grilling party: It just wouldn't be as much fun without rough picnic tables and paper goods.)

To calculate your linen needs, check to see if you have suitably sized table cloths or mats for every surface you will be using, including dining table, buffet table, sidebars, or beverage-service tables.

Don't skimp on napkins. For a seated dinner party, plan on one linen napkin per guest for the main course and another table-size napkin (either linen or paper) for dessert. Have a sufficient quantity of paper napkins for cocktail hour (plan on several per guest). For a buffet, you should have preset rolls (one per guest) of a dinner-size napkin with flatware inside, with a stack of extra napkins (one for every five guests). Cloth or high-quality paper napkins are appropriate for wrapping silver. Extra napkins (paper is fine) should also be set out with the dessert buffet.

◆ What are your stemware needs?

You probably need more than you think! First, consider your predinner drinks: You will need at least two glasses per person—or more, if your cocktail period is extended. I think that stemmed glasses are appropriate for all predinner beverages, including mixed drinks and wine. Total the number you need, count what you own, and consider where you will get the balance.

To calculate stemware needs during a sit-down dinner, go through your menu. What beverages do you want to serve with each course? You will always need water glasses for each guest; the number and type of wineglasses will vary with your menu.

At a formal dinner, you should certainly have separate wineglasses for each wine poured. At other occasions, you can choose whatever you are comfortable with.

◆ How much flatware do you need? Do you need to use your real silver?

At one time, almost everybody in certain social groups received real silver flatware for their wedding. But that's not so common anymore (and not everyone gets married anyway). You can set a lovely table with silver-plate flatware or even everyday stainless knives, forks, and spoons, but the most elegant occasions demand the real thing. (See "The Formal Table Setting," page 363, for a guide to old-fashioned formal flatware service.)

Go through your menu course-by-course, counting what's needed for each place setting, and then calculate your totals. Remember that you have the option of washing between courses, especially if you have a kitchen helper. Also note that you can sometimes rent flatware in various price ranges.

◆ What dishes and china do you need?

The latest news from the designer front is that a mixed china table service is chic, even at a formal dinner party. Your personal style should dictate what you want to have at your table, whatever the occasion. (See "Initial Table Setting," page 363, for the classic arrangement of a uniform china setting.)

Assess your needs just as with flatware, going through your menu course-by-course and calculating the totals. Don't forget underliners for soup and other appetizer courses, bread-and-butter dishes, and dessert plates.

◆ Do you have the serving utensils and vessels that you need?

Again, your menu is your guide. List every item on your menu, including extras like bread and butter, sauces, and dressings, and figure out what vessel you have that will be practical and decorative. You want to carefully design the appearance of your table, especially in a buffet format. Check *your closets: You may have lovely bowls, baskets, platters, and trays that you have forgotten. (See page 130 for my method of setting up a beautiful buffet table.)*

STEP 5:
PREPARING YOUR ROOMS
FOR THE PARTY

Take another look at the spaces through which your party will flow, and consider the many ways you can make them more suitable for entertaining:

• What things can be easily moved to make more space?

• What personal, unusually valuable, or breakable items should be removed?

• How can seating be grouped for comfortable conversation?

• Where will the bar go? And what will you use for a bar?

Make sure that your bar does not block an entryway, access to the kitchen, or any other important traffic route. Consider putting it in an extra room if one is available. For smaller parties (sixteen people or fewer), an ordinary side table is probably sufficient, but for a larger group, you may have to set up a four-foot bar table.

• Where will guests' coats go?

In cold seasons and for large gatherings this is an important consideration. You may need to empty some closets, get more hangers, clear space in a bedroom, or even rent a portable coatrack.

• When will the party areas get a thorough cleaning?

Not to be left for the last minute, this is a critical entry in your game plan. Allow enough time to clean all the areas, including entryways and bathrooms, that guests will use. You will also want to police the outside grounds, such as the front and backyard, the walkways, and any place guests may wander, even if the party is indoors.

STEP 6:
DECIDE ON DECORATIONS

Plan your decor *after* you have decided on your final room arrangements. Consider all the places where flowers and/or candles will be used, calculate your total needs, and add them to your shopping list. If flowers need to be specially ordered from a florist, put that in your game plan checklist and schedule.

I discuss many more specifics of decoration—both elaborate and extremely simple—for all the different party formats and menus in Part II of this book. Of course, decor is an art of almost infinite possibility: The most important thing for your game plan is to make sure that decor planning, shopping, and arranging fits into your finite resources of time, energy, and money.

STEP 7:
STOCKING UP

Throughout the party-planning process, you will naturally be making lists of things that need to be rented, borrowed, or purchased, and all the places you need to go. Make sure you don't just keep the lists in your head, but put them down on paper.

• What food needs to be purchased?

At least a week before your party, go through your menu, recipe by recipe, and make a complete and consolidated shopping list. This will give you enough time to contact your grocer or other food purveyors to order or check on the availability of specialty foods such as custom-cut meats or fish, or specialty produce. And you will have time to make substitutions or change recipes if necessary.

• What beverage items need to be purchased?

See Chapter 14, "Basics of Beverage Service," to calculate your needs and make a shopping list. Schedule a trip to the wine merchant whenever your menu calls for special wines to accompany a great meal. Don't forget all the beverage and bar staples, such as mixers, sodas, lemons, and so forth. And if you have not put them on your grocery list, make sure you stock all the basic after-dinner beverages, including decaffeinated and regular coffee, black and herbal teas, milk, half-and-half, sugar, and honey.

• Are all the basic household items in good supply?

Don't forget all the things you will need behind the scenes, in the kitchen and bathroom: soaps of all kinds, paper towels, tissues, toilet paper, aluminum and plastic food wraps, and garbage bags. Last-minute trips to the store for the forgotten dishwasher detergent should not be part of your party preparation.

STEP 8:
THE KITCHEN SCHEDULE

Preparing an elaborate menu, especially one that includes new dishes, is a challenge to every cook, but if you are trying to give a party at the same time, getting a meal to come out perfectly can quickly bring on "frantic host" syndrome.

Your game plan for cooking—I call it the "kitchen schedule"—will save you from this terrible fate and help you produce a better meal more efficiently. It is a chronological overview of all stages of food preparation, both in the days and hours before the event, and during the party itself.

I have prepared kitchen schedules for my professional staff for years, and I believe they are even more important for a host-chef at home, especially one who is working alone. There is a kitchen schedule provided for each menu in this book that details what cooking can be completed in advance and how to coordinate the final steps at the party.

Study the kitchen schedule before you start cooking. I also suggest you copy it and post it on your refrigerator as a checklist of what you need to do. Make adjustments to suit your situation: You can choose to make as much as possible ahead of time—even to freeze and store some foods—or decide to complete more tasks on the day of the party itself.

If you are making up your own menu, try to set up a kitchen schedule patterned on mine. Analyze what steps in every recipe you can complete in advance, and how you will finish the cooking as efficiently as possible.

LAST-MINUTE MOOD SETTING

Just before your guests arrive, you will want to be sure to take a few minutes to get your home—and yourself—in the most welcoming state. If you've followed your game plan to this point, you can be confident that you have anticipated all your guests' needs and that your party will flow as planned. Enjoy adding some final touches:

◆ Do you have a well-chosen CD playing in the background?

Nothing is more deadly than walking into a silent room. But the sounds of chamber music or instrumental jazz will fill the space with pleasant vibrations.

◆ Have you adjusted the lights and lit the fire?

Your guests will appreciate that this is a special occasion.

◆ Do you have hors d'oeuvres or snacks out and the bar all set?

If you invite them to fix drinks for themselves, your guests will be relieved that they have something to do besides stand around.

STEP 10:

PLANS FOR POST-PARTY TASKS

The end of a well-planned party can be an afterglow rather than a tedious task, if you have thought through what will need to be done and have prepared for it.

◆ How and when will party cleanup be accomplished?

You can decide that you will finish the cleanup right away and wake up to a spotless house, or defer some of it to the following day. If you have a kitchen helper, he or she can complete much of the cleanup even while you extend your visit with guests. Sometimes a delay in cleaning something will cause problems later on—leaving stains in a tablecloth, for instance—so deal with such items before going to bed.

◆ Have you stored away all food and beverages?

At a casual party for close friends or family, a gift of leftover food can be a much-appreciated party favor. Plan ahead to have storage containers on hand and refrigerator space available for surplus food and open beverage bottles.

◆ Is your kitchen ready for a rest?

A final check that stoves and electrical appliances are shut off and unplugged should be the last item on your kitchen-schedule checklist.

ENOUGH TIME TO GET
IT ALL DONE

Before you have even issued an invitation, you need a certain amount of foresight to think about the end of your gala evening—bidding farewell to your guests and loading the dishwasher. But the advantage of our game-plan approach is maximized when you set it up far in advance. The more time you have to back things up—that is, to complete your list of party tasks over weeks rather than at the last minute—the easier and more effective your efforts will be. If you decide, for instance, that you will need to rent extra chairs, stemware, or a coffeemaker, that's something that can be arranged well ahead of time, freeing your last days before the party for more immediate and creative concerns, such as cooking and decorating.

Here's a suggested time frame for backing up the work of a typical game plan. This allows a generous amount of time for completing the multitude of tasks for all but the largest and most formal parties. Notice that the obvious activity starts four weeks before the event, but you will have to figure out your game plan before you start it. So, in reality, you might well begin your planning six weeks to two months before your event date. Of course, absolutely spur-of-the-moment gatherings can be pleasurable, too; but if you are a busy person and want to have a big party in a relaxed but effective way, don't cut your time frame too short.

6 TO 8 WEEKS BEFORE EVENT:

- Choose the kind of party you want to give, considering your home's entertaining capacity and your tentative guest list.
- Start developing a game plan.

4 WEEKS BEFORE EVENT:

- Send out invitations.
- Make arrangements for kitchen, serving, or cleanup help.
- Make arrangements for rental items.

3 WEEKS BEFORE EVENT:

- Plan the menu and related shopping lists.
- Start decorating plans and related shopping lists.

2 WEEKS BEFORE EVENT:

- Get wines and beverages; consult with specialty purveyors.

WEEK BEFORE P-DAY:

- Shop for food.
- Follow kitchen schedule for advance food prep.
- Site preparation and house cleaning.

NIGHT BEFORE THE PARTY:

- Set or design the table.

DAY OF THE PARTY:

- Complete cooking, following kitchen schedule.
- Complete site preparation and last-minute mood setting.
- Smile! This is entertainment!

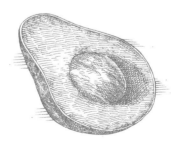

PART II

The Simplicity and Intimacy of Casual Dinners

It's hard to say what I like more about casual dinner parties: the chance to entertain and really relax with my favorite people for hours on end, or the chance to cook them a homey and delicious meal they will rave about. Here are four occasions that tempt me on both counts:

- A midwinter feast of braised lamb shanks is a heart- and soul-warming gift to visiting friends.

- February 29 comes but once every four years, so celebrate Sadie Hawkins Day with a trap for the guys in your lives: a great dinner of lemon-roasted chicken and other love-inducing delicacies.

- Summer's end brings ocean-loving pals together for a farewell supper of steamed clams and mussels, with the roar of the ocean accompanying the laughter.

- Your reading group gathers for a stimulating evening of literary discovery and dispute, inspired by a poetic presentation of cherry-glazed duck breasts accompanied by a chorus of colorful vegetable dishes.

I hope you will be tempted too! Don't worry if your occasions or settings are different from mine—use any excuse to get your friends over to enjoy the menus in this chapter. They are all tremendously adaptable and illustrate the ease and versatility of the casual dinner.

Take a few moments to create a special atmosphere in your home with simple touches: perhaps a roaring fire in the fireplace, candles flickering on the dinner table, or lanterns illuminating the deck if you are eating outside on a summer evening. If you have the time, add a fanciful air to the dinner table with the decoration ideas that accompany each menu. (If you're in a hurry, simply arrange seasonal fruits and vegetables in baskets as a dining-table centerpiece.) Read through the recipes, then choose between the one-toque or two-toque side dishes, depending on how much time you have for cooking (they are all delicious).

Remember, as with every party, to think about flow: Create a "we-are-ready-for-you" feeling to welcome your guests. Have beverage mixings all set out for self-service on a side table and hors d'oeuvre ready in the living room. Engage your guests in the shared good feeling by letting them help: pouring wine, serving up food family-style at the table, or assisting you with dessert (tell them they can lick the whipped cream bowl!). When it is time for dinner, invite your guests to seat themselves, or to find the clever place cards you may have set. Either choice is appropriate.

Follow my kitchen schedule (you will find one *after* the last recipe in each menu) for the greatest efficiency and ease in cooking and serving your meal, or create a schedule for your own menu, and follow it! This will ensure that you have as much time with your guests as possible, and still have the main meal all ready at one time for family-style serving. Fumbling around in the kitchen is no fun for anyone.

Dessert is a wonderful finale to a casual dinner party, especially when it's enjoyed while lounging in the living room. The desserts in these menus are perfect for living-room service. Bring in the coffee and take the lovely centerpiece bowl of fruit into the living room, too, as a final indulgence.

MENU 1

A Warming Welcome for Visiting Friends

THE MAIN EVENT:

Osso Buco Braised in Red Wine with Thyme

ON THE SIDE:

Toasted Barley and Orzo Pilaf

◆

Lettuce Salad with Fresh Herbs and Cheeses and Oven-Roasted Garlic-Basil Vinaigrette (page 87)

ON THE SIDE:

Shallot-Roasted Dicey Potatoes

◆

Focaccia with Onion and Herbs

THE GRAND FINALE:
A Medley of Baked Apples

PALATE TEASERS:
Wild Mushroom Fritters (page 88)

BEVERAGE RECOMMENDATIONS:
Bellinis (page 356)

◆

Barolo Marcarni "Brunate"

*T*HEY'VE TRAVELED A LONG WAY TO REACH YOUR HOME, SO YOU hustle your best friends inside as the winter winds swirl snow flurries across the street. A colorful array of primroses on the coffee table tells them they've reached an oasis of warmth and refuge from the cold. And the air is suffused with the aroma of *osso buco*—veal shanks braising in red wine—and the soul-satisfying smell of herbed focaccia, just out of the oven.

This hearty meal, full of big flavors and rustic textures, will communicate a warm and unforgettable welcome to everyone at your table. The Main Event, osso buco, is succulent from its long braising with wine, thyme, mustard, and garlic, then piqued with a final garnish of parsley and lemon.

Choose from two sets of wonderful side dishes. My one-toque choices are a simple pilaf, laced with the flavor of fennel and sweet bell pepper, with a quick and crunchy lettuce salad as a foil to the richness of the veal. Complete your meal with a basket of thick slices of European-style country bread.

When you have a bit more time, try the two-toque choices: a sweet, earthy casserole of potatoes, carrots, and turnips that matches the heartiness of the osso buco perfectly. The onion-studded focaccia is a tasty way to mop the luscious sauces, as well as great fun to make. You will need to leave time for this yeast dough to rise, but the results will be worth it.

The homey warmth of the meal is completed with the dessert medley of baked apples—a comforting treat made extra-special with different-col-ored apples, the sweetness of dried apricots and apricot brandy, and a pleasing lilt of lemon.

See the kitchen schedule on page 44 for a smart strategy on completing this menu.

SETTING THE STAGE

This occasion definitely calls for a warm hearth to gather around, so build a roaring fire in your fireplace. Another lovely way to relieve the chill is to bring a hint of springtime into your home, with its promise of warmth to come. For your dining- or coffee-table centerpiece, choose a mass of potted primrose. Arrange them in a low round basket, using moss to hide the plastic pots. And set your table with pale cloths and pastel napkins to bring some light to the dark season.

I love to serve the osso buco in large soup bowls—with an underliner plate, of course—and you will want to set out a salad dish for the lettuce salad, too. See my serving suggestions following The Main Event recipe.

Osso Buco Braised in Red Wine with Thyme

MAKES 8 SERVINGS

You will want to buy meaty, good-sized veal shanks for this wonderful dish.

SPECIAL COOKWARE

*Extra-large (8–10-quart) ovenproof Dutch oven or heavy
    casserole with lid*
Butcher's twine

*8 veal shanks, about 13 ounces each, with bone,
    tied with butcher's twine*
1/2 teaspoon salt, plus additional salt to taste
*1/4 teaspoon freshly ground black pepper, plus additional
    pepper to taste*
1/2 cup all-purpose flour
5 tablespoons olive oil
2 medium onions, peeled and finely chopped
5 cloves garlic, peeled and finely minced
2 teaspoons Dijon mustard
*2 (28-ounce) cans Italian whole peeled plum tomatoes,
    coarsely chopped with their liquid*
1 tablespoon tomato paste
2 1/2 cups chicken broth, homemade or low-sodium canned
2 cups full-bodied, dry red wine
1 tablespoon finely chopped fresh thyme
1 tablespoon finely minced flat-leaf parsley
1 tablespoon finely grated lemon

1. Preheat the oven to 350°.

2. Generously season the veal shanks with salt and pepper. Place the flour on a large plate and coat the veal shanks well on all sides.

3. Heat 3 tablespoons of the oil over medium heat in a large Dutch oven or heavy ovenproof casserole. Brown the veal shanks, a few at a time, until they are golden brown, about 3–4 minutes on each side. Keep the flame low under the shanks to ensure that the flour coating does not burn. Drain on paper towels.

4. Add the remaining olive oil to the casserole and sauté the onions over medium heat until they have wilted, about 3–5 minutes. Add 1 tablespoon of the minced garlic and continue to sauté for 1 minute more. Add the mustard, plum tomatoes, tomato paste, chicken broth, red wine, and thyme to the pan. Cook the sauce over medium-high heat until it has thickened slightly, 12–15 minutes.

5. Return the veal shanks to the casserole and coat well with the sauce. Cover and braise in the oven until the shanks are tender, about 1 1/2 hours.

6. Remove the casserole from the oven, remove the shanks to a baking sheet, and remove and discard the butcher's twine. Reduce the oven temperature to 250°. Cover the shanks with foil and place in the oven.

7. Allow the sauce to sit at room temperature for 10 minutes, until all the fat rises to the top. Skim off and discard the fat. In a food processor fitted with the knife blade, puree the sauce in several batches until it has thickened but is not entirely smooth. Season with salt and pepper to taste. *(The shanks can remain in the warm oven, covered, for about 45 minutes, or they can be cooled in the sauce and refrigerated for a day. Reheat in a 350° oven for 25–30 minutes.)*

8. Combine the remaining garlic with the parsley and grated lemon and set aside.

I like to bring the osso buco to the table arranged around the inside edge of a large serving platter. Mound the Toasted Barley and Orzo Pilaf or the Shallot-Roasted Dicey Potatoes in the center of the platter. Garnish each shank with the reserved blend of garlic, grated lemon, and parsley.

The Inventive Chef

THIS RECIPE IS ALSO A WONDERFUL PREPARATION FOR LAMB SHANKS. USE FRESH ROSEMARY TO SEASON THE LAMB INSTEAD OF THE THYME, AND OMIT GRATED LEMON FROM THE FINAL GARNISH.

ON THE SIDE
Toasted Barley and Orzo Pilaf

MAKES 8 SERVINGS

3 cups chicken broth, homemade or low-sodium canned
1 cup white wine
$^1/_4$ cup plus 2 tablespoons olive oil
1 cup minced fennel leaves (mince and reserve the green tops)
4 scallions, green stems only, finely minced
$^1/_2$ cup pearl barley
$^1/_2$ cup orzo
2 cloves garlic, peeled and finely minced

1 yellow bell pepper, seeded and finely diced
1 red bell pepper, seeded and finely diced
$^1/_4$ cup freshly grated Parmigiano Reggiano
Grated zest of 1 lemon
2 teaspoons fresh lemon juice
Salt to taste
Freshly ground pepper to taste

1. Bring the chicken broth and white wine to a simmer in a medium saucepan.
2. Heat $^1/_4$ cup of the olive oil in a large skillet over medium-high heat. Add the fennel and scallions and sauté 2 minutes. Add the barley and orzo and sauté, stirring often, until they become a light nutty brown, approximately 3 minutes. Add the garlic and cook 1 minute.
3. Slowly add the hot chicken broth and wine to the sauté pan, blending well. Simmer, uncovered, over medium heat, until the grains absorb all the liquid, about 25 minutes. (At this point, *the pilaf can be held, covered, in a warm oven for 1 hour. If prepared ahead and refrigerated, reheat in the top of a double boiler.*)
4. While the pilaf is simmering, pour the remaining 2 tablespoons of olive oil into a medium skillet. Sauté the yellow and red peppers for 3 minutes, until lightly wilted. Remove from the heat and reserve.
5. Toss the cooked grains with the peppers, grated cheese, minced fennel greens, lemon zest, and juice. Season with salt and pepper to taste.

FINISHING TOUCHES AND
TABLE PRESENTATION

See above for service.

ON THE SIDE

Shallot-Roasted Dicey Potatoes

MAKES 8 SERVINGS

SPECIAL COOKWARE

One large roasting pan, 17 by 11 inches, or two smaller
roasting pans

1 1/2 pounds medium new potatoes, unpeeled, washed, and
cut into 1/2-inch dice
2 1/2 pounds carrots, peeled and cut into 1/3-inch dice
1 pound turnips, peeled and cut into 1/3-inch dice
6 large shallots, peeled and quartered lengthwise
1 large red onion, peeled and cut into 1/2-inch dice
1/2 cup olive oil
2 teaspoons chopped fresh rosemary
3/4 teaspoon salt
1/2 teaspoon freshly ground black pepper
1/4 cup chicken broth, homemade or low-sodium canned
1/4 cup dry white wine

1. Preheat the oven to 450°.
2. Place the potatoes, carrots, turnips, shallots, and
red onion in a roasting pan large enough for the
vegetables to have room to brown and not steam. (*Two*

roasting pans can be used if you do not have one large enough.)
Toss the vegetables well with the oil, rosemary, salt,
and pepper.
3. Place on the lowest rack of the oven and bake until
the vegetables are browned and tender, about 30
minutes. Stir the vegetables twice while roasting to
ensure they brown evenly.
4. Add the chicken broth and white wine to the
roasting pan and roast for 10 minutes more. Check
the seasonings and add salt and pepper to taste.

FINISHING TOUCHES AND
TABLE PRESENTATION

See page 40 for service.

Focaccia with Onion and Herbs

MAKES 8 SERVINGS

SPECIAL COOKWARE

9-inch round cake pan

THE FOCACCIA

6 tablespoons plus 2 teaspoons olive oil
1 cup warm water (105°–115°)
1 package dry yeast (2 1/2 teaspoons)
2 3/4–3 cups all-purpose flour
1 teaspoon salt

THE HERBED ONION TOPPING

2 tablespoons olive oil
1 medium red onion, peeled and cut into 1/4-inch dice
3 cloves garlic, peeled and finely minced
1/2 teaspoon salt
1 teaspoon finely chopped fresh basil
1/2 teaspoon finely chopped fresh oregano
1 teaspoon finely chopped flat-leaf parsley
1/2 teaspoon freshly ground black pepper

GARNISH

1 tablespoon freshly grated Parmigiano Reggiano

1. Oil the cake pan with 2 teaspoons of the olive oil. Reserve the rest.

2. Place the warm water in a small bowl. Sprinkle the yeast over the water. Set the mixture aside for 5 minutes or until the yeast and water begin to foam. Add 4 tablespoons of the remaining olive oil.

3. In a large bowl, stir together 2 3/4 cups of flour, the salt, and the water-yeast-oil mixture. Mix the dough until it comes together into a ball. Place the dough on a lightly floured surface and, if it is too wet to work with, gradually knead in the remaining 1/4 cup of flour. Knead until you have a somewhat sticky, soft dough, about 3 minutes. Form the dough into a ball. Coat a large bowl with the remaining 2 tablespoons of olive oil and rub the dough around in the bowl to coat it well with the oil. Cover the bowl with plastic wrap and let the dough rise in a warm place for about 1 hour, or until it has almost doubled in size.

4. While the dough is rising, prepare the topping: Heat the olive oil in a medium skillet over medium heat. Sauté the onion until it is soft and translucent, about 4–6 minutes. Add the garlic and sauté for 1 minute. Season with the salt and remove from the heat.

5. Punch down the doubled dough with your hands, press it into a 9-inch, generously oiled, round cake pan, and let it rise for another 45 minutes to 1 hour, until it is almost doubled in size.

6. While the dough is rising, preheat the oven to 400°.

7. Make indentations over the surface of the risen dough with your fingertips and spread it with the reserved onion and garlic. Sprinkle with the basil, oregano, parsley, and pepper. Bake on the middle rack of the oven until it is golden, about 30–35 minutes. Cool on a wire rack for 15 minutes and remove from the pan to a work surface.

FINISHING TOUCHES AND
TABLE PRESENTATION

Dust the foccacia with Parmigiano. With a serrated knife, cut the foccacia into wedges and place it on the table in a flat napkin-lined basket.

The Inventive Chef

FOR ADDED COLOR AND TASTE, SAUTÉ ½ CUP OF JULIENNED RED AND YELLOW PEPPERS WITH THE ONIONS AND GARLIC.

THE GRAND FINALE

A Medley of Baked Apples

MAKES 8 SERVINGS

SPECIAL COOKWARE
Apple corer
Baking dish approximately 8 by 12 inches

THE FILLING
½ cup almonds, skin removed
1 egg, beaten
½ cup dried apricots
½ cup dried currants
¼ cup orange marmalade
1 teaspoon pure vanilla extract
2 tablespoons apricot brandy
Zest of 1 lemon, finely minced
Juice of 1 lemon
1 teaspoon ground cinnamon

THE APPLES
4 medium red apples, such as McIntosh or red Delicious
4 medium green or yellow apples, such as Granny Smith or golden Delicious
1½ cups fresh orange juice

1. Preheat the oven to 350°.
2. Put all the filling ingredients into a food processor fitted with a metal cutting blade, and pulse until the mixture is coarsely chopped. Set aside at room temperature.
3. Wash the apples and remove the cores, being careful not to go through the bottom. Scoop out a 1½-inch opening in each center and fill it with about 3 tablespoons of the reserved filling, stuffing the apples to their tops. Arrange the apples in the baking dish, which should be just large enough to hold them. Pour the orange juice around the apples and bake for 45 minutes or until the apples are tender.

FINISHING TOUCHES AND
TABLE PRESENTATION

Transfer the warm apples to a large, round serving platter, alternating the green and red colors. Coat the apples with the pan juices and serve with Ginger Cream, page 101, or your favorite ice cream or sorbet.

The Inventive Chef

GIVE SOME DELICIOUS CRUNCH TO THIS DESSERT: BROWN 3 TABLESPOONS OF COOKIE CRUMBS AND 3 TABLESPOONS OF CHOPPED WALNUTS IN 1 TABLESPOON OF BUTTER. TOP EACH APPLE WITH THE CRUMBS BEFORE SERVING.

KITCHEN SCHEDULE

2 OR 3 DAYS BEFORE THE PARTY

MAIN EVENT   Veal   Prepare onions and garlic; store covered in refrigerator.

TOQUE 1   Pilaf   Prepare fennel and scallions; store covered in refrigerator.

  Salad   Prepare vinaigrette; store covered in refrigerator.

TOQUE 2   Focaccia   Prepare onion and garlic; store covered in refrigerator.

THE DAY BEFORE THE PARTY

MAIN EVENT   Veal   Prepare recipe through step 8; cover veal with the sauce, and cool; store covered in refrigerator. Refrigerate mixture of garlic, parsley, and lemon in a well-covered container.

TOQUE 1   Pilaf   Prepare recipe through step 3 and cool; store covered in refrigerator.
Prepare fennel leaves, peppers, and lemon zest; store covered in refrigerator.

TOQUE 2   Potatoes   Prepare potatoes, carrots, turnips, shallots, onion, and rosemary as instructed in ingredient list. Store potatoes and turnips, covered with cold water, in refrigerator separately. Store remaining ingredients, covered, in refrigerator.

  Focaccia   Prepare basil, oregano, and parsley.
Prepare recipe and cool; store covered in refrigerator.

Strategic Maneuvers: Fill creamer; cover and store in refrigerator.

Fill sugar bowl.
Set table.
Place Main Event liners at each place.
Check table decor.
Check ice and beverages.
Locate teas.
Chill wine if white.
Set garnishes for each recipe.
Locate and label all serving bowls, platters, and utensils.

THE DAY OF THE PARTY

MAIN EVENT   Veal   Set at room temperature.

TOQUE 1   Salad   Prepare greens, set in bowl; store covered in refrigerator.
Bring vinaigrette to room temperature.
Arrange cheeses and croutons; cover well.

  Pilaf   Warm in top of double boiler. Complete step 4.

TOQUE 2   Potatoes   Prepare recipe through step 3; set aside.

  Focaccia   Set at room temperature.

GRAND FINALE   Apples   Prepare through step 3; set aside.
Prepare Ginger Whipped Cream (if you plan to serve it); cover and refrigerate or locate ice cream.

15 MINUTES BEFORE GUESTS ARRIVE:

Preheat oven to 350°.

30 MINUTES BEFORE DINNER:

MAIN EVENT	Veal	Place in oven for 25–30 minutes, until heated through.
TOQUE 1	Pilaf	Complete step 5; heat over simmering water.

20 MINUTES BEFORE DINNER:

		Plug in coffee.
TOQUE 1	Salad	Toss with vinaigrette. Place in bowl with servers.
TOQUE 2	Potatoes	Warm in oven.
	Focaccia	Warm in oven.

JUST BEFORE DINNER:

MAIN EVENT	Veal	Garnish with garlic, parsley, and lemon mixture. Bring out steaming hot platters and bowls of food. Invite guests to dinner.

DURING DINNER SERVICE:

GRAND FINALE	Apples	Reduce oven to 300° Warm in oven.

BEFORE DESSERT SERVICE:

Prepare ice cream or quickly rewhip cream with wire whip.

DESSERT SERVICE:

Set dessert plates on the table. Bring apples and whipped cream to table and serve.

AFTER SERVICE:

Unplug coffee. Turn off oven.

A Savory Seduction on Sadie Hawkins Day

THE MAIN EVENT:

Lemon-Roasted Chicken

ON THE SIDE:

Leek and Potato Soup

◆

Spinach, Strawberries, and Figs

ON THE SIDE:

Oyster and Wild Mushroom Chowder

◆

Braided Tarragon Bread

◆

Adam and Eve Salad with Spiced Walnuts and Herbed Cheese Soufflé

THE GRAND FINALE:

Sour Cherry Cake with Black Cherry Ice Cream

PALATE TEASER:

Crusty Sausage-Filled Bread (page 164)

BEVERAGE RECOMMENDATION:

Margaritas with a Hint of Cranberry (page 355)

◆

Beaujolais-Villages, Georges Duboeuf

THE UNSUSPECTING OBJECT OF YOUR DESIRE MAY NOT HAVE REAL-ized that the calendar said February 29. But the legendary day when gals make their pitch to the guys of their dreams is a perfect occasion to snare him with a romantic supper. The roses and the soft music may begin to tell him something is up, but it's likely that his attention will be distracted by the steaming bowl of oysters and wild mushrooms, and then by an incredible salad of strawberries, figs, and spinach. Of course, he's not the only one who will succumb. By the time you serve your Sour Cherry Cake with Black Cherry Ice Cream, you'll be getting adoring glances from everyone at the table.

Is there a better way to woo a special some-one than with a sensuous meal in a romantic set-ting? I was inspired by the racy rituals of Sadie Hawkins Day to create a delicious menu with many foods noted for their stimulating—if not ab-solutely aphrodisiacal—qualities. But this dinner is so good you should not wait four years to make it. And you will enjoy serving it to any group of guests—and any special someone, even someone you've been married to for decades!

The meal will start with a tempting soup, of course. You might choose the silky leek and potato or the more extravagant chowder of oysters and wild mushrooms. It's not The Main Event here will also show off your culinary skills: a perfectly crisp-skinned roast chicken and a gorgeous braided loaf of homemade bread, infused with tarragon. And certainly you will overpower any remaining resistance with either of two sensuous salads: a simple mélange of strawberries and figs tossed with spinach, or the lushness of a creamy cheese soufflé mingling with the fresh tastes of apples, grapes, and ginger in the Adam and Eve Salad.

Your mastery of sweetness is amply demon-strated by the fresh Sour Cherry Cake and its ice cream accompaniment. As you will want to keep your eye on your special guest, follow the kitchen schedule on page 56, and don't waste time in the kitchen!

SETTING THE STAGE

If you have the time, you will enjoy reflecting the sensuality of the meal itself in your room and table decor. Lush and romantic are your goals: Soft mu-sic and flickering candlelight are musts. Drape your table with a cloth in deep jewel tones—amethyst, emerald, or ruby—with coordinated napkins. A centerpiece of anemones, rich-colored tulips, or roses will be stunning.

You will have a chance to use a lot of colorful tableware with this dinner: soup bowls and salad plates, soup tureens and nice platters.

Lemon-Roasted Chicken

MAKES 8 SERVINGS

SPECIAL COOKWARE

One extra-large roasting pan, 16 1/2 by 11 by 2 1/2 inches,
*   or two large roasting pans, 14 by 10 by 2 inches*
Butcher's twine

2 (4–5-pound) capons or roaster chickens
2 teaspoons salt, plus 1/4 teaspoon to season the tops
*   of the birds*
1/2 teaspoon freshly ground black pepper, plus 1/8 teaspoon
*   to season the tops of the birds*
2 large lemons, each cut into 6 wedges
6 sprigs fresh rosemary
4 cloves garlic, peeled and quartered
4 tablespoons salted butter, melted
1/3 cup fresh lemon juice
1/4 cup orange juice concentrate, defrosted
3 pounds butternut or hubbard squash,
*   cut into 1 1/2-inch cubes*
6 large shallots, peeled and quartered lengthwise
2 large red onions, peeled and medium chopped
1/4 cup olive oil

GARNISH

1 large lemon or 2 small lemons, cut into 8 wedges
8 fresh rosemary sprigs

1. Preheat the oven to 450°.
2. Wash the birds' cavities and pat them dry with paper towels. Rub the inside of each cavity with 1 teaspoon of the salt and pepper, and place half the lemon wedges, rosemary, and garlic inside each bird.
3. Fold back the wings so that they secure themselves underneath the birds and truss the chickens by tying the legs together securely in front of the cavity, using about 12 inches of butcher's twine for each bird. Sprinkle with salt and pepper.
4. Mix the melted butter, lemon juice, and orange juice together. Generously brush most of the mixture over the entire surface of the birds. Reserve 2 tablespoons.
5. Toss the squash, shallots, and onions with the olive oil and the remaining teaspoon salt. Scatter the vegetables over the bottom of the roasting pan.
6. Place the chickens over the vegetables and roast for 20 minutes. Baste the birds with the remaining citrus-butter mixture and reduce the oven temperature to 350°. Continue to roast until the chickens are golden brown and the juices in the thigh run clear when pierced with a fork, about 55–75 minutes more.
7. Transfer the birds to a cutting board. Remove and discard the trussing twine. Let the birds rest for 15 minutes before removing the lemon wedges, rosemary, and garlic from the cavities. Return the vegetables in the roasting pan(s), covered with foil, to a 200° oven to keep warm while carving the chicken.

FINISHING TOUCHES AND
TABLE PRESENTATION

TO CARVE THE CHICKEN: Separate the legs and thighs by cutting through the thigh joint. Slice and place the thigh meat on a large serving platter. Cut off the wings, laying open the surface of the breast meat. Carve the breast meat into 1/4-inch slices and arrange in the center of the platter over a bed of the squash, shallots, and onions. Surround the carved meat with the legs and wings. Place lemon wedges with sprigs of rosemary around the edge of the platter. Place the pan juices in a bowl on the side.

ONE-TOQUE: Place the Leek and Potato Soup in a tureen on a serving table and fill bowls with steaming soup. Serve the Spinach, Strawberries, and Figs with the Lemon-Roasted Chicken. See detailed directions, page 50.

TWO-TOQUE: Place the Oyster and Wild Mushroom Chowder in a tureen on a serving table and serve the steaming soup to your guests. Place the Adam and Eve Salad on the dinner plate with the Lemon-Roasted Chicken. See detailed directions, pages 50 and 51. Slice the Braided Tarragon Bread with a serrated knife. Arrange it in a napkin-lined basket and pass at the table with the butter crock.

The Inventive Chef

YOU CAN HAVE A COMPLETE DINNER PREPARED IN ONE PAN IF YOU ADD COARSELY CHOPPED CARROTS, TURNIPS, AND POTATOES TO THE ROASTING PAN WITH THE CHICKENS. SERVE ALL THE VEGETABLES.

ON THE SIDE

Leek and Potato Soup

MAKES 8 SERVINGS

5 leeks, white parts only
$^1/_4$ cup salted butter plus 2 tablespoons
4 cloves garlic, peeled and minced
8 cups chicken broth, homemade or low-sodium canned
1 smoked ham bone or ham hock
$2^1/_2$ pounds (about 10 large) Red Bliss potatoes, scrubbed well, unpeeled, and cut into $^1/_2$-inch dice

4 medium carrots, peeled and cut into $^1/_4$-inch dice
1 tablespoon minced curly parsley
1 French baguette, cut into $^1/_4$-inch croutons
$^1/_2$ teaspoon salt, or to taste
$^1/_4$ teaspoon white pepper, or to taste

1. Preheat the oven to 375°.
2. Cut each leek lengthwise into $^1/_4$-inch pieces. Soak well until all the dirt is removed, and drain. Heat 2 tablespoons of butter in a skillet and sauté the leeks over medium heat for 3–4 minutes, until soft and translucent. Add the garlic and sauté for 1 minute more. Set aside.
3. Heat the chicken broth with the ham bone in a large stockpot over medium-high heat and simmer for 10 minutes before adding the potatoes, carrots, and the reserved leeks and garlic. Simmer the vegetables in the broth, uncovered, until they are tender but have not lost their shape, about 20–25 minutes. Remove from the heat and cool slightly, about 5 minutes.
4. While the soup is simmering, warm the $^1/_4$ cup butter over low heat in a saucepan. Remove from the heat, add the parsley, and blend well.
5. Using a pastry brush, coat each crouton well with the parsley butter. Place the croutons on a baking sheet and bake until golden brown, about 6–8 minutes. Set aside at room temperature.
6. Remove the ham or hock bone from the stockpot and discard. Puree half the broth and vegetables in batches in a food processor fitted with a knife blade. *(This will produce a thick, smooth soup.)*
7. Return the pureed soup to the stockpot with the remaining clear broth and vegetables and stir to mix. Season with salt and pepper to taste and reheat before serving if necessary.

I like to fill a soup tureen with the steaming soup and bring it to the table. Guests pass their bowls to the head of the table, and I fill each bowl and garnish the soup with the croutons.

ON THE SIDE

Spinach, Strawberries, and Figs

MAKES 8 SERVINGS

1/2 cup Kirschwasser or brandy
3/4 pound dried figs, quartered
2 pounds fresh spinach
1 quart medium strawberries, washed, stemmed, and quartered
1 recipe Mint Vinaigrette (page 264)
1 pint large strawberries, washed, stems on

1. Heat the Kirschwasser or brandy in a saucepan over medium heat until it just begins to simmer. Place the figs in a bowl, pour the brandy over them, and plump the figs for 15 minutes. Set aside at room temperature.

2. While the figs are soaking in the brandy, pick through the spinach and discard any brown leaves. Remove the stems, tear the large leaves into smaller pieces, and wash and dry the spinach well (preferably with a salad spinner). Place it in a covered bowl in the refrigerator until ready for service.

TO ARRANGE THE SALAD: Toss the spinach in a large bowl with the figs, any remaining soaking brandy, the quartered strawberries, and the vinaigrette. For a formal salad, make a pretty mound on each of 8 small plates and place a ring of whole strawberries, stem-side up, around each salad. For casual service, as Sadie Hawkins Day, place the salad next to the Lemon-Roasted Chicken.

> ## The Inventive Chef
>
> SHREDS OF COOKED CHICKEN AND DUCK PERFECTLY COMPLEMENT THE FLAVORS AND TEXTURES OF THIS SALAD AND WILL TRANSFORM IT INTO A FINE ENTRÉE.

ON THE SIDE

Oyster and Wild Mushroom Chowder

MAKES 8 SERVINGS

SPECIAL COOKWARE
Heavy-bottomed 8-quart stockpot
1/2–2-quart liquid measuring cup

9 tablespoons salted butter, softened
1 large onion, peeled and finely chopped
4 leeks, white parts only, cut in half lengthwise, washed, dried, and cut into 1/8-inch slices

3 medium carrots, peeled and cut into $^1/_4$-inch dice

$1^1/_2$ quarts fresh oysters, shelled and cleaned (purchased from the fish market in their liquid)

$1^1/_2$ quarts chicken broth, homemade or low-sodium canned

5 large new potatoes, washed, unpeeled, and cut into $^1/_4$-inch dice

2 bay leaves

2 generous pinches ground saffron

$3^1/_2$ cups dry white wine

$1^1/_2$ pounds wild mushrooms, such as shiitake or oyster, cut into $^1/_2$-inch dice

$1^1/_2$ teaspoons balsamic vinegar

1 teaspoon salt, or to taste

$^1/_8$ teaspoon cayenne pepper

$^1/_4$ cup all-purpose flour

1 cup heavy cream

1. Heat 3 tablespoons of the butter over medium heat in a heavy-bottomed 8-quart stockpot. Add the onion and leeks and sauté until they are translucent, about 5 minutes. Add the carrots and continue to sauté for 3 minutes more.

2. Pour the oyster juices into a liquid measuring cup and add enough chicken stock to make $1^1/_2$ quarts. Pour this mixture into the stockpot with the onion and leeks and cook over medium heat until the liquid begins to simmer, about 4 minutes. Add the diced potatoes, bay leaves, and saffron and simmer until the potatoes are tender but still crisp to the bite, about 12–15 minutes. Remove and discard the bay leaves. (*If not serving immediately, let the soup cool to room temperature and refrigerate, covered.*)

3. While the soup is simmering, heat the wine in a large saucepan over medium heat. When the wine begins to simmer, add the oysters and poach them, uncovered, until the edges curl, about 2–4 minutes. Set aside. (*If you are serving the soup immediately, the oysters*

can remain at room temperature until they are added. If you are preparing the soup early in the day, refrigerate the oysters in the wine broth.*)

4. Heat 2 tablespoons of the butter in a large skillet over medium-high heat and sauté the mushrooms briskly for 4–5 minutes, until they are tender but still crisp to the bite. Add the balsamic vinegar and season with the salt and cayenne pepper. Set aside. (*Follow the same storage rules for the mushrooms as recommended above for the oysters.*)

5. Make a paste by combining the remaining 4 tablespoons of softened butter with the flour in a medium bowl until well combined and lump-free. Set aside at room temperature for up to 4 hours or until ready to finish the soup.

6. A half hour before service, heat the soup over medium heat until it begins to simmer, about 6 minutes. Whisk $^1/_2$ cup of the warm soup into the reserved butter-flour paste to make it smooth and thin it down. Add the softened paste to the pot of warm soup, whisking constantly to prevent lumps. Add the oysters with their wine liquid, the mushrooms, and the heavy cream. Continue to heat the soup, without letting it boil, until it is piping hot, about 5 minutes. Taste and adjust the seasoning with salt and pepper.

FINISHING TOUCHES AND
TABLE PRESENTATION

Ladle the hot chowder into deep terra-cotta or white bowls set over underliners. Pass the Braided Tarragon Bread. Encourage your guests to dunk the bread into the chowder.

Braided Tarragon Bread

MAKES 1 LARGE BRAIDED LOAF

2 packages dry yeast

2/3 cup warm water (not over 110°)

8 tablespoons plus 2 tablespoons salted butter

1/3 cup sugar

2 teaspoons salt

1 cup whole milk

3 large shallots, peeled and finely chopped

1/2 teaspoon finely chopped fresh tarragon

3 eggs, beaten

5–6 cups all-purpose flour

1/4 cup vegetable oil

*1/4 cup egg wash (1 egg yolk beaten with 1 tablespoon
    water)*

GARNISH

8 ounces lightly salted butter, room temperature

1. Sprinkle the yeast over the water in a small bowl. Let it stand for 5–8 minutes until foamy.

2. Place 1 stick of the butter, the sugar, and the salt in a large bowl. Scald the milk in a medium saucepan over medium-high heat and pour it over the ingredients in the bowl. Stir until the butter has melted and the milk is at room temperature

3. Heat the remaining 2 tablespoons of butter in a small skillet over medium-high heat. Sauté the shallots until they are soft and translucent, about 3–4 minutes. Add the shallots, yeast, and tarragon to the milk mixture.

4. Place the milk mixture in the large bowl of an electric mixer. On medium speed, using the paddle beater, slowly add the beaten eggs. Lower the speed and gradually add half the flour; beat until smooth. Gently beat in the remaining flour to make a wet, sticky dough. *(The full amount of flour may not be required to reach the sticky consistency.)*

5. Turn the dough onto a lightly floured board and knead well until it becomes elastic, shiny, and smooth. *(Dusting your hands with flour makes kneading an easy process.)* Moisten a paper towel with the oil and grease the inside of a large bowl. Place the dough in the bowl and cover the top with a kitchen towel. Let the dough rise in a warm place (not over 80 degrees) until it has doubled, about one hour.

6. Divide the dough into three equal pieces. Roll each piece into a log 12–14 inches long. Braid the dough loosely. Join the braided ends together with egg wash and place the bread on a greased or nonstick baking sheet. Let the braided bread rise for a second time, for 35 minutes. Brush the entire braid with egg wash.

7. While the braid is rising, heat the oven to 375°. Bake the bread for 30 minutes, or until it is light to the touch and golden. Transfer it to a rack to cool.

FINISHING TOUCHES AND
TABLE PRESENTATION

For Sadie Hawkins Day dinner, cut the bread into
1¹/₂-inch slices. Place the slices in a basket and pass with
the butter spooned into a crock.

ON THE SIDE

*Adam and Eve Salad with
Spiced Walnuts and
Herbed Cheese Soufflé*

MAKES 8 SERVINGS

1 cup walnuts, broken in pieces
3 tablespoons olive oil
¹/₂ teaspoon ground cinnamon
¹/₂ teaspoon ground cumin
¹/₂ teaspoon powdered ginger
¹/₄ cup finely chopped onion
2 large zucchini, cut in half lengthwise, then cut into
  ¹/₄-inch semicircles
salt and freshly ground pepper to taste
2 apples, Granny Smith or greenings
1 cup seedless red grapes, halved
4 bunches watercress, washed,
  stemmed, and dried
¹/₄ cup coarsely chopped curly parsley
Herbed Cheese Soufflé (recipe follows)
Lemon-Lime Vinaigrette (page 202)

1. Preheat the oven to 400°.
2. Place the walnuts in a bowl and toss with 1¹/₂

tablespoons of the olive oil, cinnamon, cumin, and
ginger. Place the nuts on an ungreased baking sheet
and bake until they are lightly browned and crisp,
about 3–4 minutes. Set aside.
3. Heat the remaining oil in a large skillet and sauté
the onion over medium heat until translucent, about
3 minutes. Add the zucchini to the pan and continue
to sauté the vegetables, stirring often, until the
zucchini begins to become translucent and is crisp to
the bite, about 2–3 minutes. *(The zucchini will become
limp if it is overcooked.)* Season with salt and pepper to
taste and cool to room temperature.
4. Cut each apple in half vertically and remove the
core. Cut each half into 2 pieces, and each quarter
horizontally into ¹/₄-inch slices. Toss the walnuts,
onions, zucchini, apple slices, grapes, watercress, and
parsley with ¹/₂ cup of Lemon-Lime Vinaigrette to
coat the greens lightly.

The Inventive Chef

THIS SALAD AND THE CHEESE SOUFFLÉ MAKE A
COLORFUL BUFFET PRESENTATION.

ON THE SIDE

Herbed Cheese Soufflé

MAKES 8 SERVINGS

SPECIAL COOKWARE
Eight 6–8-ounce ramekins

Vegetable oil spray, such as Pam

1 large shallot, peeled and minced

1 tablespoon olive oil

1/4 pound (about 6 medium spears) asparagus, tough ends removed, finely diced

Salt and black pepper to taste

1 cup heavy cream

1 cup whole milk

3 large eggs

2 teaspoons peppercorn Dijon mustard

1/4 teaspoon cayenne pepper

4 ounces chèvre, cut into 1/2-ounce medallions

1. Preheat the oven to 450°. Spray the ramekins with vegetable oil spray.

2. In a small skillet over medium heat, sauté the shallot in the olive oil until translucent, about 1 1/2 minutes. Add the asparagus to the pan and continue to sauté, stirring frequently, until the asparagus is tender, about 2 minutes more. Season with a pinch of salt and pepper and remove from the heat. Cool to room temperature.

3. While the asparagus cools, whisk the heavy cream, milk, eggs, mustard, cayenne pepper, and 3/4 teaspoon salt together in a large bowl. Beat until all ingredients become a well-blended custard.

4. Line the bottom of each ramekin with a slice of chèvre.

5. Stir the cooled asparagus and shallots into the custard and, mixing well, ladle the custard over the chèvre in the ramekins, filling them 3/4 full. Place the ramekins in a roasting pan and fill the pan with hot tap water until it comes halfway up the sides of the ramekins.

6. Bake the soufflés in the upper half of the oven for 30 minutes, or until the soufflés are puffed and golden. *(The soufflés will fall as they cool but they will look beautiful unmolded on the salad plate.)*

Unmold the soufflés by inverting each ramekin and allowing the soufflé to slip out onto a flat plate. Mop up any liquid from the ramekin with paper towels.

For formal service, I like to arrange individual 8- or 9-inch plates in the kitchen. Picture your plate as the face of a clock. Place the warm soufflé at 6 o'clock on the plate or in the middle of the salad.

For Sadie Hawkins Day dinner, place the salad with the chicken on the dinner plate. Place the chicken at 12 o'clock, the salad at 3 o'clock, and the soufflé at 6 o'clock.

The Inventive Chef

ADD 2 TABLESPOONS GORGONZOLA AND 2 TABLESPOONS OF GRUYÈRE TO THE CUSTARD BEFORE LADLING IT INTO THE RAMEKINS. TRY SERVING THE SOUFFLÉS WITH FRESH APPLE OR PEAR SLICES OR A SMALL BUNCH OF SEEDLESS RED OR GREEN GRAPES.

THE GRAND FINALE

Sour Cherry Cake with Black Cherry Ice Cream

MAKES 8 SERVINGS

SPECIAL COOKWARE

8-inch springform pan

1 tablespoon unsalted butter

2 cups plus 1 tablespoon all-purpose flour

2 cups water

1 teaspoon freshly grated nutmeg

1 cup dried sour cherries

1 1/2 teaspoons baking powder

1/2 teaspoon baking soda

1/4 teaspoon salt

7 ounces (1 3/4 sticks) unsalted butter

1 1/2 cups granulated sugar

Zest of 1 orange

2 large eggs

1 cup buttermilk

1 teaspoon vanilla extract

1 tablespoon cherry liqueur

1/4 cup sifted confectioners' sugar

2 quarts black cherry ice cream

1. Preheat the oven to 350°. Butter and flour the baking pan.

2. Cut the cherries in half and place in a bowl.

3. Bring the water and nutmeg to a boil in a small saucepan and pour over the cherries. Let sit for 15 minutes. Drain the cherries and discard the liquid. Dry the cherries with paper towels.

4. Sift together 2 cups of the flour, the baking powder, baking soda, and salt. Set aside.

5. Cut the butter into 1-inch pieces and, in an electric mixer with the paddle attachment at medium speed, beat the butter, sugar, and orange zest for about 10 minutes. Occasionally scrape the sides of the bowl with a rubber spatula.

6. Add the eggs, one at a time, at 1-minute intervals.

7. Combine the buttermilk, vanilla extract, and cherry liqueur in a small bowl.

8. Reduce the mixer speed to low. Add the dry-ingredient mixture alternately with the wet-ingredient mixture, dividing the dry ingredients into 4 parts and the liquids into 3 parts, starting and ending with the flour mixture. Mix only until incorporated after each addition. After both wet and dry ingredients have been added, mix an additional 20 seconds.

9. Add the remaining 1 tablespoon of flour to the cherries and toss to coat them well. Fold the cherries into the batter with a rubber spatula.

10. Pour the batter into the prepared pan and bake in the preheated oven about 50 minutes, or until a toothpick inserted in center comes out clean.

11. Remove the cake from the oven. Let the cake cool in the pan set on a rack, for 10 minutes.

12. Run a knife around the sides of the cake and remove the outside ring. Let the cake cool completely, about 30 minutes, and then invert to remove the bottom of the pan.

13. Dust the top of the cake with confectioners' sugar.

14. Scoop the ice cream into 8 generous balls and place them in the freezer on a baking sheet.

FINISHING TOUCHES AND
TABLE PRESENTATION

Redust the cake with confectioners' sugar and present it on a large, round serving plate. Place the ice cream in a serving bowl. Cut the cake into 8 generous wedges and serve it with the balls of black cherry ice cream.

The Inventive Chef

I LIKE TO SERVE THIS CAKE WHILE IT IS STILL WARM. AND FOR A MOIST TREAT, WARM 1/4 CUP OF CHERRY LIQUEUR AND BRUSH IT ON THE ENTIRE CAKE BEFORE SERVING.

KITCHEN SCHEDULE

2 OR 3 DAYS BEFORE THE PARTY

TOQUE 1   Salad   Prepare vinaigrette; store covered in refrigerator.

TOQUE 2   Chowder   Prepare onion, leeks and carrots; store separately, covered, in refrigerator. Prepare potatoes; cover with cold water; store covered in refrigerator.

             Salad   Prepare vinaigrette; store covered in refrigerator.

THE DAY BEFORE THE PARTY

MAIN EVENT   Chicken   Prepare the recipe through step 5; store covered in refrigerator. Cover and refrigerate remaining citrus butter. Prepare garnishes; store covered in refrigerator.

TOQUE 1   Soup   Prepare through step 4; store covered in refrigerator. Prepare croutons through step 5; set aside in an air-tight container.

             Salad   Wash and dry spinach; store in refrigerator in plastic bag.

TOQUE 2   Chowder   Prepare through step 5, refrigerating the oysters and mushrooms.

             Bread   Prepare and bake the bread through step 7. Cool to room temperature. Place in plastic bag and refrigerate.

             Salad   Prepare through step 2.

GRAND FINALE   Cake   Prepare through step 5, but do not sprinkle with confectioners' sugar. Cool; store covered in refrigerator.

Strategic Maneuvers: Fill creamer; cover and store in refrigerator.
Fill sugar bowl.
Set table.
Place soup underliners on the table.
Check ice and beverages.
Locate teas.
Chill wine if white.
Set garnishes for each recipe.
Locate and label all serving bowls, platters, and utensils.

THE DAY OF THE PARTY

MAIN EVENT   Chicken   1 ½ hours before guests arrive, set chicken at room temperature

             Bread   Set at room temperature

TOQUE 1   Soup   Ready for heating.

             Salad   Prepare strawberries; store covered in refrigerator. Set vinaigrette at room temperature.

TOQUE 2   Chowder   Prepare step 6

             Salad   Prepare step 3. Prepare grapes, watercress, and parsley as instructed.

             Soufflé   Prepare and bake soufflés through step 6. Remove from water bath and set aside at room temperature.

GRAND FINALE   Cake   Bring to room temperature. Locate and scoop ice cream; return to freezer.

45 MINUTES BEFORE GUESTS ARRIVE:

	Heat oven to 450°.
Chicken	Roast chicken as instructed for 20 minutes.

30 MINUTES BEFORE GUESTS ARRIVE:

MAIN EVENT	Chicken	Turn down oven to 350° and continue to roast chicken.
TOQUE 1	Soup	Warm over low heat. Locate croutons.
TOQUE 2	Chowder	Finish recipe; set up for reheating.
	Soufflé	Set ramekins in water bath for reheating

15 MINUTES BEFORE DINNER:

		Plug in coffee.
MAIN EVENT	Bread	Warm in oven, slice. Fill bread baskets, cover lightly with foil.
TOQUE 1	Soup	Put croutons in bowl for serving.
	Salad	Toss with vinaigrette.
TOQUE 2	Chowder	Warm over low heat.
	Salad	Prepare apples, add to salad, and toss. Place in serving bowl.
	Soufflé	Warm in oven in warm water bath for 15 minutes; unmold on flat plate and set out pie server for transferring to dinner plates.
GRAND FINALE	Cake	Dust with confectioners' sugar.

BEFORE DINNER IS SERVED: TURN DOWN OVEN TO 250°.

MAIN EVENT	Chicken	Carve chicken; place over bed of vegetables; arrange on platter. Cover lightly with foil and place in the oven with the door ajar about 4 inches.

JUST BEFORE DINNER:

Fill bowls with hot soup. Serve and pass the bread.

DINNER SERVICE:

After soup is cleared, bring all food to the table. Plate and serve Main Event.

15 MINUTES BEFORE DESSERT:

Place ice cream balls in serving bowl and refrigerate.

DESSERT SERVICE:

Set dessert plates on table. Bring cake to table with ice cream and serve.
Serve coffee.

AFTER SERVICE:

Unplug coffee.
Turn off oven.

MENU 3
An End-of-Summer Seafood Spree

THE MAIN EVENT:

A Brimming Steamer with Shellfish, Potatoes, and Ale

ON THE SIDE:

Cabbage Slaw with Sour-Cream Dressing

◆

Roasted Corn in the Husk

ON THE SIDE:

Black-eyed Peas and Avocado Salad

◆

Red and Yellow Tomato Stacks with Pesto

THE GRAND FINALE:
Spiced Fruit Crumble

PALATE TEASER:
Shrimp, Red Onion, and Monterey Jack Quesadillas (page 316)

BEVERAGE RECOMMENDATION:
McSorley's Ale
Grolsch Premium Lager

OU HAVE BEEN COLLECTING SHELLS EVERY DAY ON YOUR BEACH walks and they're all on display on your picnic table and along the rails of your deck. Before you pack up and head home, you and your beach buddies must celebrate the beauty and bounty of the sea and garden. Big bowls of coleslaw and roasted corn are already out on the table when you emerge from inside the cottage with your favorite old steamer, chockfull of clams and mussels, sausage and potatoes, and steaming ale.

The Main Event on this fabulous seasonal menu is really the defining element of a great dinner party. Wherever you serve up your steamers, whether it's right on the beach or on an apartment dining table, enjoy the communal casualness of the occasion. Everyone will help themselves from the giant platters of shellfish, sausage, and potatoes—and will be well protected with bibs and loads of napkins!

The brimming steamer and its accompaniments (both the one- and two-toque menus) are simple and enjoyable to prepare. You'll have fun layering ingredients into the cooking pot—pay attention to the cooking times—and the wafting aroma of steaming ale will create an unforgettable party atmosphere. Complementing the sweet shellfish are tangy side dishes: coleslaw with sour-cream dressing (zesty with mustard and horseradish) and moist, roasted corn brushed with a terrific gingered herb butter.

You'll also use summer's best vegetables in my two-toque side dishes, first assembling a wonderfully textured salad of black-eye peas, sweet peppers, and avocado. And you will absolutely thrill your guests (and yourself) with luscious, multicolored tomato sandwiches filled with pesto and smoked mozzarella, artistically arrayed on a serving platter.

Later, as the sea breezes pick up, and the stars come out over the ocean, or wherever you are, you will please everyone all over again by bringing Spiced Fruit Crumble (really easy!) to the table, still warm enough to melt a big scoop of vanilla ice cream.

SETTING THE STAGE

You can lend a touch of the ocean to this party with a display of seashells. Select the prettiest and most varied and arrange them in a low wicker basket for a centerpiece.

Eager eating is the main activity of this ultra-casual dinner party, and you will be wise to provide lobster bibs and plenty of paper towels, napkins, and moist towelettes to keep everyone clean and comfortable while they dig in! As you will see in the recipes, there are lots of bowls of food, and every guest will need an extra-large dinner plate, about 12 to 14 inches, to hold the shellfish, side dishes, and salad. Be sure to provide big bowls for discarding the shells.

THE MAIN EVENT

A Brimming Steamer with Shellfish, Potatoes, and Ale

MAKES 8 SERVINGS

This spectacular main course is a snap to make, but for those who have not had much experience with shellfish, see my shopping and handling notes below.

SPECIAL COOKWARE
Large (10–12-quart) stockpot with lid
Cleaning brush

4 dozen littleneck or steamer clams
3¹/₂ pounds mussels
¹/₄ cup salt
2 pounds very small (1-ounce) fingerling potatoes, such as Red Bliss or Yukon Gold, scrubbed and cut in half

24 ounces light or dark ale
3 cloves garlic, peeled and minced
2 Spanish onions, peeled and diced small
2 tablespoons minced fresh thyme
¹/₄ cup finely minced flat-leaf parsley
20 whole black peppercorns
2 lemons, cut into 8 wedges each
1¹/₂ pounds kielbasa sausage, cut into 2-inch pieces
1 pound salted butter
3 tablespoons fresh lemon juice

GARNISH
2 lemons, cut into 16 wedges

PURCHASING THE CLAMS AND MUSSELS
When you select your shellfish, make sure that each shell is completely closed, indicating that it is alive. Ask the fishmonger for cultivated mussels as they will be less likely to have sand in their shells.

CLEANING THE CLAMS AND MUSSELS
Scrub the clams and mussels well under cold running water with a stiff brush. Pull and scrape the beards from each mussel. Place the clams and mussels in a large pot with cold water to cover and add the ¹/₄ cup of salt. Soak the shellfish for 10 minutes. The clams and mussels will release their sand residue when soaked in salted water. Drain the shellfish through a colander and place in the refrigerator.

CONCOCTING THE BREW
1. Layer the potatoes in the bottom of the large stockpot and cover with the ale. Scatter the garlic, onions, thyme, parsley, peppercorns, and lemons over the potatoes.

2. Layer the sausage over the herbs, the clams over the sausage, and the mussels over the clams. *(Discard any opened shellfish if it does not pull closed when you press it lightly together with your fingers.)*

3. Tightly cover the stockpot and bring the ale to a boil over medium heat. Lower the heat and simmer the brew for about 15–18 minutes, or until all the clams and mussels have opened.

4. While the shellfish are simmering make the lemon butter: Melt the butter in a medium saucepan over medium heat, and stir in the lemon juice, reserve for the butter crocks.

FINISHING TOUCHES AND TABLE PRESENTATION

This is the best time to use 14-inch dinner plates. Fill two large platters with the clams, mussels, potatoes, and sausage and place them on the table. Carefully strain the broth into small bowls. Surround the platters with the bowls of broth, plates of lemon wedges, and fill the crocks of lemon butter. Let your guests help themselves. Don't forget the towelettes.

ONE-TOQUE: Place half the Cabbage Slaw and half the Roasted Corn in the Husk at each end of the table.

TWO-TOQUE: Place half the Black-eyed Peas and Avocado Salad and half the Red and Yellow Tomato Stacks at each end of the table.

ON THE SIDE

Cabbage Slaw with Sour-Cream Dressing

MAKES 8 SERVINGS

SPECIAL COOKWARE
Food processor with shredding disk or large hand-grater

THE SLAW
1 head (about 1 1/2 pounds) white cabbage
8 scallions, green and white parts, minced
1 cup finely diced fennel (1 large fennel bulb equals 5 ounces)
1/2 cup finely diced red bell pepper (1 medium pepper equals 5 1/2 ounces)
1 large cucumber, peeled, seeded, and diced
8 large radishes, trimmed and finely chopped
1 tablespoon finely chopped fresh dill
3 tablespoons finely chopped flat-leaf parsley

THE DRESSING
1 1/2 tablespoons Dijon mustard
2 tablespoons well-drained white horseradish
1/4 cup red wine vinegar
2 tablespoons fresh lemon juice
1 cup sour cream
1/4 teaspoon mustard seeds
1/4 teaspoon celery seeds
1 teaspoon sugar
1 teaspoon salt, or to taste
1 teaspoon freshly ground black pepper, or to taste

THE SLAW
1. Discard the outer leaves of the cabbage. Remove the core, then slice the cabbage into wedges that will

fit through the feeding tube of the food processor. Shred the cabbage using the shredding disk of the food processor (or on the large side of a hand-grater).

2. Toss the cabbage in a large bowl with the scallions, fennel, red pepper, cucumber, radishes, dill, and parsley. Set aside.

THE DRESSING

1. In a small bowl, whisk together the mustard, horseradish, vinegar, and lemon juice and toss with the slaw, blending well. Let rest for 20 minutes. Drain and discard any liquids that may have accumulated in the bottom of the bowl.

2. In another bowl, blend together the sour cream, mustard seeds, celery seeds, and sugar and season with the salt and pepper. Toss the seasoned sour cream with the cabbage slaw and blend very well. Season to taste once more.

FINISHING TOUCHES AND TABLE PRESENTATION

Serve the cabbage slaw from two funky pottery bowls, one at each end of the table. With all that seafood, you probably won't have any room on your dinner plate, so stack additional salad-size plates on the table.

The Inventive Chef

THIS CABBAGE SLAW IS A GREAT SIDE DISH WITH BAKED HAM, FRIED CHICKEN, ROAST TURKEY, OR ROAST PORK. HERE IT IS SEASONED WITH DILL TO COMPLEMENT THE SHELLFISH, BUT YOU CAN ALSO USE TARRAGON, SAGE, OR THYME INSTEAD OF DILL FOR A DELICIOUS SLAW.

ON THE SIDE

Roasted Corn in the Husk

MAKES 8 SERVINGS

8 ears of young corn
1/2 cup (1 stick) butter
1 plum tomato, finely diced
2 tablespoons finely chopped fresh chives or scallions
1 small shallot, minced
1 tablespoon minced fresh ginger
1 teaspoon salt, or to taste
1/2 teaspoon freshly ground white pepper,
  or to taste

1. Preheat the oven to 350°.

2. Pull down the husks from each ear of corn, exposing the silk threads, but make sure you leave the husks attached to the ears of corn. Remove and discard the silk threads. Cover again with the husks and soak the corn in cold water for 15 minutes.

3. While the corn is soaking, melt the butter in a small skillet or saucepan. Remove it from the heat and blend in the tomato, chives, shallot, and ginger. Season with salt and pepper and set aside.

4. Remove corn from water. Pull down the husks and dry the corn kernels well with paper towels. Brush each ear of corn well with the herbed butter. Enclose the kernels again with the husks and place on a baking sheet. Bake the corn for 45 minutes.

FINISHING TOUCHES AND TABLE PRESENTATION

Serve the corn, with the husks left on, on round dinner

plates. The cobs stay moist wrapped in their blanket of leaves.

ON THE SIDE

Black-eyed Peas and Avocado Salad

MAKES 8 SERVINGS

2¹/₂ cups dried black-eyed peas
4 cups chicken broth, homemade or low-sodium canned
2 cups dry white wine
¹/₂ cup olive oil
¹/₂ teaspoon ground cumin
1 tablespoon finely chopped fresh cilantro
3 tablespoons fresh lime juice
¹/₂ teaspoon dark brown sugar, firmly packed
1 small yellow pepper, seeded and cut in medium dice
10 radishes, trimmed and cut in small dice
2 scallions, white and green parts, trimmed and thinly
    sliced
¹/₂ teaspoon salt, or to taste
¹/₈ teaspoon cayenne pepper, or to taste
2 large ripe avocados

1. Rinse the black-eyed peas in a colander under cold water, removing any stones. Place the peas in a large saucepan with water to cover and soak overnight. *(If you are in a hurry, bring the peas to a boil in a large saucepan with 6 cups of water over high heat and simmer rapidly for 2 minutes. Cover the pan, remove from the heat, and let stand at room temperature for 1 hour.)* Strain the peas through a colander and discard the soaking water.

2. Combine the chicken broth and wine in a large saucepan and bring to a boil over medium-high heat. Lower the heat, add the drained peas, and cook at a slow boil, uncovered, for 20–30 minutes, or until the peas are tender but crisp to the bite. Drain the peas once more. Discard the broth and wine and cool the peas to room temperature, about 20 minutes.

3. In a large bowl, toss the peas with the oil, cumin, cilantro, lime juice, and brown sugar. Stir in the yellow pepper, radishes, and scallions. Season with salt and cayenne pepper and refrigerate for 2–3 hours.

4. To keep the avocados green and fresh-looking, prepare them just before service. Peel and pit the avocados and cut them into medium dice.

FINISHING TOUCHES AND
TABLE PRESENTATION

Gently blend in the freshly cut avocado and reseason the salad to taste. With a slotted spoon, transfer the salad to two glass or crockery bowls. Place one at either end of the table.

ON THE SIDE

Red and Yellow Tomato Stacks with Pesto

MAKES 8 SERVINGS

4 red beefsteak tomatoes, cut into 4 slices each
2 yellow beefsteak tomatoes, cut into 4 slices each
16 1/4-inch slices smoked mozzarella (about 1 pound)
1 cup tightly packed basil leaves
2 cloves garlic, peeled
3 tablespoons pine nuts
2 teaspoons drained capers
2 tablespoons pitted and chopped Niçoise olives
2 tablespoons freshly grated Parmigiano Reggiano
1/2 cup olive oil
1/4 teaspoon salt, or to taste

GARNISH
8 large basil leaves
Freshly ground black pepper

1. Place the sliced tomatoes and mozzarella cheese on a baking sheet lined with waxed paper or plastic wrap. Cover with plastic wrap and set aside.

2. Place the cup of basil leaves, garlic, pine nuts, capers, olives, and Parmigiano in the bowl of a food processor fitted with the metal cutting blade. With the processor on, slowly drizzle the olive oil through the feeding tube until the pesto has emulsified and thickened. Add salt to taste.

3. To make the stacks: Place 8 slices of red tomato on a work surface. Spread a generous layer of pesto over the tomatoes. Cover the pesto with a slice of cheese. Place a slice of yellow tomato over the cheese. Spread

another layer of pesto over the yellow tomatoes. Place a second piece of cheese over the pesto and cover with the final slices of red tomato.

FINISHING TOUCHES AND TABLE PRESENTATION

Transfer the stacks in a zigzag pattern to two round dinner plates or platters. Garnish each tomato stack with a basil leaf and sprinkle with black pepper. If the stacks are refrigerated before service, make certain to bring them to room temperature before serving. Place a platter of tomato stacks at each end of the table.

The Inventive Chef

THERE ARE SO MANY WAYS TO VARY THESE STACKS: LAYER THE TOMATOES IN A DIFFERENT COLOR PATTERN; USE SLICES OF MONTEREY JACK OR HAVARTI CHEESE; OR TOP EACH STACK WITH AN ANCHOVY PLACED OVER THE BASIL LEAF. A WONDERFUL TOUCH IS TO PLACE THE STACKS ON A LIGHTLY OILED BAKING SHEET AND WARM THEM IN A 350° OVEN FOR 8-10 MINUTES.

Spiced Fruit Crumble

MAKES 8 SERVINGS

SPECIAL COOKWARE
2¹/₂-quart ovenproof decorative baking dish

2 pints blueberries
2 pints strawberries, washed, hulled, and halved
6 medium nectarines (about 1 pound total), pitted and cut into ¹/₂-inch pieces
¹/₄ cup fresh orange juice
Grated zest of one orange
1 teaspoon pure vanilla extract
1 teaspoon powdered ginger
1 teaspoon ground cinnamon
¹/₄ cup apricot preserves
¹/₂ cup light brown sugar, packed
¹/₄ cup rolled oats
³/₄ cup all-purpose flour
4 tablespoons unsalted butter, chilled
8 large scoops good-quality vanilla ice cream or Ginger Cream (page 101)

1. Preheat the oven to 375°.
2. Place the blueberries, strawberries, nectarines, orange juice, orange zest, vanilla, ¹/₂ teaspoon of the ginger, ¹/₂ teaspoon of the cinnamon, and the apricot preserves together in a large bowl. Toss and blend all the ingredients well and set aside at room temperature.
3. Combine the brown sugar, oats, flour, the remaining ¹/₂ teaspoon ginger and ¹/₂ teaspoon cinnamon in a medium-size bowl and blend well. Add the butter in small pieces, mixing well with your fingers or a pastry cutter until the mixture resembles coarse, sticky crumbs.
4. Pour the fruit mixture into a 2¹/₂ quart ovenproof decorative, deep baking dish. Cover the fruit with the brown sugar–oat topping. Bake the crumble for 40–45 minutes, until the top is golden brown.

FINISHING TOUCHES AND
TABLE PRESENTATION

Serve the crumble warm on dessert plates. Top the warm fruit with real vanilla bean ice cream or Ginger Cream.

The Inventive Chef

THIS IS A YEAR-ROUND DESSERT. USE OTHER SUMMER FRUITS, SUCH AS PEACHES, PLUMS, RASPBERRIES, OR BLACKBERRIES. IN WINTER, FRUITS SUCH AS PEARS, APPLES, AND PLUMS, WITH THE ADDITION OF DRIED CHERRIES, MAKE WONDERFUL CRUMBLES. AND YOU CAN ADD A HEARTY TWIST WITH THE ADDITION OF WALNUTS OR PECANS, OR BY STEEPING THE FRUIT IN A RICHLY FLAVORED BRANDY SUCH AS CALVADOS.

KITCHEN SCHEDULE

2 OR 3 DAYS BEFORE THE PARTY

MAIN EVENT	Shellfish	Order shellfish.

THE DAY BEFORE THE PARTY

MAIN EVENT	Shellfish	Prepare potatoes, garlic, onions, thyme, parsley, sausage, and lemon wedges as instructed in ingredient list; store covered in refrigerator.
TOQUE 1	Slaw	Prepare all vegetables as instructed in ingredient list; store covered in refrigerator. Combine mustard, horseradish, vinegar, and lemon juice; store covered in refrigerator. Combine sour cream, mustard seeds, celery seeds, and sugar; store covered in refrigerator.
	Corn	Prepare the tomato, chives, shallot, and ginger. Store covered in refrigerator.
TOQUE 2	Black-eyed Peas	Prepare through step 2; toss with the oil, cumin, cilantro, lime juice, and brown sugar; store covered in refrigerator. Trim and cut yellow pepper, radishes, and scallions; store covered in refrigerator.
	Tomatoes	Slice mozzarella; store covered in refrigerator. Prepare step 2; store covered in refrigerator.
GRAND FINALE	Fruit Crumble	Prepare steps 2 and 3; store covered in refrigerator. Prepare Ginger Cream; store covered in refrigerator. Or, if

		serving ice cream, make sure you bought it.
Strategic Maneuvers:		Fill creamer; cover and store in refrigerator.
		Fill sugar bowl.
		Set table.
		Check table decor.
		Check any special necessities for the shellfish (such as tons of napkins for buttery fingers and bowls for discarding the shells).
		Put moist towelettes on table in two 9 1/2-inch plates.
		Check ice and beverages.
		Locate teas.
		Chill wine if white.
		Check garnishes for each recipe.
		Locate and label all serving bowls, platters, and utensils.

THE DAY OF THE PARTY

MAIN EVENT	Shellfish	Clean clams and mussels; store covered in refrigerator. Make certain all ingredients are ready for steaming. Arrange lemon-wedge garnish for serving on two 9-inch plates; store covered in refrigerator. Heat butter with lemon juice; set aside at room temperature.
TOQUE 1	Slaw	Toss and store covered in refrigerator.
	Corn	Prepare through step 3.

TOQUE 2	Black-eyed Peas	Finish recipe through step 3; store covered in refrigerator.
	Tomatoes	Slice tomatoes and finish recipe; store covered in refrigerator. *Do not garnish.*
GRAND FINALE	Fruit Crumble	Finish recipe and bake.

15 MINUTES BEFORE GUESTS ARRIVE:

		Preheat oven to 350°.
MAIN EVENT	Shellfish	Arrange main event ingredients in pot for steaming.

45 MINUTES BEFORE DINNER:

MAIN EVENT	Shellfish	Steam shellfish. Warm Citrus Butter.
TOQUE 1	Slaw	Set on table.
	Corn	Prepare step 4.
TOQUE 2	Tomatoes	Set tomatoes on table and garnish.

JUST BEFORE DINNER:

Place citrus butter in 4 bowls and set with plates of lemon wedges on table.
Add avocado to black-eyed peas. Set on table and garnish.

DINNER SERVICE:

Plug in coffee.

GRAND FINALE	Fruit Crumble	Lower oven to 200°. Place fruit crumble in oven to warm while guests are eating.

If serving ice cream, remove it from freezer and let soften at room temperature 15 minutes before service.

DESSERT SERVICE:

Bring out dessert plates and serve.
Serve coffee.

AFTER SERVICE:

Unplug coffee.
Turn off oven.

MENU 4

A Taste of Paris with Gertrude Stein

THE MAIN EVENT:

Cherry-Glazed Duck Breasts with Tart Mango Chutney

ON THE SIDE:

*Warm Bitter Greens and Rice Salad
with Calvados Mustard Vinaigrette*

◆

Spiced Carrot Puree

ON THE SIDE:

Flageolets, Roasted Garlic, and Spinach

◆

Red Cabbage, Baby Beets, and Apples

THE GRAND FINALE:
Lemon-Glazed Spiced Pumpkin Cake

PALATE TEASER:
Pecan-Studded Cheddar Wafers (page 304)

BEVERAGE RECOMMENDATIONS:
*Madeira, Leacock's Rainwater
Pommard, Bouchard Père et Fils*

The questions—and opinions—are flying even as the aperitif is poured: Was Gertrude really a . . . genius? (She thought she was!) Do you think she might have secretly been in love with Picasso? (You're joking!) Before the literary lions and lionesses in your book club explore the secrets of Paris in the twenties, serve a meal as pretty and flavorful as the ones Alice B. Toklas cooked for the legendary Saturday salons. And while your pals are showering you with compliments on the perfect pairing of duck breasts and a salad of warm bitter greens and rice, you imagine Hemingway (or is that Scott Fitzgerald?) smiling at you, and passing his plate for seconds . . .

Treat your friends to this marvelous French-inspired menu—whether for a late lunch or an early dinner before your learned conversation, or just as a delightful casual supper. They will thrill to the lovely play of flavors and colors you have assembled on one plate.

This meal is easy to prepare (check the kitchen schedule on page 77) and full of techniques and ingredients you will enjoy. The duck breasts gain flavor from roasting with fresh herbs, then more roasting with a luscious and spicy glaze of cherry preserves, mustard, and ginger. The glistening slices are just gorgeous, and terrific paired with a tart mango chutney.

The sides are also full of fresh and interesting flavor juxtapositions (you may have a hard time deciding which to make). There's a lovely bitterness in the greens and rice salad, tinged with the apple flavor of the Calvados vinaigrette, that sets off the sweetness of the duck. Or try the rustic stew of flageolets—my favorite French beans—hearty with roasted garlic, spinach, and notes of coriander, bay leaf, and thyme. Your plate will be brilliantly colorful with either the smooth puree of carrots or the tangy and vivid mix of red cabbage and beets.

This menu's great tastes will give everyone plenty to talk about, so take a break and repair to the living room before you indulge in the sweet complexities of dessert: a perfectly spiced pumpkin cake with more than a touch of tartness in the lemon glaze.

SETTING THE STAGE

With so much color on the plate and so much conversation in the air, you can set a simple table for this meal: A neutral cloth with beautiful napkins would suffice. The menu is full of autumn foods, so a basketful of harvest fruits and produce would be a great centerpiece, or you could mass small green plants for a different effect. Here's a cute touch for a book-club event: Purchase inexpensive bookmarks for each guest and slip them inside place cards set on each plate. Be sure to seat the most contentious literary combatants on opposite sides of the table!

Cherry-Glazed Duck Breasts with Tart Mango Chutney

MAKES 8 SERVINGS

Purchase four 4$\frac{1}{2}$–5-pound ducks. Have the butcher separate the breasts as instructed below. Freeze the legs and thighs for future use. If preferred, purchase four 1$\frac{1}{2}$-pound boneless duck breasts from a butcher or in a supermarket.

4 whole skinless, boneless duck breasts, halved
   (duck skin and breast bones reserved)
4 shallots, peeled and diced
2 large cloves garlic, peeled and diced
2 large carrots, peeled and cut in $\frac{1}{2}$-inch dice
1 tablespoon minced fresh thyme
$\frac{1}{2}$ tablespoon minced fresh sage
Salt and freshly ground black pepper to taste
1 cup cherry preserves
$\frac{1}{4}$ cup Dijon mustard
2 teaspoons fresh lemon juice
Zest of 1 lemon, finely chopped
1 teaspoon powdered ginger
$\frac{3}{4}$ cup chicken broth, homemade or low-sodium canned
Delicious Duck Cracklings (optional, page 71)
Tart Mango Chutney (recipe follows)

1. Preheat the oven to 400°.
2. Place the reserved duck bones, the shallots, half the garlic, and the carrots in the bottom of a large roasting pan. Place a roasting rack over the vegetables in the pan.
3. Mix together the remaining garlic, the thyme, and the sage and rub the herb mixture over each duck breast. Lightly season the meat with salt and pepper. Place a piece of the reserved duck skin over each piece of breast. Make sure that most of the meat is covered by the skin, which will keep the meat moist. Place the breasts, about 2 inches apart, on the roasting rack, then place the roasting pan on the top rack of the oven. Roast for 20 minutes.
4. While the breasts are roasting, prepare the cherry glaze: Combine the cherry preserves, mustard, lemon juice, lemon zest, and ground ginger in a medium-size saucepan. Simmer the glaze over low heat for 5 minutes. Cover the saucepan and set the glaze aside at room temperature.
5. After the duck has roasted for 20 minutes, remove the roasting pan from the oven. Do not turn off the oven. Pour the drippings that have accumulated in the bottom of the pan into the cherry glaze; mix well. (If following the kitchen schedule, turn off oven at this time.)
6. Remove the duck skins and reserve for use in the crackling recipe below, or discard. Brush each duck breast well with the cherry glaze, reserving the left-over glaze. Return the breasts to the oven and roast for 10–12 minutes more, or until their juices run clear. Remove the duck breasts to a cutting board and let them rest for 5 minutes to allow the juices to settle.
7. Add the chicken broth to the cherry glaze remaining in the saucepan and simmer over medium-high heat until it begins to resemble syrup. Prepare duck cracklings if desired and add to the glaze. Season with salt and pepper to taste and keep warm.

FINISHING TOUCHES AND TABLE PRESENTATION

Bring all the food and the serving pieces to the table and let your guests pass the platters and bowls. Carve the duck into $1/4$-inch slices and arrange them in overlapping pieces on a white platter. Coat the duck with the reduced cherry glaze. Fill a bowl with the Tart Mango Chutney and let your guests help themselves.

ONE-TOQUE: Toss the greens and place them in a colorful round bowl. Place the carrots in an oval, round, or square bowl about 2 inches deep.

TWO-TOQUE: Place the flageolets in a colorful bowl. Place the cabbage in an oval or square bowl.

The Inventive Chef

SUBSTITUTE CURRANT JELLY FOR THE CHERRY PRESERVES.

Delicious Duck Cracklings:

I CAN'T RESIST THE ROBUST FLAVOR OF DUCK CRACKLINGS, AND I MAKE THEM WHENEVER I GET THE CHANCE. CHOP THE RESERVED DUCK SKIN INTO $1/4$-INCH PIECES AND SAUTÉ OVER MEDIUM HEAT, STIRRING CONSTANTLY, UNTIL CRISP AND GOLDEN. DRAIN ON PAPER TOWELS, SEASON WITH SALT AND PEPPER, AND ADD TO THE GLAZE.

Tart Mango Chutney

MAKES 8 SERVINGS

2 large ripe mangoes, peeled and cut into $1/8$-inch dice
2 tablespoons finely diced red onion
2 tablespoons fresh lime juice

$1/2$ tablespoon minced fresh cilantro
1 teaspoon raspberry vinegar
Pinch of cayenne pepper
$1/4$ teaspoon salt, or to taste

Blend the mangoes, onion, lime juice, cilantro, vinegar, and cayenne together in a medium bowl and season with salt to taste.

The Inventive Chef

THIS IS ALSO FANTASTIC USING FRESH RIPE PAPAYA INSTEAD OF MANGO.

ON THE SIDE

Warm Bitter Greens and Rice Salad with Calvados Mustard Vinaigrette

MAKES 8 SERVINGS

You can prepare the rice well ahead of time, so the final cooking of this delicious and unusual salad is truly a breeze.

SPECIAL COOKWARE
Extra-large skillet, 14–16 inches

THE SALAD
1 pound Swiss chard, tough stems removed
2 tablespoons olive oil
1 clove minced garlic
2 cups cooked basmati or long-grained rice, room temperature

3 bunches arugula, stemmed, washed, and dried
2 heads chicory, core removed, washed, dried, and torn into
   large pieces
1/8 teaspoon salt, or to taste
1/8 teaspoon ground black pepper, or to taste
1/2 cup Calvados Mustard Vinaigrette (recipe follows)

1. Wash the Swiss chard and dry it well, preferably with a salad spinner. Try not to tear the leaves. Heat the olive oil in an extra-large skillet over medium-high heat. Add the garlic and cook for 30 seconds. Add the Swiss chard, toss, and cook the leaves until they have wilted, about 4 minutes. Add the rice and continue to sauté until the rice is warm.

2. Toss the arugula and chicory with the Swiss chard and rice in the skillet for 1–2 minutes, until all the greens have wilted slightly. Season with the salt and pepper and remove from the heat.

FINISHING TOUCHES AND TABLE PRESENTATION

Fifteen minutes before serving dinner, put the greens mixture in a large bowl and toss with 1/2 cup of the warm Calvados Mustard Vinaigrette to lightly coat the leaves. Reserve the remaining vinaigrette in the refrigerator for another use.

The Inventive Chef

I LOVE TO SERVE THIS SALAD WITH CHICKEN, CORNISH HENS, AND GOOSE AS WELL AS DUCK. DRIED CURRANTS AND WALNUTS ARE ALSO GREAT ADDITIONS.

Calvados Mustard Vinaigrette

MAKES ABOUT 1 CUP

2 cloves garlic, peeled
1 1/2 teaspoons black-peppercorn or plain Dijon mustard
3 tablespoons red wine vinegar
2 teaspoons sugar
3/4 cup olive oil
1 1/2 tablespoons Calvados or apple liqueur
1/4 teaspoon salt, or to taste
1/8 teaspoon ground black pepper, or to taste

1. Place the garlic, mustard, vinegar, and sugar in the bowl of a food processor fitted with the cutting blade. Process for 30 seconds, until the ingredients are well blended. With the machine still running, pour the oil *very slowly* through the feeding tube, until vinaigrette has thickened. Stir in the Calvados and season with salt and pepper.

2. Transfer the vinaigrette to a small saucepan. When ready to dress the salad, warm the dressing very gently over low heat. *Do not boil the vinaigrette or it will separate.*

ON THE SIDE

Spiced Carrot Puree

MAKES 8 SERVINGS (ABOUT 3 1/3 CUPS)

3 1/2 cups chicken broth, homemade or low-sodium canned
3 large shallots, peeled and coarsely chopped
2 pounds (about 10) large carrots, peeled and quartered

6 tablespoons butter, at room temperature
3 tablespoons heavy cream
Dash of ground cloves
1/4 teaspoon salt, or to taste
1/8 teaspoon cayenne pepper, or to taste

1. In a 4-quart saucepan bring the chicken broth to a boil with the shallots over high heat. Add the carrots, cover, and simmer briskly for 15–20 minutes, or until the carrots are soft enough to pierce easily with a fork. Drain the vegetables and discard the liquid. Place the carrots and shallots in the bowl of a food processor fitted with the knife blade and puree until smooth. Use a rubber spatula to scrape down the sides of the bowl.

2. Add the butter, cream, cloves, salt, and cayenne pepper through the feeding tube of the processor and process until the puree mounds and clings to a metal spoon like whipped cream. If the mixture is too thick, add more cream and process.

3. Transfer the puree to the top of a double boiler and keep it warm over simmering water, stirring occasionally.

The Inventive Chef

I LOVE TO USE BROCCOLI, CAULIFLOWER, OR BEETS TO PRODUCE PUREES WITH VIBRANT COLOR AND TASTE. IT IS FUN TO SERVE TWO PUREES, SUCH AS CAULIFLOWER AND BEETS, TO CREATE ELECTRIFYING COMBINATIONS.

ON THE SIDE

Flageolets, Roasted Garlic, and Spinach

MAKES 8 SERVINGS

The rich flavors of this dish come from cooking the beans in chicken broth and then briefly sautéing them with aromatic vegetables, herbs, and roasted garlic.

2 cups dried flageolets or Great Northern beans
2 quarts plus 1/2 cup chicken broth, homemade
    or low-sodium canned
2 bay leaves
1 large yellow onion, peeled and chopped medium
1/8 teaspoon ground coriander
1 1/2 teaspoons salt
1/2 teaspoon freshly ground black pepper
1/4 cup extra virgin olive oil
5 shallots, peeled and finely chopped
3 ribs celery, washed and finely chopped
3 carrots, peeled and finely chopped
3 heads roasted garlic, mashed fine (page 87)
1 pound fresh spinach, washed, stems trimmed,
    and finely chopped
3/4 cup dry white wine, such as Soave or Chablis
1 teaspoon minced fresh thyme
1 tablespoon butter

1. Soak the beans in a large saucepan with cold water to cover for 3 hours or overnight. Drain the beans.

2. Bring 2 quarts of the chicken broth to a simmer in a saucepan. Add the beans, bay leaves, onion, coriander, salt, and pepper. Simmer the beans, uncovered, for 50 minutes or until they are tender but still resistant to the bite. Drain the beans through a colander, discard the bay leaves and broth, and return the beans to the pan. Set aside at room temperature.

3. Heat the oil in a large skillet. Add the shallots and celery. Sauté until the vegetables are translucent, about 3 minutes. Add the carrots and cook for 4 minutes more. Stir the mashed garlic and spinach into the vegetables. Add the white wine and the remaining $1/2$ cup of chicken broth and simmer for 3 minutes or until the spinach is bright green, wilted, and most of the liquid is absorbed.

4. Toss the reserved beans in the skillet with the vegetables. Add the thyme and butter and heat briefly until the butter has melted. Adjust the seasoning to taste.

The Inventive Chef

THESE BEANS ARE DELICIOUS WITH ANY ROASTED MEAT OR POULTRY. USE DIFFERENT HERBS, SUCH AS ROSEMARY OR TARRAGON, TO COMPLEMENT THE SEASONINGS IN THE OTHER DISHES.

ON THE SIDE

Red Cabbage, Baby Beets, and Apples

MAKES 8 SERVINGS

The delightful sweet-and-sour tang of this dish comes from balanced additions of brown sugar and vinegar. It is a perfect complement to the duck.

SPECIAL COOKWARE
3–4-quart flameproof casserole with lid

$1^1/2$ pounds small beets (about 2 inches in diameter), scrubbed clean and trimmed
Pinch of salt
3 tablespoons vegetable oil
1 large red onion, peeled and diced small
3 large cloves garlic, peeled and finely minced
$1^1/2$ pounds red cabbage, cored and shredded with a sharp knife to $1/8$-inch thick
1 tablespoon balsamic vinegar
1 tablespoon tarragon vinegar
3 tablespoons light brown sugar
$1/2$ cup plus 3 tablespoons dry red wine
3 large apples, such as McIntosh or Baldwin, cored and cut in $1/4$-inch dice
$1/8$ teaspoon ground cloves
1 tablespoon caraway seeds
2 tablespoons salted butter, softened
$1/2$ teaspoon salt
$1/4$ teaspoon freshly ground black pepper, or to taste

1. In a medium saucepan, cover the beets with water, add a pinch of salt, and simmer over medium heat for 25 minutes, until the beets are tender when pierced with a fork. Drain the beets and let cool. Peel and cut the beets in half, then cut each half into $^1/_4$-inch slices. Set aside at room temperature.

2. Preheat the oven to 375°.

3. In a large skillet, heat the oil over medium heat. Sauté the onion for 2–3 minutes, until it begins to soften. Add the garlic and cook 1 minute more.

4. Add the red cabbage and $^1/_3$ cup of water to the onions in the skillet. Cook, stirring, over medium heat, until the cabbage begins to wilt, about 3–5 minutes. Increase the heat, and add the balsamic vinegar, tarragon vinegar, sugar, and 3 tablespoons of the wine. Simmer until the sugar has completely dissolved, about 1 minute.

5. Place the cabbage mixture, the reserved beets, and the apples in a 3–4 quart flameproof casserole. Add the remaining $^1/_2$ cup of wine, cover the casserole, and bake for about 30 minutes.

6. Remove the casserole from the oven, toss in the cloves, caraway seeds, and butter, and season with salt and pepper to taste.

The Inventive Chef

THIS IS ANOTHER DISH YOU CAN TURN INTO A ROBUST ENTRÉE WITH THE ADDITION OF DICED BAKED HAM OR OTHER COOKED MEATS. YOU CAN ALSO ADD SOME COOKED DICED ROOT VEGETABLES, SUCH AS CARROTS OR PARSNIPS, TO THE CASSEROLE BEFORE YOU PUT IT IN THE OVEN.

THE GRAND FINALE

Lemon-Glazed Spiced Pumpkin Cake

MAKES 12 CAKE SQUARES

You make this luscious cake with canned pumpkin, but if small fresh pumpkins are available, use them as a charming part of dessert service.

SPECIAL COOKWARE
Baking pan, 13 by 9 by 2 inches
Flour sifter

THE CAKE
1 tablespoon unsalted butter for greasing cake pan
2 $^1/_2$ cups all-purpose flour
$^1/_2$ teaspoon salt
1 teaspoon baking soda
2 tablespoons baking powder
2 teaspoons powdered ginger
$^1/_2$ teaspoon ground nutmeg
$^1/_2$ teaspoon ground cloves
1 teaspoon ground cinnamon
1 tablespoon instant espresso dissolved in $^1/_2$ cup boiling water
1 cup canned pumpkin puree, unsweetened
$^3/_4$ cup molasses
8 tablespoons unsalted butter, at room temperature
1 cup sugar
2 large eggs

2 tablespoons brandy
1/2 cup crystallized ginger (purchased on spice shelves in markets), *chopped medium*

THE GLAZE

1 cup confectioners' sugar
1 tablespoon fresh lemon juice
Few drops of boiling water
Grated zest of one lemon

GARNISH

1 recipe Ginger Cream (page 101)
2 miniature pumpkins or 1 small pumpkin (optional)
8–10 lemon leaves (optional)

THE CAKE

1. Preheat the oven to 350°. Butter the baking pan.
2. Sift together the flour, salt, baking soda, baking powder, ginger, nutmeg, cloves, and cinnamon into a bowl. In another bowl, blend together the dissolved espresso, pumpkin puree, and molasses.
3. Beat the butter in a large bowl with an electric mixer on medium speed, using the paddle attachment, until it is creamy, about 2 minutes. Add the sugar and beat until well blended. Add the eggs and continue to beat until the ingredients are well combined.
4. On low speed, mix in *1/3* of the dry ingredients and *1/2* the pumpkin mixture. Beat the ingredients only to mix. Add *1/3* more of the dry ingredients and the rest of the pumpkin. Blend just to mix. Add the last *1/3* of the dry ingredients. Blend just to mix. *(Gently blending the ingredients will make the cake light.)*
5. Stir in the brandy and crystallized ginger. Pour the batter into the prepared cake pan, spreading it evenly. Bake the cake for 40–50 minutes, until a cake tester inserted in the center comes out clean. Let the cake cool in the pan while preparing the lemon glaze.

THE GLAZE

1. Combine the sugar and lemon juice in a small bowl. Add the boiling water, a few drops at a time, until the glaze has reached a thick but pouring consistency.
2. Mix the lemon zest with the glaze, then pour over the cake. Smooth the top of the glaze evenly with a rubber spatula. *(It is perfectly fine if some of the pumpkin cake shows through; the glaze is translucent.)*

FINISHING TOUCHES AND TABLE PRESENTATION

When the cake is completely cool and still in the pan, cut it into twelve 2*1/2*-by-3-inch pieces. Before the meeting, arrange the pieces on a platter lined with lemon leaves (if available). I serve the Ginger Cream on the side, presented in a glass serving bowl or in the pumpkins. To use the miniature pumpkins: With a sharp knife, cut a *1/2*-inch top from the miniature pumpkins or a 1*1/2*-inch top from the small pumpkin. With a small metal teaspoon or grapefruit spoon, scrape the pits and strings from the inside of the pumpkins. Place an underliner under the pumpkins and fill them with the Ginger Cream. I like to lean the pumpkin tops between the pumpkins and the side of the underliner plate.

KITCHEN SCHEDULE

1 WEEK AHEAD

GRAND FINALE	Cake	Prepare through step 5. Cover and freeze.

2 OR 3 DAYS BEFORE THE PARTY

MAIN EVENT	Duck	Order from butcher. Make cherry glaze through step 4; store covered in refrigerator.

THE DAY BEFORE THE PARTY

MAIN EVENT	Duck	Prepare shallots, garlic, carrots, thyme, and sage; store covered in refrigerator.
	Chutney	Prepare recipe; store covered in refrigerator.
TOQUE 1	Salad	Prepare rice; cool and store covered in refrigerator. Prepare vinaigrette; store covered in refrigerator.
	Puree	Prepare recipe; cool and store covered in refrigerator.
TOQUE 2	Flageolets	Prepare through step 2; cool and store covered in refrigerator.
	Cabbage and Beets	Prepare recipe; prepare shallots, celery, carrots, garlic, spinach, and thyme; store separately, covered, in refrigerator. Cool and store in covered casserole in refrigerator.
GRAND FINALE	Cake	Defrost in refrigerator. Prepare pumpkins for garnish; store covered in refrigerator.
Strategic Maneuvers:		Fill creamer; cover and store in refrigerator.

Fill sugar bowl.
Set table.
Check ice and beverages.
Locate teas.
Chill wine if white.
Check garnishes for each recipe.
Locate and label all serving bowls, platters, and utensils.
Place serving pieces on table.

THE DAY OF THE PARTY

MAIN EVENT	Duck	Prepare through step 5; set aside.
	Chutney	Bring to room temperature and place in bowl with ladle or spoon.
TOQUE 1	Puree	Bring to room temperature.
	Salad	Prepare through step 2; set aside. Set up vinaigrette in saucepan for warming.
TOQUE 2	Flageolets	Finish recipe through step 4; set aside at room temperature.
	Cabbage and Beets	Bring to room temperature in casserole.
GRAND FINALE	Cake	Make lemon glaze, coat cake; refrigerate. Whip cream and store in refrigerator in serving bowl.

1 HOUR BEFORE GUESTS ARRIVE:

GRAND FINALE	Cake	Cut cake and arrange on platter. Cover well and set at room temperature.

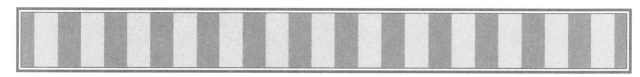

Fill pumpkins or glass bowl with whipped cream and refrigerate.

30 MINUTES BEFORE GUESTS ARRIVE:

		Preheat oven to 400°.
		Plug in coffee.
MAIN EVENT	Duck	Finish recipe, reduce oven temperature to 300°; keep warm in oven.
TOQUE 1	Salad	Warm vinaigrette over very low heat.
	Puree	Set in top of a covered double boiler over simmering water.

30 MINUTES BEFORE DINNER:

| TOQUE 2 | Flageolets | Warm in skillet. |
| | Cabbage and Beets | Warm with duck in oven. |

15 MINUTES BEFORE DINNER:

| MAIN EVENT | Duck | Carve and arrange. |
| TOQUE 1 | Salad | Toss with warm vinaigrette; place in serving bowl. Place all side dishes and condiments in serving bowls. |

DINNER SERVICE:

Bring all food to the table. Let guests help themselves.

DESSERT SERVICE:

Bring cake plates to table and serve guests.
Don't forget the Ginger Cream.
Serve coffee.

AFTER SERVICE:

Unplug coffee.
Turn off oven.

The Drama and Celebration of Formal Dinners

Want to start a ripple of excitement through your circle of friends and acquaintances? Send a select group of them a lovely invitation to dinner, with a subtly tempting (and probably unexpected) phrase such as, "We eagerly await your appearance at eight o'clock. Creative black-tie please." The growing anticipation for your event will be thrilling!

When you host a formal dinner (whether you call for black-tie or another dressy standard), you are putting on a show and inviting your guests to be both part of the drama and the privileged audience. And there's plenty to show off, in addition to the finery that everyone is wearing. Your home is glowing with soft candlelight, your table is set with care and artistry. Most important, you serve a spectacular menu, with special-occasion foods presented as a lovely gift to your guests.

In this chapter, I propose celebrating a few great moments in life with people whom you hold in the highest esteem. Reward them with one of these four sumptuous menus, each with a stunning main event and superb supporting acts:

◆ A royal platter of succulent roast beef will honor the woman who has led you to the biggest success in your career: your boss!

◆ Twelve months have gone by, you love each other more than ever, so bring back your bridesmaids and groomsmen to dress up again for a first-anniversary feast featuring cranberry-glazed Cornish hens.

◆ Your best friend has just had her latest romance novel published, so fete her with a magnificent dinner of roast lamb with Moroccan spices and sensual side dishes.

◆ Is there any news more exciting than the impending arrival of your first grandchild? Welcome your children to the proud state of parenthood with a picture-book vegetarian dinner, crowned with an extravagant strudel filled with melting goat cheese and wild mushrooms.

Use Place Cards to Pamper Your Guests . . . and Avoid Panic

As I have noted, people are a bit like kindergarten children when they come to a party: If they don't know where they are supposed to go, or what they are supposed to do, they feel lost. It is the host's job—especially at formal parties—to take care of them in the most gracious way. Guests don't want to "sit wherever they want." They want *you* to give them a "home" for dinner.

There is an easy, elegant, and time-honored solution to where-am-I-supposed-to-sit panic: the place card. I believe that you *must* use place cards anytime you are hosting a formal, seated party for more than four people. Here are some things to consider about the use of place cards:

◆ Shake up the mix: Don't seat people together who already know each other intimately. Most of all, don't seat couples together. I will admit (as much as I love him!), that it's boring to sit next to my husband all the time.

◆ Place guests in proximity to others (on their left *and* right) with whom they might enjoy great conversation.

◆ I advise using place cards at seated-buffet parties, where guests take a seat at a table (not a piano bench) after filling their plates. For instance, I set place cards at our family Thanksgiving to avoid a chaotic scramble for seating.

◆ Place cards are not *necessary* at casual dinners (especially among small groups of good friends), but they can be a lovely touch, particularly if the cards fit into the decor or theme of the occasion.

◆ Formal place cards can be found at most good stationery stores. Lovely handwriting in colored inks (to match the room or table decor) gives them an elegant appearance. Set them in the middle of the dinner plate, at the setting where you want the guest to be.

◆ Be creative and reflect the theme of your party by finding materials or objects that can serve as place cards. Use a pretty cut-out paper heart, a seashell, or a lemon leaf—in fact, any surface on which you can write clearly.

Theatrical as they are, formal dinners are not occasions for dramatic conflict. Rather, I suggest you direct your production as a smooth-flowing, elegant comedy. And this is no place for experimental improv either! Your game plan must include a well-written script with specific stage directions and all props ready in the wings, too.

Start the entertainment with a flute of fine Champagne or another festive drink, and a decidedly fancy *amuse-gueule*, or palate teaser.

To avoid panicky moments on entering the dining room and to encourage dinner conversation (if you have more than four people), be sure you set out place cards. The first breathtaking course will be on the table already or well on its way. And (if you follow my kitchen schedules) you will smoothly and effortlessly direct the clearing of the first course, the plating of the main course, and its dramatic presentation.

At a formal dinner, desserts, coffee, and tea should be served at the dining table (you will have prepared all the necessities on your previous trips to the kitchen). Then, with a final flourish, you will repair with your guests to the living room for a sweet and a Sauternes or a cognac, and perhaps a demitasse of espresso. By now you will have completed almost all the hosting work except for the final cleanup, and you will be ready to take a few bows.

A King of Roasts for a Beef-Loving Boss

THE MAIN EVENT:

Rib Roast of Beef

THE OPENING ACT:

Sun-dried Tomato Guacamole in Radicchio Cups

ON THE SIDE:

Asparagus with Lemon Butter

◆

Horseradish Mashed Potatoes

THE OPENING ACT:

*Endive with Roasted Asparagus, Ribbons of Cantaloupe,
and Oven-Roasted Garlic-Basil Vinaigrette*

ON THE SIDE:
Herbed Potatoes with Two Cheeses

◆

Wild Mushroom Fritters

THE GRAND FINALE:
Blood Orange Crème Brûlée

PALATE TEASER:
Mussels with Parsley and Horseradish Mayonnaise (page 302)

BEVERAGE RECOMMENDATIONS:
Vodka Martinis (page 357)
Cabernet Sauvignon, California, Franciscan Vineyards

*T*HERE WERE MANY LONG DAYS AND NIGHTS—AND TAKE-OUT DIN-
ners—while the entire team worked on the final design specs, and your boss
was there at every hour, sleeves rolled up, leading the charge. Why does she
always order a burger and fries? you wonder, until it hits you that she is a meat-and-pota-
toes kind of gal . . . patient, good-humored, and rock-solid. When the contract comes
through—just as she said it would—you decide to reward her with a royal rib roast and
the richest gratin of potatoes imaginable. And everyone on the design team comes, dressed
to the nines in silk dresses and tailored suits.

You will want your guests to see the magnificent main event—a deeply crusted roast, spicy
with its mustard glaze—before you carve it. This
beef preparation, enhanced with a sweet and tangy
red onion marmalade, will certainly be one of the
most deeply flavored and succulent you've ever
tried. As you finish the onions in the roasting pan
while the beef rests, the combined aromas will
drive the meat lovers at your table wild.

Divert their attention with the beautiful first
courses on either the one- or two-toque menu.
The tangy guacamole, piqued with sun-dried
tomatoes, is whipped up in a flash, and presented
in a clever cup of radicchio leaves. From the two-
toque menu, choose the flower-like arrangement of
roasted asparagus, endive leaves, and shimmering
ribbons of melon. It is just stunning with colorful
touches of mint and a tiny dice of red pepper.

Complement the rich sweetness of the beef
with either of two great potato creations. Try
mashed potatoes with horseradish, sour cream,
and a bit of mustard, or the luscious casserole of
scalloped potatoes flavored with thyme and parsley and Parmigiano and Gruyère. The other accompaniments offer delightful taste and texture
contrasts—either simple and fresh asparagus with
lemon butter or exquisite mushroom fritters.

The Blood Orange Crème Brûlée is a fitting
Grand Finale to this rich feast. Balancing sweetness with citrus tang—its heavenly creaminess hidden under a crisp veil of caramelized sugar—this
unforgettable custard glows with the colors of a
sunset.

SETTING THE STAGE

This beautiful and celebratory meal will be wonderful presented on a table with cloth and napkins
in a neutral color accented with sparkling crystal
and polished flatware. A simple yet eye-catching
floral centerpiece might be an assortment of blush
roses in a silver bowl. Or consider a more colorful display of several dozen tulips in a fishbowl
vase—very dramatic! (Remember, though, to

avoid flowers with a strong fragrance. You don't want them to compete with the wonderful aromas of the meal.)

Add some tall tapered candles in silver or glass holders. Formal place cards can be inscribed in a colored ink that matches your flowers or room decor.

Rib Roast of Beef

MAKES 8 SERVINGS

SPECIAL COOKWARE
Meat thermometer
Serving tray fitted with a cutting board

1 (4-rib) roast, trimmed of excess fat (about 8 pounds after trimming)
2 teaspoons coarse kosher salt
1 1/2 teaspoons freshly ground black pepper
1/4 cup plus 1 teaspoon Dijon mustard
1 large yellow onion, peeled and finely diced
3 tablespoons butter
3 large red onions, peeled, quartered, and sliced 1/4-inch thick
1/2 cup dry red wine
Salt to taste

1. Preheat the oven to 450°.
2. Rub the entire top and underside of the beef with the kosher salt and 1 teaspoon of the pepper. Spread the 1/4 cup mustard over the entire surface of the beef.
3. Place the beef on a rack in a roasting pan, fat side up. Roast the beef for 30 minutes.
4. Reduce the oven temperature to 350°. Scatter the

yellow onion around the beef, and continue to roast for 1 1/4 to 1 3/4 hours, or until a meat thermometer reaches 130° for a medium-rare roast. Let the beef sit for 20 minutes at room temperature in the roasting pan before carving.
5. While the beef is roasting, heat the butter in a skillet and sauté the red onions over medium heat until they are translucent, about 5–8 minutes. Cover the pan with a lid and continue cooking the onions, stirring occasionally, over low heat for 15–20 minutes more. (Add more butter if the onions get too dry.)
6. Place the roast on a serving tray with a carving-board insert. Deglaze the roasting pan over a burner on medium-high heat using the red wine and a wooden spoon to scrape up the meat drippings. Stir in the 1 teaspoon of Dijon mustard and add the reserved red onions to the pan. Season with the salt and remaining pepper. Transfer this onion marmalade to a serving dish.

FINISHING TOUCHES AND
TABLE PRESENTATION

ONE-TOQUE: Use your largest dinner plates, preferably 12 to 14 inches, and make sure to give your boss the end cut or a rib. Carve the roast into 1/2-inch slices and serve 2 slices to each person. Bring the onions to the table in a pretty bowl and smother the slices of beef generously. Place the asparagus with the spears all falling the same way on a decorative flat plate and serve 6 or 7 to each guest. Pile the mashed potatoes into a round bowl and serve with the beef.

TWO-TOQUE: Use your largest dinner plates, preferably 12 to 14 inches, and make sure to give your boss the end cut or a rib. Carve the roast into ¹/₂-inch slices and serve 2 slices to each person. Bring the onions to the table in a pretty bowl and smother the slices of beef generously. Serve each guest 5 fritters, dusted with the parsley. Serve the potatoes from the baking dish.

Sun-dried Tomato Guacamole in Radicchio Cups

MAKES 8 SERVINGS

¹/₄ cup sun-dried tomatoes, packed in olive oil, finely chopped and drained

3 ripe avocados, peeled, pits removed

2 tablespoons fresh lime juice

1 tablespoon fresh lemon juice

¹/₂ medium red onion, peeled and finely diced

1 large clove garlic, peeled and minced

1 teaspoon Dijon mustard

2 tablespoons finely chopped fresh cilantro

¹/₄ teaspoon salt, or to taste

6–8 drops Tabasco sauce

GARNISH

16 radicchio leaves, washed and dried

¹/₂ cup seeded and finely chopped fresh tomatoes

1 recipe Black-and-White Sesame Wontons (page 313)

1. Put the ingredients (not including garnishes) in the bowl of a food processor fitted with the knife blade and pulse until the mixture is mostly smooth but slightly chunky.

FINISHING TOUCHES AND TABLE PRESENTATION

In the kitchen, lay out 8 salad plates and arrange 2 radicchio leaves into a cup in the center of each plate. Heap a generous ¹/₄ cup of the guacamole into each radicchio cup. Garnish with the chopped tomatoes. Arrange the wontons in a silver bowl, ready to pass to guests. Present the salad plates on top of the underliner plates already set in front of each guest.

The Inventive Chef

THIS TANGY GUACAMOLE IS ALSO A GREAT DIP FOR CRUDITÉS. TRY IT AS AN ADDITION TO SALADS, TOO. WE TOP OUR FAJITAS WITH GOBS OF THIS GUACAMOLE.

Asparagus with Lemon Butter

MAKES 8 SERVINGS

SPECIAL COOKWARE
Extra-large skillet

4 pounds medium asparagus spears

7 tablespoons butter

1 large clove garlic, finely minced

Zest of 2 lemons, finely minced

1 teaspoon Dijon mustard

³/₄ teaspoon salt, or to taste

¹/₂ teaspoon freshly ground black pepper

2 teaspoons finely chopped flat-leaf parsley

1. Wash the asparagus; snap off and discard the tough ends. Peel about 1 inch of the stalk ends with a vegetable peeler. Fill an extra-large skillet with enough water to cover the asparagus, and bring it to a boil. Simmer the spears over medium heat for 3–5 minutes, until they are tender but crisp to the bite. *(The cooking time will depend on the size of the asparagus.)*

2. While the asparagus are cooking, set a bowl of ice water on a counter. Drain and shock the asparagus in the bowl of ice water. Drain the asparagus *again* and dry on paper towels; return them to the skillet and set aside.

3. While the asparagus are cooking, heat the butter in a small saucepan over medium heat. When the butter is almost fully melted, add the garlic, lemon zest, mustard, salt, and pepper, and simmer rapidly for 1 minute to combine all the flavors.

4. Pour the lemon butter over the asparagus in the skillet and cook over high heat just until the spears are heated through, about 1 1/2 minutes. Garnish with the chopped parsley.

The Inventive Chef

FOR ASPARAGUS WITH ADDED TEXTURE AND A NUTTY FLAVOR, ADD 1/2 CUP COARSELY CHOPPED PECANS TO THE LEMON-BUTTER MIXTURE WHILE IT IS SIMMERING.

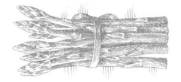

ON THE SIDE

Horseradish Mashed Potatoes

MAKES 8 SERVINGS

These luscious potatoes should be served *hot* so you can really enjoy the biting taste of the horseradish and mustard!

3 1/2 pounds potatoes, russet or Yukon Gold, peeled and cut into 2-inch dice
1 1/2 cups heavy cream
4 tablespoons butter
1 1/4 cups sour cream
1 teaspoon Dijon mustard
2 1/2 teaspoons white horseradish, drained and squeezed dry
3/4 teaspoon salt
1/2 teaspoon freshly ground pepper
2 tablespoons finely chopped chives

1. Place the potatoes in a large saucepan or stockpot with water to cover. Bring the water to a boil over high heat, lower the heat to medium, and simmer the potatoes until they are soft, about 15–20 minutes. Drain the potatoes and transfer them to the bowl of an electric mixer.

2. In a small saucepan, over low heat, warm the heavy cream with the butter until the butter is melted and the cream is hot. Remove from the heat.

3. Beat the potatoes with the paddle attachment on low until they are crumbled. With the mixer on medium, slowly add the warmed heavy cream and butter. Once the potatoes are softened, add the sour cream, mustard, horseradish, salt, and pepper. Adjust the seasoning to suit your taste.

4. Transfer the whipped potatoes to the top of a double boiler set over simmering water. The potatoes can stay warm partially covered, over the simmering water, for 30 minutes. Garnish with the chives just before serving.

Endive with Roasted Asparagus, Ribbons of Cantaloupe

MAKES 8 SERVINGS

THE SALAD

48 medium (about 3 pounds) asparagus spears, washed and trimmed
2 tablespoons olive oil
1/4 teaspoon salt
1/8 teaspoon freshly ground pepper
1 large cantaloupe, peeled, cut in half, and seeded

GARNISH

5 heads endive, leaves separated, washed and dried (at least 48 petals)
2 tablespoons red bell pepper, seeded and finely diced
8 mint sprigs

1. Preheat the oven to 400°.

2. Toss the asparagus with the olive oil, salt, and pepper. Divide the asparagus and place them loosely on two baking sheets. Roast in the lowest part of the oven for 12 minutes, or until the asparagus are cooked through. Remove from the oven and place the asparagus on a platter.

3. Dress the roasted asparagus by coating the spears with 2 tablespoons of the Oven-Roasted Garlic-Basil Vinaigrette (recipe follows).

4. Randomly peel thin ribbons of flesh from the cantaloupe with a vegetable peeler.

FINISHING TOUCHES AND TABLE PRESENTATION

I like to use 8- or 9-inch floral-patterned plates to present this gorgeous first course. Place 6 endive leaves in a concentric circular pattern, like the spokes of a wheel, around each salad plate, tips pointing out. Put one asparagus spear into each endive leaf, with the tip facing out. Divide the melon ribbons into 8 bunches. Heap the ribbons in the center of each plate to form a hub for the endive petals. Drizzle each leaf with vinaigrette, sprinkle the spears with red pepper, and garnish the melon with a mint sprig.

The Inventive Chef

YOU CAN VARY THIS SALAD WITH OTHER MELONS AS AN ACCENT. IF YOU USE A GREEN-FLESHED MELON, USE RADICCHIO LEAVES INSTEAD OF THE ENDIVE FOR ADDED COLOR. FOR A HEARTIER FIRST COURSE OR A LIGHT LUNCHEON, TUCK SLIVERS OF PROSCIUTTO OR SMOKED DUCK BETWEEN THE PETALS OF THIS DESIGN.

Oven-Roasted Garlic-Basil Vinaigrette

MAKES ABOUT $^3/_4$ CUP OF VINAIGRETTE

THE ROASTED GARLIC

1 head garlic, unpeeled
2 teaspoons olive oil

1. Preheat the oven to 400°.
2. Place a 12-by-12-inch piece of foil on a counter. Slice and discard about $^1/_4$ inch from the top of the garlic head and place the bulb of garlic in the center of the foil. Coat the garlic well with the 2 tablespoons of olive oil. Fold the edges of the foil over the garlic to make a sealed package. Place on a small baking sheet and bake for 40–60 minutes, until the flesh of the garlic is very soft. Remove the foil package from the oven and allow the garlic to cool slightly. Carefully press down at the base of the garlic to squeeze the softened cloves out of their skins. Reserve the roasted garlic.

THE VINAIGRETTE

$^1/_4$ cup tightly packed fresh basil leaves
2 tablespoons fresh orange juice
1 teaspoon Dijon mustard
$^1/_2$ teaspoon drained capers
1 tablespoon balsamic vinegar
$^1/_2$ cup olive oil
Salt and freshly ground black pepper to taste

1. Put the roasted garlic, basil leaves, orange juice, mustard, capers, and vinegar in the bowl of a food processor. Blend, pulsing, until the ingredients form a smooth puree. With the motor running, slowly pour the olive oil into the feeding tube, until the dressing has thickened.
2. Season with salt and black pepper to taste.

ON THE SIDE

Herbed Potatoes with Two Cheeses

MAKES 8 SERVINGS

SPECIAL COOKWARE

4-quart ovenproof decorative baking dish
8 tablespoons butter plus additional to grease the baking dish

3 pounds large russet potatoes
2 shallots, peeled and finely minced
3 cloves garlic, peeled and finely minced
2 teaspoons finely chopped fresh thyme
2 tablespoons finely chopped fresh curly parsley
$^1/_2$ teaspoon salt
$^1/_2$ teaspoon freshly ground pepper
$^1/_2$ cup freshly grated Parmigiano Reggiano
$^1/_2$ pound finely grated Gruyère
$1^3/_4$ cups heavy cream
2 teaspoons finely chopped curly parsley

1. Preheat the oven to 375°. Butter the bottom and sides of a 3-quart ovenproof baking dish.

2. Peel and slice the potatoes into $^1/_8$-inch circles. Put the potatoes in a bowl and cover with cold water.

3. Heat the 8 tablespoons of butter in a small skillet over medium-high heat. Add the shallots and sauté until they are soft, about 2 minutes. Add the garlic and sauté for 1 minute more. Remove the skillet from the heat and mix in the thyme, parsley, salt, and pepper. Blend well.

4. Drain and discard the water from the potatoes. Dry the potatoes well with paper towels and return them to the bowl. Toss the potatoes with the herb-butter mixture until all the slices are well coated.

5. Place half the potatoes, in one layer, in the bottom of the baking dish. Scatter half the Parmigiano and Gruyère over the potatoes. Layer the remaining potatoes over the cheese. Sprinkle the other half of the cheeses over this layer. Pour the heavy cream over the potatoes. *(The cream will not necessarily cover all the potatoes.)*

6. Bake the potatoes in the oven for about 45 minutes, until they are tender when pierced with a fork and the top is a golden brown. Garnish with chopped parsley just before serving.

The Inventive Chef

THESE EXTRAVAGANTLY RICH POTATOES ARE WONDERFUL WITH SIMPLY BROILED CHICKEN OR FISH.

ON THE SIDE

Wild Mushroom Fritters

MAKES 8 SERVINGS

The key to delicious, grease-free fritters is maintaining the frying oil at the correct temperature . . . so use a deep-fat thermometer!

SPECIAL COOKWARE
Deep-fat-frying thermometer

3 large eggs, separated
1 teaspoon salt, plus additional to taste
$^3/_4$ teaspoon finely chopped fresh tarragon
1 tablespoon vegetable oil
$1^1/_3$ cups beer, at room temperature
$2^3/_4$ cups all-purpose flour
$1^1/_2$ pounds medium-size cremini or white button mushrooms
$^1/_2$ teaspoon freshly ground black pepper, or to taste
$1^1/_2$ tablespoons fresh lemon juice
$^1/_4$ teaspoon cayenne pepper
Peanut or corn oil for frying
$^1/_4$ cup finely chopped flat-leaf parsley

1. With a whisk, beat the egg yolks in a large bowl with $^1/_2$ teaspoon of the salt, tarragon, vegetable oil, and beer. Blend well.

2. Continue to beat, slowly adding the flour. Let the batter rest at room temperature for 30 minutes.

3. While the batter is resting, cut the stems off the mushrooms $^1/_4$ inch below the caps. Wipe the mushrooms well with a damp kitchen towel. In a large bowl, toss the mushroom caps with the remaining $^1/_2$ teaspoon of salt, the $^1/_2$ teaspoon of black pepper,

the lemon juice, and the cayenne pepper and, let them marinate for 10–20 minutes.

4. Lightly pat the mushrooms dry with paper towels. To finish the batter, whip the egg whites in the bowl of an electric mixer until they are stiff but not dry, and with a rubber spatula, fold the whites into the yolk mixture.

5. Heat about 2–2$^1/2$ inches of oil in a deep saucepan or skillet until the temperature on a deep-fat-frying thermometer reaches 375°.

6. Dip the mushrooms in the batter and fry them, 5 or 6 at a time, about 2–3 minutes, until they are golden brown. For a crisp, golden fritter, do not overcrowd the pan. If the batter becomes too thick, add more beer.

7. With a slotted spoon, place the fritters on paper towels to drain. Transfer them to a baking sheet and keep warm in a 250° oven for up to 25 minutes. Garnish with the chopped parsley just before serving.

The Inventive Chef:

MAKE FRITTERS USING SMALL RATHER THAN MEDIUM MUSHROOMS FOR A FINE HORS D'OEUVRE.

Blood Orange Crème Brûlée

MAKES 8 SERVINGS

SPECIAL COOKWARE
Eight 10-ounce ramekins

2 cups heavy cream
2 cups whole milk
Grated zest of 2 blood oranges
6 egg yolks
4 eggs
1 cup plus 3 tablespoons sugar
$^2/3$ cup blood orange juice (from 2–3 oranges)◆
1$^1/2$ tablespoons orange liqueur, such as triple sec or Grand Marnier

GARNISH
8 candied mint leaves (purchased from gourmet markets)
16 blood orange sections, skin and pith removed, from 2 oranges◆

1. Preheat the oven to 350°. Arrange the 8 10-ounce ramekins set into a large roasting pan. Set aside.

2. In a medium saucepan, heat the heavy cream, milk, and orange zest over medium heat until the liquid just starts simmering. Remove from the heat, allowing the mixture to steep while you prepare the custard.

3. Whisk the egg yolks and whole eggs with the 1 cup of sugar in a large bowl, until they are well blended. Whisk in the orange juice.

4. Reheat the cream mixture until it begins to simmer.

◆Blood orange juice can be found in the gourmet section of many markets or fancy food stores. Substitute regular orange zest and juice if you have trouble finding the blood orange.

Very slowly, pour a little of the hot cream into the eggs while whisking constantly. Blend well. Gradually pour the rest of the cream into the eggs. *If you add the hot liquid all at once to the cold egg base, the eggs will scramble.* Continue whisking the mixture until the sugar has dissolved, about 1 minute, then blend in the liqueur.

5. Strain the custard through a fine sieve into a large mixing bowl. Fill the ramekins in the roasting pan with the liquid. Fill the roasting pan with hot water to come halfway up the sides of the ramekins. *Carefully place the baking pan in the hot oven.* Bake the custards for 1 hour, or until a knife inserted along the outer edge comes out clean. The center will be a little moist.

6. Carefully remove the roasting pan from the oven and remove the ramekins from the water bath. Place the ramekins on a tray and cool them at room temperature. Refrigerate, lightly covered, for at least 2 hours. *(The custards can be made the day before serving and refrigerated.)*

7. When ready to continue the recipe, preheat the broiler. Put the ramekins on a baking pan. Sprinkle the 3 tablespoons of sugar evenly over the tops, and place the custards under the broiler, approximately 3 inches from the heat, until the sugar melts and begins to caramelize, about 1–2 minutes. Remove from the broiler and set aside.

FINISHING TOUCHES AND
TABLE PRESENTATION

Set the ramekins on decorative 8–9-inch dessert plates. Garnish each with a candied mint leaf. Arrange 2 pieces of blood orange sections on each plate.

The Inventive Chef

CHOCOLATE CRÈME BRÛLÉE IS EASY: SUBSTITUTE 6 OUNCES OF UNSWEETENED CHOCOLATE FOR THE ORANGE ZEST AND JUICE. MELT THE CHOCOLATE WITH THE CREAM AND MILK AS IT SIMMERS IN STEP 2, AND CONTINUE.

2 OR 3 DAYS BEFORE THE PARTY

TOQUE 1	Guacamole	Make wontons and store as directed.
	Mashed Potatoes	Peel potatoes; cover with water, and store covered in refrigerator.
TOQUE 2	Endive and Asparagus	Roast garlic and prepare vinaigrette; store covered in refrigerator.
	Herbed Potatoes	Peel potatoes; cover with water, and store covered in refrigerator. Grate Parmigiano and Gruyère; store covered in refrigerator.

THE DAY BEFORE THE PARTY

MAIN EVENT	Beef	Season the roast and cover with mustard; store covered in refrigerator. Prepare yellow and red onions; store covered in refrigerator.
TOQUE 1	Guacamole	Mince garlic; store covered in refrigerator. Wash and dry radicchio leaves. Store covered in refrigerator.
	Asparagus	Peel asparagus and prepare as in step 1; dry and store covered in refrigerator.
TOQUE 2	Endive and Asparagus	Roast asparagus; store covered in refrigerator. Prepare red-pepper garnish; store covered in refrigerator. Separate mint sprigs.
	Herbed Potatoes	Prepare garlic, shallots, thyme, and parsley; store covered in refrigerator.
GRAND FINALE	Crème Brûlée	Prepare through step 6; store covered in refrigerator.

Strategic Maneuvers: Fill creamer; cover and store in refrigerator. Fill sugar bowl. Set table. Check table decor. Set underliners for Opening Act, if being used. Prepare and set place cards. Check ice and beverages. Locate teas. Chill wine if white. Check garnishes for each recipe. Locate and label all serving bowls, platters, and utensils.

THE DAY OF THE PARTY

MAIN EVENT	Beef	4 hours before guests arrive, set at room temperature. If you are having a cocktail hour, place the beef in the oven 2 hours before guests are due to arrive. If you are planning to eat soon after guests arrive, place roast in oven $2^{1}/_{2}$ hours beforehand. Beef will rest while first course is served. Prepare onions as in step 5; cover and store at room temperature.
TOQUE 1	Guacamole	Prepare guacamole; store covered in refrigerator. Chop tomato garnish; store covered in refrigerator.
	Asparagus	Prepare lemon butter as in step 2; set aside at room temperature.

	Mashed Potatoes	Late in the day, prepare potatoes through step 4. Set aside, covered, at room temperature. Prepare chive garnish.
TOQUE 2	Endive and Asparagus	Wash endive. Set aside.
		Prepare melon. Arrange salad as indicated in presentation instructions. *Do not dress.* Refrigerate lightly covered.
	Herbed Potatoes	Prepare potatoes through step 6; set aside at room temperature.
	Fritters	Make batter through step 2; store covered in refrigerator. Prepare mushrooms as in step 3; store covered in refrigerator. Ready oil for frying.
GRAND FINALE	Crème Brûlée	Before putting roast in oven, preheat broiler and prepare as in step 7; store covered in refrigerator.

30 MINUTES BEFORE GUESTS ARRIVE:

TOQUE 1	Guacamole	Finish and plate; refrigerate plates, covered.

30 MINUTES BEFORE DINNER:

MAIN EVENT	Beef	When beef is cooked to your liking, remove from oven and let rest. Reduce oven temperature to 300°. Heat sautéed onions in covered oven-proof casserole, stirring occasionally.
TOQUE 1	Mashed Potatoes	Heat potatoes over simmering water.
	Asparagus	Warm lemon butter over very low heat.
TOQUE 2	Herbed Potatoes	Heat potatoes in 300° oven.

	Fritters	Prepare fritters; keep warm in low oven. Warm dinner plates.

15 MINUTES BEFORE FIRST-COURSE SERVICE:

TOQUE 1	Guacamole	Set on table over underliners.
TOQUE 2	Endive and Asparagus	Dress and set on table on underliners. Plug in coffee. Warm dinner plates.
MAIN EVENT	Onions	Make sure onions are getting hot in oven.
TOQUE 1	Asparagus	Sauté as in step 3.
	Mashed Potatoes	Make sure potatoes are getting hot.
TOQUE 2	Herbed Potatoes	Make sure potatoes are getting hot.
	Fritters	Let kitchen helper fry mushroom fritters.

20 MINUTES INTO FIRST COURSE:

Remove first-course plates; set dinner plates.
Bring food to table as detailed in Main Event; serve main course.
Place Crème Brûlée at room temperature.

DESSERT SERVICE:

Remove dinner plates and serve dessert, as instructed, and coffee.

AFTER SERVICE:

Unplug coffee.
Turn off oven.

Fancy Flourishes on Your First Anniversary

THE MAIN EVENT:

Cranberry-Glazed Cornish Hen

THE OPENING ACT:

Salad of Field Greens with Crumbled Goat Cheese

ON THE SIDE:

Savory Rice Pilaf with a Duet of Herbs

THE OPENING ACT:

Spicy Shrimp with Savory Tomatoes

ON THE SIDE:

Butternut Squash Ratatouille

THE GRAND FINALE:

Chocolate Pudding with Ginger Whipped Cream

PALATE TEASER:

Tortilla Wraps with Smoked Salmon and Asparagus (page 297)

BEVERAGE RECOMMENDATIONS:

Champagne

Alsace Riesling, Wehlener Sonnenuhr, Trimbach, Hugel

*I*T TOOK A YEAR, BUT AT LAST THE LOVELIEST AND MOST LUX-urious of your wedding gifts are all in service: the silver platters, the hand-blown goblets, the raku pottery. And you have your bridesmaids and groomsmen around you again—they're still your best friends. But this time it's almost bet-ter than the wedding—less nervousness and distraction and even more love. This time the feast is from your own kitchen: elegant plates full of color and drama. Ruby-glazed roast Cornish hens sitting on golden beds of butternut squash ratatouille.

I have always loved the simple elegance of a whole Cornish hen presented on a dinner plate. It is the perfect centerpiece for a special-occasion dinner, and here, with its deep cranberry glaze—and the sweet and tart flavors from the fruit—the hen has an especially wonderful succulence and vi-sual impact.

The one-toque dishes complete a dinner that is both simple to prepare and suitably impressive for a formal event. The first course is a crunchy and refreshing salad of flavorful lettuces with a terrific citrus-ginger vinaigrette and a sprinkle of goat cheese. The rice pilaf, with its duet of pars-ley and tarragon, provides a delicious cushion for the main course.

If you want to start your dinner with a display of culinary prowess, choose the shrimp for your first course. Palates will wake to the dazzling con-trast between the sizzling and spicy shrimp and the fresh tomato salad. It is just beautiful as well. With this menu, the sweet and golden cubes of vegetables in the ratatouille form a sensational ring around the hen. Breathtaking!

Finally: chocolate pudding for dessert. Sound humble? You have never had a pudding quite like this—lush and melting in the mouth. As befits the occasion, serve this in your precious handblown goblets or any crystal stemware that will show off the irresistible dark chocolate topped with a tow-ering layer of gingered cream and golden shreds of candied ginger.

SETTING THE STAGE

Be inspired by the deep and jewel-toned colors of this menu—cranberry, green, gold, and chocolate: create a centerpiece of flowers in vibrant shades of red, purple, and rose. Nestle the flowers in a crys-tal or silver bowl, surrounded by a ring of votive candles (unscented, of course). The candles add a lovely low light and reflect beautifully off the shining crystal.

If you are celebrating any anniversary, be sure to use and enjoy your wedding gifts at the table—and it is a particular pleasure to display a gift from one of your guests. For a first anniversary, it may also please everyone to sample the top of your wedding cake, which has been saved and frozen.

Freezers and wraps being what they are, though, it might be wiser just to gaze at it—and remember the wedding!

Cranberry-Glazed Cornish Hen

MAKES 8 SERVINGS

The marvelous marinade that gives so much flavor to these hens also creates a gorgeous glaze. Brush it on generously while the hens are roasting. When buying hens: Ask the butcher to split them in half and, if possible, have him remove the breast and rib bones, too. This will make a more elegant entrée.

THE MARINADE

2 tablespoons olive oil
2 cloves elephant garlic, peeled and quartered
$1/2$ cup orange juice concentrate, defrosted
$1^1/2$ cups currant jelly
$1/4$ cup balsamic vinegar
$2/3$ cup dried cranberries
$1/2$ cup dry red wine
$1/2$ cup chicken stock, homemade or low-sodium canned
$2^1/2$ teaspoons minced fresh ginger
1 tablespoon Dijon mustard
1 tablespoon chopped fresh rosemary
1 teaspoon salt
$1/2$ teaspoon freshly ground white pepper

THE HENS

8 Cornish hens (14–16 ounces each), split in half
Salt and freshly ground black pepper to taste

3 lemons, cut into 8 wedges each
16 sprigs fresh rosemary
3 large white onions, cut into $1/2$-inch wedges
1 cup chicken stock, homemade or low-sodium canned

GARNISH

16 sprigs fresh tarragon or rosemary—see presentation
16 $1/8$-inch slices of lemon, from 2 medium lemons

1. Heat the oil in a small skillet over medium-high heat. Reduce the heat and sauté the garlic for about 1–1$1/2$ minutes, until golden and soft. *Be careful not to let it burn.* Remove from the heat and set aside to cool.
2. In a medium saucepan, combine the orange juice, currant jelly, vinegar, cranberries, red wine, chicken stock, ginger, mustard, rosemary, salt, and pepper. Simmer over medium heat for 10 minutes.
3. Place the marinade and the reserved garlic in the bowl of the food processor or blender and process to a smooth puree. *(The marinade can be made 2 days ahead and refrigerated in a covered container. Reheat gently before using.)*
4. Season the hens with salt and pepper. Place the hens in two large roasting pans and brush them generously with the marinade. Scatter the lemon wedges, rosemary sprigs, and onion wedges around the hens. Cover the pans lightly with foil and refrigerate for at least 6 hours, or overnight. Reserve the remaining marinade.
5. Bring the hens to room temperature. Preheat the oven to 350°. Pour $1/2$ cup of chicken stock into each of the pans and place the hens, uncovered, in the preheated oven.
6. Roast for 20 minutes, then baste the hens with the remaining marinade. Return to the oven for an additional 25–30 minutes, until the birds are golden and the juices run clear. Remove the hens to a warm

platter and allow them to rest for 10 minutes, covered lightly with foil.

7. Strain the lemons, rosemary, onions, and pan juices through a fine-mesh strainer into a medium saucepan. Add the juices that have accumulated around the hens on the platter and simmer for 2 minutes.

FINISHING TOUCHES AND
TABLE PRESENTATION

I use 12-inch dinner plates for this presentation.

ONE-TOQUE: Fill the center of each plate with a generous bed of the Savory Rice Pilaf. Arrange two overlapping halves of hen over the pilaf, and stand two sprigs of rosemary between the halves. Pass the sauce.

TWO-TOQUE: Fill the center of each plate with a generous bed of Butternut Squash Ratatouille. Arrange a hen as above, over the ratatouille. Place two slices of lemon over each hen. Pass the sauce.

FAMILY SERVICE: I like to arrange the hen halves on an oval platter. Lemon slices look wonderful placed on each breast. Garnish the platter with the bouquets of rosemary. The Savory Rice Pilaf and the Butternut Squash Ratatouille should be served from decorative oval or round bowls.

THE OPENING ACT

Salad of Field Greens with Crumbled Goat Cheese

MAKES 8 SERVINGS

THE VINAIGRETTE

1 small shallot, peeled and coarsely chopped
2 tablespoons balsamic vinegar
1 1/2 tablespoons Dijon mustard
2 tablespoons fresh orange juice
1 teaspoon honey
2 teaspoons fresh lemon juice
1 teaspoon finely grated fresh ginger
3/4 cup olive oil
Salt to taste
Freshly ground black pepper to taste

THE GREENS

3/4 pound assorted field greens (lollo rossa, baby Bibb, red oak, radicchio, or mâche)
2 bunches arugula
8 ounces fresh soft goat cheese, crumbled into small pieces

1. Place the shallot, vinegar, mustard, orange juice, honey, lemon juice, and ginger in the bowl of a food processor fitted with a metal cutting blade. With the motor running, *slowly* add the oil until the vinaigrette thickens. *(If you pour the oil too quickly, the vinaigrette will not thicken.)* Season with salt and pepper.

2. Gently break apart the field greens and arugula leaves. Wash and dry them well in a salad spinner. Place in plastic bags and refrigerate.

FINISHING TOUCHES AND TABLE PRESENTATION

For this formal menu, serve the salad on individual plates. Toss the greens in a large bowl with vinaigrette to taste. Arrange portions of greens loosely on the plates and sprinkle each with a generous serving (at least 2 teaspoons) of crumbled goat cheese. Before your guests are seated, set the plates on 10-inch underliners at each place.

For casual dining, dress the salad, sprinkle the goat cheese, and serve the greens directly from a large salad bowl. If you enjoy your salad lightly dressed, there will be vinaigrette left for another menu.

The Inventive Chef

TRY OTHER SOFT CHEESES, SUCH AS A RIPE GORGONZOLA, ON THIS SALAD. SERVE WITH TOASTED BAGUETTE CRISPS AND FRESH FRUIT.

ON THE SIDE

Savory Rice Pilaf with a Duet of Herbs

MAKES 8 SERVINGS

$1/4$ cup olive oil
1 medium red onion, peeled and finely chopped
1 large clove garlic, peeled and minced
2 cups basmati rice, rinsed and drained
$3 1/2$ cups chicken broth, homemade or low-sodium canned
$1/2$ cup dry white wine
$1/2$ bunch finely chopped flat-leaf parsley
1 teaspoon finely chopped fresh tarragon
1 tablespoon unsalted butter
2 tablespoons freshly grated Parmigiano Reggiano
$1/2$ teaspoon salt, or to taste
$1/8$ teaspoon freshly ground black pepper, or to taste
Small bouquet of tarragon sprigs (optional)

1. In a medium saucepan, heat the oil over medium heat. Add the onion and sauté for 3–5 minutes, until the onion is soft and translucent. Add the garlic and cook for 30 seconds. Add the rice and sauté, mixing constantly, until all the kernels are coated with oil, about 1 minute.

2. Add the chicken broth and wine and bring the mixture to a boil over medium-high heat. Immediately lower the heat, cover the saucepan, and simmer the rice for 12–15 minutes, or until all the broth has been absorbed.

3. Fluff the rice with a fork and add the parsley, tarragon, butter, and cheese. Season with the salt and pepper. (*The rice can be prepared early in the day, cooled, and reheated in the top of a double boiler.*) If serving from a bowl, garnish with the tarragon bouquet.

> ### The Inventive Chef
>
> I LIKE TO ENHANCE THE PILAF WITH THIN SLICES OF WILD OR DOMESTIC MUSHROOMS SAUTÉED IN OLIVE OIL OR BUTTER. SEASON THE MUSHROOMS WITH SALT AND PEPPER AND ADD THEM TO THE RICE ALONG WITH THE HERBS.

THE OPENING ACT

Spicy Shrimp with Savory Tomatoes

MAKES 8 SERVINGS

THE MARINADE
3/4 cup olive oil
3 tablespoons minced red bell pepper
3 tablespoons minced yellow bell pepper
2 tablespoons peeled and minced garlic (about 6 cloves)
1/4 cup fresh lime juice

2 tablespoons honey
1 teaspoon chili powder
1 teaspoon powdered ginger
1 teaspoon ground cumin
1 tablespoon Tabasco sauce
1/4 teaspoon freshly ground black pepper

THE SHRIMP
32 shrimp (about 2 pounds, 16–20 count), peeled and deveined (ask fish monger to do this), tails left on.
2 tablespoons fresh lime juice
Salt to taste

THE TOMATOES
4 beefsteak or other large tomatoes, cored and cut into 1/2-inch chunks
1/4 cup minced red onion
1/8 teaspoon ground cloves
1/4 teaspoon powdered ginger
1/4 cup orange juice concentrate, defrosted
1 tablespoon red wine vinegar
2 teaspoons olive oil
2 teaspoons finely chopped fresh cilantro (optional)
Salt to taste
Freshly ground pepper to taste

GARNISH
Finely julienned zest of 1 lime

1. To make the marinade: Heat the olive oil in a medium skillet over moderate heat. Add the red pepper, yellow pepper, and garlic. Briskly simmer the vegetables for 2 minutes. Lower the heat and add the lime juice, honey, chili powder, ginger, cumin, Tabasco sauce, and ground pepper. Simmer for 1 minute more. Cool the marinade and refrigerate covered if you are not using it immediately.

2. Place the shrimp in a large stainless steel or glass

mixing bowl and toss them with the marinade until well coated. Refrigerate, covered, for two hours.

3. Toss the tomatoes, red onion, cloves, ginger, and orange juice concentrate together in a mixing bowl. Refrigerate, covered.

4. Preheat the broiler or prepare a charcoal fire and let it burn until the coals are gray. Remove the shrimp from the marinade and place them on a baking sheet, leaving $^1/_2$ inch between each shrimp *(The shrimp will be placed directly on the grill, if this is the cooking method you choose.)* Broil or grill the shrimp about $1^1/_2$ minutes on each side, just until the center is opaque. *(Overcooked shrimp will be tough.)* Remove from the heat and sprinkle with the lime juice and salt to taste.

5. Just before serving, toss the tomato salad with the vinegar, olive oil, and cilantro, and season it with salt and pepper.

FINISHING TOUCHES AND
TABLE PRESENTATION

This is a thrilling presentation on a 9-inch white plate. Arrange 4 shrimp in the center of each plate with the tails facing out. Surround the shrimp with a ring of tomato salad and scatter the julienned lime zest over the shrimp. Before your guests are seated, set the plates directly on the table or over a 10–12-inch underliner.

The Inventive Chef

BROILED OR GRILLED SEA SCALLOPS CAN BE PREPARED THIS WAY. AND TRY THE TOMATO SALAD WITH A JUICY STEAK, REPLACING THE CLOVES IN THE SALAD WITH FRESH TARRAGON OR BASIL. IT'S A PERFECT MATCH!

ON THE SIDE

Butternut Squash Ratatouille

MAKES 8 SERVINGS

SPECIAL COOKWARE
One large skillet, at least 12 inches, or two smaller skillets, 8 inches

3 leeks, white parts only
3 tablespoons salted butter
$^1/_2$ teaspoon ground cinnamon
$^1/_8$ teaspoon ground cloves
$^1/_4$ teaspoon ground nutmeg
$^3/_4$ cup fresh orange juice
1 tablespoon grated orange zest
$2^1/_2$ cups chicken broth, homemade or low-sodium canned
1 butternut squash, about $1^1/_2$ pounds, peeled, seeded, and cut into $^1/_2$-inch cubes
2 yams, peeled and cut into $^1/_2$-inch cubes
2 small turnips, peeled and cut into $^1/_2$-inch cubes
3 firm pears, Anjou or Bosc, cut into large dice
$^1/_4$ cup pure maple syrup
$^1/_2$ teaspoon salt, or to taste
$^1/_8$ teaspoon ground white pepper, or to taste
2 tablespoons finely chopped fresh chives

1. Wash the leeks well under cold running water, dry them well, and dice fine.

2. Heat the butter in a large skillet over medium heat. Add the leeks and sauté until they have softened, about 3 minutes. Add the cinnamon, cloves, and nutmeg, and stir for $1/2$ minute. Add the orange juice, orange zest, and $1/2$ cup of the chicken broth and bring to a gentle simmer.

3. Add the squash, yam, and turnips to the skillet. Add the remaining broth and simmer, stirring occasionally, until the flesh of the vegetables is resistant to the tines of a fork, about 20 minutes. Add the pears and maple syrup and cook for 5–8 minutes more, until the pears have softened. Season with salt and white pepper to taste. Remove from the heat and stir in the chives.

The Inventive Chef

SERVE THIS LUSCIOUS RATATOUILLE WITH POT ROAST OR STEW. OR ADD LEFTOVER SHREDDED CHICKEN OR HAM FOR A SIMPLE BUT DELICIOUS ENTRÉE. SERVE IN SOUP BOWLS ACCOMPANIED BY A CRUNCHY SALAD.

THE GRAND FINALE

Chocolate Pudding with Ginger Whipped Cream

MAKES 8 SERVINGS

SPECIAL COOKWARE
Eight 10-ounce ramekins or one $2^{1}/2$-quart casserole dish
Roasting pan to accommodate all the ramekins or the casserole dish

3 cups half-and-half
2 cups heavy cream
8 ounces semisweet chocolate, cut into bite-size pieces
8 egg yolks
$3/4$ cup plus 2 tablespoons sugar
2 tablespoons Amaretto liqueur or brandy
2 teaspoons pure vanilla extract

GARNISH
Ginger Whipped Cream (recipe follows)
2 tablespoons finely julienned crystallized ginger
8 stemmed large strawberries

1. Preheat the oven to 350°.

2. In a heavy-bottomed saucepan, heat the half-and-half and cream until it just comes to a simmer. Add the chocolate and blend well, stirring until the chocolate has completely melted. Remove the saucepan from the heat and set it aside at room temperature.

3. In a medium bowl, combine the egg yolks and the sugar; whisk well until blended. Add the chocolate-cream mixture very slowly to the egg mixture, whisking constantly. Add the liqueur and vanilla.

4. Strain the cream through a fine sieve into a large mixing bowl and carefully skim off and discard any foam floating on the top. Pour the cream into the eight 10-ounce ramekins or an oven-to-table casserole dish.

5. Set the ramekins in a roasting pan. Add hot water to the pan until it reaches halfway up the sides of the ramekins.

6. Carefully place the roasting pan into the hot oven. Bake for 1–1$1/4$ hours, until a knife inserted in the center of the custard comes out clean. Carefully remove the roasting pan from the oven and transfer the ramekins to a tray. Cool to room temperature, cover lightly, and refrigerate for at least 2 hours.

FINISHING TOUCHES AND TABLE PRESENTATION

For an elegant presentation, set the ramekins on decorative underliners. Top each ramekin with a nice dollop of Ginger Whipped Cream and sprinkle the top with the finely julienned candied ginger. Place a strawberry on each underliner. If you have made the pudding in a casserole dish, spoon it into a pastry bag fitted with a large open star tip and pipe it decoratively into eight glass balloon goblets. Top with a dollop of Ginger Whipped Cream, a sprinkling of crystallized ginger, and a perfect strawberry.

> ## The Inventive Chef:
>
> IF YOU LOVE THE COMBINATION OF CHOCOLATE AND COFFEE, YOU MIGHT ADD 2 TABLESPOONS OF ESPRESSO AND 2 TABLESPOONS OF DARK RUM TO THE CUSTARD MIXTURE INSTEAD OF THE AMARETTO.

Ginger Whipped Cream

MAKES ABOUT 2 CUPS

1 1/2 cups heavy cream
2 1/2 tablespoons confectioners' sugar
1 1/2 tablespoons crystallized ginger (purchased on spice shelves in markets) *minced well*
2 teaspoons Amaretto liqueur

1. Using the whip attachment, beat the cream with an electric mixer on medium-high until it stands in soft peaks.
2. Gradually beat in the sugar, ginger, and Amaretto until the cream holds its shape but is not too stiff. Refrigerate until needed.

2 OR 3 DAYS BEFORE THE PARTY

MAIN EVENT	Hens	Prepare marinade; store covered in refrigerator.
TOQUE 1	Salad	Prepare vinaigrette; store covered in refrigerator.
	Rice	Prepare herbs and garnish; store covered in refrigerator.
TOQUE 2	Shrimp	Prepare marinade and tomatoes; store covered in refrigerator.
	Squash	Prepare squash, yams, turnips; store covered in refrigerator.

THE DAY BEFORE THE PARTY

MAIN EVENT	Hens	Marinate hens as in step 4. Prepare garnish; store covered in refrigerator.
TOQUE 1	Salad	Wash, dry, and refrigerate salad greens in plastic bags.
	Rice	Prepare rice and cool to room temperature; store covered in refrigerator.
TOQUE 2	Shrimp	Prepare garnish; store covered in refrigerator.
	Squash	Complete recipe, cool to room temperature; store covered in refrigerator.
GRAND FINALE	Pudding	Prepare and bake pudding; store covered in refrigerator.
Strategic Maneuvers:		Fill creamer; cover and store in refrigerator. Fill sugar bowl. Set table. Check table decor. Set underliners for Opening Act, if being used. Prepare and set place cards. Check ice and beverages.

Locate teas.
Chill wine if white.
Check garnishes for each recipe.
Locate and label all serving bowls, platters, and utensils.

THE DAY OF THE PARTY

MAIN EVENT	Hens	2 hours before guests arrive, take hens out of refrigerator to reach room temperature.
TOQUE 1	Salad	Set up goat cheese for salad. Set salad in bowl or on individual plates. Place in refrigerator.
	Rice	Bring rice to room temperature and reheat. Cover with foil. Leave at room temperature.
TOQUE 2	Squash	Bring to room temperature.
	Shrimp	Prepare the tomatoes as in step 3; store covered in refrigerator.
GRAND FINALE	Pudding	Make Ginger Cream and fill decorative bowl; refrigerate covered.

30 MINUTES BEFORE GUESTS ARRIVE:

Preheat the oven to 350°.

45 MINUTES BEFORE FIRST-COURSE SERVICE:

MAIN EVENT	Hens	Place hens in middle of oven.
TOQUE 1	Rice	Place rice on stovetop.
TOQUE 2	Squash	Place ratatouille in oven.

20 MINUTES BEFORE FIRST-COURSE SERVICE:

Warm dinner plates.

Plug in coffee.

Remove ratatouille from oven and keep covered.

If you have only one oven, remove hens from oven.

Turn on broiler and broil shrimp: place at room temperature and finish recipe. Immediately return oven to *bake* and continue cooking hens.

TOQUE 1   Salad   Toss and plate salad; add cheese; place on underliners at each setting.

TOQUE 2   Shrimp   Arrange shrimp as directed. Place on underliners at each setting.

20 MINUTES INTO FIRST COURSE:

Test that all food is hot.

Remove first-course plates.

Plate food in kitchen according to presentation notes; bring to table.

DESSERT SERVICE:

Remove dinner plates.

Garnish puddings; put on liners, and bring to table.

Serve coffee.

AFTER SERVICE:

Unplug coffee.

Turn off oven.

A Storybook Supper with a Touch of Spice

THE MAIN EVENT:

Exotically Spiced Moroccan Lamb

THE OPENING ACT:

Basil-Scented Apples of Love

ON THE SIDE:

Sautéed Potatoes with Carrots, Onions, and Pea Pods

THE OPENING ACT:

Crab and Fennel Chowder

ON THE SIDE:

*Minted Couscous with Sautéed Eggplant,
Zucchini, and Currants*

THE GRAND FINALE:

Tangy Lemon Tart

PALATE TEASER:

Broccoli and Portobello Mushroom Custard Tart (page 318)

BEVERAGE RECOMMENDATIONS:

*Lillet, white or red
Châteauneuf-du-Pape, Cabernet Sauvignon, Kendall Jackson*

ER NOM DE PLUME IS ISABELLA LAWFORD, BUT YOU KNOW her as Deb. The publisher is calling her "the new queen of romance" because of her spicy prose, but you know that nothing really excites her like a great meal, filled with new tastes. As you celebrate your friend's acclaimed new novel, take her and your other guests on a sophisticated culinary adventure. Who knows what passions will be stirred by the scent of licorice wafting from bowls of crab and fennel chowder? What new plot is she concocting as the room fills with the tantalizing aroma of cumin, cardamom, and other exotic spices emanating from platters of Moroccan lamb draped over a mound of mint-flecked couscous? Perhaps your lemon tart will earn a place in her next book—as her heroine's secret weapon!

Leg of lamb is always a treat, and when it is infused with the flavor of a great marinade, as is this Main Event, it is something sublime (unless you overcook it, which is terribly easy to do!). For this stylish preparation, plan on lots of time for the meat to rest, refrigerated, in the Moroccan-inspired mix of yogurt, wine, lemon, honey, and aromatic spices—overnight is best. But also plan ahead for a short roasting time, coordinated with serving your hors d'oeuvre and first course. Carefully follow the recipe and my kitchen schedule so that you serve the meat at its pinnacle of pink succulence.

You will already have thrilled your guests with the first course. The Basil-Scented Apples of Love is an unusual and beautiful salad of barely sautéed fresh plum tomatoes napped with a rich sauce of fresh basil puree. It is so sensual you will immediately understand why tomatoes were, for centuries, regarded as scandalously aphrodisiacal—and referred to as *love apples*. Or make the luscious crab and fennel chowder—equally sensual and rich, and deeply warming, too.

In this menu, either delicious side choice serves as a beautiful "on the bottom" bed for the lamb—adding more terrific flavors and great texture contrasts. The one-toque mix of sautéed potatoes, carrots, and peas is perfumed with rosemary, and is temptingly crisp and golden. For more exoticism, prepare the chewy couscous—so easy yet such a delicious accompaniment for meat. My version is just loaded with flavorful treasures: fine cubes of eggplant, carrots, zucchini, currants, feta cheese, and refreshing bits of chopped mint.

The brilliant ending to this meal, and a tangy foil to all the spices, is the smooth lemon tart with sparkling notes of orange and lime. The pastry crust is rich and crumbly, filled with a citrus luscious custard, then topped with toasted shreds of sweet coconut. This trio of textures is a truly heavenly mouthful to end your meal.

Heighten the sensuality of this exotic meal with romantic decorative undertones. I would dress the table with a color scheme of deep reds and purples—or perhaps pale pink and lilac—in the cloth, napkins, and floral centerpiece.

A striking centerpiece would be a cluster of small potted tulips, narcissus, or hyacinths in complementary colors. Elevate the flowers slightly, using inverted ashtrays or low tumblers as pedestals at varying heights. Then drape the whole display in coordinating cloth napkins or other gorgeous fabrics to hide the pots.

THE MAIN EVENT

Exotically Spiced Moroccan Lamb

MAKES 8 SERVINGS

Have your butcher prepare the lamb as directed, but be sure you take home the bones for the lamb stock.

SPECIAL COOKWARE
Butcher's twine

THE STOCK
Lamb bones, reserved from boning the leg
1/2 cup dry red wine

1 large onion, peeled and studded with 8 cloves
1 large clove garlic, peeled
1 carrot, sliced thick
4 sprigs flat-leaf parsley

THE MARINADE
3/4 cup plain yogurt
1/4 cup dry red wine
Grated zest of 2 lemons
2 teaspoons Dijon mustard
1/4 teaspoon ground turmeric
1 teaspoon ground cumin
1/4 teaspoon ground cardamom
1/2 teaspoon ground cinnamon
1/2 teaspoon powdered ginger
1 teaspoon salt
1/2 teaspoon freshly ground black pepper
1 1/2 tablespoons honey

THE LAMB
1 (5-pound) leg of lamb, boned and tied, all interior
*   fat removed (bones reserved)*
3 tablespoons olive oil
2 large onions, peeled and coarsely chopped
3 cloves garlic, peeled and diced small
Salt and freshly ground black pepper to taste

1. Preheat the oven to 400°. Place the lamb bones in a roasting pan and brown them in the oven for 30 minutes. Remove the bones to a stockpot. Pour the wine into the roasting pan and deglaze the pan over a burner on medium-high heat, scraping up all the bits and pieces that have accumulated. Add these deglazed meat drippings, along with the onion, garlic, carrot, and parsley to the stockpot with the bones. Cover with about 3 quarts of cold water. Simmer the stock over medium heat until it has reduced by half, about 30 minutes. Strain, chill, and reserve the stock.

2. Combine all the marinade ingredients in a bowl large enough to hold the lamb, blending them well. Add the lamb, turning to coat it well on all sides. Marinate the lamb in the refrigerator, turning it several times, for at least 4 hours or overnight.

3. Remove the lamb from the marinade and let it sit at room temperature for about 30 minutes. Discard any left-over marinade.

4. Preheat the oven to 450°.

5. Heat the olive oil in a large skillet and sauté the onions until they are translucent, about 3–5 minutes. Add the garlic, sauté for 1 minute more, and set aside.

6. Season the lamb with salt and pepper and set it in a large roasting pan. Roast the lamb for 15 minutes. Reduce the oven temperature to 350° and add the onions and garlic around the roast in the pan. Return the lamb to the oven and roast until the internal temperature reaches 130° on a meat thermometer, an additional 45–60 minutes. The lamb will be medium-rare and pink. Let the lamb rest at room temperature on a carving board for 10 minutes, allowing the juices to settle. Cut the white butcher's twine and discard.

7. While the lamb is resting, make the sauce. Skim off any accumulated fat in the roasting pan with a ladle. Add 2^{1}/$_{2}$ cups of the stock to the roasting pan. Place the pan over a burner on high heat. Stirring constantly scrape up all the pan juices, cooking briskly until the sauce has thickened slightly; strain the sauce, skim off any remaining fat, and season with salt and pepper. Transfer the sauce to a small saucepan, add the onions and garlic, and keep warm over low heat until ready to serve.

FINISHING TOUCHES AND
TABLE PRESENTATION

Carve the lamb in the kitchen or at the dinner table, depending on your expertise with a carving knife. Arrange approximately ^{2}/$_{3}$ cup of the Sautéed Potatoes or the Minted Couscous in the center of each plate. Place two ^{1}/$_{4}$-inch, overlapping slices of lamb over the vegetables or couscous. Mask the lamb with the onion sauce.

The Inventive Chef

ROAST A LOIN OF PORK OR VEAL FOLLOWING THE SAME RECIPE. THE INTERNAL TEMPERATURE FOR THE PORK SHOULD BE ABOUT 162°–165° WHEN IT IS FINISHED, AND THE VEAL SHOULD BE 140°–145°.

OPENING ACT

*Basil-Scented Apples
of Love*

MAKES 8 SERVINGS

1 tightly packed cup basil leaves

6 tablespoons olive oil

3 tablespoons chicken broth, homemade or low-sodium
    canned

^{1}/$_{2}$ teaspoon salt, or to taste

^{1}/$_{2}$ teaspoon freshly ground black pepper, or to taste

2^{1}/$_{2}$ pounds (about 12) small plum tomatoes, halved
    lengthwise

2 medium cloves garlic, peeled and minced

2 bunches arugula, washed and dried
$^{1}/_{2}$ cup Niçoise or Kalamata olives, pitted
$^{1}/_{4}$ pound mozzarella, julienned

1. Place the basil leaves, 2 tablespoons of the olive oil, and the chicken stock in the bowl of a food processor fitted with the cutting blade. Process until the mixture becomes a coarse puree. Season with $^{1}/_{4}$ teaspoon salt and $^{1}/_{4}$ teaspoon pepper, or to taste. Set aside at room temperature.

2. Heat the remaining olive oil in a large skillet over medium-high heat. Add the tomatoes and sauté, turning once, a total of 3 minutes, until the tomatoes have started to wilt. Add the garlic and cook for 1 minute more. Remove from the heat and drain off any excess liquid. Gently toss the basil puree together with the tomatoes. Season with the remaining $^{1}/_{4}$ teaspoon salt and $^{1}/_{4}$ teaspoon pepper, or to taste. Blend well and set aside at room temperature.

FINISHING TOUCHES AND
TABLE PRESENTATION

Arrange a bouquet of arugula (4 or 5 stems) across a salad plate. Arrange 3 or 4 tomato halves in the center of each plate. Scatter the olive and mozzarella garnishes over the arugula and tomatoes.

The Inventive Chef

I LOVE THESE BASIL-SCENTED TOMATOES, CHEESE, AND OLIVES MIXED WITH AL DENTE LINGUINE, SERVED AS AN ENTRÉE OR AS A SIDE DISH WITH GRILLED STEAK. DON'T FORGET THE PARMIGIANO!

ON THE SIDE

Sautéed Potatoes with Carrots, Onions, and Pea Pods

MAKES 8 SERVINGS

$2^{1}/_{2}$ pounds small new potatoes, washed, unpeeled, and cut into $^{1}/_{4}$-inch circles
5 tablespoons butter
1 pound small thin carrots, peeled, halved lengthwise, and cut into 2-inch pieces
1 medium yellow onion, peeled and cut into medium dice
$^{1}/_{2}$ pound snow-pea pods, stringed and tipped
2 teaspoons finely chopped fresh rosemary
$^{1}/_{4}$ teaspoon salt, or to taste
$^{1}/_{4}$ teaspoon freshly ground black pepper, or to taste

1. Crisp the potatoes for 10 minutes in a large bowl with cold water to cover. Meanwhile, heat 2 tablespoons of the butter in a large skillet over medium heat. Sauté the carrots, shaking the pan often, until they are crisply cooked, about 8 minutes. Remove the carrots and set them aside in large bowl.

2. Drain the potatoes and blot them dry with paper towels. Add 2 tablespoons of butter to the skillet and sauté the potatoes over medium-high heat, shaking the skillet often as with the carrots, for 12 minutes, until golden brown. Add the potatoes to the carrots.

3. Add the remaining 1 tablespoon of butter to the skillet and sauté the onion over medium-high heat, until golden brown, about 5 minutes.

4. Return the carrots and potatoes to the pan with the onion and add the snow-pea pods. Sauté the vegetables for 3 minutes, stirring often, to blend all the flavors and crisply cook the snow peas. Blend the rosemary with the vegetables and season with salt and pepper.

> ### The Inventive Chef
>
> I LIKE TO SERVE RARE BEEF WITH THESE SAUTÉED VEGETABLES AND LET THE MEAT JUICES ADD TO THEIR FLAVOR.

THE OPENING ACT
Crab and Fennel Chowder

MAKES 8 SERVINGS

$^1/_4$ cup vegetable oil
1 large onion, peeled and finely chopped
1 $^1/_2$ cups fennel, chopped into $^1/_8$-inch pieces
1 large clove garlic, peeled and minced
1 quart chicken broth, homemade or low-sodium canned
$^1/_2$ cup dry vermouth
2 large russet potatoes, peeled and chopped into $^1/_4$-inch
    pieces
2 large carrots, peeled and chopped into $^1/_8$-inch pieces
1 $^1/_2$ cups heavy cream
3 large tomatoes, peeled, seeded, and diced
1 tablespoon finely chopped fresh cilantro
$^3/_4$ pound lump crabmeat, picked clean of shell and cartilage
1 teaspoon salt, or to taste
$^1/_2$ teaspoon ground white pepper, or to taste
Pinch cayenne pepper, or to taste

GARNISH
$^1/_4$ cup finely chopped scallions, green part only

1. Heat the vegetable oil over medium heat in a large, heavy saucepan. Add the onion and fennel, and sauté the vegetables until they are translucent, about 4 minutes. Add the garlic and cook 1 minute more.
2. Add the chicken broth and vermouth to the saucepan and cook over high heat until the broth has come to a boil. Add the potatoes and carrots. Reduce the heat to medium and simmer for 10 minutes.
3. Add the heavy cream, tomatoes, and cilantro and simmer the soup for 10 minutes more. Add the crabmeat and heat just long enough to warm the shellfish. Season with the salt, white pepper, and cayenne pepper to taste.

FINISHING TOUCHES AND TABLE PRESENTATION

Ladle the chowder with all the vegetables, evenly divided, into eight soup bowls. Garnish each bowl with chopped scallions. Place the bowls on 8- or 9-inch plates. Serve hot.

ON THE SIDE
Minted Couscous with Sautéed Eggplant, Zucchini, and Currants

MAKES 8 SERVINGS

1 $^1/_2$ cups chicken broth, homemade or low-sodium canned
1 cup instant couscous
1 tablespoon fresh lemon juice

¹/₄ cup dried currants
¹/₃ cup vegetable oil
1 small eggplant, finely diced
2 medium carrots, peeled and finely diced
2 large zucchini, finely diced
1 large clove garlic, peeled and minced
¹/₂ teaspoon salt, or to taste
¹/₄ teaspoon freshly ground black pepper, or to taste
¹/₂ cup crumbled feta
1 teaspoon finely chopped fresh mint

1. Bring the chicken broth to a rolling boil in a large saucepan. Remove it from the heat and stir in the couscous, lemon juice, and currants. Cover with a tight-fitting lid or aluminum foil and let the couscous steep in the broth until it has absorbed all the liquid, about 4 minutes.

2. While the couscous is steeping, heat the oil in a large sauté pan. Sauté the eggplant, carrots, and zucchini over medium-high heat, until they are tender but still resistant to the bite, about 3–4 minutes. Add the garlic, salt, and pepper and sauté one minute more. Remove from the heat and set aside at room temperature.

3. Fluff the couscous with a fork and toss in the vegetables, feta, and mint. Reseason, if necessary, with salt and pepper to taste.

The Inventive Chef

YOU CAN ADD LEFTOVER LAMB OR POULTRY TO THIS COUSCOUS FOR A ROBUST ENTRÉE. IT IS DELICIOUS AT ROOM TEMPERATURE, WHICH MAKES IT A LOVELY AND PRACTICAL ADDITION TO A BUFFET TABLE.

THE GRAND FINALE

Tangy Lemon Tart

MAKES 8 SERVINGS

SPECIAL COOKWARE
Pastry blender
9-inch tart pan with removable bottom
Dry beans or baking weights

THE PASTRY
1 cup sifted all-purpose flour
2 tablespoons sugar
Pinch of salt
4 ounces unsalted butter, chilled
¹/₄ teaspoon finely grated lemon zest
¹/₄ teaspoon finely grated orange zest
Ice water

THE CITRUS CUSTARD
9 egg yolks, beaten
1 ¹/₂ cups sugar
¹/₄ cup fresh orange juice
¹/₄ cup fresh lemon juice
¹/₄ cup fresh lime juice
6 ounces unsalted butter, at room temperature
1 ¹/₂ teaspoons finely grated lemon zest

GARNISH
³/₄ cup sweetened coconut flakes

TO TOAST COCONUT:
While the oven is still hot from baking the pastry, scatter the coconut flakes over a baking sheet, separating the strands. Bake in the oven until the coconut is a nutty golden brown, about 10 to 12 minutes. Set aside.

THE PASTRY

1. Combine the flour, sugar, and salt together in a mixing bowl. Break the butter into pieces the size of small marbles. With a pastry blender, or your hands, mix the butter with the flour until it resembles coarse cornmeal. Add the lemon and orange zests and just enough ice water for the dough to form a soft ball. Gather the dough, wrap it tightly with plastic wrap, and refrigerate for $1^1/_2$ –2 hours.

The dough can also be made in the food processor. Place the flour, sugar, and salt in the bowl of the processor. Add the butter, by pieces, through the feeding tube. Process briefly, using the pulse control, until the dough resembles rough cornmeal. Add the fruit zests. Add water while pulsing quickly until the dough becomes a soft ball. Remove from the bowl, cover with plastic wrap, and refrigerate for $1^1/_2$ –2 hours.

(The dough can be kept in the refrigerator for 2 days or frozen for 2 weeks.)

2. When you are ready to bake the tart shell, preheat the oven to 400°. Place the slightly chilled dough on a lightly floured work surface and roll it into a circle large enough to hang over the edges of a 9-inch tart pan. Place the dough gently into the pan, easing the dough into the sides. Roll over the top of the pan with a rolling pin to remove the excess dough. Refrigerate the tart shell for 15 minutes.

3. Line the inside of the tart shell with foil. Cover the bottom with dry beans or baking weights to hold the foil and settle the crust. Bake the tart shell for 12 minutes. Remove the foil and weights and bake for 8 minutes more, until the crust is golden brown and crisp. Set aside on a wire rack to cool.

THE CITRUS CUSTARD

1. Pour the beaten egg yolks into a medium-size heavy saucepan. Add the sugar, orange juice, lemon juice, and lime juice. Whisk the mixture constantly over low heat for about 10–12 minutes, until the custard thickens enough to coat the back of a wooden spoon. Remove from the heat and stir the custard until it has cooled slightly, about 3 minutes. Add the butter, one small piece at a time, until it has been fully incorporated into the custard. Strain the custard into a bowl and stir in the lemon zest. Cool to room temperature.

2. Pour the custard into the baked tart shell and refrigerate for 6 hours or overnight.

FINISHING TOUCHES AND TABLE PRESENTATION

One hour before you are ready to serve dessert, remove the tart ring. Sprinkle the toasted coconut over the top of the custard, covering the surface well. Place the tart on a round platter and bring it to the table with 8- or 9-inch dessert dishes. Serve your guests generous slices of tart.

The Inventive Chef

HERE'S A SIMPLE AND GORGEOUS WAY TO SERVE THIS TANGY CUSTARD: FILL CHAMPAGNE FLUTES OR RED-WINE BALLOON GLASSES WITH A LAYER OF CUSTARD, A LAYER OF GINGER CREAM (PAGE 101), THEN SECOND LAYERS OF CUSTARD AND OF WHIPPED CREAM. TOP EACH SERVING WITH FRESH STRAWBERRIES.

KITCHEN SCHEDULE

2 OR 3 DAYS BEFORE THE PARTY

MAIN EVENT	Lamb	Make stock; cool and refrigerate.
		Make marinade; store covered in refrigerator.
GRAND FINALE	Tart	Make dough, wrap tightly with plastic wrap, and refrigerate.

THE DAY BEFORE THE PARTY

MAIN EVENT	Lamb	Marinate lamb; store covered in refrigerator.
		Chop onions for lamb; store covered in refrigerator.
		Dice garlic; store covered in refrigerator.
TOQUE 1	Tomatoes	Prepare basil puree as in step 1; store covered in refrigerator.
		Slice and julienne mozzarella; place separated strips on a covered plate in refrigerator.
		Wash and dry arugula; store in plastic bag in refrigerator.
	Potatoes	Slice potatoes; store covered with cold water in refrigerator.
		Peel and cut carrots; store covered in refrigerator.
		String and tip snow peas; store covered in refrigerator.
		Peel and chop onion; store covered in refrigerator.
TOQUE 2	Chowder	Prepare onion, fennel, garlic, carrots, and potatoes; store, separately, covered in refrigerator.
		Prepare scallion garnish; store covered in refrigerator.
	Couscous	Prepare carrots, zucchini, and garlic; store, separately, covered in refrigerator.
GRAND FINALE	Tart	Bake tart shell; make custard and fill tart; store covered in refrigerator.
		Toast coconut for garnish; store at room temperature.

Strategic Maneuvers: Fill creamer; cover and store in refrigerator.

Fill sugar bowl.

Set table. Prepare and set place cards.

Place chowder underliners on table.

Check ice and beverages.

Locate teas.

Chill wine if white.

Check garnishes for each recipe.

Locate and label all serving bowls, platters, and utensils.

THE DAY OF THE PARTY

MAIN EVENT	Lamb	Three hours before party, prepare through step 5.
TOQUE 1	Tomatoes	Slice tomatoes; store covered in refrigerator.
	Potatoes	Complete recipe through step 3. Set aside, covered, at room temperature.
TOQUE 2	Chowder	Prepare through step 2.
	Couscous	Prepare through step 2.

15 MINUTES BEFORE GUESTS ARRIVE:

Preheat oven to 450°.

TOQUE 1	Tomatoes	Arrange arugula on the salad

		plates and return to refrigerator to chill.
TOQUE 2	Chowder	Finish recipe, remove from heat, and keep covered.

60 MINUTES BEFORE FIRST-COURSE SERVICE:

MAIN EVENT	Lamb	Roast lamb and set out carving utensils.

10 MINUTES BEFORE FIRST-COURSE SERVICE:

		Plug in coffee.
TOQUE 1	Tomatoes	Complete recipe and place on table.
	Potatoes	Complete step 4 and keep warm, uncovered, on top of stove over low heat.
TOQUE 2	Couscous	Complete step 3. Keep warm on top of stove. Warm dinner plates.

5 MINUTES BEFORE FIRST-COURSE SERVICE:

Fill chowder bowls.

MAIN-EVENT SERVICE:

Remove lamb from oven as first course is served and let rest.
Carve lamb. Finish sauce.
Remove first-course plates or bowls.
Just before entrée is served, place dessert at room temperature; garnish with coconut.
Bring out dinner.

DESSERT SERVICE:

Remove dinner plates.
Bring tart and plates to table and serve.
Serve coffee.

AFTER SERVICE:

Unplug coffee.
Turn off oven.

A Vegetarian Celebration
for a New Generation

THE MAIN EVENT:

Wild Mushroom and
Goat Cheese Strudels

THE OPENING ACT:
Roasted Red Pepper and Eggplant Soup

ON THE SIDE:
Quinoa Pilaf with Toasted Pecans

♦

Zucchini and Tomatoes Smothered in Onions

THE OPENING ACT:
Butternut Squash Soup

ON THE SIDE:
Broccoli, Lima Beans, Lemon, and Garlic

♦

*Tubetti Pasta with Tomatoes, Escarole,
and Toasted Pine Nuts*

THE GRAND FINALE:
Chestnut Almond Espresso Cake with Mocha Whipped Cream

PALATE TEASER:
Sun-dried Tomato Palmiers (page 314)

BEVERAGE RECOMMENDATIONS:
Peach Sangria (page 357)
Sauvignon Blanc, Napa Valley

YOUR FIRST GRANDCHILD IS ON THE WAY! AND THOUGH THE parents-to-be don't realize it yet, gracious dining, stimulating adult conversation, and normal sleep are about to become things of the past. In the "calm before the storm," treat them to an idyllic and elegant evening with adoring family and friends. What better way to honor life's essence than with a meal of brilliant vegetable and fruit creations? (And what other way to get your daughter, the vegetarian, to eat enough?) The magnificent golden strudel is bursting with a rich filling of wild mushrooms and cheeses. Surrounded with salads, grains, fruits, and pasta, it makes such a colorful and magnificent feast that no one even misses the meat!

The pleasure of serving this Main Event strudel will be matched by your enjoyment in creating it. Phyllo pastry is fun to work with (don't let it dry out, though) and the filling is chock-full of flavor and great ingredients—three kinds of mushrooms, cheeses, pine nuts, bell pepper, Nicoise olives, spinach . . . the list goes on and on. Just a short time in the oven turns the phyllo into a golden and flaky pastry that makes a gorgeous centerpiece on a formal dinner plate.

Choose either of the first-course soups to begin the meal with a burst of color. The delicious smokiness of the red pepper soup comes from oven-roasting the peppers and eggplant. The butternut squash soup on the two-toque menu is a rich butterscotch color with a luscious, thick creaminess.

Either choice of side dishes presents complementary textures and flavors for the strudel. On the one-toque menu, serve a simple, savory (and healthy!) pilaf of quinoa with toasted pecans and fresh herbs. Complete your colorful plate with a melting mix of sautéed zucchini, tomatoes, and onion.

On the two-toque menu, the strudel is served with a warm salad of crunchy lima beans and broccoli in a garlicky olive oil dressing. Its tangy complement is a vividly colored serving of tubetti pasta with tomatoes, escarole, and pine nuts.

Finally, this great meal ends with an indulgently rich two-layered torte flavored with chestnuts, almonds, and a deep note of espresso—all swathed in Mocha Whipped Cream. After this, your only duty as host will be to graciously acknowledge the acclaim of your guests.

SETTING THE STAGE

In any season, and on any occasion, a display of vegetables, fruits, and flowers would be a fitting centerpiece for this bountiful feast of natural flavors. Create a still life worthy of a classic painting with the loveliest and most colorful pieces you can find!

Should you, in fact, have the good fortune to celebrate a new baby, here are some cute touches that will bring sweet thoughts to the table: Make place cards from tiny picture frames, with an insert displaying the guest's name. After the party (or after the baby arrives) give your guest a photo of the "blessed event" that fits into the frame.

Here's a whimsical centerpiece for the occasion: Fill a straw basket with a variety of baby items: tiny books, alphabet blocks, booties, bibs, miniature stuffed animals, and small rattles. Tie a wide pink or blue bow around the basket and use a matching narrow ribbon around each napkin. At the end of the evening, you can present this lovely piece to the proud new parents!

THE MAIN EVENT

Wild Mushroom and Goat Cheese Strudels

MAKES 8 SERVINGS

SPECIAL COOKWARE
Two baking sheets, 11 by 17 inches
Extra-large skillet

Butter for greasing two baking sheets
¹/₂ cup pine nuts
¹/₂ cup plus 3 tablespoons butter
1 medium red onion, peeled and minced

2 cloves garlic, peeled and minced
³/₄ pound fresh wild mushrooms (shiitake, cremini, or oyster) stemmed, washed, dried, and cut into ¹/₂-inch pieces
1 small red bell pepper, seeded and finely diced
10 ounces fresh spinach, stemmed, washed, dried, and coarsely chopped
2 tablespoons dry white wine (Chablis or sauvignon blanc)
2 tablespoons Nicoise olives, pitted and diced (optional)
6 ounces soft goat cheese
¹/₄ pound ricotta
1 teaspoon finely chopped fresh rosemary
1 teaspoon finely chopped fresh tarragon
2 tablespoons finely chopped flat-leaf parsley
2 eggs, beaten
1 teaspoon salt, or to taste
¹/₂ teaspoon freshly ground black pepper, or to taste
8 fresh or frozen phyllo leaves (a standard package contains 20 phyllo leaves)

GARNISH
8 sprigs fresh tarragon

1. Preheat the oven to 375°. Butter two 11-by-17-inch baking pans, or use nonstick pans, and set aside.
2. Spread the pine nuts over a small ungreased baking sheet. Bake them until they become golden brown, about 4–5 minutes. Set aside.
3. Heat 3 tablespoons of the butter in an extra-large skillet. Sauté the onion until translucent, about 3 minutes. Add the garlic and cook for 1 minute more. Add the mushrooms and pepper and cook until the vegetables have softened slightly, about 3 minutes.
4. Add the spinach and wine in batches and cook, stirring often, until all the spinach has wilted, about 3 minutes. Remove from the heat and let cool.
5. In a large bowl, blend the roasted pine nuts, olives, goat cheese, ricotta, rosemary, tarragon, parsley, all but

3 tablespoons of the eggs, and the salt and pepper until well blended. Stir the cooled vegetables into the cheese mixture, mixing well. Cover and set aside.

6. Melt the remaining 1/2 cup of butter and keep it warm in a double boiler over hot water.

7. Unroll the phyllo leaves, cover with plastic wrap, and cover the plastic wrap with a slightly damp towel. *(Respect phyllo. It is delicate and dries out quickly when exposed to the air.)* Place one leaf of phyllo on a work surface and lightly brush the entire top with melted butter◆. Place a second sheet of phyllo pastry on top of the buttered sheet and butter the top of the second sheet. Repeat this process until you have a total of four sheets. Brush the top of the fourth sheet with butter.

8. Using a sharp knife, cut the phyllo in half horizontally and vertically so that you have four equal rectangles.

9. To form individual strudels: Place a generous 1/2 cup of filling 2 inches from the short end of each phyllo rectangle. Fold the end over the filling, tucking in the edges of each side. Fold the phyllo away from you into a log shape with the seam of the phyllo placed under the strudel. *(The butter on the phyllo will keep the strudel together. Fold the ends of the phyllo strudel closed as if you were wrapping a package, and press the folds together with your finger to seal them closed.)* Repeat this process with the remaining phyllo leaves, butter, and filling.

10. Transfer the strudels to the baking sheets, brush the tops with the reserved egg, bake in the oven for 20–25 minutes, until crisp and golden brown. Remove from the oven and cool slightly before serving.

◆When removing individual leaves of phyllo from the stack, don't get frustrated if some of the phyllo doesn't peel off nicely. You only need 8 good leaves for this recipe, so you can discard any sheets that don't cooperate.

FINISHING TOUCHES AND TABLE PRESENTATION

Picture the dinner plate as the face on a clock:

ONE-TOQUE: Place the strudel at 12 o'clock and garnish with a sprig of tarragon at the center point of the plate. Arrange the Quinoa Pilaf with Toasted Pecans beginning at 9 o'clock and the Zucchini and Tomatoes Smothered in Onions beginning at 3 o'clock, flowing down, and filling out the center and bottom of the plate.

TWO-TOQUE: Place the strudel at 12 o'clock and garnish with a sprig of tarragon at the center point of the plate. Arrange the Broccoli and Lima Beans beginning at 9 o'clock and the Tubetti Pasta with Tomatoes, Escarole, and Toasted Pine Nuts beginning at 3 o'clock, filling out the center and bottom of the plate. Garnish the broccoli with lemon wedges.

The Inventive Chef

THESE STRUDELS CAN BE EATEN WARM OR AT ROOM TEMPERATURE, AND THEY ARE GREAT TO TAKE ALONG ON A PICNIC. YOU CAN ALSO USE YOUR FAVORITE VEGETABLES IN THE FILLINGS— JUST MAKE SURE THEY ARE COMPLETELY COOKED.

Roasted Red Pepper and Eggplant Soup

MAKES 8 SERVINGS

1 large eggplant (about 1¹/2 pounds), ends trimmed and
    coarsely chopped
2 large red bell peppers, cored, seeded, and coarsely
    chopped
1 bulb fennel, top removed, cored, and coarsely chopped
1 medium red onion, peeled and coarsely chopped
6 cloves garlic, peeled and coarsely chopped
¹/2 cup olive oil
2 teaspoons balsamic vinegar
4 cups tomato juice
2 cups vegetable broth, canned (available at health food
    stores or large supermarkets)
1 teaspoon salt, or to taste
³/4 teaspoon freshly ground black pepper, or to taste

GARNISH
¹/2 cup plain yogurt
8 large basil leaves

1. Preheat the oven to 350°. In a large bowl, toss the
eggplant, peppers, fennel, onion, and garlic with the
oil and vinegar, covering all the vegetables well.
2. Spread the vegetables in 2 or 3 large roasting pans
and roast them in the oven for about 30–35 minutes,
until they are very soft.
3. Place the vegetables in batches that fit comfortably
into the bowl of a food processor. Add about 1¹/2
cups of tomato juice, and process to a smooth puree.
The consistency of the puree should be thick and cling

to the spoon.✦ Pour each finished batch into a large
saucepan. Add 1–2 cups of the vegetable broth
depending on how thick you like your soup.
4. Set the pan over medium-low heat for 5 minutes
and season the soup with salt and pepper. If preparing
the soup the day before, cool to room temperature and
refrigerate covered.

✦The soup should be thick and of a consistency to coat a spoon. Add
just enough of the remaining tomato juice to reach this thickness.

FINISHING TOUCHES AND
TABLE PRESENTATION

Serve the soup in 8- or 10-ounce decorative bowls set
on 8- or 9-inch underliners. Garnish each serving with
a tablespoon of plain yogurt and a basil leaf.

The Inventive Chef

ZUCCHINI AND YELLOW BELL PEPPERS MAKE
FINE ADDITIONS TO THIS SOUP.

Quinoa Pilaf with Toasted Pecans

MAKES 8 GENEROUS $^3/_4$-CUP SERVINGS

2 cups (12-ounce package) quinoa (available at health
   food stores and supermarkets)
3 cups vegetable broth, canned (available at health food
   stores or large supermarkets)
1 cup dry white wine
2$^1/_2$ tablespoons butter
1 large Spanish or white onion, peeled and finely chopped
2 large stalks celery, washed and cut into $^1/_4$-inch dice
2 medium carrots, peeled and cut into $^1/_4$-inch dice
2 cloves garlic, peeled and minced
$^1/_2$ cup pecans, coarsely chopped
1 cup currants
$^1/_3$ cup flat-leaf parsley, coarsely chopped
1$^1/_2$ teaspoons minced fresh thyme
6 scallions, trimmed and cut into $^1/_8$-inch circles
1$^1/_2$ tablespoons fresh lemon juice
1 teaspoon salt, or to taste
$^1/_2$ teaspoon freshly ground black pepper, or to taste

1. Place the quinoa in a fine mesh strainer and rinse it
thoroughly under cool running water. Shake the
strainer over the sink to remove any excess water.
2. Place the quinoa, vegetable broth, and wine in a
large saucepan and bring to a boil over medium-high
heat. Reduce the heat to low, cover the saucepan, and
simmer the grain until all the broth has been
absorbed, about 15 minutes. (When the quinoa is cooked,
it will look transparent.)
3. While the quinoa is cooking, melt the butter in a

large skillet over medium heat. When the butter is
sizzling, add the onion and sauté, until it begins to
soften, about 2 minutes. Add the celery and carrots
and continue to sauté, stirring frequently, for an
additional 4 minutes, or until the celery and carrots
have softened but are still crisp to the bite.
4. Stir in the garlic, pecans, and currants and cook for
1 minute more.
5. Remove the skillet from the heat and toss the
vegetables into the saucepan with the quinoa. Stir in
the parsley, thyme, scallions, lemon juice, salt, and
pepper. Serve the quinoa warm or at room
temperature. (You may want to increase the lemon juice, salt,
and pepper if the pilaf is served at room temperature.)

The Inventive Chef

RED AND YELLOW PEPPERS, TOMATOES,
BROCCOLI, AND SNAP PEAS ARE FINE
VEGETABLES TO ADD TO THE QUINOA IN THIS
RECIPE.

Zucchini and Tomatoes Smothered in Onions

MAKES 8 SERVINGS

6 tablespoons olive oil
1 medium yellow onion, peeled and medium chopped
2 large red onions, peeled and medium chopped
3 cloves garlic, peeled and finely minced
2 pounds (about 4 large) zucchini, cut into $^1/_4$-inch rounds

2¹/₂ pounds plum or beefsteak tomatoes, sliced into ¹/₄-inch
   rounds
¹/₂ teaspoon salt, or to taste
¹/₄ teaspoon freshly ground black pepper, or to taste
2 tablespoons finely chopped fresh basil
1 tablespoon finely chopped flat-leaf parsley
¹/₄ teaspoon ground oregano

1. Heat 3 tablespoons of the oil in a large skillet over medium heat. Add the yellow and red onions and the garlic and sauté the vegetables for 1 minute. Cover the skillet and cook, or sweat the onions and garlic over low heat for 10 minutes.

2. While the onions are cooking, sauté the zucchini, covered, in the remaining 3 tablespoons of oil over medium heat in a second large skillet, or two medium skillets, for 5 minutes, until it is tender but still crisp.

3. Add the tomatoes to the zucchini and continue to sauté over medium heat, covered, for 5 minutes more.

4. Blend the onion mixture and ¹/₃ of the sweated juices with the zucchini and tomatoes in a large saucepan. Add the salt, pepper, basil, parsley, and oregano, and cook over low heat for 2 minutes, just to blend the flavors. Taste and season again with the salt and pepper, if needed.

> ## The Inventive Chef
>
> SERVED CHILLED, THIS IS A PERFECT SUMMER
> DISH. YOU CAN VARY THE MARKET-FRESH
> VEGETABLES, BUT ALWAYS HAVE LOTS OF
> SWEATED ONIONS FOR THE UNFORGETTABLLY
> INTENSE FLAVOR OF THEIR JUICES.

OPENING ACT

Butternut Squash Soup

MAKES 8 SERVINGS

SPECIAL COOKWARE
Large (5-quart) heavy-bottomed saucepan

4 large shallots, peeled and finely diced
2 tablespoons vegetable oil
2 cloves garlic, peeled and minced
2 quarts canned vegetable broth (available in health food
   stores and large supermarkets)
2¹/₂ pounds butternut squash, peeled, seeded, and chopped
   into ¹/₄-inch pieces
4 large carrots, peeled and chopped into ¹/₄-inch pieces
2 parsnips, center core removed, peeled and chopped into
   ¹/₂-inch pieces
2 large zucchini, washed and chopped into ¹/₂-inch pieces
¹/₄ teaspoon ground sage
³/₄ teaspoon ground nutmeg
1¹/₂ teaspoons salt, or to taste
¹/₄ teaspoon freshly ground black pepper, or to taste

GARNISH
¹/₂ cup sour cream or crème fraîche
1 teaspoon ground nutmeg

1. Sauté the shallots in the oil in a large (5-quart) heavy-bottomed saucepan for 3 minutes, until they are translucent. Add the garlic and sauté for 1 minute more.

2. Place the vegetable broth, squash, carrots, and parsnips in the saucepan. Simmer the soup for 25 minutes. Add the zucchini, sage, nutmeg, salt, and pepper and simmer for 6 minutes, until the zucchini is slightly tender. Remove from the heat.

3. Being careful to reserve both the broth and the vegetables, strain the vegetables from the pot and set aside about 2 cups for garnish. Place the remaining vegetables in the bowl of a food processor fitted with the metal knife blade and puree. Slowly add the strained broth, a little at a time, until you have a thick soup. Pour any remaining broth and the contents of the food processor bowl back into the saucepan and stir. Readjust the seasonings to suit your taste. *(If preparing soup one day ahead, cool completely to room temperature and refrigerate covered.)*

FINISHING TOUCHES AND TABLE PRESENTATION

Serve the soup, piping hot, in decorative 8- or 10-ounce *soup* bowls placed on 8- or 9-inch underliners. Garnish each serving with a tablespoon of sour cream or crème fraîche and a sprinkle of nutmeg.

The Inventive Chef

WITH CHUNKS OF TURKEY OR CHICKEN ADDED TO THIS SOUP, IT CAN BE THE CENTERPIECE FOR A FINE NONVEGETARIAN SUNDAY-NIGHT SUPPER. POUR THE HOT SOUP INTO A PREHEATED THERMOS AND SERVE IT IN MUGS AT A GAME OR AN OUTING ON A COLD, CRISP FALL DAY.

ON THE SIDE

Broccoli, Lima Beans, Lemon, and Garlic

MAKES 8 SERVINGS

SPECIAL COOKWARE
Extra-large skillet, 14 inches

$1^1/2$ cups dry lima beans
2 large bunches (about $3^1/2$ pounds) broccoli
$^1/2$ cup extra virgin olive oil
4 large cloves garlic, peeled and finely minced
1 teaspoon salt, or to taste
$1^1/2$ –2 teaspoons freshly ground black pepper, or to taste
$^1/4$ cup fresh lemon juice, or more to taste

GARNISH
6 lemon wedges

1. Place the lima beans in a large saucepan. Pour enough boiling water to cover the beans, and soak them off the heat for 1 hour. Drain through a colander and put the beans back in the saucepan.

2. Add 2 quarts of water to the lima beans. Simmer the beans over medium-low heat, uncovered, until they are tender but still crisp to the bite, about 25–35 minutes. Drain the liquid and cool the lima beans to room temperature. When the beans are cool enough to handle, use your fingers to press the tender beans out of their tough skin jackets. Discard the skins and set the beans aside.

3. While the beans are simmering, cut the tops of the broccoli into bite-size pieces. Cut off and discard the tough end of the stalks. Scrape the remaining stalks with a vegetable peeler and cut them into bite-size pieces.

4. Place the broccoli in a large saucepan of boiling water. Lower the heat to a simmer and cook over medium heat for 1 1/2 minutes. Drain the broccoli and shock it in a large bowl of ice water to keep the bright green color. Strain and reserve the broccoli.

5. Heat 1/4 cup of the olive oil in an extra-large skillet over medium heat. Sauté the garlic for 1 minute. Add the broccoli and continue to cook, stirring often, for 3 minutes. Remove the skillet from the heat and add the reserved lima beans to the broccoli. Mix well and toss with the remaining 1/4 cup of olive oil, the salt, pepper, and lemon juice to taste. Serve warm or at room temperature.

The Inventive Chef

FOR MORE COLOR, ADD 2 YELLOW AND 2 RED PEPPERS, MEDIUM CHOPPED, TO THE VEGETABLES JUST BEFORE TOSSING WITH THE OLIVE OIL AND LEMON JUICE. SERVE THIS GARLICKY, CRUNCHY COMBINATION WARM OR AS A SALAD. BOTH RENDITIONS HAVE A TANTALIZING EFFECT ON THE TASTE BUDS.

Tubetti Pasta with Tomatoes, Escarole, and Toasted Pine Nuts

MAKES 8 SERVINGS

THE SAUCE

1/3 cup pine nuts
2 medium heads (about 1 1/2 pounds) escarole
2 large leeks, white parts only
4 cloves garlic, peeled and finely minced
2 (28-ounce) cans whole peeled tomatoes in thick tomato puree
3 tablespoons balsamic vinegar
2 teaspoons sugar
1 teaspoons salt, or to taste
1/4 teaspoon freshly ground black pepper, or to taste
1/4 teaspoon red pepper flakes
1/2 teaspoon dried oregano

THE PASTA

8 quarts boiling water
1 teaspoon salt
1 1/2 pounds small tubetti pasta

GARNISH

1/2 cup finely grated Asiago

1. Preheat oven to 375°.

2. Place the pine nuts on an ungreased baking sheet and toast them in the oven until they are golden brown, about 4–5 minutes. Set aside and cool to room temperature.

3. Remove any blemished outer leaves from the escarole and cut off about 1¹/₂ inches from the stem ends. Holding the head together with one hand, use a sharp knife to cut vertically across the escarole in ¹/₄–¹/₂-inch slices. Place the escarole in a sink filled with cold water.

4. Remove and discard the green stems from the leeks. Cut each white portion in half lengthwise. Cut each half in half lengthwise and chop the pieces into ¹/₄-inch dice. Place in the sink of water along with the escarole.

5. Wash the escarole and leeks by stirring them around in the water to loosen any sand or dirt. Drain, and rewash. Remove the vegetables to a colander.

6. Place the still-wet escarole and leeks in a large (about 8-quart) stockpot and cover with a tight-fitting lid. Steam the vegetables over medium-high heat for 10 minutes, stirring once. The vegetables are done when they are soft but not fully cooked. Remove the lid and cook over high heat for about 5 minutes to allow most of the accumulated water to cook off while the escarole continues to soften. Stir in the garlic during the last minute of cooking.

7. While the vegetables continue to cook, pour the tomatoes with their puree into a large bowl and break the tomatoes apart with a wooden spoon. Add the tomatoes to the leeks and escarole along with the balsamic vinegar, sugar, salt, pepper, red pepper flakes, and oregano, and simmer over medium heat for 10 minutes.

8. To thicken the consistency and richness of the sauce, remove about ¹/₂ the sauce and puree it in two batches in the bowl of a food processor fitted with a cutting blade. Use the pulse button to ensure that it is left somewhat chunky. Return the pureed sauce to the pan and continue to heat over low heat until piping hot.

9. Stir in the toasted pine nuts and taste for salt and pepper.

10. Bring the pasta water to a rolling boil over high heat in a large 10- or 12-quart kettle or stockpot. Add the salt and then the pasta. Lower the heat to medium-high and cook the pasta at a rapid simmer until it is al dente, about 8–10 minutes. *(Reheat the cooked pasta by plunging it into a pot of boiling water, or prepare it just before you are ready to serve.)*

11. Strain the cooked pasta through a colander and return it to the stockpot. Toss the pasta with about ¹/₂ the sauce. Ladle the remaining sauce, as desired, on each individual serving.

The Inventive Chef:

THIS PASTA CAN STAND BY ITSELF AS A HEARTY ENTRÉE, BUT MEAT-EATERS WILL LOVE IT WITH SAUTÉED PANCETTA, GROUND BEEF, OR SHRIMP. ADD THESE ADDITIONS TO THE SAUCE AFTER STEP 8.

THE GRAND FINALE

Chestnut Almond Espresso Cake with Mocha Whipped Cream

MAKES 8 SERVINGS

SPECIAL COOKWARE
Two 9-inch round cake pans

1/2 cup almonds, skinless

1 tablespoon unsalted butter

1 tablespoon all-purpose flour

1 pound fresh chestnuts or 1 cup unsweetened chestnut
puree (available in gourmet stores or baking
departments of large supermarkets)

6 large eggs, separated

1 cup sugar

1 teaspoon pure vanilla extract

1/4 cup brewed triple-strength French-roast coffee, at room
temperature

Pinch of salt

Mocha Whipped Cream (recipe follows)

1. Place the almonds in the bowl of a food processor fitted with a knife blade and pulse until the nuts are finely ground. Set aside in a small dish.

2. Preheat the oven to 325°. Butter and flour two 9-inch round cake pans.

3. If you are using fresh chestnuts, place them in a saucepan with water to cover. Simmer the chestnuts until they are tender, about 40 minutes. Be sure to keep the water level over the chestnuts as they cook. Drain the chestnuts, reserving one cup of the liquid, and set aside 6 whole nuts. When they are cool enough to handle, peel the skin with a paring knife. Puree the chestnuts in the bowl of a food processor and remove the puree to a small bowl. *(If you need more liquid for a smooth puree, add some of the reserved cooking liquid. The puree should be as stiff as peanut butter.)*

4. Beat the egg yolks with the sugar in the bowl of an electric mixer on medium speed for 5 minutes or until the mixture forms ribbons when you raise the beater from the batter. On low speed, blend in the chestnut puree, almonds, vanilla, and coffee.

5. With the whisk attachment, beat the egg whites in a bowl of your electric mixer with the pinch of salt

until they form soft peaks. *Do not overbeat.* Add 1/4 of the whites to the egg batter and blend well; carefully fold in the remaining egg whites until you have a fluffy batter.

6. Fill the cake pans evenly with the batter. Gently rap the pans on the counter to settle the batter. Bake the cake layers on the center rack of the oven for about 35 minutes, or until a cake tester inserted in the center of each layer comes out clean. Allow the cakes to cool 10 minutes in their pans, then invert them onto wire cooling racks.

7. Place one cake layer on a large round silver, pottery, or china cake platter. Frost the sides and top of the bottom layer with Mocha Whipped Cream. Place the top layer over the cream and frost the rest of the cake with the remaining cream. Cut the reserved whole chestnuts in half and arrange them over the cake. Chill the cake for at least 1 hour. Remove it from the refrigerator 15 minutes before serving.

FINISHING TOUCHES AND
TABLE PRESENTATION

Bring this elegant cake to the table on your most beautiful cake plate. Serve generous slices to your guests on 8- or 9-inch dessert plates. Using a serrated knife is a good idea. Fill a bowl with the remaining Mocha Whipped Cream (recipe follows) and ladle a healthy dollop next to each slice of cake.

Mocha Whipped Cream

2 cups heavy cream
8 ounces semisweet chocolate, broken into bite-size pieces
1 teaspoon instant espresso coffee dissolved in ¼ cup
  boiling water

1. Combine the cream, chocolate, and espresso in a heavy saucepan. Cook, stirring, over moderate heat until the chocolate has melted and the mixture thickened. Transfer the mixture to the bowl of an electric mixer and refrigerate until the mocha cream has chilled, about 30 minutes.

2. Whip the cream until stiff.

K I T C H E N   S C H E D U L E

2 OR 3 DAYS BEFORE THE PARTY

MAIN EVENT	Strudel	Prepare through step 10; freeze unbaked on a baking sheet, covered.

THE DAY BEFORE THE PARTY

MAIN EVENT	Strudel	Defrost in the refrigerator
TOQUE 1	Red Pepper Soup	Prepare through step 4; Cool to room temperature; store covered in refrigerator.
	Quinoa	Prepare through step 5 but *do not add the parsley, thyme, green onions, lemon juice, salt, and pepper;* store covered in refrigerator.
TOQUE 2	Squash Soup	Prepare soup completely but do not garnish; cool to room temperature; store covered in refrigerator.
	Broccoli and Lima Beans	Prepare through step 4; cool; cover and refrigerate beans and broccoli, separately.
	Pasta	Toast pine nuts; store at room temperature well covered.
GRAND FINALE	Chestnut Cake	Prepare and bake cake through step 6; wrap well and refrigerate. Prepare Mocha Whipped Cream; store covered in refrigerator.
Strategic Maneuvers:		Fill creamer; cover and store in refrigerator. Fill sugar bowl. Set table. Prepare and set place cards. Check table decor. Set soup underliners on table. Check ice and beverages. Locate teas.

Chill wine if white.
Check garnishes for each recipe.
Locate and label all serving bowls, platters, and utensils.

THE DAY OF THE PARTY

2 HOURS BEFORE GUESTS ARRIVE:

MAIN EVENT	Strudel	Bake strudels; set aside at room temperature.
TOQUE 1	Red Pepper Soup	Put in top of double boiler. *Do not heat.*
	Quinoa	Bring to room temperature. Add parsley, thyme, green onions, lemon juice, salt, and pepper. Set in double boiler for reheating.
	Zucchini	Prepare and finish recipe; set aside at room temperature.
TOQUE 2	Squash Soup	Put in top of double boiler. *Do not heat.*
	Broccoli and Lima Beans	Finish recipe; store covered in refrigerator.
	Pasta	Make sauce; set aside at room temperature.
GRAND FINALE:	Chestnut Cake	Frost cake with whipped cream and refrigerate.

45 MINUTES BEFORE GUESTS ARRIVE:

		Fill bottoms of double boilers with water.
TOQUE 2	Pasta	Cook pasta, but do not combine with sauce.

126 ◆ *Invitation to Dinner*

15 MINUTES BEFORE FIRST-COURSE SERVICE:

		Plug in coffee.
		Preheat oven to 300°.
		Warm dinner plates.
		Ready bowls for soup.
		Check that all foods are at correct temperature.
MAIN EVENT	Strudel	Warm in oven.
TOQUE I	Red Pepper Soup	Heat over simmering water in double boiler.
	Quinoa	Heat slowly over low heat in double boiler.
	Zucchini	Heat over low heat.
TOQUE 2	Squash Soup	Heat over simmering water in double boiler.
	Pasta	Combine pasta with sauce; keep warm over low heat.

5 MINUTES BEFORE FIRST-COURSE SERVICE:

Fill soup bowls; garnish; bring to table.

Put broccoli at room temperature.

FIRST-COURSE SERVICE:

Remove cake from refrigerator; store in cool place.

Warm dinner plates.

MAIN-EVENT SERVICE:

Remove first-course plates.

Arrange and present Main Event.

DESSERT SERVICE:

Remove dinner plates.

Bring dessert plates and cake to table and serve dessert.

Serve coffee.

AFTER SERVICE:

Unplug coffee.

Turn off oven.

The Bounty and Beauty of Buffet Dinners

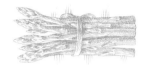

A lavish buffet is an exciting gift for your guests and, for a host who loves to cook, an exciting way to give a large dinner party or entertain a crowd. The more food you make, and the more tempting choices you provide, the greater will be your guests' gusto and sheer pleasure in abundance—and the more passionate will be their gratitude to you! There is also a special thrill in the beauty of a buffet—a fabulous tableau of food, table setting, and decorations to delight the eye as well as the palate.

For me, planning a buffet party is a distinct pleasure, one that is quite different from a served sit-down dinner. In this chapter I present four wonderful occasions with menus so delicious and bountiful that I hope you will try them all (even if you don't have to feed a crowd):

• Celebrate Easter with a colorful and formal buffet dinner of roasted veal, broiled salmon, and an array of Mediterranean flavors.

• At a down-home family reunion in the country, load the picnic tables with pans of lobster corn pudding, trays of skewered chicken, and bowls of summer salads and other specialties.

• Host a banquet in the spirit of San Gennaro's feast, challenging your guests to choose from veal, cornish hen, stuffed breads, calzones, pasta, lasagna, and vegetable dishes.

• Celebrate a daughter-in-law's academic achievement with a scintillating spread of sweet-and-sour prawns, fried Malaysian chicken, banana dumplings, and other Asian delicacies.

These events demonstrate the tremendous versatility of the buffet format, which can be as casual or as formal as the occasion demands, and can accommodate any number of guests. All the menus in this chapter are designed to serve sixteen adults. To feed more people, simply expand the recipes proportionally.

As discussed more extensively in Part I, a lap-service buffet is a party where guests fill their plates and sit anywhere they please. Obviously, you can accommodate the greatest number of guests this way, with the least disruption to your home. Set up your gorgeous food display on the dining room table (or other surface) following my tips on "Creating a Beautiful Buffet"

Creating a Beautiful Buffet

When I invite my guests to serve themselves from a buffet, people always stop first to admire the table and ask, "How did you get it to look like that?" I can honestly answer that creating a fabulous display is really quite simple.

First, plan your buffet table well ahead of the party! At least the day before the event, or even earlier, select the surface where the food will go. If space permits, always try to set up the food on a large table in the middle of a room—as with a conventional dining table—so that guests can walk around it, giving them a dramatic view of all the food and making self-service much quicker. Then select a lovely serving vessel for every single item that will go on the buffet: Go through your menu, list each food item, and choose the tray, platter, dish, basket, or bowl to contain it. (Don't forget such extra items as bread, butter, cream, sugar, and other condiments; and don't forget to look in your closets and on your top shelves for great serving pieces that are gathering dust.)

Next, compose your layout. The key to a visually powerful buffet design is *height*. You must plan and build different levels on which to place your serving pieces and thus create a dramatic and varied display. This is easy and fun: Use ordinary household items to serve as the supports. Find common sturdy objects of varying heights, such as flowerpots, heavy cardboard boxes, baking pans, ice buckets, and plastic containers.

Lay out your collection of supports, upside down, and arrange your chosen serving pieces on top of them. Make sure you have enough space for each piece, and that they are steady on their pedestals.

Arrange your tiers so that the highest point is in the middle of the table, or in the back if your display is against a wall. Be creative in arranging the shapes on their different levels. Remember to allow space for the serving utensils that go with each dish (I like to set out small dishes as resting places for drippy serving spoons and forks). Of course, you will need room for the stacks of dinner plates, and rolls of napkins and flatware, too.

Now it is time to drape the table with linens. Remove your serving pieces but leave your supporting items in place (and make sure your table surface is protected with pads or an extra cloth). Place your fine tablecloth over all the supports and arrange it to fall smoothly and beautifully. It is a good idea to place a small card noting the spot where each serving dish is to go, so you don't have to hesitate when the real meal is ready!

Be creative in filling the spaces between the dishes. I like to use such natural decorations as beautiful leafy greens, small whole fruits and vegetables, nuts in their shells, gourds, pinecones, and seashells. Now is the time to create gorgeous centerpieces. I like to fill a large basket with flowering branches, mixed flowers, or whatever is in season. You can arrange tiers of potted plants as well. I give further suggestions for centerpieces and other table decorations along with each of the menus in this chapter.

Knowing that you have created a sensational buffet will inspire your final cooking. At your party, when you bring the serving pieces to the table—this time filled with your beautifully arranged and garnished food—you will be able to quickly assemble a masterpiece of color, texture, and height that will have your guests gasping!

(page 130), and direct your guests to seat themselves wherever they choose.

For a seated or formal buffet—such as my Mediterranean Easter feast—you need to formally set a table (or several tables) for dining *in addition to* the table used to display the meal. Outdoor buffets, similarly, can be either lap-service or seated. Indoors or out, the first step in your game plan for a large buffet is to calculate the seating and capacity of your home and to determine your needs for rental equipment and linens.

Be sure to think about the flow of your buffet party. For any buffet, whether informal or quite elegant, you need to provide drinks and welcoming food in a comfortable area that won't interfere with your last-minute cooking and presentation chores. When the food is ready to be served, set up your grand display and invite the crowd in to feast their eyes—and then themselves.

If this is a seated buffet, you will, of course, join your guests at table. In a more casual or very large event, you may have to stay on your feet to replenish food and beverages and to meet special requests—unless you have hired helpers. In any case, it is your responsibility as host to judge when seconds or thirds have been finished, to direct the clearing of the buffet, and then to make the presentation of the dessert course and hot beverages. With all the foods at a buffet, even though the actual cooking has been long completed, you will still need to consult your kitchen schedule to make sure you haven't forgotten anything!

A Fancy Easter with a Mediterranean Flavor

THE MAIN EVENTS:

Roasted Breast of Veal
Citrus-Scented Broiled Salmon
Lettuce Salad with Fresh Herbs and Cheeses
and Oven-Roasted Garlic-Basil Vinaigrette

ON THE SIDE:

Marinated Eggplant, Red Peppers, Spiced Olives, and Feta Cheese

◆

*Confetti of Radicchio, Red Bliss Potatoes, and Green Beans
with Arugula, Lemon, and Garlic Vinaigrette*

ON THE SIDE:

Mushroom and Pepper Phyllo Triangles

◆

Spaghetti Squash with Currants, Dates, and Almonds

THE GRAND FINALE:
Praline Cheesecake with an Oatmeal Crust

PALATE TEASERS:
Sun-dried Tomato Palmiers (page 314)
Mussels with Parsley and Horseradish Mayonnaise (page 302)

BEVERAGE RECOMMENDATIONS:
Bellinis (page 356)
Pinot Noir, California, Talus

*T*HERE'S BOTH SOLEMNITY AND FESTIVITY IN A GRAND EASTER Sunday celebration, filled with sacred meaning and the joyous renewal of springtime. When you bring family and friends together on this most important occasion, welcome them to a house filled with light and flowers, and a huge, beautifully appointed dining table with a formal place setting for every person. Your meal will be a lavish and spirited feast, served from a dazzling buffet full of the sprightly flavors, spicy aromas, and sunny colors of the Mediterranean.

Mediterranean cookery, with its treasure of produce, meats, cheeses, herbs, spices, fruits, and nuts, has always inspired me, and I could probably fill a score of buffets with my ideas. But this menu alone has a wonderful range of choices for you as cook and, of course, for your guests.

There are three Main Events for this occasion. I have loved roast breast of veal since childhood—tantalized by the fragrance of roasting meat, wine, and rich broth wafting through the house whenever my mom prepared it. For this menu, I have given it an Italian savor with a stuffing of pancetta, porcini or cremini mushrooms, orzo pasta, and authentic Parmigiano Reggiano. Rolled, tied, braised in the oven, then sliced into gorgeous medallions, it is a fitting centerpiece for the buffet.

You will also enjoy quickly broiled salmon fillets, brightly flavored with a marinade of fresh citrus juices, capers, currants, and coriander. A three-part salad presentation completes the Main Event: a bowl of mixed green and red lettuces, tangy with roasted garlic dressing, accompanied by crisp French bread croutons and an assortment of cheeses. (Many guests will want to enjoy the salad offering as a separate course, so stack salad plates near the bowl of greens.)

Either menu's dishes contribute to the tempting display. Sautéed eggplant, crisp red pepper strips, onion, and garlic are tossed with feta cheese and black olives. Simply accented with balsamic vinegar, the mix is delicious either chilled or at room temperature. Another burst of flavor, color, and texture comes in a great glass bowl full of radicchio confetti with tender young green beans and matchsticks of cooked new potatoes, all moistened with a warm vinaigrette of arugula, lemon, and garlic.

If you enjoy baking (and have time before the party) choose to make the savory pastry triangles. The melting filling of mixed cheeses, mushrooms, red peppers, and eggs (with a spicy note of cumin) is enclosed in crisp, buttery layers of phyllo. And everyone at your party will relish the golden threads of spaghetti squash tossed with a sweet mélange of eggplant, currants, dates, and almonds piqued with ginger and coriander for a wonderful play of textures and flavors.

An easy-to-make cheesecake, dusted with hazelnut praline, is the luscious Grand Finale to this feast.

Bring the glory of spring into your home with flowers everywhere: yellow daffodils, white narcissus, and lilies. A vase of tall flowering forsythia branches makes an elegant centerpiece for the buffet. Fill in the spaces between your platters and bowls with baskets of breads and eggs (a symbol of Easter and renewal) and lovely Mediterranean foods such as lemons, grapes, nuts, and other produce.

If you're having a large number of guests, consider renting tables for seating (and linens, too), and set the buffet on the dining table. Choose colors that match the season and occasion: perhaps a pale green tablecloth with an array of pastel napkins in pink, lavender, and pale yellow. But if you possibly can, try to accommodate your guests at one table: Bringing everyone together at the table will enhance the specialness of the day.

THE MAIN EVENT
Roasted Breast of Veal

MAKES 16 SERVINGS

SPECIAL COOKWARE
One large roasting pan, 16 by 11 inches, or two medium
*   roasting pans*
Butcher's twine
Meat pounder

³/₄ pound pancetta, finely chopped
2 large onions, peeled and finely chopped
6 cloves garlic, peeled and finely minced
2 pounds wild mushrooms, cremini or shiitake, coarsely
*   chopped*
3 cups orzo, cooked
¹/₄ cup finely chopped flat-leaf parsley
1 tablespoon finely chopped fresh sage
1 cup freshly grated Parmigiano Reggiano
3 teaspoons salt
1¹/₂ teaspoons freshly ground black pepper
2 breasts of veal, boned, all excess fat removed, and
*   flattened (about 7 pounds each before boning), bones*
*   reserved and cut into 2¹/₂-inch pieces*
¹/₄ cup olive oil
4 carrots, peeled and cut into large dice
2 medium onions, peeled and cut into medium dice
1¹/₂ cups dry white wine
5 cups chicken stock, homemade or low-sodium canned

GARNISH
12 sprigs fresh sage

1. Sauté the pancetta in a large skillet over medium-high heat until it is very crisp and brown, about 7 minutes. Remove the pancetta and drain it on paper towels; set aside. Pour all but 3 tablespoons of the fat rendered from the pancetta into a large bowl and reserve it at room temperature.

2. Heat the 3 tablespoons of the reserved pancetta fat in the skillet over medium heat. Add the finely chopped onions and sauté for 4–6 minutes, until they are translucent and soft. Add 4 cloves of the garlic and sauté for 1 minute more. Add the mushrooms and continue to cook until the mushrooms are tender, about 5 minutes.

3. Transfer the sautéed vegetables to the bowl with the reserved pancetta and its drippings and mix in the

orzo, parsley, sage, and Parmigiano. Season with
1 teaspoon of the salt and $^1/_2$ teaspoon of the pepper.

4. Preheat the oven to 350°.

5. Lay the veal breasts open and flat on a work surface.
Pound them with a meat pounder to increase their
surface area. The meat should be about 2 inches thick.
Spread the sautéed vegetable mixture over the meat and
roll the breasts up like jelly rolls, seam-sides down. Tie
the breasts in four places with the butcher's twine.
Season the outside generously with the remaining
2 teaspoons of salt and 1 teaspoon of pepper.

6. Heat 2 tablespoons of the olive oil in the bottom
of a large roasting pan set on 1 or 2 burners over
medium-high heat. Brown the veal breasts one at a
time on all sides until golden brown, about 3 minutes
on a side. Remove the meat from the pan and set it
aside. Add 2 more tablespoons of oil to the pan and
brown the reserved veal bones until golden brown.
Remove the bones from the pan and add the carrots,
remaining garlic, and medium-diced onion. Sauté over
medium heat for 2 minutes.

7. Pour the white wine into the roasting pan. With
the heat on high, deglaze the drippings by using a
wooden spoon to scrape up all the bits of meat and
vegetables on the bottom of the pan.

8. If your roasting pan is large enough to
accommodate the two pieces of veal, place them back
into the roasting pan, along with the browned bones
and the chicken stock. If you need to use two
roasting pans, make sure you divide the vegetables,
veal bones, and chicken stock evenly between the
pans. Add the veal breasts to the roasting pan(s) and
roast in the oven for $2^1/_2$ hours, or until the veal is
very tender.

FINISHING TOUCHES AND TABLE PRESENTATION

Remove the veal breasts from the pan(s) and allow them
to rest on a cutting board for 20 minutes. While the
veal is resting, strain the pan juices into a small saucepan
and keep warm over low heat. Cut the butcher's twine
and discard. Slice the veal into 1-inch medallions and
arrange in overlapping slices on two large platters garnished with the sprigs of sage. Place the pan juices in a
serving dish. Place a small foil container or a small plate
in the back of the platters under the tablecloth. Let the
end of the platters rest, slightly tilted, on the foil container to give the platters height on the buffet.

THE MAIN EVENT
Citrus-Scented Broiled Salmon
MAKES 16 SERVINGS

8 (8-ounce) fillets of salmon, $1^1/_2$ inches thick, halved
$^1/_2$ teaspoon salt
$^1/_2$ teaspoon freshly ground black pepper
$^1/_4$ cup fresh lemon juice
5 tablespoons olive oil
$^1/_4$ cup drained capers
2 tablespoons currants
$^1/_4$ cup fresh orange juice
$1^1/_2$ teaspoons whole coriander seeds
Grated zest of 1 lemon
Grated zest of 1 orange

GARNISH
6 lime wedges

6 lemon wedges
2 bunches of watercress, well washed, long stems removed

1. Preheat the broiler.
2. Combine the capers, currants, orange juice,
3 tablespoons of the olive oil, coriander seeds, and
lemon and orange zests in the bowl of the food
processor. Process the ingredients with the knife blade
until they are pureed.
3. Place the salmon on a baking sheet with sides and
season it with the salt and pepper. In a small bowl,
combine the lemon juice and 2 tablespoons of the olive
oil, and brush the pieces of salmon well with the
marinade. Set aside at room temperature.
4. Broil the fish 4 inches from the heat for
7 minutes. Spread the caper mixture over the salmon
and return it to the broiler for another 9 minutes.
(Salmon is moist and juicy cooked 10 minutes to the inch.)

FINISHING TOUCHES AND TABLE PRESENTATION

Arrange the salmon fillets in rows on large cutting
boards. Garnish the boards between the fillets with
wedges of lemon and lime and the watercress.

Lettuce Salad with Fresh Herbs and Cheeses and Oven-Roasted Garlic-Basil Vinaigrette

MAKES 16 SERVINGS

2 long French baguettes, sliced horizontally in 1-inch-thick
   pieces
3 pounds mixed greens (Bibb, curly endive, radicchio, and
   red-leaf lettuces), cored, trimmed, washed, dried, and
   torn into bite-size pieces
1¼ cups Oven-Roasted Garlic-Basil Vinaigrette (page 87)
2 pounds mixed cheeses (a combination of chèvre, Brie,
   Saga blue, and Camembert), cut into wedges

GARNISH
16 rosemary sprigs

1. Preheat the oven to 400°.
2. Arrange the French bread pieces on baking sheets
and toast it in the oven for 3 minutes on each side,
until crisp and golden. Set the croutons aside at room
temperature or store them in an airtight container.

FINISHING TOUCHES AND TABLE PRESENTATION

Put the greens in a large salad bowl and, just before dinner, toss them with the vinaigrette. Set salad servers
over the greens and a pepper mill in front of the salad
bowl. Arrange the toasted croutons in a napkin-lined

basket next to the salad. Place the cheese wedges with cheese knives on a marble or wood cheese board in front of the salad bowl and basket of croutons. Garnish the cheeses with rosemary sprigs. Place the salad plates to the side of the salad. Guests can eat the salad as a separate course, if they wish.

The Inventive Chef

IT IS A GOOD IDEA TO LEAVE SOME OF THE GREENS UNDRESSED FOR FUSSY SALAD EATERS. PROVIDE LEMON WEDGES FOR THEIR SALAD.

ON THE SIDE

Marinated Eggplant, Red Peppers, Spiced Olives, and Feta Cheese

MAKES 16 SERVINGS

6 tablespoons olive oil
2 medium red onions, peeled and finely chopped
4 cloves garlic, peeled and finely minced
1 large eggplant, cut into 1-inch cubes
$^1/_3$ cup chicken or vegetable broth, homemade or low-sodium canned
4 red bell peppers, seeded, cored, and cut into $^1/_2$-inch squares
$^1/_4$ cup balsamic vinegar
$^1/_2$ teaspoon salt, or to taste
$^1/_2$ teaspoon pepper, or to taste

1 cup black olives, Kalamata or Niçoise, pitted and chopped
1 cup crumbled feta
$^1/_4$ cup feta, cut into 1-inch chunks
12 whole Kalamata or Niçoise olives

1. Heat 2 tablespoons of the oil in a large skillet over medium-high heat. Reduce the heat to moderate and sauté the onions until they are translucent and wilted, about 4–5 minutes. Add the garlic and sauté for 1 minute more. Remove the onion and garlic to a large bowl and set aside.

2. Heat $1^1/_2$ tablespoons of olive oil in the skillet over medium heat. Add half the eggplant and cook, stirring, over medium-high heat, until the skillet is dry. Add half the broth and continue cooking until the eggplant becomes translucent and soft, about 4 minutes. Add the eggplant to the bowl with the onions and garlic. Repeat with another $1^1/_2$ tablespoons of olive oil and the remaining eggplant and broth.

3. Add the red peppers and the remaining 1 tablespoon of oil to the skillet and sauté over medium-high heat for 3–4 minutes, until the peppers are tender yet crisp to the bite. Add the peppers, balsamic vinegar, salt, and pepper to the eggplant and blend well.

FINISHING TOUCHES AND TABLE PRESENTATION

Toss the eggplant mixture with the chopped olives and crumbled feta. Spoon the vegetables onto a large round or oval, white or terra-cotta platter. Garnish the top with the additional chunks of feta cheese and whole olives. Serve chilled or at room temperature.

ON THE SIDE

Confetti of Radicchio, Red Bliss Potatoes, and Green Beans with Arugula, Lemon, and Garlic Vinaigrette

MAKES 16 SERVINGS

1 teaspoon salt
2 1/2 pounds young green beans or haricots verts, *stemmed*
2 1/2 pounds Red Bliss potatoes, unpeeled, cut into 1/4 inch rounds, then cut into 1/4-inch julienne strips
1 cup Arugula, Lemon, and Garlic Vinaigrette (below)
2 large heads radicchio, cored, washed and cut into 1/2-inch julienne strips

GARNISH
8 large basil leaves

1. Pour 1 quart of the water into a large saucepan with 1/2 teaspoon of the salt and bring to a boil over medium-high heat. Pour the second quart of water into a large saucepan with the remaining salt and bring to a boil over medium-high heat.

2. When the water comes to a boil, add the beans to one saucepan and the potatoes to the other. Lower the heat and simmer the beans, uncovered, for 3–4 minutes, until they are tender but still crisp to the bite. Drain and shock the beans in cold water. Drain them again and set aside in a large bowl.

3. Cook the potatoes until they are fork-tender but still crisp to the bite, about 4 minutes. Drain and shock them in cold water to stop their cooking. Drain them again and add to the beans.

4. Warm the dressing in a small saucepan over low heat.

FINISHING TOUCHES AND
TABLE PRESENTATION

Add the radicchio to the beans and potatoes. Gently toss the vegetables with the warm vinaigrette, blending 1/2–3/4 of the colors well. Reserve the remaining vinaigrette for future use. Place the salad in a glass salad bowl and decorate it with the fresh basil leaves.

Arugula, Lemon, and Garlic Vinaigrette

MAKES 1 CUP

1 large clove garlic, peeled and coarsely chopped
1 teaspoon grated zest of lemon
1/2 teaspoon Dijon mustard

1 ounce arugula leaves
2 tablespoons fresh lemon juice
1 tablespoon balsamic vinegar
$1/4$ teaspoon salt
$1/8$ teaspoon freshly ground black pepper
$1/2$ cup olive oil
2 tablespoons freshly grated Parmigiano Reggiano cheese

1. Place the garlic, lemon zest, mustard, arugula, lemon juice, balsamic vinegar, salt, and pepper in the bowl of the food processor fitted with the knife blade. Blend all the ingredients until they are well mixed, about 30 seconds.

2. With the motor on, slowly pour the olive oil through the feeding tube until the vinaigrette has thickened, about 10 to 15 seconds. Pour the vinaigrette into a small bowl. Blend in the Parmigiano and season with salt and pepper to taste.

3. Warm the dressing in a small saucepan before dressing the Confetti of Radicchio, Red Bliss Potatoes, and Green Beans (page 138).

ON THE SIDE

Mushroom and Pepper Phyllo Triangles

MAKES 16 SERVINGS

SPECIAL COOKWARE
Pastry brush

4 tablespoons olive oil
1 medium onion, peeled and finely chopped

2 cloves garlic, peeled and finely chopped
1 pound domestic or wild mushrooms, washed, dried, and
    cut into $1/4$-inch dice
2 medium red bell peppers, cored, seeded, and finely
    chopped
5 ounces feta, crumbled
$1/2$ cup freshly grated Parmigiano Reggiano
$1/3$ cup finely chopped flat-leaf parsley
$3/4$ teaspoon ground cumin
2 eggs, beaten, at room temperature
$1/2$ teaspoon salt
$1/4$ teaspoon freshly ground black pepper
8 sheets fresh or frozen phyllo pastry
5 tablespoons salted butter, melted

GARNISH
1 bunch flat-leaf parsley

1. Preheat the oven to 350°.
2. Heat the oil in a large skillet over medium-high heat. Add the onions and sauté for 3–5 minutes, until translucent. Add the garlic and continue to cook over the medium-high heat for 30 seconds.
3. Add the mushrooms and cook over medium heat, stirring often, until they begin to soften, about 3 minutes. Add the red peppers and cook, stirring, for 3 minutes more.
4. Place the mushroom filling in a large bowl and let it cool for 5 minutes, then stir in the feta, Parmigiano, parsley, cumin, eggs, salt, and pepper. Blend well and set aside.
5. Place one sheet of phyllo on a cutting board with the short end facing you. (*Cover the remaining phyllo sheets with a piece of plastic wrap topped with a slightly damp towel. The phyllo will dry out if left uncovered.*)
6. With the short end of the phyllo sheet facing you, cut it in half, crosswise, forming two rectangular strips. Immediately brush each of the strips with melted

butter. Fold each strip in half lengthwise and brush the tops with butter. Place 2 generous tablespoons of the mushroom mixture one inch from the bottom of each rectangle. Fold the bottom end of the phyllo over the mixture. Continue folding the phyllo back and forth into a triangle, like folding a flag, until you reach the end of the strip. Do the same with the remaining strip. Brush the tops with butter and place the pastries on a buttered baking sheet 1 1/2 inches apart.

7. Repeat this assembly until all the filling and pastry have been used.

8. Bake the triangles for about 20 minutes, until they are puffed and golden brown.

FINISHING TOUCHES AND
TABLE PRESENTATION

The triangles can be served warm. Arrange them in a basket, on marble, or on white china. I like a simple garnish of small parsley bouquets at one end of the platter.

The Inventive Chef

ONCE YOU HAVE MASTERED THE KNACK OF CREATING THESE TRIANGLES, YOU WILL MAKE THEM AGAIN AND AGAIN. SPINACH, SAUTÉED GROUND BEEF, LAMB, OR CHICKEN ARE JUST SOME OF THE FILLINGS TO USE IN THE PASTRIES.

ON THE SIDE

Spaghetti Squash with Currants, Dates, and Almonds

MAKES 16 SERVINGS

SPECIAL COOKWARE
Very sharp large knife for cutting squash
Two large roasting pans, 17 by 11 inches

2 large spaghetti squash, halved lengthwise, stemmed, and seeded
6 cups fresh orange juice
2/3 cup honey
1/3 cup olive oil
2 medium red onions, peeled and finely diced
2 large eggplants, peeled and cut into 1/2-inch dice
1 tablespoon finely minced fresh ginger
3/4 teaspoon ground coriander
3/4 cup currants
3/4 cup preserved dates, seeded and coarsely diced
1 1/4 cup slivered toasted almonds (page 330)
1 teaspoon salt, or to taste
1/2 teaspoon freshly ground black pepper, or to taste

1. Preheat the oven to 375°.

2. Place the squash, flesh side down, in the roasting pans. Blend the orange juice with the honey. Add enough of the orange juice to each pan to cover the bottom of the squash by 1/2 inch. Bake the squash until it is tender and can be easily pierced with a fork, about 45–55 minutes. Reserve about 3 cups of the cooking liquid.

3. While the squash is in the oven, heat 2 tablespoons of the oil in a large skillet. Add the onions and sauté over medium-high heat until they are golden, about 5 minutes. Add the eggplant in batches with additional olive oil as necessary (about 3 tablespoons). Continue to cook the vegetables, stirring often, until the eggplant softens, about 7–9 minutes.

4. Reduce heat to medium, add the ginger, coriander, currants, dates, and $^3/_4$ cup of the almonds to the eggplant and onions, and sauté the vegetables for about 3 minutes, until all the flavors are blended. Add additional olive oil, if needed, to keep pan moist. Set aside, covered, off the heat.

5. When the squash has cooled slightly and is easy to handle, scrape the flesh lengthwise with a fork into a second large skillet. *(The cooked flesh of the squash resembles long threads of spaghetti.)*

6. Place the skillet with the strands of spaghetti squash, along with the reserved cooking liquid, over medium heat until the squash is hot, and season it with $^1/_2$ teaspoon salt and $^1/_4$ teaspoon pepper, or to taste.

7. Return the skillet with the eggplant mixture to one burner and cook over high heat for 2 additional minutes, or until hot. Season with $^1/_2$ teaspoon salt and $^1/_4$ teaspoon pepper, or to taste.

FINISHING TOUCHES AND
TABLE PRESENTATION

Combine the contents of the two skillets and heap the vegetables into a white or light-colored crockery bowl or platter to exaggerate the marvelous golden color of the squash. Scatter the remaining $^1/_2$ cup of slivered almonds over the top.

> *The Inventive Chef*
>
> PLACE THE SPAGHETTI SQUASH TOSSED WITH BUTTER IN THE CENTER OF A ROUND PLATE. SURROUND THE SQUASH WITH A MEDLEY OF LARGE DICED ZUCCHINI AND RED AND YELLOW PEPPERS SAUTÉED IN OLIVE OIL. SEASON WITH SALT AND PEPPER.

THE GRAND FINALE

Praline Cheesecake with an Oatmeal Crust

MAKES 16 SERVINGS

SPECIAL COOKWARE
10-inch springform pan
Pastry brush

THE CRUST
$^1/_4$ cup crystallized ginger (purchased on spice shelves in markets)
$^3/_4$ cup blanched hazelnuts, toasted (see page 331)
$^3/_4$ cup quick oats
$^3/_4$ cup light brown sugar
$^1/_8$ teaspoon ground cinnamon
$^1/_4$ cup melted unsalted butter

THE CHEESE FILLING
2 pounds plus 3$^1/_2$ ounces cream cheese, at room temperature
$^1/_2$ pound plus 1 tablespoon mascarpone cheese, at room temperature
1$^1/_3$ cups sugar
2 eggs

2 teaspoons vegetable oil
³/₄ cup blanched hazelnuts, toasted (see page 331)
¹/₄ cup sugar
1 tablespoon unsalted butter
¹/₄ teaspoon pure vanilla extract

GARNISH

1 pint large strawberries with stems

1. Preheat the oven to 350°.

2. *To make the crust:* Place the ginger and nuts in the bowl of a food processor fitted with the knife blade and process until the mixture is finely chopped.

3. Place the nut mixture in a medium-size mixing bowl with the oats, brown sugar, cinnamon, and butter. Mix well and press into the bottom of a 9-inch springform pan. Bake for 20 minutes and set aside at room temperature.

4. *To make the filling:* In the large bowl of an electric mixer, beat the cream cheese and mascarpone with the paddle beater on medium speed, until the cheeses are smooth. Slowly add the sugar and continue to beat for 2 minutes. Add the eggs, one at a time, beating well after each addition. Pour the cheese mixture into the crust and place the pan in the middle of the 350° oven.

5. Fill a medium-size cake pan with water and place it on the rack below the cheesecake. Bake the cheesecake for 30 minutes, until it is almost set. (*The cake will be a little moist in the center when it has finished baking.*)

6. Remove the cake from the oven, loosen the sides of the springform pan with a small metal spatula or knife, and cool for 30 minutes at room temperature while preparing the topping.

7. *To make the topping:* Line a baking sheet with aluminum foil and brush the foil with the vegetable oil.

8. In a skillet, combine all the topping ingredients. Cook over medium-high heat, shaking the pan, until the sugar melts, about 3 minutes. Reduce the heat to low and continue to cook the glaze, stirring often, until the sugar has caramelized to a golden brown.

9. Pour the nut mixture onto the foil-lined baking sheet and cool for 10 minutes. Break the nuts into chunks and put the chunks in the bowl of a food processor fitted with the knife blade. Pulse the nuts 3 or 4 times until they reach a medium-chop consistency. Sprinkle the mixture around the edge of the cheesecake and refrigerate.

FINISHING TOUCHES AND
TABLE PRESENTATION

Place the cake on a 12-inch round, silver or pottery cake stand or platter. Surround the cake with the strawberries placed stem side up. To level the strawberries, cut a sliver off the bottom of each. If your guests are "cheesecake" enthusiasts, make two cakes and enjoy the luscious seconds.

1 WEEK AHEAD

TOQUE 2	Phyllo Triangles	Prepare steps 2 through 7. *Do not bake.* Place on baking sheet, cover well, and freeze.

2 OR 3 DAYS BEFORE THE PARTY

MAIN EVENT	Salad	Prepare vinaigrette; store covered in refrigerator.
TOQUE 1	Confetti	Prepare vinaigrette; store covered in refrigerator.
GRAND FINALE	Cheesecake	Prepare entire recipe and refrigerate.

THE DAY BEFORE THE PARTY

MAIN EVENTS	Veal	Prepare through step 3; cool; store covered in refrigerator. Set up sage garnish; store covered in refrigerator.
	Salmon	Prepare step 3; store covered in refrigerator. Prepare garnishes; store covered in refrigerator.
TOQUE 1	Eggplant	Prepare onions, garlic, peppers, and olives; store separately, covered, in refrigerator.
	Confetti	Prepare through step 3; store covered in refrigerator. Prepare radicchio; store covered in refrigerator.
TOQUE 2	Phyllo Triangles	Defrost in refrigerator.
	Squash	Prepare ginger; store covered in refrigerator. Prepare dates and almonds, set aside at room temperature.

Strategic Maneuvers:

Fill creamers; cover and store in refrigerator.

Fill sugar bowls.

Set table. Locate buffet decor.

Check ice and beverages.

Locate teas.

Chill wine if white.

Check garnishes for each recipe.

Locate and label all serving bowls, platters, and utensils.

THE DAY OF THE PARTY

MAIN EVENT	Veal	Prepare steps 4 to 7.

2 HOURS AND 20 MINUTES BEFORE GUESTS ARRIVE:

MAIN EVENTS	Veal	Roast as in step 8.
	Salad	Prepare greens, set in bowl; store covered in refrigerator. Bring vinaigrette to room temperature. Arrange cheeses and croutons, cover well.
TOQUE 1	Eggplant	Finish recipe; cool; arrange and store covered in refrigerator. *Do not garnish.*
	Confetti	Set vinaigrette in saucepan ready to warm.
TOQUE 2	Squash	Prepare and finish recipe; set aside (and later serve) at room temperature.

30 MINUTES BEFORE GUESTS ARRIVE:

Complete steps 1 and 2 of salmon.

JUST BEFORE GUESTS ARRIVE:

Garnish eggplant and set at room temperature.

Bake phyllo triangles.

20 MINUTES BEFORE DINNER:

Plug in coffee.

Finish and arrange veal.

Finish broiling salmon and arrange.

Toss salad; set out cheeses and croutons.

Warm pesto vinaigrette for confetti and toss.

Bring cheesecake to room temperature.

DINNER SERVICE:

Place salmon on left side of buffet table.

Arrange the veal after the salmon.

Place eggplant and confetti, or triangles and spaghetti squash, after the veal. End the buffet with the lettuce salad and cheeses.

DESSERT SERVICE:

Serve coffee.

AFTER SERVICE:

Unplug coffee.

Turn off oven.

An Old-Fashioned Country Feast
at the Family Reunion

THE MAIN EVENTS:

Lobster Corn Pudding

Mushroom-Studded Panfried "Ham" Burgers

Peach-Glazed Skewered Chicken

ON THE SIDE:

Cabbage Slaw with Sour-Cream Dressing
(double recipe on page 61)

◆

Beefsteak Tomatoes, Red Onion, and Basil

ON THE SIDE:

A Mosaic of Summer Squashes and Roasted Peppers

◆

Brown-Sugar Baked Beans

THE GRAND FINALE:

Crunchy Coconut Ice Cream Scoops with
Mocha-Rum Sauce

PALATE TEASERS:

Pungent Meatballs Glazed in Green (page 299)

Parsley-Dusted Wild Mushroom–Stuffed Eggs (page 315)

BEVERAGE RECOMMENDATIONS:

Mint Juleps (page 355)

Chardonnay, California, Estancia Vineyards

*T*HE OLD BARN LOFT WHERE YOU JUMPED FROM THE RAFTERS into the haymow is now your cousin's architecture studio. And in the farmhouse, your grandma's old kitchen counter, where you ate pancakes and cheese sandwiches, is now gleaming with marble. But the old smells and sounds return when the far-flung cousins and their families get together for a long-planned reunion. The screen door slams open and shut with kids running through the house, and the kitchen is again a beehive of activity, producing crocks of lobster pudding and baked beans, and bowls of slaw and summer squashes—all carried out to the huge old picnic tables under the maple tree.

Whether or not you're having a family gathering, you will love this celebration of great American country cooking. The luxury of big chunks of lobster meat (without the mess) is only one appeal of my indulgent Lobster Corn Pudding. Its creamy texture and deep, sweet flavor are enhanced by a puree of roasted corn kernels, and it is traditionally rich with eggs, milk, butter, and cream.

There's a different down-home flavor and texture in the panfried "ham" burgers, a wonderful creation (kids will help!) of chopped ham steak, sautéed mushrooms, mashed potatoes, and more. They will be a sizzling hit on the buffet table. The last Main Event is also a showstopper: colorful broiled skewers of fresh peaches and chicken breast, glazed with a tangy sauce of fruit preserves and mustard.

Big bowls of side dishes complete a colorful display on the buffet and a hearty feast on the dinner plate. My slaw is a crisp and creamy salad of cabbage with added zing from scallions, fennel, red pepper, cucumber, radishes, dill, and parsley.

And I have combined juicy slices of beefsteak tomato, red onion, and basil leaves with a simple vinaigrette for a vibrantly colored and refreshing dish that takes no time at all.

You *will* need some time (but little effort) to bake the great old-fashioned beans on the two-toque menu. They are sweet with fresh tomato, brown sugar, and molasses; tangy with mustard, salt pork, and onions; and the flavors come together during hours and hours of slow cooking. They are superb with all the main courses, and well-paired with the mosaic of multicolored squashes and peppers, lightly cooked and tossed with olive oil and fresh lemon juice. With a generous garnish of fragrant tarragon, this dish brings brilliant color to the table.

There's a bit of summertime heaven in this feast's Grand Finale: a magnificent mound of ice cream scoops coated with coconut and served with a Mocha Rum Sauce that even kids consider yummy. And speaking of kids—this is a perfect dish for them to help create. It may be hard for them to see the coated ice cream scoops disappear into the freezer for several hours, but they will be the first ones at the buffet table—to choose the scoops they made, and drown them in sauce.

SETTING THE STAGE

You might be lucky enough to have the perfect place for this great meal: a gorgeous country lawn, easy access to a big kitchen, lots of big picnic tables, and a sweet-smelling empty barn in case it rains. If so, you won't have to do another thing!

But this menu, perfect for casual entertaining, is delightful served just about anywhere, on tables simply adorned with plain checkered cloths and napkins. Flowers and fresh produce are suitable centerpieces for both buffet and dining tables. Put silverware in baskets and tie them up with large bandannas for a rustic touch.

Here's a cute idea: Stuff the bottom of a metal or enamel chowder pot with crumpled newspaper, then fill the pot with partially shucked ears of corn, bell peppers, tomatoes, squashes in a variety of colors, onions, leeks, and baby eggplants. Fill in the arrangement with bunches of basil, parsley, and other fresh herbs. (A few large sunflowers tucked in the pot would add a whimsical note!)

THE MAIN EVENT

Lobster Corn Pudding

MAKES 16 SERVINGS

SPECIAL COOKWARE
5 1/2–6-quart ovenproof decorative baking dish
Large roasting pan, 17 by 11 inches

1 tablespoon salted butter
6 ears corn
3 tablespoons butter, melted
3 cups whole milk
12 eggs
5 egg yolks
9 scallions, white and green parts, chopped fine
1 large red bell pepper, cored, seeded, and diced
3 cups grated jalepeño Monterey Jack
4 1/2 cups heavy cream
3 pounds freshly cooked lobster meat, purchased from fish market, picked through for shells, coarsely chopped
2 tablespoons coarsely chopped fresh cilantro
2 tablespoons finely chopped flat-leaf parsley
1 1/2 teaspoons salt
3/4 teaspoon freshly ground black pepper

GARNISH
2 bunches flat-leaf parsley
1 steamed 1 1/2-pound lobster, left whole

1. Preheat the oven to 375°. Butter a large (5½–6 quart) ovenproof decorative baking dish.

2. Remove the tough outside leaves of the husks and the silk from the corn. Pull the remaining husks down to expose the corn, but do not remove them. Brush the corn kernels with the melted butter and recover with the husks. Bake the corn on a baking sheet for 40 minutes. Remove the husks and scrape the kernels off the cob with a sharp knife.

3. Place 1 cup of the corn kernels and the milk in the bowl of a food processor fitted with the knife blade and process until the mixture is pureed.

4. In an extra-large bowl, whisk together the eggs and egg yolks; then add the corn puree, scallions, red pepper, cheese, cream, and the remaining whole corn kernels. Stir in the lobster meat, cilantro, and parsley. Season with the salt and pepper. Transfer the mixture to the buttered baking dish.

5. Set the baking dish in a large roasting pan and add enough hot water to the outer pan to come halfway up the sides of the dish. Bake in the 375° oven for 1–1¼ hours, until a tester inserted in the center of the pudding comes out clean. *(Cover the top of the pudding with foil if it browns before the custard has set.)* Let the pudding rest at room temperature about 5 minutes before serving.

FINISHING TOUCHES AND
TABLE PRESENTATION

Place a 6–8 inch plate on the left side of the buffet *under* the tablecloth. Rest one end of the lobster pudding baking dish over the plate to give it height by raising it on the buffet.♦

♦Arrange the parsley as a heaping bed. Place the lobster over the bed on one side of the front of the casserole.

The Inventive Chef

ADD LUMP CRABMEAT AND SAUTÉED WILD MUSHROOMS TO THE PUDDING FOR ADDED ELEGANCE. (MAKE CERTAIN TO REDUCE AMOUNT OF LOBSTER.) ALLERGIC TO SHELLFISH? SUBSTITUTE A THICK, FIRM-FLESHED FISH SUCH AS HALIBUT OR SCROD.

THE MAIN EVENT

Mushroom-Studded Panfried "Ham" Burgers

MAKES 16 SERVINGS

3 tablespoons butter

1 large onion, peeled and finely chopped

6 cups domestic or wild mushrooms, (about 1¼ pounds) washed and cut into ¼-inch dice

2 pounds low-sodium fully cooked boneless ham steak, all visible fat removed, coarsely chopped

½ cup sour cream

3 large eggs, beaten

1 tablespoon finely chopped fresh rosemary

1 cup cooked and mashed Idaho potatoes (mashed without liquid), cooled

2 teaspoons Dijon mustard

1 teaspoon freshly ground black pepper

⅛ teaspoon cayenne pepper

3¼ cups unseasoned bread crumbs

1 large Granny Smith apple, washed, unpeeled, cored, and diced small

6 whole scallions, white and green parts, finely chopped

¾ cup peanut oil for panfrying

¹/₂ bunch fresh rosemary sprigs
¹/₂ bunch fresh rosemary, finely chopped
16 (4-inch) dinner rolls
1 cup honey mustard
2 cups sour cream

1. Heat the butter over medium-high heat in a skillet. Add the onion and sauté until soft and translucent, about 3–5 minutes. Add the mushrooms and continue to sauté until they are golden and dry, about 7 minutes. Set aside and cool.

2. Place half the ham in a food processor fitted with the knife blade and quickly pulse, chopping the ham into small pieces that resemble the texture of ground beef. *(Be careful not to over-process the ham or it will become pureed and lose its rougher texture.)* Place the ground ham in a large bowl and repeat the chopping process with the second batch of ham.

3. Mix in with the ham the reserved mushrooms and onions, the sour cream, eggs, rosemary, mashed potatoes, mustard, black pepper, cayenne pepper, 1¹/₂ cups of the bread crumbs, the apple, and the scallions. Stir the mixture until all the ingredients are well combined.

4. Form the ham mixture into sixteen ¹/₂-inch-thick, 4-ounce burger patties approximately 4 inches in circumference. Place the patties on a baking sheet lined with waxed paper or plastic wrap, and refrigerate, covered, for at least 1 hour or overnight.

5. Preheat the oven to 325°.

6. When ready to cook, dredge both sides of the patties lightly in the remaining bread crumbs.

7. Spread a thin film of oil in the bottom of a frying pan over medium-low heat. With a metal spatula, place the burgers in the pan and fry until golden brown, about 2¹/₂ minutes on each side. Drain the burgers on paper towels, place them on a baking sheet, and bake in the oven for 9–12 minutes, or until the burgers are piping hot. *(The burgers can be kept warm in a 250° oven for 20 minutes if necessary.)*

FINISHING TOUCHES AND
TABLE PREPARATION

Arrange the burgers in two copper or metal skillets garnished with the rosemary sprigs. Sprinkle the top of the burgers with the chopped rosemary. Fill napkin-lined baskets with the dinner rolls. Place the honey mustard in a 10-ounce crock to the right of the burgers. Place the sour cream in a bowl with a small ladle. Guests enjoy helping themselves.

THE MAIN EVENT

Peach-Glazed Skewered Chicken

MAKES 16 SERVINGS

SPECIAL COOKWARE
Meat pounder
32 (6–8-inch) wooden skewers, soaked in water, or metal skewers
Pastry brush

4 large cloves garlic, peeled
1¹/₄ cups peach preserves
³/₄ cup apricot preserves
¹/₃ cup dark soy sauce
2 tablespoons Worchershire sauce

2 tablespoons fresh lemon juice

2 tablespoons fresh lemon juice
$^1/_3$ cup Dijon mustard
$^3/_4$ teaspoon ground cloves
Dash of cayenne pepper
3$^1/_2$–4 pounds skinless and boneless chicken cutlets,
*   lightly pounded*
4 large ripe peaches, cut in half, pitted, each half
*   cut in quarters*

GARNISH
1 bunch curly parsley

1. In the bowl of a food processor fitted with the metal knife blade, puree the garlic, $^1/_2$ of the peach preserves, apricot preserves, soy sauce, Worcestershire sauce, lemon juice, mustard, cloves, and cayenne pepper to make a smooth basting sauce.
2. Cut the chicken into 32 4-inch-long-by-1-inch-wide strips.
3. Preheat the broiler.
4. Thread a piece of peach followed by a piece of chicken and a second piece of peach onto each of the 32 skewers. Place the skewers on foiled-lined baking sheets, allowing 1 inch between each skewer. (*If the skewers are too tightly packed on the baking sheet, the juices of the chicken will run together and steam the chicken.*) Generously brush both sides of the chicken and peaches with the basting sauce.
5. Heat the remaining peach preserves over low heat until it has thinned to a glaze, about 3 minutes, and keep it warm over very low heat while the skewers are cooking.
6. Broil the skewers 3 inches from the heat, turning them once, until both sides are golden, about 5–7 minutes total.
7. Brush the broiled skewers with the warm peach glaze.

FINISHING TOUCHES AND
TABLE PRESENTATION

Arrange the skewers in spirals on round or oval serving platters and garnish with small bouquets of bright green curly parsley to accent the delicate color of the peaches.

ON THE SIDE

Beefsteak Tomatoes, Red Onion, and Basil

MAKES 16 SERVINGS

THE VINAIGRETTE
$^1/_2$ cup tarragon vinegar
2 cups extra virgin olive oil
$^3/_4$ teaspoon salt, or to taste
$^1/_2$ teaspoon freshly ground black pepper, or to taste

THE SALAD
8 large ripe beefsteak tomatoes, each cut into 4 slices
3 large red onions, peeled and each cut into 6 slices

GARNISH
1 cup large fresh basil leaves

In a medium bowl whisk together the vinegar, olive oil, salt, and pepper until blended.

FINISHING TOUCHES AND
TABLE PRESENTATION

Arrange a circular pattern of 2 overlapping slices of
tomatoes and 1 slice of onion in a continuous pattern on
two round platters. Thirty minutes before serving, drizzle the dressing over the tomatoes and onions. Scatter
the basil leaves over the top.

> *The Inventive Chef*
>
> ENHANCE THE SALAD WITH THE ADDITION OF
> CRISPLY BLANCHED ZUCCHINI ROUNDS OR
> CREATE A BORDER AROUND THE TOMATOES
> WITH CRISPLY BLANCHED SUGAR SNAP PEAS.

ON THE SIDE

A Mosaic of Summer Squashes and Roasted Peppers

MAKES 16 SERVINGS

2 green bell peppers
3 yellow bell peppers
3 red bell peppers
³/₄ cup extra virgin olive oil
¹/₃ cup fresh lemon juice
1 bunch finely chopped fresh chives (if unavailable, use
  6 scallions, finely chopped)
1 teaspoon salt, or to taste
¹/₂ teaspoon freshly ground black pepper, or to taste

1 pound (about 2 large) summer squash, washed, trimmed,
  and cut into 1-inch cubes
1 pound pattypan squash, about 14–16, washed, trimmed,
  and cut into 1-inch cubes
1 pound (about 2 large) zucchini, washed, trimmed, and
  cut into 1-inch cubes

GARNISH
3 tablespoons coarsely chopped fresh tarragon

1. Preheat the broiler.
2. Place the peppers on a foil-lined baking sheet
about 3–4 inches from the broiler. Broil the peppers
on two sides, turning them with tongs or a kitchen
fork, until they have blackened, about 5 minutes. Broil
the other sides until blackened, about 2 minutes. (Do
not walk away from the broiler or you will have scorched
peppers.)
3. Place the blackened peppers in a large bowl and
quickly seal the top of the bowl with plastic wrap to
hold in the steam. Let the peppers steam under the
plastic wrap for 20 minutes. Strain and reserve any
juice that has accumulated at the bottom of the bowl.
4. Carefully peel skins off the peppers, using your
hands or a sharp paring knife.
5. Whisk together then set aside the olive oil, lemon
juice, chives, and reserved pepper juice.
6. Cut the peppers in half and remove the stems,
seeds, and ribs. Cut the peppers into ¹/₂-inch-wide
strips. Toss the strips with half the dressing and
season them with ¹/₂ teaspoon of the salt and
¹/₄ teaspoon of the pepper, or to taste.
7. Place the summer, pattypan, and zucchini squashes
in a 6-quart saucepan with ¹/₂-inch of boiling water.
Steam, covered, tossing the squash often, until it is
slightly tender but still crisp, about 3–4 minutes.
Drain the squash and toss it with the remaining

An Old-Fashioned Country Feast at the Family Reunion ◆ 151 dressing, the remaining $^1/_2$ teaspoon salt, and the remaining $^1/_4$ teaspoon pepper, or to taste.

FINISHING TOUCHES AND
TABLE PRESENTATION

Strain off any excess dressing from the squash. Heap the squash in the center of a 12- or 14-inch rectangular or square platter. Arrange the multicolored strips of pepper around the squash. Scatter the chopped tarragon over the squash. Served chilled or at room temperature.

The Inventive Chef

THE SQUASH AND PEPPERS MAKE A COLORFUL AND SPICY ADDITION TO AN ANTIPASTO PLATTER.

ON THE SIDE

Brown-Sugar Baked Beans

MAKES 16 SERVINGS

SPECIAL COOKWARE

6-quart ovenproof casserole with lid or aluminum foil
   to cover

2$^1/_2$ pounds dried navy beans
3 large red onions, peeled and finely chopped
6 cloves garlic, peeled and finely minced
$^1/_4$ cup tomato paste

3 cups fresh tomatoes, cut in medium dice
3 cups dark brown sugar, loosely packed
$^2/_3$ cup dark molasses
3 tablespoons Dijon mustard
1 teaspoon ground cloves
1 tablespoon salt
1$^3/_4$ pounds salt pork, cut into 2-inch dice

1. Soak the beans overnight at room temperature in cold water to cover. The next day, rinse the beans and discard any pebbles. (*Or do the quick-soak method: Rinse the beans and discard any pebbles. Put them in a large pot covered with cold water and bring to a boil. Boil for 2 minutes. Remove from the heat, cover, and let sit for 1 hour. Drain and rinse.*)

2. Place the beans in a stockpot or large saucepan and cover them with fresh cold water. Bring the water to a boil over high heat. Reduce the heat and simmer the beans, uncovered, until they are tender but still crisp to the bite, about 1 hour if the beans were soaked overnight and about 40 minutes if you used the quick-soak method.

3. Preheat the oven to 300°.

4. Drain the beans, reserving the liquid, and place them in a 6-quart ovenproof casserole. Blend in the onions, garlic, tomato paste, tomatoes, brown sugar, molasses, mustard, cloves, and salt. Add only enough of the reserved cooking liquid to cover the beans well; *the beans should be completely covered with the liquid.* Mix in the diced salt pork.

5. Cover the casserole and bake in the oven for a total of about 4$^1/_2$–5$^1/_2$ hours, depending on how soft or crisp you enjoy your baked beans. Stir and check the beans after 2 hours and add more of the reserved liquid if necessary to keep them just covered by the liquid.

6. After 3$^1/_2$ hours of cooking, uncover the casserole and raise the oven temperature to 375°. Bake the beans for 1–2 hours more, stirring occasionally, and adding more reserved cooking liquid if they start to cook dry. *(The beans may be cooked one day ahead and reheated very slowly, lightly covered, in a 325° oven. I make the beans ahead because they taste better after 1 day.)*

FINISHING TOUCHES AND
TABLE PRESENTATION

Serve the beans right from the casserole. Don't try to clean up any of the caramelized brown-sugar crust that clings to the casserole. The homier it looks the better the buffet will look. I like to place the casserole on a large platter. To give the baked beans some height and protect the table from burning, place the platter on a trivet.

THE GRAND FINALE

*Crunchy Coconut
Ice Cream Scoops with
Mocha-Rum Sauce*

MAKES 16 SERVINGS

SPECIAL COOKWARE
4-ounce ice cream scoop

2 cups shredded, unsweetened coconut
2 quarts pistachio ice cream♦
2 quarts chocolate fudge ice cream♦

♦Or substitute your own choice of ice creams.

Mocha-Rum Sauce (recipe follows)

GARNISH
1 bunch lemon leaves
1 coconut

1. Preheat the oven to 350°.
2. Scatter $3/4$ cup of the coconut on a baking sheet and bake it in the oven for 8–10 minutes, stirring once or twice, until evenly golden brown. Cool to room temperature. Reserve the unbaked coconut.
3. Place the toasted and untoasted coconut on two separate sheets of aluminum foil.
4. Scoop out 16 balls of pistachio and 16 balls of chocolate fudge ice cream using a 4-ounce scoop. *(There will be extra scoops for people indulging in seconds.)*
5. Roll the pistachio ice cream in the toasted coconut and the chocolate fudge ice cream in the untoasted coconut. Put the coconut-rolled ice cream scoops on the trays in the freezer and cover them lightly with foil.

FINISHING TOUCHES AND
TABLE PRESENTATION

Arrange the ice creams, alternating the toasted and un-toasted scoops, in 2 glass, ceramic, or silver punch bowls. Place the warm sauce in 2 bowls with small ladles or spoons. Arrange the lemon leaves around the bowls. Cut the coconut in half and place the 2 halves, cut-side-up, on the lemon leaves.

The Inventive Chef

USE VANILLA, STRAWBERRY, AND BLUEBERRY ICE CREAMS TO CARRY THROUGH A FOURTH OF JULY THEME. SUBSTITUTE SORBETS FOR THE ICE CREAM, OR TRY MIXING SORBETS AND ICE CREAMS. GILD THE LILY WITH WHIPPED CREAM OR OTHER DESSERT SAUCES.

Mocha-Rum Sauce

MAKES 2 CUPS

12 ounces bittersweet chocolate, chopped in bite-size pieces
1 cup brewed espresso or dark coffee
$^1/_3$ cup dark brown sugar, firmly packed
$^1/_3$ cup heavy cream
1 tablespoon rum, or to taste

1. Melt the chocolate with the espresso and sugar in the top of a double boiler over simmering water, about 5 minutes.
2. Stir in the cream, blend well, and add the rum.

1 WEEK AHEAD

GRAND FINALE	Ice Cream	Prepare recipe through step 4; freeze, covered with foil.

2 OR 3 DAYS BEFORE THE PARTY

MAIN EVENT	Lobster	Prepare through step 3; store covered in refrigerator.
	Chicken	Prepare step 1; store covered in refrigerator.
TOQUE 1	Tomatoes	Prepare vinaigrette; store covered in refrigerator.
TOQUE 2	Beans	Soak and drain beans; store covered at room temperature.

THE DAY BEFORE THE PARTY

MAIN EVENT	Lobster	Prepare scallions, pepper, cheese, lobster, cilantro, and parsley as directed in ingredient list; store separately, covered, in refrigerator.
	Burgers	Prepare through step 4; store covered in refrigerator.
	Chicken	Cut chicken; store covered in refrigerator.
TOQUE 1	Slaw	Prepare all vegetables as instructed in ingredient list; store covered in refrigerator. Combine mustard, horseradish, vinegar, and lemon juice; store covered in refrigerator. Combine sour cream, mustard seeds, celery seeds, and sugar; store covered in refrigerator.
TOQUE 2	Squashes and Peppers	Prepare through step 4; store covered in refrigerator.

		Prepare squashes; store covered in refrigerator.
	Beans	Prepare through step 4; store covered in refrigerator.
GRAND FINALE	Ice Cream	Make mocha sauce; cool; store covered in refrigerator.
Strategic Maneuvers:		Fill creamers; cover and store in refrigerator.
		Fill sugar bowls.
		Set table. Locate buffet decor.
		Check ice and beverages.
		Locate teas.
		Chill wine if white.
		Check garnishes for each recipe.
		Set out and label all serving bowls, platters, and utensils.

THE DAY OF THE PARTY

MAIN EVENT	Lobster	Prepare step 4; refrigerate custard. Set up water bath. Do not fill baking dish.
	Chicken	Thread on skewers through step 4. Set the $1/2$ cup of the peach preserves in top of double boiler.
TOQUE 1	Slaw	Toss and store covered in refrigerator.
	Tomatoes	Prepare recipe and arrange, but *do not dress;* store covered in refrigerator.
TOQUE 2	Squashes and Peppers	Finish recipe; arrange and refrigerate, covered.
	Beans	Bake beans and set aside.
GRAND FINALE	Ice Cream	Set mocha sauce in top of double boiler to reheat.

Arrange ice cream in serving bowl, *if* room in freezer.

Place the lobster on the left side of the buffet.

Arrange the burgers next to the lobster, followed by the chicken.

Arrange the slaw and tomatoes after the chicken.

Arrange the beans and squashes after the chicken.

45 MINUTES BEFORE GUESTS ARRIVE:

Preheat oven to 375°.

MAIN EVENT Lobster Prepare step 5. Complete recipe.

Slaw Place slaw in bowl.

30 MINUTES BEFORE DINNER:

Burgers Complete recipe; transfer to service skillets and hold in 250° oven. (If just one oven, reduce heat when pudding is finished and keep burgers warm.)

TOQUE 1 Tomatoes Dress and garnish.

TOQUE 2 Beans Keep warm in oven or covered with foil in warm place.

20 MINUTES BEFORE DESSERT:

Arrange ice cream and place in refrigerator.

Warm sauce in double boiler.

DESSERT SERVICE:

Set up as directed.

15 MINUTES BEFORE DINNER:

Plug in coffee.

Finish chicken recipe, arrange, and garnish.

Arrange buffet food.

AFTER SERVICE:

Unplug coffee.

Turn off oven(s).

MENU 3

An Italian Buffet
for the Festival of Festivals

THE MAIN EVENTS:

Veal Scallops with the Bite of Lemon
Rock Cornish Hens, Pancetta, and Mushrooms

ON THE SIDE:

Pasta Caprese

◆

Stewed Green Beans and Potatoes with Fresh Plum Tomatoes

◆

Crusty Sausage-Filled Bread

ON THE SIDE:

Eggplant and White Bean "Lasagna"

◆

Broccoli, Lima Beans, Lemon, and Garlic (page 121)

◆

Zucchini, Olive, and Sun-dried Tomato Calzones

THE GRAND FINALE:

Rice Pudding with Sambuca-Drenched Raisins

PALATE TEASERS:

Zucchini and Spinach-Tortellini Skewers (page 298)
Prosciutto, Chicken, and Honey-Mustard Bundles (page 317)

BEVERAGE RECOMMENDATIONS:

Cetamuro Coltibuono, 1995
Chianti Classico, Castello di Fonterutoli

*I*T'S SEPTEMBER, TIME FOR THE FAMOUS FEAST OF SAN GEN-naro—the Festival of Festivals. If you lived in Naples you might join the throngs waiting for the annual miracle of their patron saint. If you live in Manhattan, you might go to Little Italy and eat your way up the exciting half-mile *festa* along Mulberry Street, stuffing yourself from the booths selling sausages and peppers, zeppole, and *sfogliatelli*. But if you're far from a subway, and have a house full of hungry guests, you will set out this absolutely groaning buffet and watch a miracle take place as it all disappears.

There's one guiding principle underlying this Italian-inspired menu: *abbondanza*—abundance! This buffet is loaded with delicious, hearty, and filling dishes, and if your guests aren't as wonderfully stuffed as the sausage bread or calzones you've prepared, there's something wrong with them! In fact, there would be nothing wrong with *you* if you decided to make all the dishes from the one-toque *and* two-toque menus and put both the sausage bread and the calzones on the buffet!

You will enjoy making these two Main Event dishes. The succulent veal scallops are enhanced with a rich breading, a light sauté, and a brief bake in the oven with a tangy sauce of butter, lemon juice, and white wine. Halved Rock Cornish hens are rubbed with rosemary, sautéed until golden, then baked under a generous pile of wine-infused mushrooms, pancetta, and onions. The loaded platters of veal and poultry will look sensational.

The one-toque menu is a feast in itself. Pasta Caprese is a bountiful casserole of penne baked in a sauce of fresh tomatoes and eggplant, laced with

Fontina and Parmigiano cheeses. And there's a marvelous stew of fresh green beans, plum tomatoes, and potatoes, piqued with pine nuts, balsamic vinegar, and oregano. You (and all the kids at the party) will especially enjoy the sausage bread. Made with store-bought pizza dough, and stuffed with sausage and cheeses, it is a breeze to prepare and even more fun to eat.

The "lasagna" on the two-toque menu is a fabulous vegetable creation, layering strips of sautéed eggplant and zucchini, a luscious puree of white beans and Asiago cheese, and a zesty tomato sauce. It is accompanied with a warm salad of crunchy lima beans and broccoli in a garlicky olive oil dressing. For this menu, you will also use store-bought pizza dough to make the calzones, which are filled with a tangy mix of zucchini, sun-dried tomatoes, olives, and two cheeses.

The festival is not over until the Grand Finale is devoured: a cinnamon-infused creamy rice pudding, studded with raisins soaked in orange juice and anise-flavored sambuca liqueur. People will find room!

The aromas from the kitchen will immediately tell your guests what they are supposed to do: Eat! Eat! Eat! Have the food ready when they arrive and maintain a flow that invites feasters to return to the buffet as often as they like.

Food is the celebration *and* the decoration: Fill baskets with Italian breads (and put out crocks of roasted garlic, page 87, for spreading). Present cutting boards with meats, sweet peppers, bulbs of fresh fennel, and heads of radicchio, and supply a sharp knife so guests can help themselves. When you set out the rice pudding dessert, put big bowls of fruits and nuts on the buffet, too.

You can create a gorgeous centerpiece of food: Use long loaves of Italian bread (or dried meats) in a big basket as a support, and fill in with peppers of different colors, squashes, tomatoes, and other vegetables. Fill four glass jars with dried large and small penne pasta for an interesting buffet display. Of course, garnish your display with fresh basil, rosemary, parsley, and lots of garlic (whole heads) tucked into small spaces. Pepper mills can also be used as table decorations.

You don't need fancy tableware for this occasion—only big plates! Simple crockery and rustic serving ware are fine, as are tablecloths and napkins in neutral colors. A nice touch would be to combine red and green napkins with a white cloth—and to tie each napkin and silverware bundle with red and green ribbons—to show the Italian colors. If you're really in a festival mood, string small colored lights over the buffet, just as they do at the *festa* on Mulberry Street.

Veal Scallops with the Bite of Lemon

MAKES 16 SERVINGS

SPECIAL COOKWARE
Meat pounder

THE VEAL
3/4 cup all-purpose flour
5 eggs, beaten
1 teaspoon salt
1/2 teaspoon freshly ground black pepper
2 1/2 cups unseasoned bread crumbs
16 veal scallops, 3 ounces each, cut from the round and pounded 1/8-inch thick
5 tablespoons salted butter
5 tablespoons olive oil

GARNISH
32 slices of lemon, 1/8-inch thick (about 4 lemons)
1/4 cup minced curly parsley
1 bunch curly parsley
1 lemon, cut in half crosswise

1. Preheat the oven to 325°.

2. Spread the flour on a piece of aluminum foil, at least 12 inches by 12 inches, or use a shallow dish for easy cleanup.

3. Place the beaten eggs in a pie plate.

4. Mix the salt and pepper with the bread crumbs.

5. Spread the seasoned bread crumbs on a piece of aluminum foil 12 inches by 12 inches, or in a shallow dish.

6. Dredge each veal scallop in the flour, then coat it with the beaten egg, then with the bread crumbs.

Place the breaded scallops in a single layer on a baking sheet (the veal will have to be cooked in batches).

7. Place a large skillet over medium-high heat and heat 1½ tablespoons of the butter and 1½ tablespoons of the oil. When the butter is melted and foamy, add as many of the veal scallops as will fit comfortably in the pan without touching each other. Sauté them on both sides, about 1 minute on each side or until golden. Place the scallops on paper towels to drain, and continue sautéing the batches of veal, using the remaining butter and olive oil. Strain the butter/oil mixture between batches, to keep the mixture clean and ensure a golden coating on the veal.

THE SAUCE

1 stick (4 ounces) butter
3 tablespoons fresh lemon juice
3 tablespoons dry white wine
1 tablespoon finely chopped fresh basil
½ tablespoon finely chopped flat-leaf parsley
Salt to taste
Freshly ground black pepper to taste

In a small saucepan over low heat, melt the stick of butter with the lemon juice and white wine. Stir in the basil and parsley, and season with salt and pepper to taste. Arrange the veal scallops in a single layer in two shallow baking pans. Pour the lemon sauce over the scallops and bake them in the 325° oven about 5–8 minutes, or until the veal is just warmed through.

FINISHING TOUCHES AND TABLE PRESENTATION

Arrange the veal scallops in overlapping slices on a large white platter. Place 2 slices of lemon in the center of each scallop and dust the top with the chopped parsley. Place a foil container or a saucer under the tablecloth to tilt the end of the veal platter. Set the bunch of curly parsley in front of the veal platter. Nestle the lemon halves in the parsley.

THE MAIN EVENT

Rock Cornish Hens, Pancetta, and Mushrooms

MAKES 16 SERVINGS

1½ teaspoons salt
¾ teaspoon freshly ground black pepper
1 teaspoon finely chopped fresh rosemary
8 rock Cornish hens (about 1–1¼ pounds each),
   cut in halves
3 tablespoons salted butter, melted
5 tablespoons olive oil
1 pound pancetta, cut into ¼-inch dice
2 large red onions, peeled and finely chopped
3 large garlic cloves, peeled and minced
1 pound portobello or cremini mushrooms, washed and
   coarsely chopped
⅔ cup dry red wine
2 tablespoons balsamic vinegar

GARNISH

2 bunches fresh rosemary
½ pound whole shiitake or cremini mushrooms

1. Preheat the oven to 375°.
2. Mix the salt, pepper, and chopped rosemary together. Rub the hens on both sides with the spices.

Combine the butter and 4 tablespoons olive oil in a small bowl.

3. Heat 2 tablespoons of the butter and oil mixture in a large skillet over medium-high heat. Sauté the hens in batches, adding more butter and oil to the pan for each batch. Cook skin-side down until golden brown, about 6–8 minutes, then transfer the birds, skin-side up, to two large, shallow baking pans and bake in the oven for 25 minutes.

4. Wipe the hen skillet dry with paper towels and sauté the pancetta in the pan, over medium heat, until it is golden brown, about 10–12 minutes, stirring often. Remove the pancetta with a slotted spoon to drain on paper towels. Using the fat remaining in the skillet, sauté the onions until translucent, 4–5 minutes, over medium-high heat. Add the garlic and continue to cook for 30 seconds.

5. Add the mushrooms to the skillet. If the pan is dry, add the remaining 1 tablespoon of olive oil. Sauté the mushrooms for 4–6 minutes, or until they have softened. Blend the red wine, balsamic vinegar, and reserved pancetta with the mushrooms and onions and stir briskly over high heat for 30 seconds to combine all the flavors.

6. Divide the vegetable-pancetta mixture evenly between the pans of hens, spooning the mixture on top of and around the birds, and bake them in the oven for about 20–25 minutes more, or until the juices from the birds' thighs run clear.

FINISHING TOUCHES AND TABLE PRESENTATION

Transfer the hens to a round terra-cotta or silver platter or to two 12- or 14-inch silver skillets or shallow casserole dishes. Spoon the pancetta, onions, and mushrooms over the birds, literally smothering the tops. Garnish the serving vessel(s) with the bunches of rosemary and the whole mushrooms.

> ### The Inventive Chef
>
> THE MUSHROOMS, PANCETTA, ONIONS, AND GARLIC MAKE A RICH ADDITION TO PASTAS. ADD PARMIGIANO CHEESE AND FRESHLY GROUND BLACK PEPPER.

ON THE SIDE
Pasta Caprese

MAKES 16 SERVINGS

One magical sun-soaked summer, I ate this pasta at three different restaurants on Capri. Each version was infused by the individual chef's stroke of genius. If possible, use fresh basil just off the vine. In winter, this may encourage you to grow your own in the warmth of your kitchen. While you are doing all this prep work, rest assured that this recipe makes a generous amount, so there will be plenty left for the next day.

SPECIAL COOKWARE
Extra-large skillet
One large (6-quart) ovenproof casserole or two large
  3-quart ovenproof casseroles

1¹/₂ pounds small penne pasta
1 cup olive oil
Salt, for the eggplant
3 medium eggplants, unpeeled and cut into 1-inch cubes

3 Spanish onions, peeled and chopped small
5 large cloves garlic, peeled and minced
7 large ripe tomatoes, coarsely chopped
1 cup dry red wine
1 cup finely chopped fresh basil
2 1/2 teaspoons salt
2 teaspoons freshly ground black pepper
6 tablespoons balsamic vinegar
1 pound Fontina or Harvarti, cut into 1/4-inch dice
1 1/3 cups coarsely grated Parmigiano Reggiano or Asiago

GARNISH
16 large fresh basil leaves

1. Preheat the oven to 350°.

2. Cook the pasta according to package directions until tender to the bite. Drain the pasta, coat it with 1 tablespoon of the olive oil, and set it aside at room temperature.

3. While the pasta is cooking, lightly salt the diced eggplant and spread the pieces on paper towels to drain, about 15 minutes. The eggplant will release its water, which promotes even cooking.

4. While the eggplant drains, heat 1/3 cup of the oil in a large stockpot. Sauté the onions until they are translucent, about 4–6 minutes. Add the garlic and cook for 1 minute more.

5. Add the tomatoes and heat for 6–8 minutes or until they soften and release their juices. Add the red wine and cook for 2 minutes more. Remove from the heat, stir in the basil, season with 1 1/2 teaspoons of the salt and 1 teaspoon of the pepper, or to taste, and put the tomato-onion sauce into one 6-quart or two 3-quart oven-to-table casseroles.

6. Pat the eggplant dry and, using an extra-large skillet, sauté the eggplant over high heat, in batches, using about 3 tablespoons of olive oil per batch, until

the pieces are transparent and lightly browned, about 6–8 minutes per batch.

7. Return all the cooked eggplant to the skillet and season it with the remaining 1 teaspoon salt and 1 teaspoon pepper, or to taste. Add the balsamic vinegar and cook briskly for 30 seconds. Transfer the eggplant to the casserole(s) with the tomato sauce, and set them aside at room temperature.

8. Stir the pasta into the tomato sauce and eggplant in the casserole(s), along with the Fontina and 2/3 cup of the Parmigiano. Blend all the ingredients well. Taste, and adjust the seasonings if necessary. Sprinkle the top(s) with the remaining 2/3 cup Parmigiano and bake the casserole(s) in the oven for 30 minutes, or until the cheeses have melted and all the ingredients are hot. Cover the top(s) with foil if the pasta starts to dry out during cooking.

FINISHING TOUCHES AND
TABLE PRESENTATION

Garnish the top of the pasta with the basil leaves and serve piping hot.

The Inventive Chef

ADD DICED PANCETTA TO THE PASTA FOR A SLIGHTLY SMOKY TASTE. ZUCCHINI, BELL PEPPERS, AND SLIVERS OF FENNEL ARE LIVELY SUBSTITUTES FOR THE EGGPLANT.

ON THE SIDE

*Stewed Green Beans
and Potatoes with Fresh
Plum Tomatoes*

MAKES 16 SERVINGS

SPECIAL COOKWARE
*One extra-large (8–10 quart) ovenproof casserole or two
(3-quart) ovenproof casseroles*

*¹/₂ cup olive oil
2 large onions, peeled and finely chopped
8 cloves garlic, peeled and minced
5 pounds Red Bliss potatoes, washed, unpeeled, cut into
¹/₂-inch cubes
5 pounds (approximately 14 large) ripe fresh plum
tomatoes, washed, ends removed, chopped into coarse
dice
4¹/₂ cups chicken, beef, or vegetable stock, homemade or
low-sodium canned
2¹/₂ pounds fresh green beans, stemmed, washed, and cut
into ¹/₂-inch lengths
2 teaspoons ground oregano
¹/₄ cup balsamic vinegar
1 cup toasted pine nuts (page 122)*

*1¹/₂ teaspoons salt, or to taste
1 teaspoon freshly ground black pepper, or to taste*

GARNISH
*¹/₂ pound fresh green beans, stems on
8 fresh plum tomatoes
1 bunch flat-leaf Italian parsley, washed and dried*

1. Preheat the oven to 200°.
2. Heat 2 tablespoons of the olive oil in each of two
large skillets and divide the onions between the skillets.
3. Sauté the onions over medium-high heat for
3–5 minutes. Divide the garlic between the skillets and
continue to cook until the garlic just starts to turn
golden, about 2 minutes.
4. Add half the potatoes to each skillet and allow
them to cook for 3 minutes over high heat, stirring
often. Divide the tomatoes between the two pans and
continue cooking, adding ¹/₂ cup of stock whenever
the pan gets too dry, until the tomatoes soften and the
potatoes are just cooked through, about 8–10 minutes.
5. Remove the vegetables to one or two ovenproof
casseroles. Cover the top(s) loosely with foil and keep
warm in the oven while cooking the green beans.
6. Wipe the skillets clean with paper towels. In each
of the two skillets heat 2 tablespoons of oil over high
heat. Add half the green beans to each skillet and
sauté for 2 minutes. Add 1¹/₄ cups of stock to each of
the skillets and continue cooking over high heat,
stirring frequently, adding a little more stock if needed,
for 6–10 minutes or until the green beans are just
cooked through.
7. Add the oregano, balsamic vinegar, pine nuts, salt,
and pepper to the beans; blend well. Remove the
vegetables from the oven. Stir the stewed green beans
into the dish(es), taste, and adjust the seasonings if
necessary.

Place an arrangement of whole, blanched and drained green beans in front of each serving bowl. Surround the beans with the whole plum tomatoes.

The Inventive Chef

ADD ANOTHER DIMENSION TO THE STEWED VEGETABLES WITH DICED COOKED PANCETTA. IT IS SMOKY AND WONDERFUL.

ON THE SIDE

*Crusty Sausage-
Filled Bread*

MAKES 2 BREADS

1 1/2 pounds ground pork sausage
3 eggs, lightly beaten
2 teaspoons finely chopped fresh basil
1/4 teaspoon ground cloves
1/4 teaspoon ground allspice
1/4 teaspoon ground sage
1/2 teaspoon salt
1/4 teaspoon freshly ground black pepper
2 cups coarsely grated mozzarella
1 cup freshly grated Parmigiano Reggiano
*2 (1-pound) packages pizza dough (available in dairy
    refrigerator case of most supermarkets)*
*1/4 cup all-purpose flour,
    for working the dough*

GARNISH
2 cups whole-grain mustard

1. Preheat the oven to 375°.
2. Break up the sausage into small pieces and sauté it in a skillet over medium-high heat until completely brown and cooked through. Remove it from the pan with a slotted spoon and drain on paper towels. When drained, place the cooled sausage in a bowl with the eggs, basil, cloves, allspice, sage, salt, pepper, mozzarella, and Parmigiano. Mix well.
3. Set one pound of the pizza dough on a lightly floured board. *(A small amount of olive oil rubbed between your hands will assist in handling the dough.)* Sprinkle the top of the dough lightly with flour and roll it out into a 10-inch-by-12-inch rectangle, 1/2-inch thick. *(The dough will form an uneven rectangle as it is rolled.)*
4. Spread half the sausage filling over the dough, allowing a 1 1/2-inch border on all sides.
5. Fold in the 1 1/2-inch border of dough and press down. Roll the dough into a jelly roll, beginning with a short side. Place the dough, seam-side down, on a baking sheet. Make the second filled bread with the remaining ingredients and place it on the same baking sheet. Bake the breads about 40–45 minutes, until they are crusty and brown. Cool the breads on a wire rack.

FINISHING TOUCHES AND
TABLE PRESENTATION

Serve the breads warm, wrapped in brightly colored napkins, on cutting boards. Place a serrated knife on each board. Put the mustard into two small bowls with bread-and-butter knives for service.

ON THE SIDE

Eggplant and White Bean "Lasagna"

MAKES 16 SERVINGS

SPECIAL COOKWARE
Extra-large skillet
One 6-quart or two 3-quart decorative baking dishes

4 cups canned cannellini beans, rinsed and strained
2 teaspoons finely chopped fresh rosemary
$3/4$ cup half-and-half
3 cups finely shaved Asiago
1 teaspoon salt
$1/2$ teaspoon freshly ground black pepper
$2/3$ cup plus 1 tablespoon olive oil
2 large eggplants, unpeeled, ends removed, cut lengthwise
    into $1/4$-inch-long strips
5 medium zucchini, unpeeled, ends removed, cut lengthwise
    into $1/2$-inch-long strips
2 large yellow onions, peeled and finely chopped
6 large cloves garlic, peeled and minced
2 (35-ounce) cans peeled plum tomatoes,
    strained, juice discarded, and coarsely chopped
    (about 4 cups)
6 tablespoons finely chopped fresh basil

3 large tomatoes, cored and sliced $1/8$-inch-thick rounds
1 cup grated Parmigiano Reggiano

GARNISH
2 cups freshly grated Parmigiano Reggiano
2 small 4–6 ounce cruets of olive oil
2 bunches fresh basil
2 small eggplants

1. In the bowl of a food processor fitted with the cutting blade, puree the beans, rosemary, half-and-half, and Asiago in batches to form a smooth texture. Place the pureed bean mixture in a large bowl, season it with 1 teaspoon salt and $1/2$ teaspoon pepper, or to taste, and set aside.

2. Heat 2 tablespoons of the oil in an extra-large skillet. Sauté the eggplant and zucchini in separate batches, adding more oil as needed, turning the strips once until slightly tender but still crisp and lightly browned. Line a baking sheet with paper towels and drain the vegetables on the towels as they finish cooking.

3. To the same skillet, add 2 tablespoons of olive oil and sauté the onions until they are translucent, about 5 minutes. Add the garlic and sauté for 1 minute more. Blend in the chopped plum tomatoes and continue to cook over medium-high heat for 6 minutes. Add the fresh basil, remove from the heat and season with $1/2$ teaspoon salt and $1/4$ teaspoon pepper, or to taste.

4. Preheat the oven to 350°.

5. Lightly grease one 6-quart or two 3-quart decorative baking dish(es) with the remaining tablespoon of olive oil, and place $1/2$ of the eggplant strips over the bottom of the dish(es). Cover the eggplant with one-half of the zucchini. Cover the zucchini with $1/2$ of the bean purée. Follow with $1/2$

of the plum tomato sauce and a layer of sliced tomatoes.

6. Sprinkle about ¹/₂ the Parmigiano on top. Make a second vegetable layer combining the remaining strips of eggplant, zucchini, and the sliced tomato. Finish the lasagna by spreading the remaining plum tomato sauce over the entire dish(es), and sprinkle the top(s) evenly with the remaining Parmigiano.

7. Bake the lasagna 35–40 minutes until the cheese is melted and the dish is bubbly hot. Remove the lasagna from the oven and allow it to settle for 10–15 minutes. *(The vegetables will release their juices during the baking period. Spoon off any liquid that rises on the sides of the baking dish(es) before service.)*

FINISHING TOUCHES AND TABLE PRESENTATION

Serve the lasagna from the baking dish(es). Arrange the Parmigiano in two serving bowls with spoons. Set the pepper mills, along with the cruets of olive oil, to the left of the cheese. Arrange the bunches of basil and the eggplants to the right of the baking dish(es).

The Inventive Chef

USING THIS RECIPE, YOU CAN CREATE YOUR OWN LASAGNA WITH ANY COMBINATION OF VEGETABLES, SUCH AS YELLOW SQUASH AND BELL PEPPERS. COMBINE FONTINA AND GRUYÈRE FOR DELICIOUS CHEESE SUBSTITUTES.

ON THE SIDE

Zucchini, Olive, and Sun-dried Tomato Calzones

MAKES 16 CALZONES

SPECIAL COOKWARE
Extra-large skillet

THE FILLING
¹/₄ cup olive oil
1 large Spanish onion, peeled and diced small (about 3 cups)
3 cloves garlic, peeled and finely minced
6 medium zucchini, washed and cut into ¹/₂-inch dice (about 4 cups)
¹/₂ cup julienned sun-dried tomatoes, firmly packed
¹/₂ cup pitted and finely chopped Kalamata olives, firmly packed
1 cup coarsely grated Asiago
1 cup grated mozzarella
1 teaspoon salt, or to taste
¹/₂ teaspoon freshly ground black pepper, or to taste
3 tablespoons finely chopped fresh basil

THE CALZONES
2 (1-pound) packages pizza dough (available in dairy refrigerator case of most supermarkets)
2 large eggs mixed with 1 tablespoon milk (egg wash for sealing and glazing calzones)

1. Heat 2 tablespoons of the olive oil in an extra-large skillet over high heat. Add the onion and sauté for 2 minutes. Add the garlic and continue to sauté for 1 minute more.

2. Add the remaining olive oil to the skillet. Add the zucchini and continue to sauté until the zucchini is tender but slightly crisp, about 4–5 minutes. Stir in the sun-dried tomatoes and olives and cook for 1 minute more.

3. Remove the vegetables from the heat and cool for 5 minutes. Blend in the Asiago and mozzarella, the salt, pepper, and basil. Cool to room temperature. *(Once thoroughly cool, the filling can be made into calzones immediately or stored in the refrigerator, covered, for up to 2 days.)*

4. Preheat the oven to 350°.

5. To make the calzones, divide each pound of pizza dough into 8 (2-ounce) portions. Lightly flour your hands and roll each portion of dough on a floured work surface into a 4-inch circle. *(The dough will not form a perfect circle.)* If the dough becomes difficult to work with, let it rest for 5 minutes. *(The dough will become more pliable and much easier to handle when it is relaxed.)*

6. Place about ⅓ cup of the zucchini filling on the lower half of each dough circle. Brush around the inside edges of the dough with the egg wash. Fold the dough in half to form a crescent. Press the tines of a fork dipped in flour against the edges of each calzone. *(This crimping makes a decorative fluted edge that helps to seal the calzone.)*

7. Lightly brush the tops of the calzones with the remaining egg wash.

8. Place the calzones on two baking sheets and bake in the oven for 15–20 minutes, or until they are golden brown and crisp.

FINISHING TOUCHES AND TABLE PRESENTATION

The calzones should be served hot and can be reheated in a 400° oven for serving. I like to find red bricks and arrange them into a square resembling the bottom of a pizza oven. Place the calzones, at random, over the bricks.

The Inventive Chef

THE CALZONES ARE DELICIOUS WITH MEAT FILLINGS AS WELL AS THE VEGETABLES. THEY ARE FUN TO SERVE WITH THE CHUNKY TOMATO SAUCE (PAGE 234).

THE GRAND FINALE

Rice Pudding with Sambuca-Drenched Raisins

MAKES 16 SERVINGS

SPECIAL COOKWARE

Two 3-quart or one 6-quart oven-to-table baking or soufflé dish(es)

3 quarts whole milk
2 cinnamon sticks
4 cups uncooked short-grain rice
4 teaspoons sambuca liqueur
¼ cup fresh orange juice
2 cups golden raisins
7 cups heavy cream
2 cups sugar
8 eggs
2 teaspoons vanilla extract
1 teaspoon ground cinnamon

¹/₂ teaspoon ground cinnamon
Bowls of whole peaches, plums, apricots, apples, pears,
  grapes, and/or figs, depending on the season
2 recipes Hazelnut Biscotti (page 331)

1. Preheat the oven to 350°.

2. Bring 9 cups of the milk to a boil in a large saucepan over moderate heat. Add the cinnamon sticks and the rice. Simmer the rice, covered, over low heat, until it has absorbed all of the milk, about 20 minutes. Remove the cinnamon sticks and cool the rice to room temperature.

3. Warm the sambuca and orange juice in a small saucepan. Remove from the heat and add the raisins. Let the raisins soak and plump for 10 minutes.

4. Whisk together the remaining 3 cups of milk, the cream, sugar, eggs, vanilla, and ground cinnamon in a large mixing bowl. Add the rice and the raisins with any remaining liquid. Blend well.

5. Butter one 6-quart or two 3-quart decorative baking or soufflé dishes. Divide the rice-and-milk mixture between the dishes and place them in two roasting pans. Fill the pans with hot tap water to come halfway up the sides of the soufflé dishes. Stir the mixture once more and bake in the oven for 50 minutes, or until a toothpick inserted in the center of the pudding comes out clean. Serve warm or cool to room temperature and reheat the pudding in a water bath in a 300° oven.

FINISHING TOUCHES AND
TABLE PRESENTATION

Garnish the pudding with ¹/₂ teaspoon ground cinnamon and place it at the left of the table. Serve warm. Place bowls of whole fruit and the Hazelnut Biscotti (page 331) on the table near the rice.

The Inventive Chef

FOR A DIFFERENT TREAT, ADD CANDIED FRUITS, SUCH AS LEMON, ORANGE, OR GRAPEFRUIT PEEL, TO THE PUDDING WHEN YOU ADD THE RAISINS, OR ADD ¹/₄ TEASPOON SAFFRON THREADS TO THE MILK USED FOR COOKING THE RICE TO GIVE THE PUDDING A SUBTLE GOLDEN HUE.

1 WEEK AHEAD

| TOQUE 1 | Sausage Bread | Make bread halfway through step 5; *freeze unbaked*, covered with plastic. |

2 OR 3 DAYS BEFORE THE PARTY

MAIN EVENT	Veal	Order from butcher.
TOQUE 1	Pasta	Prepare onion, garlic, basil, Fontina, and Parmigiano; store separately, covered, in refrigerator.
TOQUE 2	Lasagna	Prepare rosemary, Asiago and Parmigiano cheeses, onion, garlic, and basil; store separately, covered, in refrigerator.
	Calzones	Prepare filling through step 3; store covered in refrigerator.
GRAND FINALE	Rice Pudding	Bake and freeze biscotti.

THE DAY BEFORE THE PARTY

MAIN EVENT	Veal	Slice lemon garnish; store covered tightly in refrigerator.
	Hens	Prepare pancetta, onions, and garlic; store separately, covered, in refrigerator.
TOQUE 1	Green Beans	Prepare pine nuts; set aside at room temperature.
	Pasta	Prepare halfway through step 8 but *do not bake;* store covered in refrigerator.
	Sausage Bread	Defrost in refrigerator overnight.
TOQUE 2	Lasagna	Prepare through step 5 but *do not bake;* store covered in refrigerator.
	Calzones	Prepare through step 7.

	Broccoli	Refrigerate covered.
		Prepare lima beans through step 2; store covered in refrigerator.
		Prepare broccoli, garlic, lemon wedges, and roasted garlic; store separately, covered, in refrigerator.
GRAND FINALE	Rice Pudding	Prepare and bake recipe; cool to room temperature; store covered in refrigerator.
		Wash fruit.
Strategic Maneuvers:		Fill creamers; cover and store in refrigerator.
		Fill sugar bowls.
		Set up buffet table decor.
		Check ice and beverages.
		Locate teas.
		Chill wine if white.
		Check garnishes for each recipe.
		Set out and label all serving bowls, platters, and utensils.

THE DAY OF THE PARTY

MAIN EVENT	Veal	Prepare through step 8 but *do not bake;* set aside, covered, in baking sheets.
	Hens	Prepare through step 6; set aside at room temperature.
TOQUE 1	Pasta	Bake and set aside at room temperature.
	Green Beans	Prepare through step 6; set aside in skillets.
	Sausage Bread	Bake the breads as in step 5.
TOQUE 2	Lasagna	Bake and set aside at room temperature.

	Broccoli	Complete recipe and set aside at room temperature.
GRAND FINALE	Pudding	Locate two roasting pans for reheating. Set fruits in bowls. Arrange biscotti.

15 MINUTES BEFORE GUESTS ARRIVE:

Preheat oven to 350°. Make sure remaining foods are at room temperature.

50 MINUTES BEFORE DINNER:

Bake Calzones.
Heat lasagna, and pasta until piping hot. Adjust heating foods to availability of space in ovens.

20 MINUTES BEFORE DINNER:

Finish veal in oven.
Heat hens. Complete finishing touches and presentation.
Heat breads.
Heat green beans. Complete finishing touches and presentation.

JUST BEFORE DINNER:

Plug in coffee.
Place puddings in roasting pans. Set oven at 300°.
Fill pans halfway with water and warm puddings in oven during dinner.

DINNER SERVICE:

Bring out all the food at once. Place hens on the left side of buffet, followed by the veal, then the pasta, green beans, and sausage bread, or the lasagna, broccoli, and calzones. Set up the garnishes specified in the recipes to fill the table. Guests can help themselves.

DESSERT SERVICE:

Place the warm rice pudding, bowls of fruit, and biscotti on the table.

AFTER SERVICE:

Unplug coffee.
Turn off oven(s).

A Graduation Celebration with Asian Sizzle

THE MAIN EVENTS:

Sweet-and-Sour Prawns
Fried Malaysian Chicken
Cucumber and Mango Salad
with Ginger and Lime

ON THE SIDE:

Nyonya Fried Rice

◆

Steamed Cabbage with Mushrooms, Carrots,
and Snow Peas

ON THE SIDE:

Chili-Spiced Noodles

◆

Spinach, Cauliflower, and Red Bell Pepper

THE GRAND FINALE:

Almond-Crusted Fried Banana Dumplings

PALATE TEASER:

Black-and-White Sesame Wontons (page 313)

BEVERAGE RECOMMENDATIONS:

Chilled dry Vermouth
Pinot Grigio, Friuli-Venezia Giulia, Jermann

*H*OW TO IMPRESS THE WORLDLY CROWD OF HUNGRY INTEL-lectuals who are coming to my daughter-in-law's commencement cele-bration? She's just earned her Ph.D., and her sophisticated friends are economists, political scientists, and sociologists who have studied all over the world—and everyone's "been there, eaten that!" My thesis: Serve up a dazzling dissertation of dishes inspired by my Asian travels, a most delicious research project. And (not to show off, of course) I will chat about *sambals, gulais,* and *acars,* classic dishes from the Nyonya kitchens of the "Straits-born" Chinese in Penang and Malacca.

The fun of this buffet starts long before the party, or even the cooking: You will have a culinary adventure visiting an Oriental food market to find the wonderful condiments, chilies, and specialty foods you will use in these tantalizing dishes. All are readily available, even in many supermarkets, and though they might seem exotic, you will love the exciting flavors they bring to these simple preparations. You will find yourself using them often in your everyday cooking, too.

Fresh red chilies, miso, and ginger—as well as generous amounts of shallots and garlic—help create the fantastic sauce that coats the Sweet-and-Sour Prawns, an extravagant Main Event. Any fresh red chili will work well in these recipes. I chose to use the long, thin red chilies that are moderately hot. Miso also comes in different forms, and you will want to use a dark style.

You will make two wonderful concoctions for the Malaysian Fried Chicken: a tangy marinade with soy sauce, lime juice, and sesame oil, and a dipping sauce with orange juice, coconut milk,

dried chilies, and other seasonings. The fabulous crust on the fried chicken comes from sweetened Japanese bread crumbs known as *panko.* Also on my Main Event menu is a hot, cool, tangy, and sweet salad of mango, cucumber, and pineapple with a dressing that includes ginger, miso, soy sauce, and guava nectar!

The spicy Asian flavor-parade continues in both menus' side dishes—and your guests' plates will look like paintings (at least until they start to use their chopsticks). Nyonya Fried Rice, like many of these dishes, is inspired by the spicy Nyonya cuisine I fell in love with in Penang, a Malaysian island. It's an easy stir-fry of cooked rice and seasonings. A pleasing contrast comes with the mild and sweet flavors and crisp textures of Steamed Cabbage with Mushrooms, Carrots, and Snow Peas.

My two-toque menu presents a terrific assortment of foods tucked into Chili-Spiced Noodles. You will stir-fry julienned strips of pork loin, napa cabbage, and bean sprouts, with oyster sauce, soy sauce, chilies, and coriander—and then toss it all with cooked Chinese noodles. It's terrific hot or at room temperature. Also on this menu is a zesty mélange of quickly sautéed spinach, cauliflower florets, red peppers, and onions.

Almond-Crusted Fried Banana Dumplings provide a luscious and unusual sweet ending to this Asian feast. You will need to deep-fry these treats while the dinner buffet is still in service, but you can hold them in the oven while your guests are enjoying the Main Events, indulging in seconds, and (don't be surprised) thirds.

SETTING THE STAGE

This dinner can be served as casually or formally as the occasion demands. For a lap-service buffet, consider purchasing bamboo or wicker trays for every guest. Available at import stores and some Asian markets, they are inexpensive and practical for all sorts of parties. Line them with black or neutral-colored napkins and stack them on the end of the buffet table. While shopping, you can certainly find tableware with Asian motifs that would be perfect for this menu, or use simple large white plates to show off all the gorgeous colors— and to hold great quantities of food. You will want to provide chopsticks, of course, as even novices will be motivated to use them. Wrap the chopsticks and conventional flatware in black napkins and arrange them in tall baskets.

There are lovely foods that can be arranged in a centerpiece or scattered about the buffet table. Fill baskets with Chinese and Japanese mushrooms and piles of different kinds of Asian noo-

dles. Fresh ginger is lovely and aromatic, and you can display many varieties and colors of chilies as well.

THE MAIN EVENT
Sweet-and-Sour Prawns

MAKES 16 SERVINGS

THE SAUCE

^{1}/$_3$ cup vegetable oil

10 large shallots, peeled and finely minced

14 cloves garlic, peeled and finely minced

2 tablespoons finely minced fresh ginger

4 large fresh red chili peppers, halved, seeded, and sliced on the diagonal

^{1}/$_4$ cup dark soy sauce

^{1}/$_4$ cup sugar

^{3}/$_4$ cup fresh lemon juice

^{1}/$_4$ cup dark miso (soy bean paste, available in Asian food stores or health food stores)

1 tablespoon cornstarch

THE PRAWNS

4 pounds jumbo prawns (under 15 count), peeled and deveined

^{1}/$_2$ cup cornstarch

1 cup peanut oil

1. First make the sauce. Heat the vegetable oil in a large skillet over medium-high heat and sauté the shallots until they are soft, about 2 minutes. Add the garlic, ginger, and chilies and continue to sauté the vegetables over medium heat for 1 minute more. Remove from the heat and set aside.

2. Blend together the soy sauce, sugar, lemon juice, miso, and cornstarch in a bowl with 2 cups of water. Mix the ingredients together until they are well blended. Pour this liquid into the skillet with the shallots and simmer, stirring, over medium heat until the sauce begins to thicken, about 1 minute. Remove it from the heat and cool to room temperature. Puree the sauce in a food processor fitted with a cutting blade. Set the sauce aside at room temperature.

3. Lightly coat the prawns with the cornstarch.

4. Heat the peanut oil in a heavy-bottomed, large, deep skillet over high heat. Add the prawns in batches and cook them for 2–3 minutes, until they are a very light golden color. Drain the prawns on paper towels as they are finished.

5. Drain any remaining oil from the skillet and wipe it clean. Stir the sauce and prawns together in the skillet and heat over medium heat until hot, being careful not to overcook the shrimp. The sauce should coat and cling to the shrimp. (*If you would like the sauce to have more "heat," sprinkle in red pepper flakes to suit your taste when heating the sauce with the shrimp.*)

FINISHING TOUCHES AND TABLE PRESENTATION

The prawns display incredibly well in a large shallow dish with an Asian motif. Don't be concerned about their cooling down to room temperature; the flavorful seasonings will continue to be intense. Place the shrimp on the left side of the buffet, followed by the chicken and the cucumbers. Place the one-toque or two-toque side dishes on the right side of the buffet. A display of Asian fans makes a fine centerpiece. I like to put each dish in a different kind of vessel, combining pottery, baskets, and copper.

The Inventive Chef

SUBSTITUTE RAW SEA SCALLOPS FOR THE SHRIMP, OR ADD COOKED LUMP CRABMEAT TO THE SAUCE IN THE FINAL STEP OF THE RECIPE.

THE MAIN EVENT

Fried Malaysian Chicken

MAKES 16 SERVINGS

SPECIAL COOKWARE
Meat pounder

THE MARINADE
1 cup dark soy sauce
$1/2$ cup fresh lime juice
$2/3$ cup honey
$1/4$ cup sesame oil
1 tablespoon minced fresh ginger
3 large cloves garlic, peeled and minced

THE CHICKEN
4 pounds boneless chicken breasts, pounded to $1/2$-inch thick and cut into pieces 2 inches wide by $2^{1}/2$ inches long

1 cup fresh orange juice
2 teaspoons cornstarch
1/2 dry red chili pepper, finely chopped
1/4 cup Worcestershire sauce
2 tablespoons light soy sauce
1/2 cup unsweetened coconut milk
1/2 tablespoon minced fresh ginger
1 tablespoon sugar
1 generous pinch Chinese five-spice powder

THE CRUST

2 cups all-purpose flour, plus additional for dredging
  chicken
1 (8-ounce) package panko (Japanese bread crumbs with
  honey, available at Asian food stores)
3 cups vegetable oil for frying

GARNISH

5 whole red chilies
5 whole green chilies

1. To make the marinade, combine all ingredients in a large glass or stainless steel bowl to blend well. Add the chicken and toss it well to coat all pieces evenly. Marinate the chicken, covered, for 2–3 hours in the refrigerator.

2. While the chicken is marinating, make the sauce. In a small bowl, whisk the orange juice into the cornstarch until the cornstarch dissolves and is free of lumps. In a 2-quart saucepan, combine the orange juice and cornstarch with the red chili, Worcestershire sauce, soy sauce, coconut milk, ginger, sugar, and five-spice powder. Stir well and bring to a boil over medium-high heat. Cook the sauce for 3 minutes or until it thickens. Remove from the heat and keep warm in the top of a double boiler.

3. Drain the chicken and discard the marinade. Pat the chicken dry with paper towels.

4. Preheat the oven to 250°.

5. To make the crust for the chicken, create a thick paste by whisking the flour with 2 cups of water in a medium-size bowl until the mixture is free of lumps. Place some dredging flour in a second medium-size bowl, and, in a third bowl, place the panko. Coat each piece of chicken first with the flour, then with the flour-water paste, and finally with the panko.

6. Heat at least 3 inches of oil in a large frying pan over medium-high heat until a drop of water sizzles when trickled into the pan. *(If the oil gets too hot, the crust will burn before the chicken is cooked; if the oil is too cool, the bread crumbs will roll off the meat.)* Fry the chicken in small batches, turning it once, until light golden in color and cooked through, about 2–2 1/2 minutes. Remove it with a slotted spoon to drain on paper towels. Hold the cooked chicken in the oven to keep warm, crisp, and moist for 30 minutes.

FINISHING TOUCHES AND
TABLE PRESENTATION

Arrange the crisp chicken on large flat platters garnished with the whole red and green chilies. Put the warm sauce in an Asian rice dish or a white pottery dish garnished with whole red and green chilies.

The Inventive Chef

DON'T HESITATE TO MAKE THIS CHICKEN FOR BEACH PARTIES OR PICNICS. CUT THE CHICKEN IN FINGER-SIZE PIECES BEFORE FRYING AND SERVE IT AS AN HORS D'OEUVRE.

Cucumber and Mango Salad with Ginger and Lime

MAKES 16 SERVINGS

THE DRESSING

$1^1/_2$ dried red chilies, stems removed, about 1 ounce
2 teaspoons finely minced fresh ginger
2 tablespoons light soy sauce
2 tablespoons fresh lime juice
$^1/_3$ cup guava nectar
$1^1/_2$ tablespoons miso (soybean paste, available in Asian
    food stores or health food stores)
$^1/_4$ cup peanut oil

THE SALAD

1 tablespoon peanut oil
$^1/_2$ cup sesame seeds
4 large cucumbers, peeled, seeded, and cut into $^1/_2$-inch
    dice
4 ripe mangoes, peeled, pitted, and cut into $^1/_2$-inch dice
2 large pineapples, peeled, cored, and cut into $^1/_2$-inch dice
1 cup coarsely chopped unsalted peanuts

1. To make the dressing, soak the dried chili in warm water to cover for 15 minutes; drain well and mince by hand.
2. Place the minced chili, ginger, soy sauce, lime juice, guava nectar, and the $^1/_4$ cup peanut oil in the bowl of a food processor fitted with knife blade and blend well. Set the dressing aside.
3. Heat the 1 tablespoon of peanut oil for the salad in a small skillet over high heat. Briskly sauté the

sesame seeds, stirring often, until they are golden, about 30 seconds. Drain on paper towels.

FINISHING TOUCHES AND TABLE PRESENTATION

Toss the cucumbers, mangoes, pineapples, and peanuts together with enough of the dressing to lightly coat the fruit. Serve in a salad bowl with an Asian motif or a glass bowl, topped with the toasted sesame seeds. Serve the extra dressing on the side.

The Inventive Chef

TO TURN THIS INTO AN UNUSUAL CHICKEN SALAD ENTRÉE, POACH 1 POUND OF SKINLESS AND BONELESS CHICKEN BREASTS. CUT THE CHICKEN INTO 1-INCH DICE, AND ADD IT TO THE FRUIT WHILE THE CHICKEN IS STILL WARM.

ON THE SIDE

Nyonya Fried Rice

MAKES 16 SERVINGS

6 tablespoons sesame oil
5 large shallots, peeled and finely minced
4 large cloves garlic, peeled and finely minced
4 fresh red chilies, seeded and finely minced, or
    $1^1/_4$ teaspoons prepared red pepper flakes
8 cups cooked basmati rice, at room temperature

2 1/2 tablespoons light soy sauce
1 tablespoon dark soy sauce
7 scallions, white and green parts, sliced on the diagonal
    into 1/8-inch rounds

1. Heat the sesame oil in a large skillet over high
heat. Add the shallots and garlic and sauté briskly for
1 minute. Lower the heat, add the chilies, and sauté
for 30 seconds.
2. Add the rice with the light and dark soy sauces.
Stir over medium heat until the ingredients are well
blended. Stir in the scallions and cook 1 minute more.

FINISHING TOUCHES AND TABLE PRESENTATION

The fried rice looks brilliant in a deep copper dish or
skillet.

The Inventive Chef

ADD DICED ROAST PORK, CHICKEN, OR COOKED
SHRIMP TO THE RICE FOR A STICK-TO-YOUR-
RIBS ENTRÉE. A LIGHT CRISP GREEN SALAD
WITH A CITRUS DRESSING IS A TANGY FOIL FOR
THE SEASONINGS IN THE RICE.

ON THE SIDE

Steamed Cabbage with Mushrooms, Carrots, and Snow Peas

MAKES 16 SERVINGS

SPECIAL COOKWARE
Extra-large skillet

5 tablespoons peanut oil
2 pounds Chinese cabbage, washed, ends removed, cut into
    1-by-1-inch julienne strips
3 large carrots, peeled and cut on the diagonal into 1/8-inch
    rounds
1 1/4 pounds domestic mushrooms, washed and quartered
1 1/4 pounds shiitake mushrooms, washed, stemmed, and
    quartered
1 pound snow peas, strings removed, quartered
1 tablespoon minced fresh ginger
1/4 cup light soy sauce
1 tablespoon sugar
1/8 teaspoon Chinese five-spice powder
1/2 teaspoon freshly ground black pepper, or to taste
1/4 teaspoon salt, or to taste (optional)

1. Heat 2 tablespoons of the oil in an extra-large
skillet over medium-high heat and sauté the cabbage,
in batches if necessary, until softened but still crisp,
about 3–5 minutes. Remove it to a large bowl and
reserve at room temperature.
2. Add the remaining 3 tablespoons of oil to the
skillet and sauté the carrots for 1 minute over
medium-high heat. Add the domestic and shiitake

mushrooms and sauté an additional 2 minutes, then add the snow peas and ginger and cook until the vegetables are slightly wilted, about 2 additional minutes.

3. Toss the cabbage with the vegetables in a colander to drain off the excess liquid. Return to the bowl and stir in the soy sauce, sugar, five-spice powder, pepper, and salt, if desired, while the vegetables are hot.

FINISHING TOUCHES AND
TABLE PRESENTATION

The cabbage can be served hot or at room temperature. The colors of the vegetables show off well on a flat oval or round platter.

The Inventive Chef

JULIENNED STRIPS OF STIR-FRIED BEEF
ENHANCE THE FLAVOR OF THE CABBAGE FOR AN
EXCELLENT ENTRÉE.

ON THE SIDE

Chili-Spiced Noodles

MAKES 16 SERVINGS

SPECIAL COOKWARE
Large wok

6 dried chilies
1 pound Chinese plain thin noodles or Italian vermicelli noodles

$^{1}/_{4}$ cup plus 1 tablespoon peanut oil
2 large yellow onions, peeled and finely minced
6 large cloves garlic, peeled and finely minced
3 pounds boneless pork loin, fat removed, sliced in $^{1}/_{4}$-inch-by-1-inch julienne strips
2 pounds bean sprouts, washed in cold water and drained well
2 pounds napa cabbage, washed, dried, and shredded $^{1}/_{4}$-inch thick
$^{2}/_{3}$ cup oyster sauce
$^{1}/_{3}$ cup dark soy sauce
2 teaspoons ground coriander
1 teaspoon salt, or to taste
Juice of 2 large limes

GARNISH
5 scallions, thinly sliced on the diagonal

1. Soak the dried chilies in warm water to cover for 15 minutes. Drain well and mince finely with a sharp knife. Stir 2 tablespoons of water into the minced chilies and set aside.

2. Bring 5 quarts of water to a rolling boil over high heat in a large stockpot. Add the noodles and boil, uncovered, for 3–4 minutes. Immediately place the noodles in a colander and rinse them with warm tap water. Drain the noodles well, return them to the stockpot, and toss with 1 tablespoon of the peanut oil until thoroughly coated.

3. Add the remaining $^{1}/_{4}$ cup of oil to a large wok and sauté the onions over high heat until lightly browned, about 4–5 minutes. Add the garlic and continue to sauté for 30 seconds.

4. Add the pork and sauté, stirring constantly, until the meat loses its pink color, about 3 minutes. Cook for 1 minute more, stirring and tossing all the ingredients together. *(If you don't have a large wok, divide the onions and pork evenly between two large skillets.)*

5. Add the bean sprouts, cabbage, reserved minced chilies and their water, oyster sauce, soy sauce, coriander, and salt to the wok with an extra tablespoon of oil if the vegetables seem dry. Stir over high heat for 1–2 minutes and blend all the flavors.

6. Add the noodles and toss to mix well.

7. Just before serving, blend in the lime juice.

FINISHING TOUCHES AND TABLE PRESENTATION

Serve the noodles hot, in a large bowl with an Asian motif, a wok, or a terra-cotta bowl. Sprinkle the top with the scallions. The noodles will probably cool down on the buffet, but I enjoy them at room temperature as much as I do served hot.

The Inventive Chef

TO ALL THE SIDE RECIPES IN THIS MENU, I ENCOURAGE ADDING COOKED DICED CHICKEN, BEEF, SHRIMP, OR CRAB. TOP THE DISH WITH DRIED CHINESE NOODLES FOR EXTRA CRUNCH.

ON THE SIDE

Spinach, Cauliflower, and Red Bell Pepper

MAKES 16 SERVINGS

SPECIAL COOKWARE
One extra-large skillet or two large skillets

3 tablespoons sesame oil
3 tablespoons vegetable oil
2 tablespoons finely minced fresh ginger
2 large cloves garlic, peeled and finely minced
2 large red onions, peeled and finely minced
4 tablespoons soy sauce
3 tablespoons oyster sauce
2 1/2 pounds cauliflower, core removed, with florets cut into
*   bite-size pieces*
3 red bell peppers, cored, seeded, and cut into 1/2-inch dice
1 1/2 pounds fresh spinach, washed, trimmed, and dried
1 teaspoon salt, or to taste
1/2 teaspoon freshly ground black pepper, or to taste

GARNISH
Grated zest of 1 large lemon

1. Heat the sesame and vegetable oils together over high heat in an extra-large skillet. Add the ginger and garlic and sauté about 30 seconds. Add the red onions and sauté another 2 minutes. Blend in 3 tablespoons of the soy sauce.

2. Mix 2 tablespoons of the oyster sauce with 1 1/4 cups of water, and add the mixture to the skillet. Simmer over medium heat for 5 minutes.

3. Add the cauliflower and peppers and cook, tossing

frequently, for 3 minutes. Add the spinach and cook until it has wilted but remains bright green, about 1–2 minutes more. Strain the vegetables through a colander to remove any excess liquid and stir in the remaining 1 tablespoon soy sauce and 1 tablespoon oyster sauce. Season with salt and pepper.

FINISHING TOUCHES AND
TABLE PRESENTATION

Arrange the vegetables on a square platter and sprinkle the top with the lemon zest.

The Inventive Chef

YOU MAY WANT TO TRY COOKING THE VEGETABLES SEPARATELY. THIS TECHNIQUE IS CERTAINLY MORE TIME-CONSUMING, BUT ARRANGING THEM IN RIBBONS OF COLOR—THE WHITE OF THE CAULIFLOWER, THE RED OF THE PEPPER, AND THE VIVID GREEN OF THE SPINACH—ADDS AN ELECTRIC SHOCK OF COLOR TO THE BUFFET.

THE GRAND FINALE

Almond-Crusted Fried Banana Dumplings

MAKES 16 SERVINGS

SPECIAL COOKWARE
Deep-fat-frying thermometer

1/2 cup almonds, skins removed
8 large ripe bananas
1 cup all-purpose flour
1/4 cup light brown sugar, firmly packed
1/3 teaspoon salt
1 teaspoon baking powder
1/2 teaspoon baking soda
Vegetable oil for frying

GARNISH
1/2 cup coconut flakes

1. Grind the almonds by pulsing them in a food processor fitted with the knife blade until they are pulverized. Set aside.
2. Peel the bananas and mash them thoroughly with a fork.
3. Place the bananas, flour, sugar, salt, baking powder, baking soda, and ground almonds in a large bowl. Mix all the ingredients together until they form a soft dough.
4. Preheat the oven to 250°.
5. Pour 2 inches of oil into a large skillet. Heat the oil until a deep-fat-frying thermometer reaches 375°. Gently place a tablespoon of the banana batter into the oil and fry the dumplings, a few at a time, turning them once, until golden brown, about 30 seconds per side. Drain on paper towels. *(The banana dumplings can be held in a 250° oven for 30 minutes.)*

FINISHING TOUCHES AND
TABLE PRESENTATION

Line a round basket with a brightly colored napkin or choose a platter with an Asian motif for the dumplings. Arrange them in the basket or on the platter and sprinkle them with the coconut flakes.

KITCHEN SCHEDULE

THE DAY BEFORE THE PARTY

MAIN EVENTS

Prawns	Prepare the sauce as in steps 1 and 2; store covered in refrigerator.
	Peel and devein shrimp; store covered in refrigerator.
Chicken	Prepare the chicken as in the ingredient list; store covered in refrigerator.
	Prepare the marinade as in step 1; store covered in refrigerator.
	Prepare the sauce as in step 2; store covered in refrigerator.
Cucumber Salad	Prepare dressing; store covered in refrigerator.

TOQUE 1

Fried Rice	Trim and slice shallots, garlic, chilies, and scallions; store separately, covered, in refrigerator.
Cabbage	Trim and slice cabbage, carrots, snow peas, and ginger; store separately, covered, in refrigerator.

TOQUE 2

Noodles	Trim and slice onion, garlic, pork, bean sprouts, and cabbage; store separately, covered, in refrigerator.
Spinach	Trim and slice ginger, garlic, onions, cauliflower, red peppers, spinach, and lemon zest; store separately, covered, in refrigerator.

Strategic Maneuvers:

Fill creamer; cover and store in refrigerator.
Fill sugar bowls.
Set table. Check buffet decor.

Check ice and beverages.
Locate teas.
Chill wine if white.
Check garnishes for each recipe.
Locate and label all serving bowls, platters, and utensils.

THE DAY OF THE PARTY

MAIN EVENT

Prawns	Warm sauce in double boiler.
Chicken	Marinate chicken for 2 hours.
Cucumber Salad	Prepare cucumbers, mangoes, and pineapple.
	Bring dressing to room temperature and toss with salad; store covered in refrigerator.

TOQUE 1

Fried Rice	Complete entire recipe; set aside at room temperature.
Cabbage	Prepare recipe through step 3; set aside at room temperature.

TOQUE 2

Noodles	Prepare through step 6 but *do not blend in lime juice.* Store covered in refrigerator.
Spinach	Prepare through step 3 but *do not garnish with the lemon zest.* Store covered in refrigerator.

GRAND FINALE

Dumplings	Set up all ingredients for recipe.

1 HOUR BEFORE GUESTS ARRIVE:

Heat oven to 250°.
Coat and fry prawns through step 4; set aside at room temperature.
Make banana dumpling batter through step 3; store covered in refrigerator.

Prepare chicken through step 6; keep warm in oven.

30 MINUTES BEFORE DINNER:

Complete prawn recipe.
Blend lime juice with noodles.
Garnish spinach with lemon zest.
Rewarm rice in the oven.
Garnish all buffet foods.

15 MINUTES BEFORE DINNER:

Fill bowl with sauce for chicken.
Arrange all food on buffet table.
Plug in coffee.

DINNER SERVICE:

Have kitchen helper fry banana dumplings. *(If there is no kitchen helper, fry dumplings 30 minutes before dessert is served and keep warm in the low oven.)*
Bring all the food out at once.
All the dishes blend well on one plate.

DESSERT SERVICE:

Fill baskets with dumplings, sprinkle with coconut, and bring to table.

AFTER SERVICE:

Unplug coffee.
Turn off oven.

CHAPTER 9

The Spark and Spice of Grilling Parties

"We're going to fire up the grill and cook something. Come on over." Now that's about the most informal invitation I can issue, but also one of the most irresistible. It really doesn't matter what I am cooking: Grill it and they will come!

I admit that I love grilling parties precisely for their come-as-you-are casualness. This is the standard for summer entertaining at my home: As long as it's warm enough to be outside, I wouldn't think of giving a dinner where I have to leave my guests and go into the kitchen to cook!

In this chapter you will find three great grilling occasions with menus perfect for partying your way through the summer:

♦ Heat things up for the Fourth of July fireworks with grilled swordfish bursting with brilliant flashes of Asian flavor.

♦ Indulge your deepest desires with a dream dinner: a summer evening, thick steaks sizzling on the fire, and a host of savory accompaniments.

♦ Create an unforgettable afternoon with a picnic feast of soulful Southern classics such as spicy spareribs, Cajun-style grilled shrimp and scallops, hush puppies, black-eyed peas, and sweet potato pie.

Aside from the fabulous food, the attraction of these menus is their versatility. Food service can be any style: Display all the dishes on a buffet near the grill, then call your guests to fill their plates and plunk themselves down on lawn chairs and picnic blankets. Or make it a family-style, pass-me-the-potatoes-please feast at the picnic table. Or you can arrange a formally set table and serve gorgeously composed plates to each guest (the steak dinner is especially wonderful for seated service).

For me, the sensuality of grilling parties comes as much from the outdoor atmosphere—perfumed air and gentle breezes, sunshine or moonlight—as it does from the savor and spice of the meal. I make every effort to keep the party completely outdoors, but in every case, your game plan *must* include the contingency of indoor service in bad weather, even if you end up grilling in the rain!

With basic decor provided by Mother Nature, you

Good Times in the Great Outdoors

The game plan for a successful grilling party—or any other alfresco meal—necessitates special consider-ations. As I advised in my chapter on "Choosing the Perfect Party" (page 19), you must be certain that your outdoor area is level and firm, that it has con-venient access to house facilities, and the capacity for seating your guests and serving your meal, including space for a tent if appropriate.

Here are a few more considerations you don't want to overlook:

• What kind of grill will you use? Does it have enough space for the amount of food you need to cook? Do you have enough fuel on hand (and a reliable way to ignite it)?

• What about the sun? You don't want your guests grilling, too. Assess the natural shade at the time of day of your party. Erect umbrellas, a tent, or another sunscreen as needed.

• What about the wind? You will know you have forgotten to ask this question when the paper napkins blow across your lawn. Make sure your table-setting items and candle flames are protected from unpredictable breezes.

• What about bugs? There are various ways to reduce bug annoyance: Consider spraying your party area with a safe insecticide the day before your event, or use insect-repellent candles or other devices.

• Do you have enough light in your outdoor dining area? You don't want to be plunged into darkness before dessert, or forced to eat in the glare of outdoor floodlights. Plan ahead for adequate ambient and decorative lighting. (A simple solution for marking walkways is to set votive candles within small paper bags filled with a few inches of sand.)

• How will you keep food and beverages cold? A smart host will save many trips to the kitchen by using coolers with an adequate supply of ice to serve as outdoor refrigeration for beverages and salads. The coolers can be hidden under the buffet table or behind the bar.

don't need much beyond simple embellishments such as fresh-cut flowers and bowls of beautiful produce as cen-terpieces. Though I occasionally set a table with color-ful china, most often I use top-quality paper products for outdoor eating. Be sure to get the sturdiest, largest plates you can buy—and real flatware, please, forget the

plastic! A caution: If the entrée needs to be cut with a knife, don't plan on a lap-service event. Having to cut steak while reclining on a picnic blanket can turn your dinner into a juggling act.

In the following menus, much of your cooking and preparation work can be done well ahead of time—see the kitchen schedules for the most efficient approach. When guests arrive, lead them right outside and have a few savory hors d'oeuvres and beverages to serve while you get the fire going. Your party will heat up along with the coals. (I give recommendations for appetizers and summer drinks in each menu.)

For these menus, the Main Event is truly that: the fiery and aromatic climax of your dinner preparation.

Putting the main course on the grill will inevitably inspire everyone to ask, "Can I help you?" You bet they can! Let them bring out prepared bowls and platters of side dishes from the kitchen or refrigerator, or even assist you with last-minute cooking chores. Since what they really want to do is stand around the fire themselves, you might let them turn the swordfish, steak, or ribs while you coordinate the assembly of dinner.

Let your dinner take its own leisurely course. Dessert can be served any time (or anywhere the bugs are not biting). If darkness descends, small lanterns or votive and citronella candles will provide a romantic glow. I hope you try all of these menus at least once. The only problem is that winter will seem interminably long until you can try them again.

MENU 1

Scintillating Fare
Before the Fireworks

THE MAIN EVENT

Grilled Swordfish and
Red Onion-Raisin
Marmalade

ON THE SIDE:

Soba Noodles with Bean Sprouts and Broccoli

◆

Tropical Gingered Fruit Kabobs

ON THE SIDE:

Tomato Bread Pudding

◆

Wheat Berries with Crunchy Vegetables

THE GRAND FINALE:
Peaches Soaked in Honey and Port

PALATE TEASER:
Lamb, Carrot, and Potato Kabobs (page 303)

BEVERAGE RECOMMENDATIONS:
Margaritas (page 355)
Chardonnay, California, Trefethen Vineyards

*A*H, FREEDOM! HERE'S A FOURTH OF JULY MENU THAT declares your independence from the usual holiday routine. Freedom from hot dogs and hamburgers! Freedom from potato and macaroni salads! Celebrate our nation's culinary liberty with Asian-spiced grilled swordfish steaks and tropical fruits on the grill, accompanied by a creamy and cheesy tomato bread pudding from the oven and juicy peaches soaked in port wine.

Before the fireworks, or for any other occasion, this delicious and easy menu affords great freedom from last-minute chores. Even the Main Event swordfish can be completed ahead of your guests' arrival—it is delicious at room temperature.

The fish steaks develop a marvelous flavor during a brief period in an Asian marinade made with ginger, soy sauce, rice wine vinegar, and honey. After grilling, they are topped with a winey marmelade of sautéed red onions and golden raisins that accents the sweet and spicy notes.

My dishes offer distinctly different but complementary accompaniments to the swordfish. I love the flavor of Japanese soba noodles dressed with a complex peanut-sesame-ginger-citrus sauce. I've added crisp broccoli, bean sprouts, and cashew nuts to the smooth noodles for a delightful texture. A lovely accent to the fish and noodles is provided by tropical fruit kabobs. Throw them on the grill when the fish comes off and they will be done in a flash. Brushed with a citrus marinade, these simple and sensational grilled fruit chunks will change your perception of how to use fruit in your meals.

Go in a different direction with the two-toque accompaniments, preparing the rich and smooth-

flavored Tomato Bread Pudding. This menu is completed with a salad of cooked wheat berries mixed with crunchy bell peppers and broccoli. Lime juice and rice wine vinegar give a brightly acidic note to the nutty flavor of the grain. This dish can be served warm or cooled, and is a delightful textural contrast to the smooth pudding.

While everyone is enjoying dinner, large ripe peach halves will be soaking in a syrup of port wine, honey, cloves, cinnamon, and orange zest. Before you go to the fireworks—or even better, after you come home—simply serve the peaches with a bit of syrup and you will know why this is a great country to live in.

SETTING THE STAGE

This menu is wonderfully versatile. You can pass the foods at the table family-style, but I think it is easiest, and perhaps best, to let your guests serve themselves from a separate buffet table. It is not necessary to have elaborate decorations for the food display: The platter of swordfish, with fruit kabobs laid out as spokes, or the cheese-laden bread pudding, along with the vegetable-studded salads, look simply gorgeous in and of themselves.

Make a centerpiece for your dining table with small pots of aromatic herbs set at different heights—cilantro, mint, basil, and dill, for example, all play a role in the meal. (There's plenty of summer left, so after the party, plant the herbs in your garden or send them home with the guests.) And there's a long lingering twilight on the Fourth of July, so have candles at the ready.

THE MAIN EVENT

Grilled Swordfish and Red Onion-Raisin Marmalade

MAKES 8 SERVINGS

SPECIAL COOKWARE
Charcoal or gas grill

2 tablespoons minced fresh ginger
2 tablespoons soy sauce
2 tablespoons honey
2 tablespoons rice wine vinegar
2 tablespoons sesame oil
1/3 cup olive oil
1 1/2 tablespoons finely chopped cilantro
8 (6-ounce) swordfish steaks, 1 1/2 inches thick

Red Onion–Raisin Marmalade (recipe follows)

1. Blend the ginger, soy sauce, honey, vinegar, sesame oil, olive oil, and cilantro together in a stainless steel or other noncorrosive bowl. Mix the ingredients well.
2. Brush both sides of the swordfish with the marinade, reaching down to the bottom of the bowl to make sure you pick up all the flavors. Marinate the swordfish in the refrigerator for 2 hours. (*Over-marinating will cause the flesh of the fish to break down and soften.*)
3. Light the charcoal and wait until the coals are ashy gray, or preheat the gas grill until it's good and hot, before you grill the fish.
4. Remove the swordfish from the marinade, pat dry, and grill it 4–6 minutes on each side, depending on the heat of the coals and the thickness of the fish. (*Do not overcook. The swordfish is done when the flesh has turned from translucent to opaque and the juices run freely.*)

FINISHING TOUCHES AND
TABLE PRESENTATION

The swordfish can be served at room temperature.

ONE-TOQUE: Arrange the swordfish steaks in concentric circles inside the rim of a large platter. Place the end of each Tropical Gingered Fruit Kabob in the center of the platter with the fruit separating each swordfish steak, as in the spokes on a wheel. Serve the marmalade at room temperature from a pottery bowl set next to the fish.

TWO-TOQUE: Fill a platter with swordfish and garnish with small bunches of fresh herbs. Serve the marmalade next to the swordfish.

Red Onion-Raisin Marmalade

MAKES ABOUT 1 1/2 CUPS

4 tablespoons olive oil
2 large red onions, peeled and finely diced
2 1/2 teaspoons sugar
3 tablespoons balsamic vinegar
3/4 cup red wine
1/2 cup golden raisins
1/4 cup finely chopped cilantro
1/8 teaspoon salt, or to taste
1/8 teaspoon freshly ground black pepper, or to taste

1. Heat the oil in a large skillet and sauté the onions over medium-high heat until they become a light golden brown, about 6 minutes. Add the sugar and balsamic vinegar and cook, stirring, until all the vinegar has been incorporated into the onions, about 30 seconds.
2. Stirring constantly, add the red wine and raisins and lower the heat. Simmer the marmalade until the wine has been absorbed, about 2 minutes. Remove from the heat, add the cilantro, and season with salt and pepper. Set aside at room temperature until ready to serve.

ON THE SIDE

Soba Noodles with Bean Sprouts and Broccoli

MAKES 8 SERVINGS

Salt
3/4 pound soba or lo-mein noodles (available dry or fresh in Asian food stores)
1/4 cup smooth peanut butter
1/4 cup soy sauce
3 tablespoons finely minced fresh ginger
1/4 cup fresh orange juice
6 tablespoons sesame oil
3 tablespoons honey
2 heads broccoli florets, cut into bite-size pieces
3 cups bean sprouts
3 tablespoons sesame seeds
2/3 cup cashew nuts
5 scallions, white and green parts, trimmed, and cut on the bias into thin slices

1. In a large pot, bring 4 quarts of water to a boil with a pinch of salt. Simmer the dry noodles for 4–5 minutes until they are tender.♦ Drain through a colander and immediately pour cold water through the noodles to stop the cooking process. Drain the noodles well again and transfer them to a large bowl.
2. In a medium-size bowl, whisk together the peanut butter, soy sauce, ginger, orange juice, sesame oil, and honey until you have a smooth dressing. Set aside.
3. Steam the broccoli in a vegetable steamer or simmer it, uncovered, in 2 cups of salted water until it is cooked crisp but not soft, about 3 minutes. Drain

♦Fresh noodles cook in 1 minute.

the broccoli and immediately immerse it in ice water to retain its bright green color. Drain once more and set aside.

4. Steam the bean sprouts for 1 minute and toss with ³/₄ of the broccoli amd the noodles.

5. Add the sesame seeds, cashews, and about ³/₄ of the scallions to the noodles and toss with the reserved dressing.

FINISHING TOUCHES AND TABLE PRESENTATION

Serve the noodles at room temperature in a colorfully decorated pottery bowl and garnish with the reserved broccoli and scallions.

> ### *The Inventive Chef*
>
> THESE NOODLES CAN BE SERVED WITH GRILLED BEEF, CHICKEN, OR PORK. I LOVE THEM HOT.

ON THE SIDE

Tropical Gingered Fruit Kabobs

MAKES 8 SERVINGS

SPECIAL COOKWARE
16 (12-inch) metal skewers
Charcoal or gas grill

1 tablespoon minced fresh ginger

¹/₃ cup light brown sugar, firmly packed
¹/₃ cup fresh lemon juice
¹/₄ cup fresh lime juice
48 seedless red grapes
4 medium mangoes, peeled, pitted, and each cut into eight 2-inch cubes
2 medium pineapples, peeled, quartered, cored, and each cut into sixteen 2-inch wedges
8 large peaches, halved, pitted, and sliced into eighths
4 kiwifruits, peeled and quartered

GARNISH
4 starfruit, cut into ¹/₂-inch slices, or sixteen 1-ounce bunches of green grapes

1. Blend together the ginger, brown sugar, and lemon and lime juices in a small saucepan and bring to a simmer over medium heat, stirring until the brown sugar is completely dissolved. Remove from the heat and set aside for basting the fruit.

2. Thread the fruits carefully onto skewers. To distribute the colors of the fruit, first thread a grape, followed by a piece of mango, a piece of pineapple, a grape, a peach half, a kiwifruit quarter, and then a second piece of mango, pineapple, a grape, and finally a peach half.

3. Brush the fruit kabobs generously with the marinade 15 minutes before you put them on the grill or under the broiler. Grill the Kabobs for a total of 5 minutes, turning them once. Remove from the heat and glaze once more with the marinade before serving.

FINISHING TOUCHES AND TABLE PRESENTATION

Serve the kabobs with the swordfish as described on page 188, or arrange them in spokes on a flat platter. Place the slices of starfruit in overlapping circles around the edge of the platter, or arrange the grapes around the edge of the platter.

The Inventive Chef

THE CHOICES FOR MIXING AND MATCHING FRUITS FOR THE KABOBS ARE LIMITLESS. HAVE FUN WITH YOUR OWN WHIMSY.

ON THE SIDE

Tomato Bread Pudding

MAKES 8 GENEROUS SERVINGS

SPECIAL COOKWARE
4-quart oven-proof decorative casserole

Nonstick spray or 2 tablespoons vegetable oil
1 small challah or brioche bread (about 1 pound), cut into
   1/2-inch cubes

3 tablespoons salted butter
4 garlic cloves, peeled and finely minced
1 small white onion, peeled and finely minced
2 shallots, peeled and finely minced
1 quart heavy cream
8 eggs
2 (2 1/2-pound) cans Italian plum tomatoes, drained
2 tablespoons finely chopped fresh basil
3/4 cup freshly grated Parmigiano Reggiano
3/4 cup Boursin or garlic-scented soft, creamy cheese
1 1/2 teaspoons salt
1/2 teaspoon freshly ground black pepper

GARNISH
1/2 cup Parmigiano Reggiano shavings
1/2 bunch fresh dill sprigs

1. Preheat the oven to 350°. Spray a 4-quart oven-proof decorative casserole or baking dish with nonstick spray or coat with the oil.
2. Place the bread cubes on a baking sheet and toast them in the oven until golden, about 5–8 minutes.
3. Heat the butter in a medium skillet over medium-high heat and sauté the garlic for 30 seconds. Add the onion and shallots and continue to sauté for 3 minutes, until the vegetables are soft and translucent. Let cool at room temperature.
4. In a large bowl, whip together the cream and eggs with the whisk attachment of your electric mixer at medium speed. Add the tomatoes, basil, Parmigiano and Boursin cheeses, and the cooled onion-and-garlic mixture. Continue to beat the custard until all the ingredients are well blended. Season with the salt and pepper.
5. Arrange the toasted bread cubes on the bottom of the prepared casserole. Pour the custard over the bread and let the pudding stand for 15 minutes at room temperature.

6. Place the casserole in a large roasting pan, fill the pan with warm water to come halfway up the sides of the casserole dish, and bake the casserole for 45–50 minutes, until a knife inserted in the center comes out clean.

FINISHING TOUCHES AND
TABLE PRESENTATION

Remove the casserole from the water bath and place it on a decorative underliner. Garnish the top with the shaved Parmigiano and the dill.

The Inventive Chef

WE SERVE THIS PUDDING WITH ROASTED BEEF, VEAL, AND CHICKEN. GIVE THE SEASONING A TWIST BY SUBSTITUTING CILANTRO FOR THE BASIL AND ASIAGO FOR THE PARMIGIANO.

ON THE SIDE

Wheat Berries with Crunchy Vegetables

MAKES 8 SERVINGS

2 cups wheat berries (available in health food stores)
1/4 cup plus 2 tablespoons olive oil
2 cloves garlic, peeled and minced
1 bunch (about 1 pound) broccoli florets, stems removed, cut into small pieces
1 medium red bell pepper, seeded and diced

1 medium yellow bell pepper, seeded and diced
1/4 cup dry white wine
1 teaspoon salt, or to taste
1/2 teaspoon pepper, or to taste
2 tablespoons rice wine vinegar
2 tablespoons fresh lime juice
4 scallions, white and green parts, cut into 1/8-inch rounds

GARNISH
6 julienned strips of red bell pepper
6 julienned strips of yellow bell pepper

1. Rinse the wheat berries under cold running water for 2 minutes. Bring 6 cups of water to a boil in a large saucepan, add the wheat berries, cover, and simmer for about 1 hour. After 45 minutes, test the berries for crispness. They should be resistant to the bite.
2. While the wheat berries are cooking, heat 2 tablespoons of the olive oil in a large skillet or wok. Add the garlic and cook over medium-high heat for 15 seconds. Add the broccoli and cook, stirring, for 1 minute. Add the red and yellow peppers and the white wine and cook, tossing constantly, for about 2 minutes, or until all vegetables are crisp-tender. Season with salt and pepper and set aside at room temperature.
3. When the wheat berries have cooked, drain them well and toss them with the rice wine vinegar, lime juice, and the remaining 1/4 cup of olive oil. Gently blend in the cooked vegetables and scallions and season again, if necessary, with salt and pepper.

FINISHING TOUCHES AND
TABLE PRESENTATION

The wheat berries can be served warm or chilled. Arrange them in a wooden or ceramic salad bowl and garnish the top with strips of red and yellow bell peppers.

THE GRAND FINALE

Peaches Soaked in Honey and Port

MAKES 8 SERVINGS

SPECIAL COOKWARE

*Noncorrosive 3-quart casserole or baking dish, 13 by 9 by
2 inches or larger*

Grated zest of 1 orange
2 cups honey
2 cups port
3 cinnamon sticks
5 whole cloves
8 large ripe peaches, stemmed

GARNISH

16 mint sprigs

1. Combine the orange zest, honey, port, cinnamon
sticks, and cloves in a 2-quart saucepan, stir well, and
bring the syrup to a low boil over medium heat. Stir
until the honey has completely dissolved and continue
cooking until the syrup has thickened, about
12–15 minutes.

2. Slice the peaches in half lengthwise. The knife will
touch the pit in the center as you slice. Twist the
peach halves in opposite directions to separate the pit.

3. Place the peach halves, skin side down, in a
2-inch-deep noncorrosive casserole or baking dish.
Pour the hot port syrup with the cinnamon sticks over
the peaches. Place the peaches, covered, in the
refrigerator for at least 6 hours or overnight. Turn
over the peaches halfway through the soaking period.

FINISHING TOUCHES AND
TABLE PRESENTATION

Place two peach halves in a 1-inch-deep dessert dish,
one skin-side up and the other skin-side down. Pour
3 tablespoons of the syrup around the peaches into each
dish. Garnish with the mint sprigs.

KITCHEN SCHEDULE

2 OR 3 DAYS BEFORE THE PARTY

MAIN EVENT	Swordfish	Prepare the marinade as in step 1; store covered in refrigerator.
TOQUE 1	Noodles	Prepare the dressing as in step 2; store covered in refrigerator.
	Fruit Kabobs	Prepare the marinade as in step 1; store covered in refrigerator.
TOQUE 2	Bread Pudding	Grate Parmigiano; store covered in refrigerator.
GRAND FINALE	Peaches	Prepare syrup through step 2; store covered in refrigerator.

Strategic Maneuvers: Check charcoal supply.

THE DAY BEFORE THE PARTY

MAIN EVENT	Swordfish	Prepare marmalade; store covered in refrigerator.
TOQUE 1	Noodles	Prepare broccoli and green onions; store separately, covered, in refrigerator.
TOQUE 2	Bread Pudding	Make and toast bread cubes, set aside covered at room temperature. Prepare garlic, onion, and shallots; store separately, covered, in refrigerator.
	Wheat Berries	Cook wheat berries, toss with wine vinegar, lime juice, and oil; store covered in refrigerator. Prepare garlic, broccoli, and peppers; store separately, covered, in refrigerator.
GRAND FINALE	Peaches	Prepare through step 4; store covered in refrigerator in the syrup.

Strategic Maneuvers: Fill creamer; cover and store in refrigerator.
Fill sugar bowl.
Set table.
Check ice and beverages.
Locate teas.
Chill wine if white.
Check garnishes for each recipe.
Locate and label all serving bowls, platters, and utensils.

THE DAY OF THE PARTY

MAIN EVENT	Swordfish	Set marinade at room temperature.
TOQUE 1	Noodles	Bring marinade to room temperature. Prepare noodles, toss with marinade, and set aside at room temperature. Prepare broccoli as in step 3; store covered in refrigerator.
	Fruit Kabobs	Prepare fruit and thread kabobs; store in refrigerator on a baking sheet, lightly covered.
TOQUE 2	Bread Pudding	Finish through step 6; remove from water bath and set aside at room temperature.
	Wheat Berries	Sauté vegetables; set aside at room temperature. Set wheat berries at room temperature in serving bowl. Set up garnishes.
GRAND FINALE	Peaches	Arrange in dessert dishes but *do not garnish with mint*; place in refrigerator.

Strategic Maneuvers: Set up charcoal grill.

2 HOURS BEFORE GUESTS ARRIVE:

Marinate and refrigerate swordfish.

Bring marmalade to room temperature and fill serving bowl.

30 MINUTES BEFORE GUESTS ARRIVE:

Light charcoal.

Preheat oven to 300°.

15 MINUTES BEFORE GUESTS ARRIVE:

Finish noodles.

Place bread pudding into water bath; put into oven to rewarm.

Complete wheat berries through step 3 and garnish.

Garnish peaches with mint; set aside at room temperature.

15 MINUTES BEFORE DINNER:

Garnish the bread pudding and set on food table.

Marinate the fruit kabobs.

Plug in coffee.

JUST BEFORE DINNER:

Light candles, check general lighting.

Bring all food to the table.

DINNER SERVICE:

Bring the swordfish out and grill with fruit kabobs in front of the guests.

Serve swordfish from the grill or arrange as instructed in Main Event.

DESSERT SERVICE:

Serve dessert.

Pour coffee.

AFTER SERVICE:

Unplug coffee.

Turn off oven and grill.

A Midsummer Night's Dream. . . of Steak

THE MAIN EVENT:

Grilled New York Strip Steaks, Sautéed Onions, and Champagne

ON THE SIDE:

Stuffed Hot Mini-Bakes

◆

Sugar Snap Peas, Endive, and Radicchio with Roasted Red Pepper Vinaigrette

ON THE SIDE:

Polenta, Mascarpone, and Chipotle Peppers

◆

Romaine, Radishes, and Daikon with Herbed Croutons and Lemon-Lime Vinaigrette

THE GRAND FINALE:

Brandied Strawberries and Bananas with Brandy-Drenched Cake

PALATE TEASER:

Drunken Shrimp with Cilantro and Tequila (page 296)

RECOMMENDED BEVERAGES:

Champagne
Cabernet Sauvignon, Santa Rita (Chile)

THIS IS THE PARTY YOU DREAMED ABOUT LAST JANUARY WHEN the wind blew drifts across the deck and your grill looked like a snowman. Now the air is so still the votive candles on the table barely flicker, and the mingled smell of searing beef and honeysuckle hang over the deck. The pop of a champagne cork is the loudest sound in the yard, other than the chirp of crickets—and you and your guests toast one another for surviving the winter.

When you set a dinner plate with a still-sizzling New York strip steak before each of your guests on a summer evening, they will forget all about winter. And I can assure you that the steaks done "my way" will be long-remembered.

You'll cook the thick-cut strip quickly, seasoned simply with some olive oil, salt, pepper, and a swipe of Dijon mustard. Then you'll gild this perfect piece of meat with a generous pile of buttery soft sautéed onions, nearly caramelized and piqued with jalapenos.

You surely want to try both side-dish menus. The Stuffed Hot Mini-Bakes are a wonderful creation using new potatoes as shells for a mashed potato filling rich with butter, sour cream, and Monterey Jack. For a colorful and crisp foil to the steak and potatoes, there's the one-toque salad of sugar snap peas, endive, and radicchio, drizzled with a crimson roasted red pepper vinaigrette.

On the two-toque menu, the color and spice in the savory polenta come from a different pepper—the chipotle chili. Cooked in chicken stock, the cornmeal is also embellished with mascarpone and Asiago cheeses and fresh basil. You will serve squares of polenta bubbling from the broiler, a glorious accompaniment to the steak. For this menu, I prepare a cool salad of romaine lettuce, radishes, and slices of crunchy daikon, with a bright citrus dressing and croutons seasoned with garlic and cumin.

The dessert tonight is as memorable as the steak: slices of light, orange-flavored sponge cake are topped with a heavenly melting layer of fresh strawberries and bananas quickly cooked in butter in brandy. You can complete the dessert in front of your guests, flaming the fruit right on the grill and lighting up the evening sky.

SETTING THE STAGE

This is a grilled menu that I like to serve with a touch of elegance. Bring your side dishes to an outdoor work table just as the steak is finishing on the grill and prepare a plate for each guest. Real tableware, rather than paper, is both fitting and practical here for the juicy steak. For an evening like this, set a table draped with a neutral cloth, but brighten the scene with an exciting display of summer flowers. Create a fiery centerpiece of hot colored dahlias and zinnias: Boldly mix colors such as bright orange, fuchsia, red, yellow, and tangerine. The flowers will reflect the flames of the grill and the candlelight.

THE MAIN EVENT

Grilled New York Strip Steaks, Sautéed Onions, and Champagne

MAKES 8 SERVINGS

SPECIAL COOKWARE
Charcoal or gas grill

8 New York strip steaks, 10 ounces each, 1 1/2 inches thick
2 tablespoons olive oil
Salt and freshly ground black pepper
6 tablespoons butter
1 pound (about 2 large) Vidalia or Spanish onions, peeled and sliced into 1/4-inch-thick rounds
1 pound (about 2 large) red onions, peeled and sliced into 1/4-inch-thick rounds
1 cup domestic dry champagne
2 serrano or jalapeño chilies, seeds and ribs removed, finely minced, about 3/4–1 ounce
3 tablespoons Dijon mustard

1. Prreheat the oven to 250°.
2. Light the charcoal and wait until the coals are ashy gray, or preheat the gas grill until it's good and hot.
3. Bring the steaks to room temperature, brush them with the olive oil, and season them with salt and pepper.

4. Divide the butter into two large skillets and melt it over medium-low heat. Add 1/2 the Vidalia or Spanish and 1/2 the red onions to each skillet with a pinch of salt and pepper. Stir often, until the onions have separated into individual limp rings and have caramelized to a golden brown color, about 18–25 minutes. Increase the heat to high, add the champagne, and cook briskly for 1–2 minutes, until the champagne has been completely absorbed.
5. Stir half the chilies into each skillet. Simmer the mixture for 1 minute. Season with salt and pepper to taste. (For a milder taste, use half the amount of chilies.)
6. Combine the onions into one skillet, cover, and keep warm in the preheated oven.
7. When the coals are ashy gray, grill the steaks on one side for 4 1/2 minutes. Turn the steaks and spread the grilled side with the mustard. Grill the steaks 4–4 1/2 minutes more for medium-rare.

FINISHING TOUCHES AND
TABLE PRESENTATION

Serve a steak to each guest on individual plates, mustard-coated side down, smothered with the onions. Or, for very casual service, serve the guests directly from the grill as the steaks are ready.

The Inventive Chef

I SERVE THE ONIONS OVER SAUTÉED CALVES' LIVER AND ON JUICY HAMBURGERS. ONION-SMOTHERED HAMBURGERS WITH A TOMATO AND FRESH BASIL SALAD, ALONG WITH YOUNG BUTTERY CORN ON THE COB, IS OUR ULTIMATE SUMMER FEAST.

Stuffed Hot Mini-Bakes

MAKES 8 SERVINGS

24 new potatoes, each about 3 inches in diameter, unpeeled,
  washed, and dried
1 tablespoon vegetable oil
2 tablespoons salted butter
¹/₄ cup sour cream
¹/₃ cup plus ¹/₄ cup grated Monterey Jack with jalapeño
2 tablespoons whole milk
¹/₂ teaspoon salt, or to taste
¹/₄ teaspoon freshly ground pepper, or to taste

1. Preheat the oven to 350°. Cut a thin slice from the bottom of each potato to create a level base. Brush the outside of the potato skins with the oil and place them on a baking sheet. Bake the potatoes for about 35–40 minutes, until they are soft when pierced with a fork.

2. Cool the potatoes at room temperature until they are ready to handle, about 5 minutes. Cut off and discard the tops of the potatoes. Use a small spoon to scoop a well about ³/₄ of the way through the flesh of each potato, leaving about ¹/₂ inch of thickness. Place the scooped-out flesh in the bowl of an electric mixer and place the potato-skin shells back on the baking sheet.

3. Add the butter, sour cream, ¹/₃ cup of the cheese, and the milk to the potato flesh, and using the paddle attachment, beat the mixture on medium speed until it is smooth and creamy. *(Add more milk if you like the mashed potatoes fluffier.)* Season with the salt and pepper to taste.

4. Using a teaspoon, heap the mashed potatoes into the potato shells. Sprinkle the tops with the remaining cheese, and bake the potatoes for 20 minutes, or until they are heated through and lightly browned.

FINISHING TOUCHES AND
TABLE PRESENTATION

Serve each guest 3 potatoes with the steak, or place the potatoes on a flat basket or tray. Make self-service easy by supplying tongs for the potatoes.

Sugar Snap Peas, Endive, and Radicchio with Roasted Red Pepper Vinaigrette

MAKES 8 SERVINGS

1 large red bell pepper
1 large clove garlic, peeled, and coarsely chopped
3 tablespoons red wine vinegar
¹/₂ teaspoon green peppercorns, drained and rinsed if packed
  in brine
¹/₂ cup olive oil
¹/₄ teaspoon salt, or to taste
1 pound sugar snap peas, stemmed
2 small radicchio, cored, leaves separated, washed,
  and dried
3 endive, trimmed and separated into petals

1. Preheat the broiler. Place the whole red pepper on a baking sheet and put it about 3–4 inches from the broiler. Broil the pepper on two sides, turning with tongs or a kitchen fork until it has blackened, about 5 minutes. Place the pepper in a large bowl and quickly seal the top of the bowl with plastic wrap to hold in the steam. Let the pepper steam under the plastic wrap for 20 minutes. Remove the plastic wrap and allow the pepper to cool, then peel back and discard the skin. Slice the pepper in half and remove and discard the seeds and pith.

2. Place the roasted pepper, garlic, red wine vinegar, and peppercorns in the bowl of a food processor fitted with the knife blade and process until the mixture is smooth. With the processor on, slowly pour the olive oil through the feeding tube until the dressing has thickened. Season with the salt and pepper and set aside.

3. Bring 4 cups of water to a boil in a medium-size saucepan over high heat. Place the sugar snap peas in the saucepan and simmer 30 seconds. Drain off the hot water and shock the peas under running cold tap water. Dry the peas on paper towels.

FINISHING TOUCHES AND
TABLE PRESENTATION

Alternate the radicchio and endive leaves around the edge of an oval or round platter. Place the snap peas in the center. Dress the salad with a plastic squeeze bottle filled with the reserved vinaigrette, or use a tablespoon to drizzle the vinaigrette over the vegetables.

The Inventive Chef

TRY THIS DRESSING ON HERO SANDWICHES OR A COLD PASTA SALAD. ONCE YOU HAVE LEARNED TO ROAST PEPPERS, YOU WILL BE HOOKED ON THE SMOKY TASTE.

ON THE SIDE

Polenta, Mascarpone, and Chipotle Peppers

MAKES 8 SERVINGS

4 tablespoons olive oil
1 large white onion, peeled and finely minced
6 cups homemade or low-sodium canned chicken broth
2 cups cornmeal
1/2 tablespoon pureed dried chipotle pepper
  (about 1 pepper)♦
4 ounces mascarpone, at room temperature
4 tablespoons salted butter, at room temperature
2 tablespoons finely chopped fresh basil
1 teaspoon salt
1/4 teaspoon freshly ground black pepper
1/2 cup freshly grated Asiago

GARNISH
1/4 cup freshly grated Asiago

♦To reconstitute the chipotle, soak it in warm water to cover for 30 minutes. Drain the water, cut the pepper in half, and remove the seeds. Pulse the pepper in a food processor fitted with the knife blade until pureed, scraping down the bowl with a rubber spatula.

1. Grease a large baking sheet with sides with 2 tablespoons of olive oil.

2. Heat the remaining olive oil in a large saucepan and sauté the onion until it is wilted and translucent. Add the chicken broth and bring to a boil over medium-high heat.

3. When the liquid comes to a boil, lower the heat and immediately add the cornmeal in a steady stream, whisking it constantly with a wire whisk. *(If you add the cornmeal all at once, it will become lumpy.)* Simmer the polenta, stirring often with a wooden spoon, until it pulls away from the sides of the pan and is very thick, about 15–20 minutes.

4. When the polenta has cooked and is steaming hot, add the pureed chipotle pepper, mascarpone, butter, basil, salt, and pepper. Remove from the heat and blend well.

5. Spread the polenta about 1 1/2 inches thick onto the greased baking sheet. Cover and refrigerate the polenta for 2 hours or overnight.

6. Preheat the broiler. Cut the polenta into 2-inch squares and sprinkle it well with the 1/2 cup of Asiago. Broil the squares until they are hot and the cheese is bubbly, about 3–4 minutes.

FINISHING TOUCHES AND TABLE PRESENTATION

Place a polenta square on each dinner plate or arrange the squares on a large, colorful platter. Scatter the 1/4 cup of Asiago over the top and serve piping hot. The juicy steaks and sautéed onions look mouth-wateringly enticing surrounded by the polenta squares.

ON THE SIDE

Romaine, Radishes, and Daikon with Herbed Croutons and Lemon-Lime Vinaigrette

MAKES 8 SERVINGS

THE CROUTONS

4 tablespoons salted butter
1 large clove garlic, peeled and finely minced
1/4 teaspoon ground cumin
1/2 teaspoon salt
1/4 teaspoon freshly ground black pepper
1 small French bread, two days old, cut into
*   1-inch cubes*

THE SALAD

1 1/2 pounds (about 2 large heads) romaine lettuce, washed
*   and torn into bite-size pieces*
10 large red radishes, trimmed, washed, cut in half, and
*   sliced thin*
1 medium daikon, peeled, cut in half lengthwise, and sliced
*   into 1/4-inch semicircles*

1. Preheat the oven to 400°.

2. Heat the butter in a small sauté pan over medium-high heat. Add the garlic and sauté for 30 seconds. Stir in the cumin, salt, and pepper and blend well.

3. Place the bread cubes in a large bowl and toss to coat them well with the seasoned butter. Transfer the cubes to a baking sheet and bake them for 5–8 minutes, until golden and crisp. Set aside at room temperature.

FINISHING TOUCHES AND TABLE PRESENTATION

In a large wooden or terra-cotta salad bowl, toss the romaine, radishes, and daikon together with the vinaigrette. Scatter the croutons throughout and over the top of the salad.

> *The Inventive Chef*
>
> TRY THIS SALAD WITH ASIAN FOOD. THE CRISPNESS AND TANG OF THE RADISHES SEEM TO ACT AS A PERFECT FOIL FOR EXOTIC SEASONINGS. WE ALSO CRUNCH ON THIS SALAD WITH THE GRILLED SWORDFISH (PAGE 188).

Lemon-Lime Vinaigrette

MAKES ABOUT ²/₃ CUP

1 tablespoon fresh lemon juice
1 tablespoon fresh lime juice
1 teaspoon Dijon mustard

3 tablespoons fresh orange juice
¹/₂ teaspoon well-drained white horseradish
¹/₂ cup olive oil
2 tablespoons finely chopped chives
¹/₄ teaspoon salt, or to taste
¹/₈ teaspoon freshly ground black pepper, or to taste

1. Put the lemon juice, lime juice, mustard, orange juice, and horseradish in the bowl of a food processor and process with the knife blade to blend the ingredients.

2. With the motor running, add the olive oil slowly through the feeding tube until the dressing has thickened. Stir in the chopped chives and season with salt and pepper to taste.

> *The Inventive Chef*
>
> THE NATURAL FLAVORS IN FISH EXPLODE WITH FRESHNESS WHEN YOU USE THIS VINAIGRETTE AS A MARINADE BEFORE GRILLING.

THE GRAND FINALE

Brandied Strawberries and Bananas with Brandy-Drenched Cake

MAKES 8 SERVINGS

SPECIAL COOKWARE
9-inch springform pan

THE CAKE
2 teaspoons vegetable oil
8 eggs, separated, at room temperature

2 cups sifted sugar

1/2 cup fresh orange juice, heated to a simmer

1 1/2 teaspoons pure vanilla extract

1/2 teaspoon almond extract

4 tablespoons brandy, or orange liqueur, triple sec, or Cointreau

2 cups cake flour, sifted

1 pinch salt

1/4 teaspoon cream of tartar

THE FRUIT

1 1/2 quarts strawberries

5 ripe bananas

1/4 cup unsalted butter

1/4 cup granulated sugar

1/2 cup light brown sugar

3 tablespoons fresh lemon juice

1 tablespoon finely grated lemon zest

1/4–1/3 cup brandy or orange liqueur, or to taste

1. Preheat the oven to 350°. Lightly grease and flour a 9-inch springform pan.

2. In the bowl of an electric mixer, using the whip attachment, beat the egg yolks until they have thickened and are a bright lemon color, about 3 minutes. Slowly add the sugar and continue beating 3 minutes more.

3. With the mixer on, gradually add the hot orange juice in a slow stream. *(If you add it too fast, the eggs will scramble.)* Beat until the mixture has cooled to room temperature, about 1 minute. Add the vanilla, almond extract, 2 tablespoons of the liqueur and beat to mix.

4. With the beater on low, gradually add the flour to the yolk batter. Mix gently until the ingredients are blended.

5. In a clean bowl, beat the egg whites with the whisk attachment of an electric mixer until foamy,

about 1 minute. Add the salt and cream of tartar and continue to whip until the whites are stiff but not dry, about 2 minutes more. Using a rubber spatula, gently fold the egg whites into the cake batter. Pour the mixture into the prepared cake pan and bake on the middle rack of the oven for 35–45 minutes, or until the cake is golden and a tester inserted in the center comes out clean. Cool to room temperature in the pan set on a cooling rack.

6. Run a thin metal spatula or sharp flat knife between the cake and the edge of the cake pan to loosen the cake. Open the spring mechanism and invert the cake onto a cooling rack.

7. Slice the cake in half horizontally with a serrated knife. Brush each half with the remaining liqueur and cut each half into 4 wedges.

8. Stem the strawberries and cut them in half lengthwise. Peel the bananas and cut them on the bias into 1 1/2-inch wedges.

9. Warm the butter in a large skillet. Add the granulated sugar and warm it over medium heat for 3 minutes, or until the sugar starts to brown and caramelize. Immediately add the banana slices, the brown sugar, lemon juice, and zest. Gently turn the bananas as they cook and begin to turn a golden brown, about 2 minutes. Set aside at room temperature. This all can be done on the grill.

Place wedges of the cake in the bottom of each balloon glasses or large dessert bowls. Place the strawberries and brandy in bowls and bring out to the grill. Bring the dessert wine glasses or bowls out to the grill. Place the skillet with the caramelized bananas on the grill and heat until bubbly. Add the strawberries and warm the fruits, stirring for 1 minute. To flambé the fruit, pour the brandy carefully into the skillet and light it with a match. Stir until the alcohol stops burning. Immediately spoon the warm fruits into the glasses.

The Inventive Chef

THE GOOD NEWS IS THAT YOU *CAN* FREEZE THE CAKE. THIS RECIPE WORKS PERFECTLY FOR A JELLY ROLL. BAKE THE CAKE ON AN 11-BY-17-INCH JELLY ROLL PAN. SPRINKLE A KITCHEN TOWEL WITH CONFECTIONERS' SUGAR. INVERT THE CAKE FROM THE WIRE RACK ONTO THE TOWEL. IMMEDIATELY ROLL THE CAKE.

KITCHEN SCHEDULE

2 OR 3 DAYS BEFORE THE PARTY

MAIN EVENT	Steak	Check charcoal supply; clean grill.
TOQUE 1	Mini-Bakes	Grate Monterey Jack; store covered in refrigerator.
	Sugar Snaps	Prepare vinaigrette through step 2; store covered in refrigerator.
TOQUE 2	Polenta	Reconstitute chipotle; store covered in refrigerator. Grate Asiago; store covered in refrigerator.
	Romaine Salad	Prepare lemon-lime vinaigrette; store covered in refrigerator.
GRAND FINALE	Cake	Prepare cake through step 5; cool and refrigerate well covered, or freeze up to 7 days ahead.

THE DAY BEFORE THE PARTY

MAIN EVENT	Steak	Peel and slice onions; store covered in refrigerator. Mince serrano or jalapeño chilies; store covered in refrigerator.
TOQUE 1	Sugar Snaps	Snap and stem peas; store covered in refrigerator. Prepare radicchio; store covered in refrigerator.
TOQUE 2	Polenta	Complete recipe through step 5; store covered in refrigerator.
	Romaine Salad	Prepare romaine, radishes, and daikon; store covered in refrigerator.

GRAND FINALE	Cake	If cake is frozen, defrost overnight in refrigerator.
Strategic Maneuvers:		Fill creamer; cover and store in refrigerator. Fill sugar bowl. Set table. Set up table decor. Check ice and beverages. Locate teas. Chill champagne and wine if white. Check garnishes for each recipe. Locate and label all serving bowls, platters, and utensils. Set up charcoal grill.

THE DAY OF THE PARTY

MAIN EVENT	Steak	Prepare onions and chilies as in steps 4–5; set aside at room temperature.
TOQUE 1	Mini-Bakes	Prepare through step 4 and set aside.
	Sugar Snaps	Prepare endive. Prepare peas as in step 3. Arrange salad but do not dress; store covered in refrigerator. Bring vinaigrette to room temperature.
TOQUE 2	Polenta	Cut into squares, sprinkle with cheese, and set up for broiling.
	Romaine Salad	Prepare croutons and set aside at room temperature. Toss salad in bowl but *do not dress;* store covered in refrigerator.

GRAND FINALE Cake   Prepare steps 6–7; cover well
and set aside at room
temperature.
Prepare strawberries as in step
8; store covered in refrigerator.
Arrange bananas on a tray. Set
all ingredients for flambéing in
bowls on a tray.

30 MINUTES BEFORE GUESTS ARRIVE:

Preheat broiler.
Open wine if red.

10 MINUTES BEFORE GUESTS ARRIVE:

Light charcoal.
Broil polenta. Set aside at room
temperature.
Preheat oven to 325°.
Season steaks; set aside at room
temperature.

30 MINUTES BEFORE DINNER:

Warm mini-bakes in oven,
covered in foil.
Reheat onions in oven.

15 MINUTES BEFORE DINNER:

Plug in coffee.
Uncork champagne.

Toss sugar snap peas or romaine
salad and place on table.
Light candles, check general
lighting.

DINNER SERVICE:

As guests watch steaks broil,
warm polenta in oven, and load
up the groaning board with all
the food.

BEFORE DESSERT SERVICE:

Prepare step 9 and the finishing
touches on the grill in front of
your guests.

DESSERT SERVICE:

Serve dessert.
Pour coffee.

AFTER SERVICE:

Unplug coffee.
Turn off oven and grill.

Southern Comfort
on an August Afternoon

THE MAIN EVENTS:

Spicy Barbecued Spareribs
Cajun-Rubbed Grilled Shrimp
and Sea Scallops

ON THE SIDE:

Red-hot Hush Puppies

◆

Red Lentils, Scallions, and Peppery Pecan Salad

◆

Beefsteak Tomatoes, Red Onion, and Basil (page 150)

ON THE SIDE:

Black-eyed Peas and Avocado Salad (page 63)

◆

Bourbon-Buttered Grilled Corn on the Cob

◆

Cheesy Biscuits

THE GRAND FINALE:
Coconut-Crusted Sweet Potato Pie

PALATE TEASER:
Zucchini and Spinach-Tortellini Skewers (page 298)

BEVERAGE RECOMMENDATIONS:
Peach Sangria (page 375)
Pinot Noir, Mondavi

*S*T'S A MIDSUMMER AFTERNOON AND THE HEAT IS FEARSOME. The kids are running under the lawn sprinklers—and a few of your guests are there, too, not running though but lying in the wet grass, sipping peach sangria, and watching the sprinkler arc across the flower beds. It's a lazy day for the host, too: Dinner's all done, except for the biscuits baking in the oven, and you are sitting in a chaise, watching the smoke curl up from the heating charcoal. When the shadow of the maple tree covers the picnic table, you tell yourself, you'll flip that big pile of baby-back ribs, soaked with spicy marinade, onto the grill—and take a run through the sprinkler.

I love spicy barbecue, and while the Main Event baby-back pork ribs on this menu are not slow-smoked in the classic manner, they are finger-licking delectable. Given a brief period of par-boiling, a long marinade in "Abigail's original" marvelous marinade, and a spell on the grill, the pork is extraordinarily tender and flavorful. You will use my original—a tomato-based sauce with ginger, molasses, brown sugar, balsamic vinegar, a generous dose of Tabasco, and a host of other sea-sonings—as a marinade, a mop for the ribs on the grill, and a table sauce. Pass the paper napkins!

The Main Event grilled shrimp and sea scal-lops are inspired by the Cajun cookery of Louisiana. The shellfish are quickly coated in a tangy dry-rub of onion powder, garlic, paprika, cumin, and cayenne, then skewered and quickly grilled. (They will take just a few minutes after the ribs are done.)

I have adapted Southern traditions for my tangy sides, offering two wonderful bean salads, two terrific "breads," and a pair of perfect sum-mer vegetables. On the one-toque menu, you'll find an unusual lentil salad with big flavors, great

textures, and some nice surprises. The lovely red lentils are mixed with scallions and cool cucumber bits and tossed in a knockout dressing loaded with mustard, horseradish, and red wine vinegar. The surprises are peppery pecans that give crunch and heat to the salad. Southern bean cookery also in-spires my black-eyed peas, cooked in chicken broth and wine, cooled, mixed with yellow pep-pers and radishes, and then spiced up with a dressing of cumin, cilantro, brown sugar, and lime juice. The neat surprises here are soft chunks of ripe avocado.

The breads are also takes on Southern spe-cialties. Red-hot Hush Puppies are light and lus-cious fried corn breads, sparked with cayenne, paprika, and scallion. You will need to deep-fry them close to mealtime, but they can be held in the oven while you attend to the ribs. The Cheesy Biscuits are enriched with Parmigiano and Cheddar and come out of the oven puffed, golden, and bursting with melted cheese. Both hush pup-pies and biscuits are great for mopping up and dunking in the barbecue sauce (and they are fun to make, too).

This summer menu is completed with either juicy slices of beefsteak tomatoes, red onions, and basil (one-toque) or grilled corn on the cob with bourbon butter (two-toque). Cooking fresh corn right on the grill produces ears with a terrific smoky-sweet flavor.

When the afternoon finally cools into evening, serve up the Coconut-Crusted Sweet Potato Pie. The shell is made from sweet coconut and is a perfect base for the light and spicy custard, topped with Ginger Whipped Cream.

SETTING THE STAGE

This is one party where rustic fixings are fine. Have plenty of napkins or paper towels on hand, and, if you want to give everyone a giggle (and a welcome touch) offer finger bowls filled with water and a slice of lemon. The Old South was never so relaxed.

Spicy Barbecued Spareribs

MAKES 8 SERVINGS

SPECIAL COOKWARE
Charcoal or gas grill

6 tablespoons peanut oil
2 large onions, peeled and finely chopped
5 cloves garlic, peeled and finely minced
4 (1-pound) cans peeled imported plum tomatoes, with their juices
1 tablespoon tomato paste
1 tablespoon chili powder
2 tablespoons finely minced fresh ginger
3 tablespoons Dijon mustard
1 cup light brown sugar
1 cup molasses
Grated zest of 2 lemons (about 2 teaspoons)
$1/4$ cup balsamic vinegar
2 teaspoons Tabasco sauce
Salt to taste
Freshly ground black pepper to taste
8 baby back pork rib racks, about $1^3/4$ pounds each
1 large yellow onion, peeled and studded with 6 whole cloves
4 large cloves garlic, unpeeled, smashed with a knife

1. Heat the oil in a large saucepan over high heat. Add the chopped onions and sauté for 3 minutes. Add the minced garlic and sauté for 1 minute more. Add the plum tomatoes with their juices, the tomato paste, chili powder, ginger, mustard, brown sugar, molasses, lemon zest, balsamic vinegar, and Tabasco sauce. Bring the marinade to a boil, lower the heat to medium-low, and simmer for 45 minutes. Taste and add salt and pepper to taste.

2. Cool the marinade to room temperature. Pour half the marinade into the bowl of a food processor fitted with the knife blade and pulse until you have a slightly chunky, thickened marinade. Repeat the process with the remaining marinade, leaving it in two batches. *(One batch will be used to marinate, the other will be served with the cooked ribs.)* Refrigerate the marinade reserved for serving with the ribs.

3. While the marinade is simmering, place the ribs in one or two large stockpots and cover them with water. Add the clove-studded onion and smashed garlic cloves and bring the water to a simmer over medium heat. *(If using two saucepans, divide the onion and garlic between the two.)* Simmer the ribs for 30 minutes. Skim and discard any foam that may form as the ribs cook. Cool the ribs for 15 minutes in the liquid and place on baking pans. Discard the cooking liquid.

4. Brush both sides of the ribs generously with marinade, cover, and refrigerate for at least 2 hours or overnight.

5. Bring the ribs to room temperature and sprinkle them with salt and pepper. Prepare the grill, allowing the coals to burn to a gray color. Rebrush the ribs with marinade and place them on the grill, meaty side up. Grill the ribs for 8–10 minutes. Turn them, brush again with marinade, and grill until the ribs are heated through and a crusty brown, about 8–10 minutes more.

6. Warm the refrigerated marinade over medium heat and set it aside to serve with the cooked ribs.

FINISHING TOUCHES AND TABLE PRESENTATION

Place the warm marinade in a pottery bowl with a ladle on the food table. Serve one whole rack of ribs to each guest, right from the grill.

Cajun-Rubbed Grilled Shrimp and Sea Scallops

MAKES 8 SERVINGS

SPECIAL COOKWARE
Charcoal or gas grill
8 (8–10-inch) wooden skewers, soaked in water, or metal skewers

THE SPICE RUB
1 tablespoon onion powder
1 tablespoon garlic powder
1 1/2 teaspoons paprika
1 1/8 teaspoons salt
1/2 teaspoon cumin
1/4 teaspoon cayenne pepper

THE SEAFOOD
16 sea scallops (approximately 1 1/4 pounds)◆
24 large shrimp (under 15 count, approximately 2 pounds) peeled, deveined, tails removed
2 tablespoons olive oil

GARNISH
1/4 cup fresh lemon juice (from 1 large lemon)
2 lemons, halved, cut into 1/8-inch wedges

◆Remove and discard the tough muscle attached to the sea scallops.

1. Make the spice rub by combining the onion powder, garlic powder, paprika, salt, cumin, and cayenne in a small bowl. Set aside.

2. Spread the spice rub in the center of a large (approximately 14-by-12-inch) piece of aluminum foil.

Lightly press and coat both sides of the shrimp and scallops with the rub.

3. Light the charcoal and wait until the coals are ashy gray, or preheat the gas grill to high. Oil the grill grate.

4. Thread a skewer through the center of one shrimp and one scallop. Add a second shrimp and scallop and finish the skewer with a third shrimp. Continue this process until you have completed 8 seafood skewers.

5. Lightly brush both sides of each of the skewers with olive oil and place them on the oiled hot grill for about 2 minutes. Turn and grill 2 minutes longer, or until the seafood is opaque.

FINISHING TOUCHES AND TABLE PRESENTATION

Remove the skewers to a long, narrow serving platter, sprinkle them with the lemon juice, and garnish with the lemon wedges; or hand the skewers to your guests right off the grill.

ON THE SIDE
Red-hot Hush Puppies

MAKES ABOUT 36 HUSH PUPPIES

SPECIAL COOKWARE
Deep-fat-frying thermometer

1 1/2 cups yellow cornmeal
1/2 cup all-purpose flour
2 teaspoons baking powder
1/4 teaspoon cayenne pepper

1/4 teaspoon paprika
1 teaspoon salt
4 scallions, white and green parts, finely chopped
1/2 cup whole milk
1/2 cup buttermilk
1 egg, lightly beaten
Vegetable oil for deep-frying

1. In a medium bowl, sift together the cornmeal, flour, baking powder, cayenne pepper, paprika, and salt.

2. Add the scallions, whole milk, buttermilk, and egg to the dry ingredients. Stir until the ingredients are well mixed and the batter is thick. Set aside at room temperature for 10 minutes.

3. Heat 2–3 inches of oil in a large skillet until the deep-fat-frying thermometer reaches 325°. Drop the batter by teaspoons into the oil and fry for about 1 1/2 minutes, turning once, until the hush puppies are golden brown on both sides and just cooked through. *(Do not overcrowd the pan.)* Drain the hush puppies on paper towels and serve hot.

FINISHING TOUCHES AND TABLE PRESENTATION

Pile the hush puppies in a colorful cloth-lined basket.

Red Lentils, Scallions, and Peppery Pecan Salad

MAKES 8 SERVINGS

THE PEPPERY PECANS

3 tablespoons vegetable oil

1 1/2 teaspoons peeled and finely minced garlic (about
    1 large clove)

3/4 teaspoon cayenne pepper

1/4 teaspoon white pepper

3/4 teaspoon salt

1 teaspoon sugar

1 1/4 cups coarsely chopped pecan halves

THE SALAD

1 1/2 quarts homemade or low-sodium canned chicken broth

1 large onion, peeled and studded with 8 cloves

2 bay leaves

1 pound red lentils

1/4 cup red wine vinegar

4 teaspoons Dijon mustard

2 teaspoons well-drained white horseradish

1/2 teaspoon salt

1/4 teaspoon freshly ground black pepper

2/3 cup olive oil

8 scallions, sliced in 1/8-inch circles (about 3/4 cup)

1/4 cup finely chopped flat-leaf parsley

1 large cucumber, peeled, sliced in half lengthwise, seeded,
    and cut into 1/4-inch dice

1. Preheat the oven to 350°.

2. To make the pecans, heat the oil in a small saucepan over medium-low heat. Add the garlic, cayenne, white pepper, and salt. Stir the spices for one minute. Remove from heat and cool before stirring in the sugar.

3. Toss the pecans with the spice mixture, making certain all the nuts are well coated. Scatter the nuts in one layer on a baking sheet and bake for 8–10 minutes, until toasted. Set aside at room temperature.

4. While the pecans are baking, heat the chicken broth in a large stockpot over high heat until it begins to simmer. Add the clove-studded onion, the bay leaves, and the lentils. Reduce the heat and simmer the lentils for about 10–12 minutes or until they are tender but crisp to the bite. Drain the lentils. *(You may want to reserve the flavorful stock for making a soup at a later date.)* Discard the bay leaves and the onion. Shock the lentils briefly under cold running water.

5. In a medium-size bowl, whisk together the vinegar, mustard, horseradish, salt, and pepper. Blend well, and continue to whisk while slowly adding the olive oil in a steady stream until the dressing is well combined and thickened. Set aside at room temperature.

FINISHING TOUCHES AND TABLE PRESENTATION

Toss the cooked lentils, scallions, parsley, cucumbers, and baked pecans in a large salad bowl 2 hours before the barbecue. Dress with half the vinaigrette. The lentils will absorb the dressing and all the spices in the pecans to give them an electric flavor. Just before serving, toss with the remaining vinaigrette and adjust seasonings.

A Savory Seduction on Sadie Hawkins Day

A King of Roasts for a Beef-Loving Boss

An Italian Buffet for the Festival of Festivals

Southern Comfort on an August Afternoon

Making Mom's Day with Italian Delights

Sundays in the Kitchen with Friends

St. Patrick's Day Dinner by the Bite

The Team Takes Over the Ice Cream Counter

Bourbon-Buttered Grilled Corn on the Cob

MAKES 8 SERVINGS

8 large or 16 small ears corn
  (depending on availability)
1 cup salted butter
²/₃ cup bourbon
¹/₄ cup minced flat-leaf parsley
1¹/₂ teaspoons salt, or to taste
³/₄ teaspoon freshly ground black pepper, or to taste

1. Pull the husks down to the end of each ear of corn, but do not remove them. Remove and discard the silk. Re-cover the corn with the husks.

2. Soak the husks by placing the corn, stem side down, in 1 or 2 large stockpots ³/₄ full of cold water. (*The husks will absorb water while the corn stays dry.*) Set aside to soak for ¹/₂ hour.

3. While the corn husks are soaking, melt the butter in a small saucepan over medium-low heat. Add the bourbon, parsley, salt, and pepper and heat just to warm through, about 45 seconds. Set aside.

4. Light the charcoal grill and wait until the coals are ashy gray, or preheat the gas grill to high.

5. Remove the corn from the water. Shake off any excess water from the leaves and pull down the husks. Generously brush each ear of corn with the warm butter. Bring the remaining butter to the grill to keep warm.

6. Replace the husks by pulling them back up around each ear of buttered corn, and place the ears on the hot grill.

7. Cook the corn on the grill for about 20–25 minutes, turning them with tongs or a long grill fork every 5 minutes so that the ears cook evenly and the husks have a charcoal-grilled look.

FINISHING TOUCHES AND TABLE PRESENTATION

I like to serve the corn right in their husks. Wrap them in foil to keep warm as ribs are grilling. Arrange the grilled corn in a flat basket for guests to help themselves. Pour the butter into a small crock and pass it with a pastry brush.

Cheesy Biscuits

MAKES ABOUT 15 BISCUITS

SPECIAL COOKWARE
2¹/₂-inch biscuit cutter
Pastry blender

4 cups self-rising flour
¹/₂ tablespoon baking powder
¹/₂ teaspoon cayenne pepper
2 tablespoons grated Parmigiano Reggiano
2 cups grated extra-sharp Cheddar
1 cup vegetable shortening
1¹/₂ cups buttermilk

1. Preheat the oven to 425°.

2. Mix the flour, baking powder, and cayenne pepper together in a mixing bowl.

3. Add the Parmigiano Reggiano, 1 cup of the Cheddar, and the vegetable shortening. Combine the ingredients with a pastry blender or your fingers until the dough resembles coarse cornmeal.

4. Make a well in the center of the mixture and pour in the buttermilk all at once. Using your hands or a wooden spoon, quickly incorporate the milk to form a soft and slightly wet dough. (*Be careful not to overwork the dough or the biscuits will be tough.*)

5. Gather the dough into a ball and knead it on a lightly floured board for 30 seconds to obtain a consistent soft texture. With floured fingers, flatten the dough into a $1/2$-inch-thick circle. Cut the dough into $2^1/2$-inch biscuits. (*Gather leftover scraps to make more biscuits. The biscuits made from dough scraps may be a little tough, as the dough has been worked more.*)

6. Place the biscuits on a baking sheet, allowing $1^1/2$ inches between them. Bake for 8 minutes. Remove the biscuits from the oven and place 1 tablespoon of the remaining Cheddar cheese on top of each one. Return the biscuits to the hot oven and continue cooking for 4–5 minutes, or until the cheese is thoroughly melted and the biscuits are puffed and golden. Cool on a cake rack for 2 minutes.

FINISHING TOUCHES AND
TABLE PRESENTATION

Pile the biscuits in a napkin-lined basket. A good idea is to fill two baskets and set one at each end of the table.

THE GRAND FINALE

Coconut-Crusted Sweet Potato Pie

YIELDS 1 PIE, 8 SERVINGS

THE FILLING

2 cups warm, cooked sweet potato (about $1^1/2$ pounds)
5 eggs, separated
4 tablespoons sweet butter, at room temperature
$1/2$ cup light brown sugar, firmly packed
$1/4$ cup maple syrup
$1/2$ teaspoon ground cinnamon
$1/8$ teaspoon ground cloves
$1/2$ teaspoon powdered ginger
3 tablespoons Southern Comfort or peach brandy
$1/4$ teaspoon almond extract
$1/4$ teaspoon lemon extract
Salt
Pinch of black pepper

THE CRUST

1 recipe baked Coconut-Crusted Tart Shell (recipe follows)

GARNISH

Ginger Whipped Cream (page 101)

1. Preheat the oven to 425°.

2. Place the warm cooked potatoes in the bowl of an electric mixer and beat with the paddle attachment until perfectly smooth, about 5 minutes.

3. In a separate bowl, beat the egg yolks with a whisk until a light lemon color, then stir them into the sweet potatoes.

4. Add the butter, brown sugar, maple syrup, cinnamon, cloves, ginger, Southern Comfort, almond

and lemon extracts, and a pinch of salt and pepper. Beat the potatoes for 2–3 minutes.

5. Using a clean bowl and the whisk attachment of the electric mixer on medium speed, whip the egg whites with a pinch of salt until the whites hold a soft peak.

6. Gently fold the egg whites into the sweet-potato mixture. Pour the mixture into the prepared pie shell and bake for 30–40 minutes, until a knife inserted in the center comes out clean. Cool the pie for 30 minutes on a cooling rack.

FINISHING TOUCHES AND TABLE PRESENTATION

Remove the pie from the tart pan and place it on a 12–14-inch round serving platter. Bring the pie to the table with a bowl of Ginger Whipped Cream on the side. Serve the pie at room temperature.

Coconut-Crusted Tart Shell

MAKES 1 TART SHELL

SPECIAL COOKWARE
9-inch tart pan with removable bottom

1 tablespoon unsalted butter
2 cups sweetened coconut flakes, purchased in markets
2 tablespoons all-purpose flour
¹/₂ teaspoon salt
2 large egg whites
¹/₃ cup sugar

1. Preheat the oven to 375°. Butter the bottom and sides of a 9-inch tart pan with a removable bottom.

2. Toss together the coconut, flour, and salt in a medium-size bowl. In another bowl, whisk together the egg whites and sugar until the mixture is foamy. Combine the coconut and egg white mixtures until they are well blended.

3. Using a rubber spatula or your fingers, spread the bottom and sides of the tart pan with the coconut mixture. Bake in the upper third of the oven for 20–28 minutes, or until the crust is deep golden around the edges, light golden in the center, and firm to the touch. Cool on a cake rack for 20 minutes.

KITCHEN SCHEDULE

2 OR 3 DAYS BEFORE THE PARTY

MAIN EVENT	Spareribs	Prepare marinade through step 2.
	Shrimp and Scallops	Prepare rub as in step 1; set aside in bowl, covered, at room temperature.
TOQUE 1	Lentils	Prepare pecans through step 3; store covered in refrigerator.
TOQUE 2	Biscuits	Grate Parmigiano and Cheddar; store covered in refrigerator.
Strategic Maneuvers:		Check charcoal supply; clean grill.

THE DAY BEFORE THE PARTY

MAIN EVENT	Spareribs	Prepare ribs as directed in steps 3–4; store covered in refrigerator.
TOQUE 1	Lentils	Prepare lentils as in step 4; store covered in refrigerator.
TOQUE 2	Black-eyed Peas	Prepare through step 2; toss with the oil, cumin, cilantro, lime juice, and brown sugar; store covered in refrigerator. Trim and cut yellow pepper, radishes, and scallions; store covered in refrigerator.
	Corn	Make the bourbon butter as directed in step 3.
GRAND FINALE	Pie	Prepare and bake tart shell; set aside, covered, at room temperature.
Strategic Maneuvers:		Fill creamer; cover and store in refrigerator. Fill sugar bowl. Set table.

Check ice and beverages.
Locate teas.
Chill wine if white.
Check garnishes for each recipe.
Locate and label all serving bowls, platters, and utensils.
Set up charcoal grill.

THE DAY OF THE PARTY

MAIN EVENT	Spareribs	Bring to room temperature, sprinkle with salt and pepper, brush with marinade, and set aside. Set serving marinade in saucepan for warming.
	Shrimp and Scallops	Coat with rub; skewer as directed in step 4; store wrapped in plastic in refrigerator.
TOQUE 1	Hush Puppies	Blend dry ingredients and set aside. Prepare scallions and set aside. Measure and refrigerate, covered, wet ingredients. Store covered in refrigerator.
	Lentils	Prepare step 5; set aside at room temperature.
TOQUE 2	Black-eyed Peas	Finish recipe; store covered in refrigerator.
	Corn	Prepare steps 1, 2, and 5.
GRAND FINALE	Pie	Prepare through step 6; cool, cover, and refrigerate. Whip ginger cream; store covered in refrigerator.

30 MINUTES BEFORE GUESTS ARRIVE:

Preheat oven to 425°.

Prepare hush-puppy batter as in step 2 and refrigerate; set up frying pan.

Finish lentil or black-eyed pea salad.

Finish forming biscuits, put on baking sheet, refrigerate, and bake. Cool to room temperature.

45 MINUTES BEFORE DINNER:

Light charcoal.

Warm marinade sauce for ribs.

20 MINUTES BEFORE DINNER:

Put corn on grill.

15 MINUTES BEFORE DINNER:

Plug in coffee.

Have kitchen helper fry hush puppies. (*If no kitchen helper, fry them just before guests arrive and keep warm in a very low oven.*)

Brush shrimp and scallops with olive oil.

Dress lentils.

Blend avocado into black-eyed peas.

Bring all the food out to the barbecue.

Take corn off grill, cover with foil to keep warm, and grill ribs.

Light candles, check general lighting.

DINNER SERVICE:

When ribs come off grill, brush shrimp-and-scallop skewers with olive oil and grill. Serve ribs from grill and hand guests seafood skewers.

20 MINUTES BEFORE DESSERT:

Bring pie to room temperature.

DESSERT SERVICE:

Serve pie.

Don't forget whipped cream.

Pour coffee.

AFTER SERVICE:

Unplug coffee.

Turn off oven and grill.

The Warmth and Comfort of Family Dinners

Of all the things in life there are to celebrate (and you should know by now that I love celebrations), the most important to me, by far, is family. Whenever my far-flung family gets together—for an annual holiday feast or just a quick "the-kids-are-dropping-by-today" kind of visit—I cherish the unique feeling of connection and closeness. And though they can sometimes be a bit chaotic, the joy of these occasions inspires me to cook with a special sense of love for those who are at my table.

In this chapter, I share three menus of delectable family fare. They are grand enough to get the youngsters to sit at the table (minding their "party manners") yet easy enough to make without a big fuss, especially with all the help you will have in the kitchen.

◆ Here's the fabulous braised beef brisket the kids are always hoping to find on the menu at my house—and they do!

◆ Delight any mom who loves Italian food with a Mother's Day treat of oven-roasted fresh tuna—and overwhelm her with chocolate-Toblerone torte for dessert.

◆ Enjoy an extended Thanksgiving holiday with an informal feast of moist turkey sandwiches on "kid-created" cranberry biscuits, accompanied by a slew of fresh-tasting fixin's.

Ordinarily, I recommend not having "too many cooks" in a kitchen, yet it honestly seems different with family. Perhaps it is a genetic bond, a similar culinary sense, or just the comfort that blesses relatives, but these dinners can be joint efforts. Don't hesitate to assign a dish or two to others to prepare at home and bring to the party. And enjoy the hustle and bustle of cooking together to make quick work of any menu. Following the kitchen schedules will help you get everything done on time.

Of course, let the children help out, too. I make a point of finding cooking tasks for kids of all ages. Tactile chores are the best for little ones—mixing ingredients, shaping cakes with their hands, mashing vegetables. Older children can handle more skilled jobs: Young readers love to demonstrate how they can sound out a long list of ingredients and instructions while you run around following their orders! Another way to engage children is by having them set and decorate the dining table. They can learn about proper service etiquette and show off their artistic talents at the same time.

With all the help you will get (and all the natural confusion about who's in charge in any family), don't forget that you are the host. You may not be able to control the flow of a family event as you would a dinner party for friends, but you can try! As at any of my casual dinners, start with some nice hors d'oeuvre and drinks in the living room, then proceed to the dining room.

Certainly you can have the children assist with service—holding the bowls while adults fill plates, passing items, and clearing the table. When kids are present, I never have trouble recruiting some small person to help me get dessert ready and out to the dining table. Working with the children may take some of your time from adult talk, of course; but I love to give kids this kind of positive attention. And it's wonderful to see the hosts and home entertainers of the next generation learning to put on a great party.

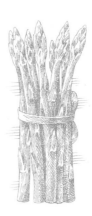

Sunday Afternoon at My House

THE MAIN EVENT:

Abigail's Top Secret Brisket of Beef

ON THE SIDE:

Sweet Peas and Sweet Leeks

◆

Mashed Golden Root Vegetables

ON THE SIDE:

Red Cabbage, Baby Beets, and Apples (page 74)

◆

Potato, Mushroom, and Roasted Garlic Pudding

THE GRAND FINALE:

Apple Pecan Torte with Calvados Whipped Cream

PALATE TEASER:

Sun-dried Tomato Guacamole in Radicchio Cups (page 84)
and tortilla chips

BEVERAGE RECOMMENDATIONS:

Strawberry Citrus Punch (page 354)
Apple juice
Merlot, California, Sebastiani Vineyards, "Sonoma Cask"

I HAVE ONE SET OF KIDS IN TENNESSEE, ONE SET IN VERMONT, one in upstate New York, and one in Connecticut. So you never know who's going to be able to come to dinner. But at least I never have to ask what they want to eat: "Let's have brisket!" Oh, some parts of the menu change: When there's a birthday, I have chocolate layer cake; if it's Hanukkah, we make potato latkes. But there's always brisket—the same tender, aromatic, long-braised pot roast of beef that I grew up with. I guess it's a tradition by now, the special dish that tells everyone we are together at home. My grandkids probably think that Grandma's house always smells this good— and come to think of it, that's how I thought my grandma's house always smelled.

The fragrance that fills the house while this brisket is cooking can make even a complete stranger feel like family. What's the secret? I like to think that my brisket—with the wine, honey, and sweet pears that I add to the more usual onions, carrots, and beef broth—offers an especially sweet welcome, and aroma.

And here's another secret: Often I make my brisket weeks ahead. The meat, vegetables, and sauce all seem to improve with time in the freezer. When I reheat the casserole in the oven, the flavor is fabulous, and the house smells great for a second time.

As my family knows, almost anything goes great with brisket. In this menu, I have shared several wonderful options. The one-toque choices are especially simple and delicious. Get the kids to help you shell fresh sweet peas to sauté with tender leeks, a touch of ginger, and brown sugar. They can also help you make the mashed vegetables—it is fun to whip up the cooked sweet potatoes, rutabagas, and butternut squash in an electric mixer, adding lots of "this and that." Everyone will love this vegetable combination, with its mild tang of sour cream, orange juice, and spices.

If you have a bit more time (or some older helpers) the two-toque choices are wonderful. Beets and cabbage are cooked separately then baked together with apple chunks in a wonderful balance of sweet, acidic, and spicy flavors. It is fun—and fancy—to make the individual puddings of mashed potato, sautéed mushrooms, and roasted garlic. Young cooks will enjoy seeing them puff in the oven and helping unmold the finished puddings. (But be careful: hot! Oven mitts and older kids only for this step.)

Every child will want to help you make the Grand Finale torte with apples and pecans. They can mix the batter and hide a layer of apples and raisins in the middle of the cake. This is wonderful served warm—so plan to make it when the kids come, even on the day of the party. They can whip the cream for dessert, too!

For a family occasion such as this Sunday get-together, the fragrance of the brisket is really all you need to create the perfect atmosphere. Of course, you and your helpers will set and decorate the table for a sit-down dinner. Aprons for young chefs are handy items today.

THE MAIN EVENT

Abigail's Top Secret Brisket of Beef

MAKES 8 SERVINGS

SPECIAL COOKWARE
6-quart oven- and flameproof casserole with lid or Dutch oven

Salt and freshly ground black pepper
1/2 teaspoon ground thyme
1/4 cup all-purpose flour
5–6 pound brisket of beef
3 tablespoons plus 2 teaspoons vegetable oil
3 large yellow onions, peeled and roughly chopped
4 large carrots, peeled and diced small
4 cloves garlic, peeled and finely chopped
3 Anjou pears, unpeeled, cored, and diced
7 cups beef broth, homemade or low-sodium canned
2 3/4 cups dry red wine
2/3 cup honey

1. Preheat the oven to 350°.

2. Mix 1/2 teaspoon of salt, 1/2 teaspoon of pepper, and the thyme with the flour. Lightly coat both sides of the brisket with the seasoned flour. Heat 3 tablespoons of the oil over medium-high heat in a large flameproof casserole dish or Dutch oven. Brown the brisket on both sides over medium heat for about 2 minutes on each side. Remove the meat to a large piece of foil on the counter.

3. Add the remaining 2 teaspoons of oil to the casserole and sauté the onions and carrots over medium heat for 6 minutes. Add the garlic and pears and cook 2 minutes more. Remove vegetables and set aside.

4. Turn the heat to high, add the beef broth, wine, and honey to the casserole. Bring to a boil, blending all the ingredients. Return the brisket to the casserole, cover, set it in the oven, and braise for 2 1/2 hours. Add the vegetables and continue to braise the brisket until it is fork tender, about 30–45 minutes more.

5. Remove the brisket to a cooling rack placed over a baking sheet to catch the juices as they settle. Strain and reserve the cooking liquid from the casserole. Place the strained vegetables in a covered dish to keep warm. *(The vegetables will be the garnish for the brisket.)* Put the cooking liquid and accumulated brisket juices back in the casserole and cook, uncovered, over high heat, until the sauce is reduced by half, becomes syrupy, and coats the back of a spoon. Season with salt and pepper to taste.

6. When the brisket is cool enough to handle, carve the meat across the grain into 1/4-inch slices. *(If the brisket is being frozen, freeze 1/4 of the sauce with the brisket and the remaining sauce with the vegetables.)* Return the slices to the casserole with the pan juices and keep the brisket warm over low heat. Warm the vegetables, covered, in the oven.

Arrange the brisket slices on a large serving platter. Surround the brisket with the vegetables, and ladle the sauce over the sliced meat or serve it separately. Serving the brisket and all the side dishes from the dining-room table allows the children to heap their plates with their favorite comfort foods.

The Inventive Chef

MAKE THE BRISKET 2 WEEKS BEFORE YOUR DINNER. SLICE THE MEAT AND FREEZE THE BRISKET AS INSTRUCTED IN STEP 6. BRING THE BRISKET TO ROOM TEMPERATURE BEFORE REHEATING. I LIKE TO REHEAT THE BRISKET IN THE OVEN TO REFRESH THE INTEGRITY OF THE ORIGINAL FLAVORS. BRISKET IMPROVES WITH AGE, BUT REMEMBER TO RESEASON THE SAUCE.

ON THE SIDE

Sweet Peas and Sweet Leeks

MAKES 8 SERVINGS

3 pounds sweet peas in their shells, or 20 ounces frozen baby peas, thawed
5 small leeks, white parts only
4 tablespoons salted butter
1 tablespoon light brown sugar

1 teaspoon minced fresh ginger
$^1/_2$ teaspoon salt, or to taste
$^1/_4$ teaspoon freshly ground black pepper, or to taste

GARNISH
2 teaspoons finely chopped flat-leaf parsley

1. Shell the peas, if using fresh. Wash the shells and reserve the peas. Simmer the shells in salted water to cover for 20 minutes. Discard the shells and cook the peas in the same water, uncovered, until they are slightly crisp to the bite, about 4 minutes. Drain the peas. If using frozen peas, proceed to step **2.**
2. Wash and dry the leeks well. Make certain all the sand hidden in the stems has been washed away. Cut the leeks into lengthwise into a $^1/_8$-inch-wide julienne.
3. Heat 3 tablespoons of the butter in a large skillet and sauté the leeks over medium heat until they are translucent, about 3–4 minutes. Add the peas, the remaining 1 tablespoon of butter, the brown sugar, ginger, salt, and pepper. Cook briskly over high heat for 1–2 minutes, until the sugar has melted and the vegetables are hot.

Serve the peas piping hot, garnished with the parsley. Bring them to the table in a deep serving dish.

Mashed Golden Root Vegetables

MAKES 8 SERVINGS

3 large sweet potatoes or yams, peeled and cut into
   2-inch pieces
2/3 pound rutabagas, peeled and cut into 1-inch pieces
1 1/3 pounds butternut squash, peeled, seeds removed, and
   cut into 2-inch pieces
1/3 cup melted salted butter
1/2 cup sour cream
3 tablespoons fresh orange juice
Zest of 2 oranges, minced (about 2 tablespoons)
3 tablespoons honey
1/4 teaspoon ground nutmeg
1/4 teaspoon powdered ginger
1/4 teaspoon ground mace
1 teaspoon salt, or to taste
1/2 teaspoon freshly ground black pepper,
   or to taste

GARNISH
Zest of 1 orange, finely julienned

1. Put the sweet potatoes or yams, rutabagas, and butternut squash in a large saucepan with enough water to cover them by two inches. Bring to a boil, then lower the heat to medium and simmer the vegetables until they are tender, about 30 minutes.
2. Drain the vegetables and put them into the large bowl of an electric mixer. Using the paddle attachment, beat the vegetables for 1 minute on medium speed.

3. Slowly add the melted butter, sour cream, orange juice, orange zest, and honey. Whip the vegetables until smooth, about 2 minutes. Season with the nutmeg, ginger, mace, salt, and pepper. Put the vegetables into a double boiler to keep warm if preparing ahead and reheating.

FINISHING TOUCHES AND
TABLE PRESENTATION

Fill a serving bowl with the mashed vegetables and serve family-style with the brisket, garnished with a sprinkle of julienned orange zest.

The Inventive Chef

SERVE THESE VEGETABLES WITH ROAST CHICKEN, PORK, OR LAMB. SINCE ANYTHING MASHED SAYS COMFORT FOOD, THESE ARE A GREAT ADDITION TO ANY SUNDAY-NIGHT SUPPER, AND A PRESCRIPTION FOR WARMTH ON A BONE-CHILLING WINTER EVENING.

Potato, Mushroom, and Roasted Garlic Pudding

MAKES 8 SERVINGS

SPECIAL COOKWARE
Eight 4-ounce oven-to-table ramekins
1 tablespoon vegetable oil

4 medium baking potatoes, peeled and cut into 1-inch dice
6 large cloves garlic, unpeeled
4 tablespoons olive oil
$1/4$ cup peeled and minced onion
$1/2$ pound fresh mushrooms, domestic or wild, trimmed,
*   washed, and coarsely chopped*
$1^1/4$ cups whole milk
2 eggs, beaten
1 teaspoon finely chopped fresh thyme
2 teaspoons finely chopped curly parsley
1 teaspoon salt
1 teaspoon freshly ground black pepper

GARNISH
2 teaspoons chopped curly parsley
1 bunch flat-leaf parsley or thyme

1. Preheat the oven to 450°. Brush eight 4-ounce ramekins with vegetable oil.

2. Put the potatoes in a saucepan with water to cover and a pinch of salt. Simmer the potatoes uncovered until they are tender, about 20 minutes. Drain and transfer the potatoes to the bowl of an electric mixer fitted with the paddle attachment.

3. While the potatoes are cooking, place the garlic in the center of a 6-by-6-inch piece of foil. Sprinkle 1 tablespoon of the olive oil over the garlic and wrap in the foil to form a small package. Place the foil on a baking sheet and roast the garlic for 25 minutes. Remove it from the oven and cool slightly. Carefully slip off and discard the peels. Reserve the roasted garlic and lower the oven temperature to 350°.

4. Heat the remaining 3 tablespoons of olive oil in a skillet and sauté the onion for 2 minutes over medium heat, stirring frequently. Add the mushrooms and cook briskly for about 2 minutes over high heat, until the

mushrooms are tender. Remove from the heat and set aside.

5. Beat the potatoes on medium speed until they become somewhat smooth, about 1 minute. With the mixer on slow, gradually add the milk, eggs, and the reserved garlic. Beat only until blended, or until the texture of the mix is acceptably smooth. (*A few lumps are definitely okay.*) With the mixer on low, blend the onions and mushrooms, thyme, parsley, salt, and pepper into the potatoes.

6. Spoon the potato mixture into the molds with a tablespoon until they are $3/4$ full. Place the molds in a large baking pan and fill the pan with warm tap water to come halfway up the sides of the molds. Bake the puddings for 30 minutes, until a knife inserted in the center comes out clean. Remove the molds from the water bath.

FINISHING TOUCHES AND
TABLE PRESENTATION

Let the puddings rest on a wire rack for 5 minutes at room temperature. Loosen the inside edge of the puddings with a knife and invert them onto a flat serving platter. Garnish the puddings with the chopped parsley, and garnish the platter with sprigs from the bunch of parsley or thyme.

The Inventive Chef
YOU CAN BAKE THE PUDDINGS A FEW HOURS BEFORE DINNER IS READY. PLACE THE RAMEKINS IN A WATER BATH AND REWARM IN A 350° OVEN.

Apple Pecan Torte with Calvados Whipped Cream

MAKES 8 SERVINGS

SPECIAL COOKWARE

10-inch tube pan with removable bottom

APPLE MIXTURE

1 tablespoon unsalted butter

2 Granny Smith or other type tart apple, peeled, cored, and cut into 1/2-inch dice.

1/4 teaspoon ground cinnamon

1/4 cup sugar

1 tablespoon fresh lemon juice

CAKE MIXTURE

2 1/3 cups all-purpose flour

1 1/2 teaspoons baking powder

1/2 teaspoon baking soda

3/4 teaspoon salt

1 teaspoon ground cinnamon

1/4 teaspoon ground nutmeg

1/4 teaspoon ground allspice

4 sticks (1 pound) unsalted butter

Zest of 1 orange

2 cups less 2 tablespoons sugar

4 large eggs

4 3/4 ounces whole milk

1 1/2 teaspoons Calvados or applejack

1 1/2 teaspoons pure vanilla extract

3 tablespoons all-purpose flour

1 cup coarsely chopped pecans

1/2 cup raisins

1/4 cup sifted confectioners' sugar

Calvados Whipped Cream (recipe follows)

1. Preheat the oven to 350°. Butter and flour the baking pan.

2. Mix the diced apple with 1/4 teaspoon cinnamon, 1/4 cup sugar, and the lemon juice. Cover and let sit for at least 30 minutes. Drain, discard liquids, and leave the apples in a colander.

3. Sift together the 2 1/3 cups of flour, the baking powder, baking soda, salt, cinnamon, nutmeg, and allspice. Set aside.

4. Cut the butter into 1-inch pieces, and in an electric mixer with the paddle attachment, at medium speed, beat the butter, orange zest, and sugar for about 10 minutes. Occasionally scrape the sides of the bowl with a rubber spatula. Add the eggs, one at a time, at 1-minute intervals. Combine the milk, applejack, and vanilla extract in a small bowl.

5. Reduce the mixer speed to low. Add the dry-ingredient mixture alternately with the wet-ingredient mixture, dividing the dry ingredients into 4 parts and the liquids into 3 parts, starting and ending with the flour mixture. Mix only until incorporated after each addition. After both mixtures have been added, mix an additional 20 seconds.

6. Add the 3 tablespoons of flour to the apples and toss to coat them well. Fold the apples, pecans, and raisins into the batter with a rubber spatula.

7. Pour the batter into the prepared pan and bake in the preheated oven about 45 minutes, or until a toothpick inserted in the center comes out clean.

8. Remove the cake from the oven. Cool cake in the pan set on a rack, 10 minutes.

9. Run a knife around sides of cake and remove the outside ring. Let the cake cool completely, about 30 minutes, and then invert cake to remove the bottom of the pan.

10. Dust the top of the cake with confectioners' sugar.

Redust the torte with confectioner's sugar and bring to the guests on a large round serving plate. Cut the cake into 8 generous wedges and serve with the Calvados Whipped Cream.

The Inventive Chef

OTHER FRUIT CAN ALSO BE USED IN THE TORTE. TRY BOSC OR CUMICE PEARS WITH AMARETTO LIQUEUR INSTEAD OF THE APPLES AND CALVADOS. SERVE THE CAKE WITH THE CALVADOS WHIPPED CREAM OR WITH ICE CREAM OR FROZEN YOGURT.

Calvados Whipped Cream

MAKES ABOUT 2 CUPS OF WHIPPED CREAM

1 cup heavy cream, well chilled
2 tablespoons confectioners' sugar
1 teaspoon pure vanilla extract
2 teaspoons Calvados liqueur

1. Beat the cream in the bowl of an electric mixer fitted with the whip attachment on medium speed until the cream stands in soft peaks.

2. On low-medium speed, slowly whip in the confectioners' sugar, vanilla, and Calvados liqueur until the cream is well blended and holds its shape.

KITCHEN SCHEDULE

1 WEEK AHEAD

MAIN EVENT	Brisket	Prepare through step 6; cool completely. Freeze as instructed in step 6.
GRAND FINALE	Torte	Prepare through step 9; cool completely; wrap tightly and freeze.

2 OR 3 DAYS BEFORE THE PARTY

TOQUE 2	Pudding	Roast garlic and cool as in step 3; store covered in refrigerator.

THE DAY BEFORE THE PARTY

MAIN EVENT	Brisket	Defrost brisket and sauce in refrigerator overnight.
TOQUE 1	Root Vegetables	Prepare sweet potatoes, rutabagas, and squash; store in airtight containers in refrigerator. Mince zest of 2 oranges and julienne zest of 1; store separately, covered, in refrigerator.
	Peas	Shell peas, if fresh; julienne leeks; mince ginger; chop parsley; store covered, separately, in refrigerator.
TOQUE 2	Cabbage	Prepare recipe through step 6; Remove from oven, cool, and store covered in refrigerator.
	Pudding	Prepare recipe through step 5; spoon into molds, cool, and store covered in refrigerator.
GRAND FINALE	Torte	Defrost in refrigerator overnight.

Strategic Maneuvers: Fill creamers; cover and store in refrigerator. Fill sugar bowls. Set up table and decor. Check ice and beverages. Locate teas. Chill wine if white. Check garnishes for each recipe. Locate and label all serving bowls, platters, and utensils.

THE DAY OF THE PARTY

3 HOURS BEFORE GUESTS ARRIVE:

MAIN EVENT	Brisket	Warm in 300° oven for 25 minutes and reseason; remove from oven and set aside at room temperature.
TOQUE 1	Root Vegetables	Prepare through step 3 and set in top of double boiler.
	Peas	Sauté leeks as in step 3; set aside at room temperature, *but do not add peas.* Set aside brown sugar, ginger, salt, pepper, and butter.
TOQUE 2	Cabbage	Set at room temperature.
	Pudding	Set puddings at room temperature; fill pan with water for baking.
GRAND FINALE	Torte	Place on baking sheet for warming; set aside. Make Calvados whipped cream; refrigerate, covered.

60 MINUTES BEFORE DINNER:

MAIN EVENT

Preheat oven to 350°.
Heat brisket, vegetables, and
sauce, covered, until piping hot
(about 25–30 minutes). Remove
from oven and hold at room
temperature, covered, to stay
hot.

40 MINUTES BEFORE DINNER:

TOQUE 1 Root Warm over simmering water.
    Vegetables
TOQUE 2 Cabbage Warm in oven or on stovetop.
    Pudding Bake as in step 6; remove from
        oven and cover lightly with
        aluminum foil.

15 MINUTES BEFORE DINNER:

MAIN EVENT Brisket Return to oven, covered.
TOQUE 1 Peas Return skillet to heat and add
       the peas, butter, brown sugar,
       ginger, salt, and pepper to leeks
       as in step 3.
TOQUE 2 Pudding Unmold onto serving platter.
GRAND FINALE Torte Turn off oven. Place torte in
       oven on a baking sheet with
       the door open about 2 inches,
       to warm through.
       Plug in coffee.

JUST BEFORE DINNER:

Arrange all foods and garnish:
Place brisket and vegetables on
a large serving platter. Ladle $1/4$
of sauce over brisket; place the
remaining sauce in a sauceboat
with a ladle.
Bring all foods to table. Invite
guests to dig in.

DESSERT SERVICE:

Dust torte with confectioners'
sugar and bring to the table—
with the whipped cream, or
with ice cream or frozen
yogurt, if desired.
Pour coffee.

AFTER SERVICE:

Unplug coffee.

Making Mom's Day with Italian Delights

THE MAIN EVENT:

Oven-Roasted Tuscan Tuna with Chunky Tomato Sauce

ON THE SIDE:

Garlicky Green Beans with Sautéed Pine Nuts

◆

Savory Linguini with Radicchio and Arugula

ON THE SIDE:

Balsamic Mixed Vegetable Roast

◆

Saffron Risotto Cakes

THE GRAND FINALE:

Brownie Torte with Bittersweet Chocolate Ganache and Toblerone Cream

PALATE TEASER:

Pungent Meatballs Glazed in Green (page 299)

BEVERAGE RECOMMENDATIONS:

Campari and soda
Chianti Classico, Viticcio Riserva 1993
Sauvignon Blanc, California, Château Potelle

*S*HHH . . . DON'T TELL HER WHAT WE'RE MAKING. MOM HINTED that she wanted to go to that new northern-Italian restaurant, but we said we would make something Italian here. She's probably expecting lasagna. Well, we could tell her there's linguine on the menu, but not that it's tossed with arugula and radicchio and a bit of chicken stock—she'd never believe it anyway. The tuna's got to be the big surprise. There's no restaurant that would roast a giant piece of tuna in a fabulous tomato sauce, and then slice it thin like wonderful meat. They can't afford to make a dish like that in a restaurant. You need a family for a meal like this! We'll just tell her there's tons of garlic . . . and then a lot of chocolate.

The main event on this menu, a spectacular roast of tuna, is a true home-cooked specialty. Coated in a savory paste of basil, oregano, and garlic, it is seared in a skillet, then baked in a casserole with a chunky, freshly made tomato sauce. Thin slices of the roasted fish are napped with the braising sauce and dusted with capers and parsley. Not only Mom, but everyone at your table, will swoon.

Side dishes are full-flavored, too. The one-toque menu offers an easy presentation of brilliantly colored green beans sautéed with garlic and pine nuts. And the linguine, mixed with wonderful bitter greens and sweet chicken stock, makes a great bed for the tuna.

The two-toque menu presents a beautiful mix of vegetables—including eggplant, zucchini, red onions, endive, and red and yellow peppers—dressed with balsamic vinegar and extra virgin olive oil, then roasted in a hot oven to soften and caramelize their natural sweetness. You will also make a wonderful risotto, colored with saffron and

embellished with black olives and Parmigiano and Boursin cheeses. But you can't eat it yet! After cooling, you will bread and fry the risotto into crunchy cakes. Get the kids to help you with this step.

The Brownie Torte with Bittersweet Chocolate Ganache and Toblerone Cream is a gift for any chocolate lover—especially for a mom when her kids have made it. The fudgy and dense cake, the glistening ganache icing, and the luscious cream (including an entire melted Toblerone chocolate bar) are simple to make and serve. No fancy decorating needed, just beautiful strawberries.

SETTING THE STAGE

Mother's Day is perfectly timed for flowers, of course. Mom will know something special is coming her way when she sees a beautiful centerpiece with masses of fresh lilacs, tulips, peonies, and roses. And, Dad, if you are setting the table, find a pastel tablecloth (and coordinating napkins) to match the floral hues.

THE MAIN EVENT

Oven-Roasted Tuscan Tuna with Chunky Tomato Sauce

MAKES 8 SERVINGS

SPECIAL COOKWARE
4-quart flameproof casserole with lid or Dutch oven

1 1/2 tablespoons fresh lemon juice
25 fresh medium-size basil leaves
2 cloves garlic, peeled
3 tablespoons dried oregano
4 1/2 tablespoons olive oil
4 pounds fresh tuna, in 1 large piece (about 4 inches thick and 7 inches long), skin removed
1 teaspoon salt
1 teaspoon freshly ground black pepper
1/4 cup all-purpose flour
2 1/2 cups Chunky Tomato Sauce (recipe follows)

GARNISH
1 tablespoon drained capers
1 tablespoon finely chopped flat-leaf parsley

1. Preheat the oven to 350°.
2. Place the lemon juice, basil leaves, garlic, and oregano into the bowl of a food processor fitted with the metal cutting blade and with the motor running, slowly drizzle 2 1/2 tablespoons of the olive oil through the feeding tube. Turn the machine off periodically to scrape down the sides of the bowl with a rubber spatula. Continue processing until the basil and garlic are finely chopped and all the ingredients are well combined.

3. Season the tuna with the salt and pepper. Spread the lemon-herb-garlic paste over the entire fish, using your fingers or a flat metal spatula and making sure to coat the tuna well, using all the paste. Pat flour around the sides and edges of the herb-pasted tuna, covering the fish well.

4. Heat the remaining 2 tablespoons of olive oil in a large flameproof casserole or Dutch oven. Using a long-handled fork, transfer the tuna to the casserole and sear it on all sides until golden, about 1 minute on each side. Pour the Chunky Tomato Sauce around the fish.

5. Bake the tuna, covered, for about 30 minutes for rare and up to 50 minutes for well-done. (*To check the fish for doneness, use a paring knife to make a small slit in the center of the fish. The flesh of the tuna will be red for rare, pink for medium, and gray for well done.*) Remove the fish to a cutting board and let it rest for 5 minutes, lightly covered with foil. Keep the sauce warm on top of the stove over very low heat.

FINISHING TOUCHES AND
TABLE PRESENTATION

Carve the fish into quarter-inch-thick slices and arrange slices, overlapping, on a square or oval platter. Spoon the tomato sauce over the fish to give it color and coat it lightly. Pour the remaining sauce into a sauceboat and pass it separately. Garnish each slice of tuna with capers and a dusting of parsley.

ONE-TOQUE: If you decide to arrange individual plates for your guests, make a heaping bed of the linguini in the center of each plate and cover it with overlapping slices of tuna.

TWO-TOQUE: Place the risotto cakes between 9 and 6 o'clock, the vegetables between 3 and 6 o'clock, and the tuna fish at 12 o'clock.

The Inventive Chef

THE NATURAL FLAVORS OF SWORDFISH, HALIBUT, COD, FLOUNDER, AND HADDOCK ARE ENRICHED WHEN BRAISED IN THIS TOMATO SAUCE. SERVE THE FISH WITH RICE, OR ROAST UNPEELED SMALL RED BLISS OR YUKON GOLD POTATOES IN THE POT WITH THE FISH.

Chunky Tomato Sauce

MAKES 1 QUART

SPECIAL COOKWARE
4-quart heavy-bottomed saucepan

1/3 cup olive oil
1 large white onion, peeled and finely chopped
3 cloves garlic, peeled and minced
2 1/2 pounds ripe plum tomatoes, peeled (if desired) and coarsely chopped
2 1/2 cups canned chopped Italian plum tomatoes, strained, juices reserved
1 cup full-bodied red wine, such as cabernet sauvignon or merlot
1 1/2 teaspoons sugar

1 teaspoon salt
1/2 teaspoon freshly ground black pepper, or to taste

1. Heat the oil over medium heat in a large heavy-bottomed saucepan and sauté the onion until translucent, about 3–5 minutes. Add the garlic and sauté for one minute more.
2. Add the fresh and canned tomatoes, 3/4 cup of the reserved tomato juice, the wine, and the sugar to the saucepan. Bring the sauce to a boil, lower the heat, and simmer uncovered for 20 minutes, or until the fresh tomatoes are tender and about 1/2 the liquid has cooked off.
3. Season with the salt and pepper and simmer the sauce for 5 minutes more. Cool the sauce to room temperature and store it in the refrigerator, covered, for up to 1 week, or in the freezer for up to 2 weeks.

ON THE SIDE

Garlicky Green Beans with Sautéed Pine Nuts

MAKES 8 SERVINGS

2 pounds young string beans, stemmed and tailed
1/4 cup extra virgin olive oil
1/2 cup pine nuts
3 large cloves garlic, peeled and finely minced
1/2 teaspoon salt, or to taste
1/2 teaspoon freshly ground black pepper, or to taste

GARNISH
1 teaspoon finely chopped flat-leaf parsley

1. Bring 2 quarts of water to a boil over high heat with a pinch of salt. Add the beans and simmer rapidly, uncovered, for 3–3$^{1}/_{2}$ minutes, or until the beans are slightly tender but crisp to the bite. Drain the beans through a colander, then shock them immediately in ice-cold tap water to stop the cooking process and keep the beans crunchy and bright green. After the beans have cooled in the ice water, drain them again and shake off all the excess water. Reserve the beans at room temperature.

2. Heat 2 tablespoons of the oil in a skillet over medium heat. Add the pine nuts and sauté, stirring constantly, until they start to turn golden brown, about 2 minutes. Add the garlic and sauté for an additional minute, making sure to stir the nuts and garlic constantly so they turn golden but do not burn.

3. Add the remaining olive oil and the reserved green beans to the skillet. Toss the beans, stirring constantly, in the garlic-and-nut mixture until they are well coated and heated through, about 1$^{1}/_{2}$ minutes. Season with the salt and pepper.

FINISHING TOUCHES AND TABLE PRESENTATION

Fill a round or square dish, about 1$^{1}/_{2}$ inches deep, with the beans and garnish them with the chopped parsley. I like to see their vibrant color set against a background of white pottery.

The Inventive Chef

YELLOW WAX BEANS ADDED TO THE GREEN BEANS BRING ANOTHER DIMENSION OF COLOR TO THE TABLE.

ON THE SIDE

Savory Linguini with Radicchio and Arugula

MAKES 8 SERVINGS

1 tablespoon plus $^{1}/_{4}$ teaspoon salt, or to taste
1 pound dried linguini
5 tablespoons olive oil
1 medium onion, peeled and finely chopped
2 large cloves of garlic, peeled and finely minced
2 large heads radicchio, cores removed, leaves cut in medium julienne
2 bunches arugula, washed, dried, and coarsely chopped
$^{3}/_{4}$ cup homemade or low-sodium canned chicken broth
$^{1}/_{8}$ teaspoon freshly ground black pepper, or to taste

GARNISH
1 cup freshly grated Parmigiano Reggiano

1. In a large saucepan or stockpot, bring 5 quarts of water with 1 tablespoon of salt to a boil over high heat. Add the linguini and cook, uncovered, stirring occasionally, for 8–10 minutes, until the pasta is al dente—slightly firm to the bite. Drain the pasta and place it in a colander. Toss the pasta with 1 tablespoon of the olive oil and keep it warm in the colander over a pot of slow-simmering water.

2. While the pasta is cooking, heat the remaining 4 tablespoons of olive oil in a large skillet over medium heat, and sauté the onion until translucent, about 2–3 minutes. Add the garlic and continue cooking for 1 minute more.

3. Add the radicchio and cook, stirring frequently, until the leaves begin to wilt, about 2 minutes. Stir in the arugula and cook for another 1 1/2 minutes, until the leaves have wilted. Blend in the chicken stock and simmer the vegetables for 1 minute. Season with salt and pepper.

FINISHING TOUCHES AND
TABLE PRESENTATION

Toss the pasta with the radicchio-and-arugula mixture in a large serving bowl. Place the Parmigiano and a pepper mill on the dining table. Pass the pasta; guests will help themselves to the cheese and the pepper.

> *The Inventive Chef*
>
> I LIKE TO SAUTÉ 3/4 POUND OF PANCETTA, DICED IN 1-INCH PIECES, AND ADD TO THE PASTA SAUCE. SERVE THIS WITH BASIL-SCENTED APPLES OF LOVE (PAGE 107).

ON THE SIDE

Balsamic Mixed Vegetable Roast

MAKES 8 SERVINGS

1 large (about 1 pound) eggplant, unpeeled, cut crosswise into 1/4-inch-thick rounds
1 1/2 teaspoons salt or more as needed to lightly sprinkle the eggplant pieces
3/4 cup extra virgin olive oil
1/3 cup good-quality balsamic vinegar

1/2 teaspoon freshly ground black pepper
1 pound (about 2 medium) zucchini, washed, dried, and cut on the bias into 1/4-inch-thick rounds
2 large red onions, peeled and sliced into 1/4-inch-thick rounds
1 large red bell pepper, cored, seeded, and cut into 3/4-inch pieces
1 large yellow bell pepper, cored, seeded, and cut into 3/4-inch pieces
4 large heads of endive, each cut into quarters

GARNISH
4 sprigs fresh basil

1. Place a layer of paper towels over a baking sheet. Arrange the eggplant in a single layer on the paper towels and sprinkle the pieces lightly with 1/2 teaspoon of the salt, or more as needed. Let stand for 30 minutes. Pat the eggplant dry with additional paper towels. *(The eggplant will release its water and become a golden brown when roasted.)*
2. Preheat the oven to 450°. Whisk together the olive oil, balsamic vinegar, 1 teaspoon of salt, and the pepper, and set aside.
3. Divide the eggplant, zucchini, red onions, red pepper, yellow pepper, and endive between two large baking pans with sides. Gently toss the vegetables well with 3/4 of the blended oil and vinegar. Place one baking sheet on the bottom oven rack and the second on the middle rack. Roast the vegetables for 15–20 minutes, turning them once and rotating the baking pans between the middle and bottom shelves after 10 minutes. The vegetables should be crisp to the bite when they are done.

FINISHING TOUCHES AND
TABLE PRESENTATION

Arrange the vegetables in bunches on a large round or oval platter with the various types mixed together to achieve a vibrant panoply of colors. Sprinkle the veggies with additional salt and pepper to your taste, and drizzle them with the remaining olive oil–balsamic vinegar dressing. Place sprigs of basil leaves in the center of the platter. Serve the vegetables hot or at room temperature.

The Inventive Chef

FOR A SUMMERTIME TREAT, GRILL THE VEGETABLES OVER WELL-HEATED CHARCOAL. BRUSH THEM WITH THE OIL AND VINEGAR AND SPRINKLE WITH SALT AND PEPPER BEFORE PLACING THEM ON THE GRILL. BRUSH AGAIN WITH THE OIL AND VINEGAR AFTER THEY ARE GRILLED.

ON THE SIDE

Saffron Risotto Cakes

MAKES 8 SERVINGS

4 1/2 cups chicken broth, homemade or low-sodium canned
1/4 teaspoon powdered saffron
8 tablespoons unsalted butter
1 medium red onion, peeled and finely chopped
2 medium cloves garlic, peeled and minced
2 cups Arborio rice

1/2 cup dry white wine, such as Soave, chardonnay, or dry vermouth
1/2 cup Niçoise olives, pitted and quartered
2 cups finely chopped radicchio leaves
1/3 cup freshly grated Parmigiano Reggiano
2 tablespoons Boursin or garlic-herbed cheese
1/2 cup plain fine bread crumbs
1/2 teaspoon salt
1/4 teaspoon ground white pepper
16 dry flat-leaf parsley leaves (optional)

GARNISH
1 cup Parmigiano Reggiano shavings

1. Bring the chicken broth to a simmer over medium-high heat in a medium saucepan. Add the powdered saffron and stir well. Turn the heat to low and allow the saffron to steep in the gently simmering broth while you complete the next step.
2. In a large, heavy-bottomed saucepan, heat 3 tablespoons of the butter over low heat. Add the onion and garlic and cook them, covered, for 5 minutes, until they are soft and translucent.
3. Add the rice to the butter, onions, and garlic. Over medium heat, cook and coat the rice with the butter mixture, stirring with a wooden spoon, for about 1 minute, until the rice is translucent. Add the wine and stir, cooking until it is all absorbed.
4. Stirring constantly, ladle about 1/2 cup of the simmering broth into the rice. Add 1/2–3/4 cup of additional broth each time the rice absorbs the liquid. Cook until the texture of the rice is al dente and thick, and all the broth in the saucepan has been completely absorbed, about 18 minutes. Remove the rice from the heat and immediately stir in the olives and radicchio. (*Unlike standard risottos, which are a little*

saucy, this risotto needs to be cooked dry in order to be formed into cakes.)

5. Off the heat, blend in the Parmigiano and Boursin cheeses and the bread crumbs. Season with salt and pepper.

6. Let the risotto cool and refrigerate, covered, for at least 2 hours or overnight.

7. Using your hands, form the chilled risotto into sixteen 3-inch cakes. Press a parsley leaf into one side of each cake. Heat the remaining butter in a large skillet. Over medium heat, sauté the cakes, a few at a time, gently turning them with a metal spatula, until they are golden brown on both sides. Set aside. *(The cakes can be reheated in a 250° oven.)*

FINISHING TOUCHES AND TABLE PRESENTATION

Make sure to arrange the cakes parsley-side up. Place them in circles on a china or crockery platter and dust them with the cheese shavings.

> ## The Inventive Chef
>
> MAKE 1 1/2-INCH RISOTTO CAKES FOR AN INTRIGUING HORS D'OEUVRE.

Brownie Torte with Bittersweet Chocolate Ganache and Toblerone Cream

MAKES 8 SERVINGS

SPECIAL COOKWARE
8-inch springform pan

1 tablespoon unsalted butter for greasing
8 ounces unsalted butter
6 ounces semisweet chocolate, coarsely chopped
4 ounces unsweetened chocolate, coarsely chopped
1/2 cup all-purpose flour
1 1/2 teaspoons baking powder
1/2 teaspoon salt
3 eggs
1 1/4 cups sugar
2 teaspoons pure vanilla extract
1 tablespoon dark rum
Bittersweet Chocolate Ganache (recipe follows)
Toblerone Cream (page 240)

GARNISH
16 large strawberries

1. Preheat the oven to 350°.

2. Grease and lightly flour the bottom and sides of an 8-inch springform pan.

3. Heat the butter with the semisweet and unsweetened chocolates in the top of a double boiler set over barely simmering water. Stir until the ingredients have completely melted. Remove the top of the double boiler and allow the chocolate to cool to room temperature.

4. Mix the flour, baking powder, and salt together in a small bowl.

5. Place the eggs in the bowl of an electric mixer and beat them with the whip attachment, on high, until they are a light lemony color. Slowly add the sugar and continue to beat until the mixture forms ribbons when the whip is lifted from the center of the bowl.

6. With the mixer on low, slowly blend in the dry ingredients until incorporated. Add the reserved chocolate, the vanilla, and rum and mix well.

7. Pour the batter into the springform pan and bake for 30–35 minutes, until a toothpick or tester inserted into the center comes out with a small amount of fudgey batter clinging to it. *(This cake resembles a dense brownie rather than a fluffy layer cake.)*

8. Remove the cake from the oven and separate the sides of the cake from the inside of the pan with a flat knife. Cool the cake for 20 minutes. Release the sides of the springform pan and invert the cake onto a cake rack. Remove the bottom of the cake pan. Invert the cake again and cool it to room temperature.

9. Glaze the top and sides with the ganache using a flat metal spatula. Refrigerate the torte for about 1 hour, until the ganache is set, before serving.

FINISHING TOUCHES AND TABLE PRESENTATION

My favorite way to serve this torte is to cut it in front of my guests and top each piece with a large dollop of Toblerone Cream and two strawberries. The torte can also be precut into 8 wedges. Place a wedge of torte in the center of individual 8- or 9-inch dessert plates and

serve with a generous spoonful of Toblerone Cream and two strawberries.

The Inventive Chef

WHEN THE TORTE IS PART OF A DESSERT BUFFET, CUT IT INTO 16 WEDGES AND PLACE THE TOBLERONE CREAM IN A GLASS OR CHINA BOWL NEXT TO A BASKET OF STRAWBERRIES. GUESTS CAN HELP THEMSELVES TO THE CREAM.

Bittersweet Chocolate Ganache

ABOUT 1 3/4 CUPS

3/4 cup heavy cream
*6 ounces good-quality bittersweet chocolate, such as
    Valrhona*
1 teaspoon pure vanilla extract
1 1/2 teaspoons dark rum (optional)

1. In a small saucepan, over low heat, gently heat the cream to a slow simmer.

2. While the cream is heating, break the chocolate into chunks and place it in the bowl of a food processor fitted with the metal cutting blade. Pulse until the chocolate is finely chopped.

3. Remove the cream from the heat and, with the food processor turned on, slowly pour the cream through the feeding tube into the chocolate. Process until the chocolate is thoroughly melted and smooth.

4. Remove the mixture to a medium-size bowl. Stir in the vanilla and rum and cool for 10 minutes.

Toblerone Cream

MAKES 1 CUP

1 bar (3.5 ounce) Toblerone milk chocolate
1 ounce semisweet chocolate
2 teaspoons powdered instant coffee dissolved in $^1/_4$ cup
    boiling water
$^3/_4$ cup heavy cream

1. Chill the bowl of the electric mixer and the whip attachment in the freezer.

2. Melt the chocolates in the coffee in the top of a double boiler set over simmering water. Stir until smooth. Remove the top of the double boiler and cool the chocolate to room temperature.

3. Remove the bowl and whip from the freezer and whip the cream until it forms soft peaks. Gently fold in the cooled chocolate mixture using a rubber spatula. Chill the cream in the refrigerator until serving.

1 WEEK AHEAD

MAIN EVENT	Tuna	Prepare tomato sauce through step 3; cool to room temperature and freeze. (Or make 2–3 days before party and store covered in refrigerator.)
GRAND FINALE	Torte	Prepare through step 8; cover well and freeze.
	Ganache	Prepare through step 4; store covered in refrigerator.

THE DAY BEFORE THE PARTY

MAIN EVENT	Tuna	Prepare capers and parsley. Store separately, covered, in refrigerator. Prepare paste as in step 3; store covered in refrigerator.
TOQUE 1	Green Beans	Prepare step 1; cool and store covered in refrigerator.
TOQUE 2	Risotto	Prepare through step 6; store covered in refrigerator. Prepare parsley; store covered in refrigerator.
GRAND FINALE	Torte	Defrost in refrigerator overnight.

Strategic Maneuvers:
Fill creamers; cover and store in refrigerator.
Fill sugar bowls.
Set up table and decor.
Check ice and beverages.
Locate teas.
Chill wine if white.
Locate and label all serving bowls, platters, and utensils.

THE DAY OF THE PARTY

MAIN EVENT	Tuna	Prepare through step 4; store covered in refrigerator.
TOQUE 1	Green Beans	Set at room temperature. Prepare step 2; set aside at room temperature.
	Pasta	Sauté onion and garlic as in step 2. Prepare radicchio and arugula for step 3; set aside at room temperature.
TOQUE 2	Vegetables	Prepare through step 3; set aside at room temperature.
	Risotto	Prepare steps 6–7; set aside at room temperature.
GRAND FINALE	Ganache	Reheat to spreading consistency in top of double boiler. Frost torte; set on a serving platter. Prepare strawberry garnish.
	Cream	Prepare through step 3; place in service bowl; store covered in refrigerator.

15 MINUTES BEFORE GUESTS ARRIVE:

TOQUE 1	Pasta	Preheat oven to 250°. Prepare step 1. Sauté the radicchio and arugula with onion as in step 3.

50 MINUTES BEFORE DINNER:

MAIN EVENT	Tuna	Finish recipe through step 5 (cooking time will depend on desired doneness of fish).

20 MINUTES BEFORE DINNER:

		Plug in coffee.
TOQUE 1	Green Beans	Prepare steps 2–3; keep warm over very low heat on stovetop.
	Pasta	Finish recipe; keep warm over very low heat on stovetop.
TOQUE 2	Vegetables	Heat in oven.
	Risotto	Reheat in oven.

10 MINUTES BEFORE DINNER:

| **MAIN EVENT** | Tuna | Carve tuna and garnish platter. Set out for service with extra sauce in a serving boat and ladle. |

DINNER SERVICE:

Bring all food to the table.

DESSERT SERVICE:

Serve torte with strawberries.
Pass cream.

AFTER SERVICE:

Unplug coffee.
Turn off oven.

Turkey with a Twist
When the Crowd Comes Home

THE MAIN EVENTS:

Turkey Sandwiches with Dried Cran-apple Chutney on Cran-orange Buttermilk Biscuits
Fennel and Celery Slaw with Red Apples and Grapes

ON THE SIDE:

Carrot and Peanut Soup

◆

Candied Yam Steak Fries

ON THE SIDE

Roasted Cauliflower Soup with Turmeric

◆

Sweet Potato and Zucchini Pancakes

THE GRAND FINALE:
Pear Custard with Apricot Sauce

PALATE TEASER:
Parsley-Dusted Wild Mushroom–Stuffed Eggs (page 315)

BEVERAGE RECOMMENDATIONS:
Champagne Punch (page 355)
Apple cider
Bordeaux Blanc, Château Bonnet

MAYBE THIS IS THE YEAR TO SKIP THE THANKSGIVING Day "parade" of preparation and party giving. Your son stayed at school to finish his paper; your daughter and her kids are going to her in-laws; and they won't all be coming home until Friday night. So have a thankful day of rest on Thursday and on Friday you'll poach a beautiful turkey breast, fix chunky cran-apple chutney, and make a luscious roasted cauliflower soup. On Saturday morning, you'll make biscuits with the kids and pear and walnut custard. So what if the gang doesn't sit down together until Saturday night for soup and sandwiches? A family holiday is better late than never, and they'll love your easy turkey supper as much as any fancy feast.

You don't have to knock yourself out to enjoy the most lasting pleasure of the Thanksgiving holiday: perfect fixings for turkey sandwiches. The Main Events here are melt-in-your-mouth sandwiches that may change your holiday cooking plans for years to come. Poaching the turkey breast my way will give you wonderfully moist and flavorful turkey with little work and absolutely no worry about roasting times, basting, and foil tents. (You will also have quarts of delicious stock for soup.)

The kids in your family will enjoy making and baking the flaky and tender Cran-orange Buttermilk Biscuits, and they can also help with the tangy Dried Cran-apple Chutney. These simple sandwiches will expand their culinary horizons as they learn about cooking and baking—working with dough and with fruit, using dried and fresh fruits, fruit juices, and zest for many marvelous flavors. A colorful slaw with fennel, celery, apples, and grapes completes the main course (and is easy to make ahead of time).

I share two hearty and warming soups for this occasion. The one-toque Carrot and Peanut Soup is a breeze, with a delightful richness derived from just a few spoonfuls of peanut butter. With a little more time, try the Roasted Cauliflower Soup with Turmeric. The depth of flavor here comes from roasting the cauliflower florets and garlic, and from a delicate spicing (which also gives it gorgeous color).

Sweet potatoes are featured on this menu, too, of course. The steak fries made from yams are simple and very indulgent, as you candy the thick potato wedges by roasting them in a rich mixture of butter, brown sugar, maple syrup, orange juice, cinnamon, and ginger. The Sweet Potato and Zucchini Pancakes are crisp and delicious, with the flavors of apple, orange, and cumin.

Whoever makes my wonderful Pear Custard will learn a fascinating technique. Soak slices of rich egg bread (such as challah or brioche) in cream, then blend them with eggs, cream, ground nuts, and cinnamon for a light, smooth, and substantial custard. Ripe pear slices form a flavorful hidden layer in the middle of the casserole. There's an easy Apricot Sauce, too, with super flavor from apricot preserves, dried apricots, apricot brandy, and apricot nectar.

SETTING THE STAGE

Without all the excess bowls and china of the usual Thanksgiving feast, you will have plenty of room on the dining table to create lovely seasonal decorations. Collect a variety of small vegetables and fruits: baby squashes, gourds, pumpkins, baby pears, lady apples, kumquats, clementines, and fresh cranberries. Also include whole nuts and dried apricots, peaches, and pineapples. You can create your arrangement right on the tablecloth, filling the entire center of the table—no bowls or vases necessary.

Turkey Sandwiches with Dried Cran-apple Chutney on Cran-orange Buttermilk Biscuits

MAKES 8 SERVINGS (OR 16 SANDWICHES PLUS ENOUGH FOR LEFTOVERS)

8–10 pounds fresh turkey breast, bone in
2 quarts homemade or low-sodium canned chicken broth
1 cup peeled and coarsely chopped carrots
1 cup washed and coarsely chopped celery
1 large white onion, peeled and coarsely chopped
1 bunch curly parsley
1 bay leaf
1/4 teaspoon salt, or to taste
1 medium head romaine lettuce, outer leaves removed, washed, cored, and torn into 16 pieces
Cran-orange Buttermilk Biscuits (page 247)
Dried Cran-apple Chutney (recipe follows)

GARNISH
Whole cranberries
1 bunch flat-leaf parsley

1. Place the turkey breast in a 6-quart stockpot and pour enough of the chicken broth over the breast to cover it completely, then add 2¹/₂ inches of additional liquid *(if you do not have enough broth, add water)*. Bring the broth to a simmer. Remove any gray foam that rises to the top of the pan.
2. Add the carrots, celery, onion, parsley, bay leaf, and salt. Simmer the turkey, partially covered, for about 1¹/₂ hours. Keep the top of the turkey breast covered

with liquid as it simmers. (*The turkey is cooked when a meat thermometer inserted into the thickest part reaches 165°.*) Remove the pan from the heat and let the turkey cool in the broth for 30 minutes. Place the turkey on a platter and cool it to room temperature. Return the turkey to the cooled broth, cover it well, and refrigerate it overnight or until ready to serve.

3. About 2 hours before serving, remove the turkey from the broth, remove the skin, and carve the breast into ¼-inch slices. Arrange the turkey in overlapping slices on a large platter. Cover and set aside.

4. Strain the vegetables, parsley, and bay leaf from the stock and discard. (*Freeze the stock, well covered, in a plastic container for up to 4 weeks. The stock makes a flavorful base for soup.*)

FINISHING TOUCHES AND TABLE PRESENTATION

Slice the Cran-orange Buttermilk Biscuits in half. Spread a thin layer of Dried Cran-apple Chutney on the bottom of each biscuit. Cover the biscuit with 2 slices of turkey breast and 1 leaf of romaine lettuce. Cover with the top half of the biscuit. Arrange the biscuits on a large shallow basket or platter garnished with the whole cranberries and flat-leaf parsley and set on the table.

The Inventive Chef

THE TURKEY BREAST WILL STAY FRESH FOR 2 DAYS IN THE BROTH IN THE REFRIGERATOR. TO KEEP THE MEAT MOIST, DON'T CARVE IT UNTIL YOU ARE READY TO MAKE THE SANDWICHES. I LIKE TO USE THIS METHOD OF COOKING TURKEY FOR A MOIST, CHUNKY TURKEY SALAD.

Dried Cran-apple Chutney

MAKES 2 CUPS

6 ounces dried cranberries
3 tablespoons sugar
½ cup cran-apple juice
⅓ cup fresh orange juice
2 Granny Smith apples, peeled, cored, and chopped small
3 tablespoons Dijon mustard
½ teaspoon powdered ginger
2 teaspoons fresh lemon juice
¼ teaspoon freshly ground black pepper, or to taste

1. Place the cranberries in a saucepan with the sugar and cran-apple and orange juices. Simmer over medium heat until the dried cranberries are plump, about 5 minutes. Add the chopped apples and simmer for 3 minutes more, until all the cranberries and apples have softened, but are not mushy.

2. Transfer the cranberry mixture, with its liquid, to the bowl of a food processor, add the mustard, ginger, lemon juice, and pepper and pulse briefly, until the chutney is slightly chunky.

Cran-orange Buttermilk Biscuits

MAKES 20–22 BISCUITS

SPECIAL COOKWARE
2 1/2-inch round biscuit cutter

4 cups self-rising flour
1/2 tablespoon baking powder
1 teaspoon salt
1/2 cup sugar
1 cup vegetable shortening
1 1/2 cups buttermilk
Grated zest of 2 oranges
1 1/4 cups coarsely chopped cranberries

1. Preheat the oven to 400°.

2. In a large bowl stir together the flour, baking powder, salt, and sugar. Using a pastry blender or your hands, blend in the shortening until the mixture resembles coarse cornmeal. Make a well in the center of the mixture.

3. In a medium mixing bowl, combine the buttermilk, orange zest, and cranberries until they are well blended.

4. Add the buttermilk mixture to the dry ingredients. Quickly mix the wet and dry ingredients with a wooden spoon until the batter is just combined.

5. Lightly flour a work surface. Gently turn the dough out onto the surface and, using floured hands, lightly pat it into a 3/4-inch-thick circle. Cut the dough into biscuits with a 2 1/2-inch round biscuit cutter. Dip the cutter into flour between cuts. Reform dough and cut additional biscuits, one time only.

6. Place the biscuits, one inch apart, on two ungreased baking sheets and bake until they are golden brown, about 12–15 minutes. Cool for 3 minutes on a wire cooling rack.

THE MAIN EVENT

Fennel and Celery Slaw with Red Apples and Grapes

MAKES 8 SERVINGS

THE DRESSING:
2 tablespoons sour cream
1/3 cup mayonnaise
1/4 cup unsweetened applesauce
1 1/2 teaspoons cider vinegar or rice vinegar
1 1/2 teaspoons poppy seeds
1/2 teaspoon salt, or to taste
1/4 teaspoon pepper, or to taste

2 medium bulbs fennel, washed, tops and bottoms removed

4 large stalks celery, washed, leaf ends and bottoms
   removed

6 scallions, green parts only, sliced $^{1}/_{8}$-inch thick on the
   diagonal

1 $^{1}/_{4}$ cups seedless red grapes, washed, stemmed, and sliced
   in half

Juice of 1 large lemon

2 large red Rome Beauty or Delicious apples, washed, skin
   on, cored, and cut into $^{1}/_{2}$-inch dice

1. In a medium-sized bowl, whisk together the sour
cream, mayonnaise, applesauce, vinegar, poppy seeds,
salt, and pepper. Blend well and reseason to taste.

2. Set aside at room temperature or store in a covered
container in the refrigerator for up to 3 days.

3. To make the slaw, cut the fennel bulbs in half
lengthwise. Slice each half into $^{1}/_{4}$-inch crosswise
pieces and place the pieces in a large bowl.

4. Cut the celery crosswise into $^{1}/_{4}$-inch slices and add
it to the fennel. Add the scallions and grapes.

5. Pour the lemon juice into a separate medium-size
bowl. Toss the apples together with the lemon juice
until all the pieces are well coated. Add the apples
with the lemon juice to the fennel mixture.

6. Toss the slaw with the reserved dressing and taste
for seasoning. (The slaw may be served immediately
after tossing or can be stored covered in the
refrigerator for up to 2 hours. If you plan to store the
slaw in the refrigerator before serving, add the apples
and lemon juice just before serving.)

FINISHING TOUCHES AND
TABLE PRESENTATION

I like to serve this colorful slaw in a large terra-cotta or
pottery bowl. The terra-cotta picks up the beautiful
color of the apples and the grapes.

ON THE SIDE
Carrot and Peanut Soup
MAKES 8 SERVINGS

3 tablespoons salted butter

1 large onion, peeled and medium chopped

2 tablespoons flour

2 quarts stock reserved from turkey recipe (page 245)
   or 2 quarts chicken stock, homemade or low-sodium
   canned, at room temperature

8 large carrots, peeled and medium chopped

$^{2}/_{3}$ cup heavy cream

1 teaspoon powdered ginger

1 teaspoon salt, or to taste

$^{1}/_{2}$ teaspoon freshly ground pepper, or to taste

8 drops Tabasco sauce

$^{1}/_{4}$ cup smooth peanut butter

GARNISH

18 (3-inch-long) thin carrot sticks, about 3–4 carrots

1. Heat the butter in a large saucepan or stockpot
over medium-high heat. Add the onion and sauté until
soft and translucent, 3–5 minutes. Blend in the flour
and cook, stirring, over low heat for 2 minutes.

2. Gradually whisk in the turkey or chicken stock.
(Whisking the stock gradually will yield a smooth
thickened mixture.) Add the chopped carrots and
simmer the soup, uncovered, over medium heat until
the carrots are tender, about 30 minutes.

3. Pour the broth and carrots into the bowl of a food

processor in batches, or use a handheld blender. *(Don't overload the processor or you will have a flood of broth and carrots all over your counter.)* Process the soup, using the knife blade, until it is a smooth puree.

4. Return the soup to the saucepan and blend in the heavy cream, ginger, salt, pepper, Tabasco, and peanut butter. Put the soup back over low heat until it is heated through. *(The peanut taste is subtle the first day, but as the soup sits the flavor becomes more intense.)*

FINISHING TOUCHES AND TABLE PRESENTATION

Fill large, wide-mouthed white crockery mugs with the soup, set 3 carrot sticks into each mug, and place the mugs on the table.

> ## The Inventive Chef
> THIS IS A GREAT SOUP TO TAKE ALONG IN HEATED THERMOSES FOR TAILGATING FESTIVITIES.

ON THE SIDE
Candied Yam Steak Fries

MAKES 8 SERVINGS

6 large yams, peeled
8 tablespoons salted butter, melted
1 cup light brown sugar
$^1/_2$ cup maple syrup
$^1/_4$ cup fresh orange juice

1 tablespoon cider vinegar
$^1/_4$ teaspoon ground cinnamon
$^1/_4$ teaspoon powdered ginger
$^3/_4$ teaspoon salt
$^1/_2$ teaspoon freshly ground black pepper

GARNISH
2 tablespoons ground cinnamon
$^1/_4$ cup finely chopped fresh chives

1. Preheat the oven to 375°. Grease two baking sheets with one tablespoon of butter.
2. Cut each yam in half lengthwise, then cut each half into 4 lengthwise wedges.
3. Combine the remaining butter, brown sugar, maple syrup, orange juice, cider vinegar, cinnamon, and ginger in a small saucepan. Cook the glaze over medium heat, stirring often, until the sugar has melted, about 4 minutes.
4. Place the yam wedges on the baking sheets and brush them well with the glaze. Sprinkle the yams with the salt and pepper and bake for 30–40 minutes, until they are tender and candied.

FINISHING TOUCHES AND TABLE PRESENTATION

Serve the yams in napkin-lined baskets, sprinkled with cinnamon and chives, and watch them disappear.

> ## The Inventive Chef
> THE YAM FRIES ARE FUN TO SERVE AT A COCKTAIL PARTY AS AN EXTRA NIBBLE.

Roasted Cauliflower Soup
with Turmeric

MAKES 8 SERVINGS

SPECIAL COOKWARE
Large (6–8-quart) stockpot

2 large heads cauliflower
8 cloves garlic, peeled and left whole
5 tablespoons olive oil
*2 large leeks, well washed, white parts only, cut into
    medium dice*
2 stalks celery, washed and cut into medium dice
2 medium carrots, peeled and cut into medium dice
2 quarts canned vegetable broth (available in health
    food stores and large supermarkets)
1 large baking potato, peeled and cut into $^1/_2$-inch dice
2 bay leaves
4 sprigs curly parsley
$^1/_8$ teaspoon ground cloves
$^1/_2$ teaspoon turmeric
$^1/_4$ teaspoon cayenne pepper
1 teaspoon salt, or to taste
$^1/_4$ teaspoon black pepper, or to taste
$1^1/_2$–$2^1/_4$ cups half-and-half or whole milk

GARNISH
$^1/_2$ cup sour cream or crème fraîche
3 tablespoons finely chopped fresh chives

1. Preheat the oven to 450°.
2. Cut the cauliflower into medium-size florets and
place them in a large bowl with the garlic cloves. Toss

well with 3 tablespoons of the olive oil to lightly coat
the vegetables.

3. Spread the cauliflower and garlic onto two large
baking sheets. *(The more room they have, the better they
will roast)*. Place the baking sheets low in the oven and
roast for 15–20 minutes, turning them once so that
the cauliflower and garlic are flecked with a roasted
brown color. Remove from the oven and turn the oven
off.

4. While the cauliflower and garlic are roasting, heat
the remaining 2 tablespoons of oil over medium-low
heat in a large, 6–8 quart stockpot. Add the leeks,
celery, and carrots and sauté for 8–10 minutes, stirring
often, until the vegetables are slightly softened.

5. Add the vegetable broth, potatoes, bay leaves, and
parsley and bring to a rolling boil over high heat.
Lower the heat, add the reserved roasted cauliflower and
garlic, and simmer the soup for 10–14 minutes, or until
the vegetables are fully cooked. Remove from the heat.

6. Puree the broth and vegetables in small batches in
the bowl of the food processor fitted with the knife
blade. *(If you have a hand-immersion blender, the soup can be
pureed directly in the pot after it has cooled slightly.)*

7. Return the pureed soup to the pot and bring it to
a simmer over medium heat. Add the cloves, turmeric,
cayenne, salt, and pepper. Add half-and-half or milk
until the soup has reached the thickness and
creaminess you desire. Continue to cook, stirring often,
until the soup is piping hot.

Ladle the soup into a large tureen or into 8 large soup mugs. Top with the sour cream or crème fraîche and a sprinkle of fresh chives, or place the garnishes in small bowls near the soup and allow your guests to help themselves.

The Inventive Chef

ROASTED ASPARAGUS, BRUSSELS SPROUTS, OR BROCCOLI ARE GOOD ALTERNATIVES TO THE CAULIFLOWER.

ON THE SIDE

Sweet Potato and Zucchini Pancakes

MAKES ABOUT 24-32 PANCAKES

SPECIAL COOKWARE
Food processor with grating disk or large hand-grater

2 pounds sweet potatoes, peeled and sliced lengthwise into ¹/₂-inch-wide pieces
1 zucchini, peeled and finely diced
4 scallions, white and green parts, finely chopped
³/₄ cup unpeeled, cored, and diced Granny Smith apple; about 1 large
Grated zest of 1 orange (approximately 1 tablespoon)
4 eggs, lightly beaten
¹/₂ cup flour
1 ¹/₄ teaspoons ground cumin

1 teaspoon salt, or to taste
¹/₈ teaspoon cayenne pepper
¹/₂ cup vegetable oil, or as needed for frying pancakes

GARNISH
Julienned zest of 1 orange
1 orange cut into ¹/₈-inch rounds

1. Shred the potatoes in the bowl of a food processor fitted with the grating blade (or use the large side of a hand grater). Transfer the potatoes to a mixing bowl and stir in the zucchini, scallions, apple, orange zest, eggs, flour, cumin, salt, and cayenne.
2. Heat 1 inch of oil in a large skillet over medium-high heat. Test the seasonings of the pancake batter by dipping 1 heaping tablespoon of the batter into the oil. Sauté for about 1–1¹/₂ minutes on each side or until the cake is golden brown. Remove the cake and the skillet from the heat. Allow the cake to cool slightly before tasting. Adjust the seasonings in the remaining batter.
3. Return the skillet to the heat and continue dropping heaping tablespoons of batter into the oil, turning each once. Make certain to allow 1 inch between the pancakes so they brown evenly. Drain the cakes on paper towels and transfer to a baking sheet.
4. If you are not serving the pancakes immediately, keep them warm in a 250° oven for not more than 30 minutes.

Serve the pancakes garnished with the julienned orange zest from a flat platter. Nestle the slices of orange around the edge of the platter.

THE GRAND FINALE

Pear Custard with Apricot Sauce

MAKES 8 SERVINGS

SPECIAL COOKWARE
2-quart soufflé dish

1 cup sugar
$^1/_4$ cup water
8 tablespoons unsalted butter
1 $^1/_2$ ounces fresh ginger root, peeled and cut into $^1/_4$-inch
    rounds
1 vanilla bean split in half lengthwise
4 Anjou or Bartlett pears, peeled, cored, and diced in
    $^1/_2$-inch pieces
$^1/_4$ cup ginger liqueur or brandy, Bols or Arrow
2 cups buttermilk
6 whole eggs
3 egg yolks
$^1/_2$ cup sugar
3 slices brioche or challah bread, crusts removed, diced in
    $^1/_4$-inch cubes
Apricot Sauce (recipe follows)

1. Preheat the oven to 325°.
2. Place the sugar and water in a small skillet or
saucepan over medium heat, stirring constantly until
the sugar comes to a boil. Stop stirring and let the
sugar cook until it reaches a rich and deep amber
color. Immediately pour into a soufflé dish and swirl
around to coat the bottom and sides of the dish. Set
aside.
3. In a small skillet, heat the butter with the ginger
slices and vanilla bean over high heat until brown and
foamy. Continue cooking until the bubbles subside and
the butter gives off a nutty aroma. Immediately strain
the butter into a medium skillet and sauté pears in this
butter. When pears begin to soften, add the ginger
liqueur. Strain the pears in a colander, reserving the
juices.
4. In a bowl, beat the eggs and egg yolks with sugar.
Mix in the buttermilk. Stir in the pears.
5. Drizzle the reserved pear juices over the bread
pieces. Stir the bread into the pear/egg mixture and
pour into the prepared soufflé dish.
6. Place the soufflé dish in a larger pan filled with
boiling water halfway up the mold and bake for about
70 minutes, or until the custard does not jiggle in the
center and the tip of a knife comes clean when
inserted in the center. Remove the soufflé dish from
the water bath and chill in refrigerator.

FINISHING TOUCHES AND
TABLE PRESENTATION

Serve the custard chilled or at room temperature from
the soufflé dish. The custard looks elegant unmolded.
To unmold, put a plate on top of the soufflé dish and,
with a quick motion, turn over the custard onto the
plate. Pass the Apricot Sauce separately.

Apricot Sauce

MAKES 1 CUP

³/₄ cup apricot preserves
1 tablespoon fresh lemon juice
Grated zest of 1 lemon
¹/₂ teaspoon almond extract
¹/₄ cup dried apricots, finely chopped
2 tablespoons apricot brandy
2 tablespoons apricot nectar or juice

1. Place the apricot preserves and lemon juice in a small saucepan over medium heat. Stir until the preserves are completely melted.

2. Put the melted preserves, the lemon zest, almond extract, dried apricots, apricot brandy, and apricot juice in the bowl of a food processor fitted with the knife blade and process until the sauce is thickened and well blended. *(Small chunks of apricot will remain and add texture to the sauce.)* Keep the sauce warm in the top of a double boiler over simmering water.

FINISHING TOUCHES AND TABLE PRESENTATION

Serve the warm apricot sauce in a glass or china sauceboat placed on an underliner. Let your guests help themselves.

> ## The Inventive Chef
>
> WARM APRICOT SAUCE ADDS JUST THE RIGHT AMOUNT OF TART BALANCE TO ICE CREAM OR A SUGARY POUND CAKE. STORE THE SAUCE IN YOUR REFRIGERATOR FOR UP TO 2 WEEKS. REWARM IT IN THE TOP OF A DOUBLE BOILER OVER SIMMERING WATER.

KITCHEN SCHEDULE

2 OR 3 DAYS BEFORE THE PARTY

MAIN EVENT

Chutney — Prepare through step 2; cool; store covered in refrigerator.

Slaw — Prepare dressing through step 2; store covered in refrigerator.

THE DAY BEFORE THE PARTY

MAIN EVENT

Turkey — Prepare through step 2; store in poaching broth covered in refrigerator.
Prepare romaine lettuce; store covered in refrigerator.

Slaw — Prepare fennel, celery, scallions, and grapes; store separately, covered, in refrigerator.

TOQUE 1

Carrot Soup — Prepare through step 4; cool; store covered in refrigerator.
Prepare garnish; place in cold water; store covered in refrigerator.

TOQUE 2

Cauliflower Soup — Prepare through step 7; cool; store covered in refrigerator.
Make chive garnish; store covered in refrigerator.

GRAND FINALE

Apricot Sauce — Prepare through step 2; cool; store covered in refrigerator.

Pear Custard — Buy challah; let stand at room temperature.

Strategic Maneuvers:

Fill creamer; cover and store in refrigerator.
Fill sugar bowl.
Set table.
Check ice and beverages.
Locate teas.
Chill wine if white.

Check garnishes for each recipe.
Locate and label all serving bowls, platters, and utensils.

THE DAY OF THE PARTY

MAIN EVENT

Turkey — Prepare step 3. Follow instructions for finishing touches in Main Event (page 246).

Chutney — Place in service bowl at room temperature.

Biscuits — Prepare through step 6; when cool, arrange for service.

Slaw — Prepare through step 6; store covered in refrigerator for up to 2 hours.

TOQUE 1

Carrot Soup — Set in top of double boiler for warming.

Yams — Prepare through step 4; set aside at room temperature.

TOQUE 2

Cauliflower Soup — Set in top of double boiler for warming.

Pancakes — Prepare through step 3; set aside at room temperature.

GRAND FINALE

Custard — Prepare through step 6; set aside at room temperature.

Apricot Sauce — Set in top of double boiler for reheating.

35 MINUTES BEFORE GUESTS ARRIVE:

Preheat oven to 250°.

MAIN EVENT

Turkey — Make sandwiches, if this is the game plan.

TOQUE 1

Carrot Soup — Reheat in top of double boiler.

| **TOQUE 2** | Cauliflower Soup | Reheat in top of double boiler. |

20 MINUTES BEFORE DINNER:

| **TOQUE 1:** | Yams | Reheat in oven. |
| **TOQUE 2** | Pancakes | Reheat in oven. |

15 MINUTES BEFORE DINNER:

GRAND FINALE	Custard	Set for service.
	Apricot Sauce	Reheat in top of double boiler.
		Plug in coffee.

JUST BEFORE DINNER:

Ready all sandwich fixings (turkey, romaine, chutney, biscuits), if this is the game plan.

Bring slaw to table.

Fill bowls with hot soup; garnish; bring to table.

Transfer yams or pancakes to table.

DESSERT SERVICE:

Bring custard to table with warm sauce.

AFTER SERVICE:

Unplug coffee.
Turn off oven.

CHAPTER 11

The Bright Feeling and Fresh Flavors of Brunch

A home-cooked brunch is a delicious and distinct entertainment, filled with the energy and excitement of a new day. If you haven't cooked for a brunch crowd in a while, you will enjoy seeing the "morning" personalities of your guests—brunch should definitely be served on the AM side of noon, in my opinion—and you'll marvel at their ravenous appetites!

Each of the brunch occasions in this chapter has enough great food to satisfy the most famished among your friends (even those who have been up since 6 o'clock, run four miles, and played two sets of tennis before your party.) But beyond the flavorful array of savory and sweet dishes, these menus show the versatility of the brunch format: You can make brunch for a big crowd or an intimate gathering, with as casual or formal a feeling as you like.

◆ Give your friends and neighbors a gift on Christmas morning: a brunch buffet featuring herbed sausage frittata, tomato bread pudding, and baked fruits with pecans.

◆ No hurry for the host on a lazy Sunday morning when banana-walnut and brown sugar pancakes are flipped off the griddle into a big stack—and gobbled up right in the kitchen.

◆ Dad likes a bit of formality on Father's Day, so pamper him with a classy three-course brunch featuring savory golden-baked acorn squash stuffed with ham, mushrooms, and pears.

In my mind, brunch means "weekend," and one of its distinct pleasures should be a *relaxed* and unhurried feeling for all, including the host. Even a multicourse meal such as the semi-formal Father's Day brunch should have a leisurely, lighthearted spirit to go with its elegant touches and plated presentation. From the moment your guests come in, make it easy for them to feel at home and help themselves. Have sparkling pitchers of chilled juices and simple platters of sliced fruits ready to satisfy their hunger pangs. If you are offering alcohol, have vodka or champagne out for self-service, with accompanying juices and garnishes.

Brunch is a meal that lends itself to easy embellishments. Along with the featured foods, provide a range of wonderful condiments—not only jams and jellies, but mustards, salsas, and other savories to go with your menu. Baskets of baked goods are also rich additions to the brunch table: You will find some terrific baking recipes here, and you can fill out the meal with fresh bagels and muffins from the bakery, too.

A relaxed brunch host is someone who has followed a well-developed game plan. The kitchen schedules will help you get as much as possible completed in the days (and night) before the party. And the spirit of relaxation will be expressed as well in your decorations and table settings. Flowers in crockery vases, and bowls of fruits and nuts, are appropriate, simple centerpieces. Set out with casual, colorful tableware and linens, everything will look naturally cheerful, saying "Good morning" to all in a welcoming manner.

A Merry Buffet for Christmas Morning

THE MAIN EVENT:

Herbed Sausage Frittata

ON THE SIDE:

Orzo Risotto with Smoked Norwegian Salmon

◆

*Endive, Watercress, Baby Carrot,
and Spiced Raisin Salad with Mint Vinaigrette*

ON THE SIDE:

*Wild and Brown Rice with Oranges, Pears,
and Strawberries*

◆

Tomato Bread Pudding (page 191)

◆

Zucchini Double-Cheese Corn Muffins

THE GRAND FINALE:

Baked Fruits with Figs and Pecans

◆

Hazelnut Biscotti (page 331)

BEVERAGE RECOMMENDATIONS:
Sunrise Mimosas (page 357)
Strawberry Citrus Punch (page 354)

*A*FTER BRUNCH IS SERVED, YOU CAN OPEN THE PRESENTS."
The children may have had visions of sugarplums dancing in their heads last night, but this morning they have eyes only for the pile of gifts under the tree. Don't prolong their torment. Pop the frittata in the oven and drop the orzo into the water. By the time the frittata is puffed and golden (and garnished with red and green peppers for the occasion), you'll have tossed the pasta with its savory sauce of cream and smoked salmon. Put the hot dishes out on the buffet with the endive salad and mint vinaigrette. As soon as your guests have filled their plates and settled into comfortable spots in the living room, the children can get down to serious Christmas business. (Save food for the kids: It will taste just great at room temperature when the gift pile is gone.)

This is a visually appealing brunch menu that's just great for buffet-style service—whether it's Christmas or any other morning. The frittata is a great crowd pleaser, a creamy egg custard loaded with chunks of breakfast sausage, sautéed onions and peppers, sharp cheese, and toasted pine nuts, all seasoned with sage and nutmeg. It bakes quickly, and is easily turned out on a buffet platter.

The orzo "risotto" is especially simple and delightful, pairing the delicate pasta (sweet from cooking in broth and wine) with luscious Norwegian salmon, fresh dill, and cream. The one-toque menu also presents a beautifully arranged salad of sliced endive, watercress, baby carrots, and spiced raisins for exciting textural and flavor contrasts.

You will also love (as I do) the look and taste of the wild and brown rices combined with fresh strawberries and chunks of orange and pear. This chewy, sweet, and bright-flavored dish is perfect for brunch—somewhere between a hearty morning ce-

real and a salad. It is complemented by a creamy, cheesy, rich casserole of Tomato Bread Pudding. The Zucchini Double-Cheese Corn Muffins harmonize well with the frittata, adding a subtle zing of chili powder and black pepper.

The buffet is completed with a casserole of baked fruits that can be set out with the Main Event or reserved as a separate course. In either case, the warm mélange of figs, pineapple, grapefruit, banana, and orange chunks—with the crunch of pecans—is heavenly in its thick fruit syrup. Dunked in coffee (or in the syrup), the accompanying Hazelnut Biscotti provide a perfect last bite.

SETTING THE STAGE

After arriving, friends and neighbors shake off the snow—this *has* to be a white Christmas—and help themselves to coffee and cocoa from insulated carafes set out in the kitchen or on the dining-room table. Fruit juices should also be available and, if you want, Sunrise Mimosas (page 357), and Bloody Marys (page 356), to spread some cheer. Set up your buffet in the dining room—with an appropriate centerpiece, of course—and let your guests find seats in the living room, where they can fully enjoy your home in all its Yuletide splendor.

Note that all these brunch recipes are written for 8 servings but can easily be expanded (make multiples of the frittata in separate pans). If you are having a large crowd, you might want to rent tables or extra chairs—and linens with a hint of the holidays, too.

THE MAIN EVENT

Herbed Sausage Frittata

MAKES 8 SERVINGS

SPECIAL COOKWARE
12-inch skillet with oven-safe handle

2 tablespoons pine nuts
³/₄ pound bulk, ground breakfast sausage
2 medium Spanish or yellow onions, peeled and finely chopped

1 medium red bell pepper, seeded and finely diced
1 medium green bell pepper, seeded and finely diced
14 eggs
1¹/₂ cups heavy cream, half-and-half, or whole milk
2 cups coarsely grated extra-sharp Cheddar or jalapeño Monterey Jack
2 teaspoons finely chopped fresh sage
1 tablespoon finely chopped curly parsley
¹/₂ teaspoon salt
¹/₈ teaspoon cayenne pepper
¹/₄ teaspoon nutmeg
Vegetable oil, to grease the skillet
¹/₂ tablespoon olive oil

GARNISH
1 small red pepper, seeded and cut into ¹/₈-inch rounds
1 small green pepper, seeded and cut into ¹/₈-inch rounds
2 tablespoons coarsely grated extra-sharp Cheddar

1. Preheat the oven to 350°.
2. Place the pine nuts on an ungreased baking pan and toast them in the oven for about 4–5 minutes, until light golden in color. Chop the nuts into small pieces. Set aside at room temperature or store, covered, in the refrigerator.
3. Break up the sausage and sauté it in a 12-inch skillet with an oven-safe handle until completely browned, about 4 minutes. Remove the browned meat with a slotted spoon, but do not drain the drippings. Set the sausage aside and let it cool to room temperature.
4. Sauté the onions in the sausage drippings until they are translucent, about 3–5 minutes. Add the diced red and green peppers and cook the vegetables until they have slightly softened, about 3 minutes. Remove from the heat and reserve in the skillet.
5. In a large bowl, beat the eggs with a whisk until they are well blended. Stir in the heavy cream,

reserved sausage, cheese, toasted pine nuts, sage, parsley, salt, cayenne, nutmeg, and the sautéed vegetables, and mix well. Using vegetable oil, generously grease the bottom and sides of the skillet. Pour the egg mixture into the skillet and cook the frittata over medium heat for 3–4 minutes, until the mixture begins to pull away from the sides of the skillet.

6. Transfer the skillet to the oven and bake the frittata until it is golden on top and set, about 25 minutes. Slip the frittata out of the skillet onto a round serving platter.

7. While the frittata is baking, heat $^1/_2$ teaspoon of olive oil in a small skillet and sauté the red and green pepper garnish over medium heat for 2 minutes, until wilted. Set aside.

FINISHING TOUCHES AND TABLE PRESENTATION

Cut the frittata into 8 pie-shaped wedges. Arrange the wedges with the grated Cheddar and pepper garnish on a round serving platter. This is the best time to use Christmas dishes or platters with winter scenes.

The Inventive Chef

USE YOUR IMAGINATION AND EXPERIMENT WITH THE FILLINGS YOU PUT INTO A FRITTATA. JUST REMEMBER THAT ANY FILLING YOU USE MUST BE FULLY COOKED BEFORE ADDING IT TO THE EGGS.

ON THE SIDE

Orzo Risotto with Smoked Norwegian Salmon

MAKES 8 SERVINGS

5 cups chicken broth, homemade or low-sodium canned
1 cup dry white wine
2 cups orzo
Pinch of salt
6 ounces smoked Norwegian salmon, finely julienned
2 tablespoons fresh lemon juice
2 tablespoons finely chopped fresh dill
1 cup light cream
$^1/_8$ teaspoon freshly ground black pepper, or to taste

GARNISH
1 cup grated Parmigiano Reggiano

1. In a large saucepan over high heat, bring the chicken broth and wine to a boil. Add the orzo with the salt. Lower the heat and simmer the orzo, uncovered, for 12–15 minutes, until it is just resistant to the bite. Drain off any remaining liquid and set the orzo aside in the saucepan, off the heat.

2. Gently toss the salmon, lemon juice, and dill with the orzo. Add the light cream and warm the mixture over moderate heat, stirring often, until it is hot. Season with the black pepper.

The orzo looks very tempting served in a large terra-
cotta or glass bowl. Place it first on the buffet, with
a dish of grated Parmigiano Reggiano and a pepper
mill.

> ## The Inventive Chef
>
> SUBSTITUTING SUN-DRIED TOMATOES FOR THE
> SMOKED SALMON WILL NOT ONLY CHANGE THE
> TASTE OF THE ORZO BUT WILL CREATE A FINE
> PASTA TO SERVE WITH VEAL OR CHICKEN.
> CHANGE THE DILL TO PARSLEY AND ADD SALT
> TO TASTE WHEN YOU SEASON.

ON THE SIDE

Endive, Watercress, Baby Carrot, and Spiced Raisin Salad with Mint Vinaigrette

MAKES 8 SERVINGS

THE RAISINS
1/4 cup fresh orange juice
1 cinnamon stick
2 whole cloves
1/2 cup dark seedless raisins

THE SALAD
*3 bunches watercress (select bunches with large leaves),
about 6 ounces each*
24 long, thin baby carrots
4 endive
Mint Vinaigrette (recipe follows)

1. To prepare the raisins, warm the orange juice with
the cinnamon stick and cloves in a medium saucepan
over moderate heat, until the juice begins to simmer.
Remove the saucepan from the heat, add the raisins,
and set aside to plump for 20 minutes while you
prepare the salad.
2. Remove the stems from the watercress. Wash and
dry the leaves.
3. Peel the carrots and remove the green tops. *(If you
can't find baby carrots, substitute large thin carrots. Cut them in
half or thirds and round the tops with a carrot peeler.)*
4. Remove any browned outer leaves from the endive
and the brown part from the bottom. Slice the endive
in half lengthwise, then cut each half in half.

FINISHING TOUCHES AND
TABLE PRESENTATION

Use a large round or rectangular platter for the salad.
Drain the raisins and discard any remaining orange juice
(all of it may have been absorbed by the raisins).
Arrange the endive quarters around the edge of the platter. Make a bed of watercress leaves in the center, and
place the carrots over the watercress in spokes, with the
stem ends facing out toward the endive. Scatter the
raisins over the endive. Just before serving, spoon the
vinaigrette (recipe follows) over the salad. Place the
salad on the table after the frittata.

ON THE SIDE

Wild and Brown Rice with Oranges, Pears, and Strawberries

MAKES 8 SERVINGS

1 cup wild rice
1 cup short-grain brown rice
3 $^{1}/_{4}$ cups chicken broth, homemade or low-sodium canned
2 $^{1}/_{4}$ cups fresh orange juice
Finely minced zest of one orange
Finely minced zest of one lemon
1 large white onion, peeled and finely chopped
2 tablespoons vegetable oil
1 tablespoon balsamic vinegar
3 oranges, Valencia or navel, peeled, pith removed,
    sectioned, each section halved, crosswise
$^{1}/_{4}$ teaspoon ground allspice
$^{1}/_{4}$ teaspoon ground nutmeg
1 tablespoon finely chopped flat-leaf parsley
3 pears, Anjou or Bartlett, unpeeled, cored, cut into
    $^{1}/_{2}$-inch cubes
1 pint strawberries, washed, hulled, and quartered
$^{1}/_{2}$ teaspoon salt
$^{1}/_{4}$ teaspoon freshly ground black pepper, or to taste

1. Place the wild and brown rices in separate mesh strainers. Wash both rices well with cold water. Drain and reserve.
2. Bring 2 cups of the chicken broth and 1$^{1}/_{4}$ cup of the orange juice to a rapid simmer over high heat in a medium saucepan. Add the wild rice and the orange zest. Lower the heat and simmer the wild rice,

Mint Vinaigrette

MAKES $^{1}/_{2}$ CUP

2 tablespoons raspberry vinegar
1$^{1}/_{2}$ teaspoons Dijon mustard
1 tablespoon chopped fresh mint
1$^{1}/_{2}$ teaspoons honey
1 tablespoon fresh orange juice
1 teaspoon fresh lemon juice
$^{1}/_{2}$ cup olive oil
$^{1}/_{4}$ teaspoon salt, or to taste
$^{1}/_{8}$ teaspoon freshly ground black pepper, or to taste

1. Place the vinegar, mustard, mint, honey, and orange and lemon juices into the bowl of a food processor. Process until the ingredients are finely pureed. With the motor running, slowly drizzle the olive oil through the feeding tube until the vinaigrette has thickened. Season with salt and pepper to taste. *(If the vinaigrette is made in advance and refrigerated, allow the dressing to come to room temperature and whisk it well before using.)*

uncovered, for about 45 minutes, until all the kernels have blossomed. Drain off any excess liquid. Reserve at room temperature.

3. Bring the remaining 1 1/4 cups chicken broth and 1 cup orange juice to a rapid simmer over high heat in a second medium saucepan. Add the brown rice and the lemon zest. Lower the heat and simmer the brown rice, uncovered, for 30 minutes. *(The kernels should have a slightly chewy texture when they are finished.)*

4. While the rices are simmering, sauté the onion in the oil until it is translucent, about 3–5 minutes. Add the balsamic vinegar and cook over high heat about 15 seconds, until the vinegar is absorbed by the onion. Set aside at room temperature.

5. Combine the wild and brown rices in a large decorative salad bowl. Add the sautéed onion, oranges, allspice, nutmeg, and parsley. Add the pears and strawberries just before serving. Blend all the ingredients well and season with the salt and pepper.

FINISHING TOUCHES AND
TABLE PRESENTATION

The rices should be served warm, not hot. If you re-frigerate the rice, the flavors will be subdued and the rice will become crunchier to the bite. The colors of the rice are more vibrant in a lightly colored pottery bowl.

The Inventive Chef

MANGO, PINEAPPLE, GRAPEFRUIT, AND CURRANTS ARE SOME OF THE FRUITS THAT CAN BE SUBSTITUTED FOR THE PEARS AND STRAWBERRIES IN THE RICE. SUBSTITUTE GINGER AND CINNAMON FOR THE ALLSPICE AND NUTMEG.

ON THE SIDE

Zucchini Double-Cheese Corn Muffins

MAKES 12 LARGE OR 24 MINI-MUFFINS

SPECIAL COOKWARE
Baking tin of 12 (2 1/2-inch) muffin cups

2 tablespoons vegetable shortening
1 1/2 cups all-purpose flour
1 cups yellow cornmeal
1/4 cup sugar
4 teaspoons baking powder
3/4 teaspoon chili powder
1 teaspoon salt
1/2 teaspoon freshly ground black pepper
2 eggs, beaten
1 cup whole milk
1/3 cup vegetable oil
1/2 cup finely grated Monterey Jack
1/2 cup finely grated sharp Cheddar
1/2 pound (about 1 medium) zucchini, washed and finely grated
2 tablespoons fresh chopped chives

GARNISH
1/2-pound wedge sharp Cheddar

1. Preheat the oven to 400°. Grease with butter 12 (2 1/2-inch) muffin cups or two mini-muffin-cup pans.

2. Place the flour, cornmeal, sugar, baking powder, chili powder, salt, and pepper in a large bowl. Mix the dry ingredients well.

3. Combine the eggs, milk, vegetable oil, grated Jack and Cheddar cheeses, grated zucchini, and chives in another bowl. Make a well in the center of the dry ingredients. Place the zucchini mixture in the well and toss with a fork until all the ingredients are moistened. *(Over-blending the ingredients toughens the texture of the muffins.)*

4. Fill the prepared muffin cups ²/₃ full with the batter and bake for 20–25 minutes for the large muffins, or 15–20 minutes for the mini-muffins. *(The muffins should be golden brown, and a toothpick inserted in the center should come out clean.)*

FINISHING TOUCHES AND TABLE PRESENTATION

Arrange the muffins in napkin-lined baskets. Place the wedge of cheese on a small cheese board with a cheese knife to the side of the muffins. Guests can help themselves to slices of cheese.

> ### The Inventive Chef
> FOR A SPICIER MUFFIN, USE MONTEREY JACK WITH JALAPEÑO PEPPERS AND INCREASE THE CHILI POWDER TO YOUR TASTE.

THE GRAND FINALE

Baked Fruits with Figs and Pecans

MAKES 8 SERVINGS

SPECIAL COOKWARE
Decorative oven-to-table baking dish, 13 by 9 by 2 inches

2 tablespoons unsalted butter
1 large (about 4-pound) pineapple, peeled, halved
 lengthwise, cored, and cut into ¹/₄-inch slices
3 medium pink grapefruits, peel and pith removed, cut into
 ¹/₄-inch rounds with a serrated knife
4 large bananas (about 1¹/₄ pounds), peeled, ends
 removed, and halved lengthwise
5 medium oranges, peel and pith removed, cut into ¹/₄-inch
 rounds with a serrated knife
1¹/₂ cups dark brown sugar
¹/₄ cup fresh orange juice
¹/₂ cup pineapple juice
2 teaspoons fresh lemon juice
¹/₂ teaspoon ground cinnamon
¹/₄ teaspoon ground nutmeg
³/₄ cup coarsely chopped dried figs
¹/₃ cup pecans, coarsely chopped
1 quart ripe strawberries, washed, hulled, and sliced in half
 lengthwise

GARNISH
1 bunch fresh mint

1. Preheat the oven to 375°. Lightly butter a 13-by-9-by-2-inch decorative oven-to-table baking dish.

2. Layer the pineapple in overlapping slices on the bottom of the baking pan. Layer the grapefruit slices

over the pineapple and the banana slices over the grapefruit. Arrange the orange slices over the banana.

3. Blend the brown sugar and orange, pineapple, and lemon juices together with a balloon whisk. Add the cinnamon, nutmeg, figs, and pecans. Spoon the sugar sauce over the fruits. *(The syrup will drip down through the fruits.)* Bake for 30 minutes, until bubbly hot. Remove the pan from the oven and scatter the strawberries over the top. Return to the oven for 3–5 minutes, just to lightly cook the berries.

4. Allow the baked fruits to rest for 4–8 minutes. Then use a baster or carefully tilt the pan to transfer most of the accumulated liquid to a medium-size saucepan. *(If you pour off the liquid, be sure to hold the fruits in the baking dish with a large spoon.)*

5. Place the saucepan over high heat and boil the sauce until reduced by half or more and *slightly* thickened, about 6 minutes. Pour enough of the reduced fruit syrup over the fruits so they are all glazed and moistened.

FINISHING TOUCHES AND
TABLE PRESENTATION

Place the baking dish of fruit on a large tray or woven mat on the brunch table; place the mint at each end of the fruit dish. Your guests will help themselves to warm—my preference—or a room-temperature fruit, which certainly makes hosting easier.

The Inventive Chef

THE INGREDIENTS IN THIS RECIPE CAN BE AS VARIED AS THE WORLD OF FRUIT. I USE PEACHES AND PLUMS WITH THE PINEAPPLE IN THE SUMMER AND LOVE TO TOP THE WARM FRUIT WITH FROSTY ICE CREAM OR SWEETENED WHIPPED CREAM.

KITCHEN SCHEDULE

2 OR 3 DAYS BEFORE THE PARTY

MAIN EVENT	Frittata	Grate Cheddar; store covered in refrigerator.
		Toast pine nuts as in steps 1–2; cool; store covered in refrigerator.
TOQUE 1	Risotto	Grate Parmigiano; store covered in refrigerator.
	Salad	Prepare vinaigrette as in step 5; store covered in refrigerator.
TOQUE 2	Bread Pudding	Grate Parmigiano; store covered in refrigerator.
	Muffins	Grate cheeses; store covered in refrigerator.
GRAND FINALE	Biscotti	Prepare through step 5; store in airtight container at room temperature.

THE DAY BEFORE THE PARTY

MAIN EVENT	Frittata	Prepare onions and red and green peppers for main ingredients and garnishes; store covered in refrigerator.
		Beat eggs; store covered in refrigerator.
		Prepare sage and parsley; store separately, covered, in refrigerator.
TOQUE 1	Risotto	Julienne smoked salmon; store covered in refrigerator.
		Chop dill; store covered in refrigerator.
	Salad	Plump raisins as in step 1; store covered in refrigerator.
		Prepare watercress and carrots

		as in steps 2–3; store separately, covered, in refrigerator.
TOQUE 2	Rice	Wash rices and set aside at room temperature.
		Prepare orange and lemon zests; store separately, covered, in refrigerator.
		Chop onion, sauté as in step 4, and cool; store covered in refrigerator.
		Section and halve oranges; store covered in refrigerator.
		Hull and quarter strawberries; store covered in refrigerator.
TOQUE 2	Bread Pudding	Make and toast bread cubes; set aside covered at room temperature.
		Prepare onion, garlic, and shallots; store separately, covered, in refrigerator.
	Muffins	Measure and place dry ingredients at room temperature.
		Prepare zucchini; store covered in refrigerator.
		Chop chives; store covered in refrigerator.
		Set up garnish of Cheddar and zucchini.
		Grease muffin pans.
GRAND FINALE	Baked Fruits	Prepare through step 4; cool to room temperature; store covered in refrigerator.
Strategic Maneuvers:		Fill creamer; cover and store in refrigerator.
		Fill sugar bowl.

Set table.
Check ice and beverages.
Set up coffee and tea service.
Check garnishes for each recipe.
Locate and label all serving dishes, bowls, and utensils.

THE MORNING OF THE PARTY

Preheat oven to 400°.
Plug in coffee. (*Expect more coffee drinkers at this hour, so make plenty.*)

MAIN EVENT Frittata Lower oven to 350°. Prepare through step 7; remove from oven and hold at room temperature; when cool, cover the top of the skillet with aluminum foil.

TOQUE 1 Risotto Prepare through step 2; keep warm in top of double boiler.

Salad Set vinaigrette at room temperature.
Prepare endive as in step 4; arrange salad but *do not dress.*

TOQUE 2 Muffins Prepare muffins through step 4; set aside at room temperature.

Rices Prepare through step 5. Do not add the pears and strawberries.

Bread Pudding Finish through step 6; remove from water bath and set aside at room temperature.

GRAND FINALE: Biscotti Arrange as in finishing touches.
Baked Place at room temperature.

Fruits Place fruit liquids in saucepan to reheat.

20 MINUTES BEFORE BRUNCH:

Lower oven to 275°. Return lightly covered frittata and muffins to the oven just long enough to heat through, about 10–15 minutes.
Garnish the bread pudding and put on food table.

10 MINUTES BEFORE BRUNCH:

Toss salad. Bring out all food and arrange platters on the table.
Add strawberries and pears to rice.

GRAND FINALE Baked Place in oven to warm,
Fruits partially covered.
Just before serving, glaze with juices.

BRUNCH SERVICE:

Bring out food.

AFTER SERVICE:

Unplug coffee.
Turn off oven.

MENU 2

Sundays in the Kitchen with Friends

THE MAIN EVENT:

Banana-Walnut and Brown Sugar Pancakes with Banana-Studded Maple Syrup

ON THE SIDE:

Turkey Sausage, Savory Vegetables, and Melted Jarlsberg

◆

Pineapple and Orange Mosaic with Strawberry Puree and Toasted Coconut

ON THE SIDE:

Smoked Bacon, Vegetable, and Cheddar Egg Custard

◆

Tart Rhubarb and Apple Sauce

THE GRAND FINALE:
Citrus Poppy-Seed Pound Cake

PALATE TEASER:
Pecan-Studded Cheddar Wafers (page 304)

BEVERAGE RECOMMENDATIONS:
Peach Sangria (page 357)
Muscat de Beaumes-de-Venise, Domaine des Coyeux

$\mathcal{M}$Y FAVORITE SUNDAY-MORNING SOUNDS: THE RUSTLE of newspaper pages; the splash of coffee in a cup; the sizzle of pancake batter as it hits the hot griddle; the clink-clink of a spoon scooping the last smidgen of fruit from a crystal bowl; a bit of Vivaldi (not too loud.) A few polite questions: "Mmm, fabulous banana pancakes . . . might I have just one more?" "You were so funny last night!" "Would you mind if I put this rhubarb and apple sauce on top of the poppyseed pound cake?" "Oh, is this fresh fennel in the sausage casserole?" "Anyone know a six-letter word for *protozoan?*"

Here's a perfect menu for a lazy and intimate weekend morning when you want your guests to relax, sit wherever they want, read the paper, and eat to their heart's content. As the conversation rises and falls freely, the dishes speak for themselves: a rich and cheesy egg casserole, colorful fresh fruit, and a tender sweet-tart pound cake. You will be the center of attention as you serve batch after batch of Banana-Walnut and Brown Sugar Pancakes hot off the griddle.

The Main Event pancakes are certainly worth waiting for. They're hearty with chopped walnuts and fresh chunks of banana, with a touch of cinnamon and allspice. Your guests will drizzle them with a Banana-Studded Maple Syrup with a tang of pineapple.

Both side casseroles are savory complements to the sweet pancakes and fruit on the menu. (You should try them both, but probably on different weekends!) On the one-toque menu, quickly broiled turkey sausage chunks are tossed with sautéed fennel, mushrooms, and tomatoes, baked with a thick topping of Jarlsberg, and perfumed with fresh sage. You could also choose the richer egg custard on the two-toque menu, which is chock-full of smoked bacon, chilies, spinach, tomatoes, zucchini, and Cheddar.

The fruit dish on each menu provides a lively balance. The mosaic is a beautiful arrangement of fresh pineapple and orange slices drizzled with a tangy and thick strawberry sauce (with a hint of brandy), then sprinkled with toasted coconut. The two-toque menu offers a chunky and brightly flavored Tart Rhubarb and Apple Sauce, which is wonderful as a condiment or enjoyed by itself.

The Grand Finale here (though some guests might choose to make it their main course) is an easy-to-bake pound cake with lemon zest and poppy seeds. It gets its real kick from a fabulous lemon syrup, with a bit of orange liqueur, that is brushed onto the cake while it cools.

SETTING THE STAGE

There's a casual air to this affair, set as it is in the kitchen, where the Main Event "pancake party" is taking place. Have plenty of flowers arranged on windowsills and counters, and (if you have the room) bring in an armchair or two to invite deep relaxation. Along with plenty of hot beverages and juices (and a spirit or two if you like), arrange the side dishes and dessert on the kitchen counters or the kitchen table. Invite your guests to fill their plates and cups at their leisure. There's no strict order to this meal, and you will want everyone to have plenty to savor and to talk about while you tend the griddle. Don't forget the Sunday papers!

T H E   M A I N   E V E N T

Banana-Walnut and Brown Sugar Pancakes with Banana-Studded Maple Syrup

MAKES 8 SERVINGS, ABOUT 20 PANCAKES

SPECIAL COOKWARE
One griddle or two 10-inch skillets

2 1/2 cups all-purpose flour
1/2 teaspoon ground cinnamon
1/2 teaspoon ground allspice
1 tablespoon baking powder
1/8 teaspoon salt
2 cups whole milk
3 large eggs
1/2 cup light brown sugar
10 tablespoons unsalted butter, melted
1/2 cup finely chopped walnuts

2 large bananas, peeled and diced small
Banana-Studded Maple Syrup (recipe follows)

GARNISH
1/2 cup sifted confectioners' sugar
4 whole bananas
12 whole walnuts

1. Preheat the oven to 250°.

2. In a large bowl, combine the flour, cinnamon, allspice, baking powder, and salt and set aside.

3. In another large bowl, whisk together the milk, eggs, brown sugar, and 6 tablespoons of the melted butter until well combined.

4. Stir the egg mixture into the dry ingredients until the batter is moistened. Fold the walnuts and bananas gently into the batter.

5. Brush some of the remaining butter onto a griddle or large skillet and heat over medium-high heat. Fill a 1/4 cup measure with batter, and drop the batter onto the griddle to form a 3 1/2-inch pancake. Cook the pancake until it is an even golden brown, about 1 minute. Turn the pancake with a spatula and cook the other side for about 45 seconds. (*The first side you cook will be a more uniform brown than the second. This is the nature of pancakes. Show the best side to your guests.*) Cook 4 or 5 pancakes at a time, transferring them to a baking sheet as they are done.

6. Continue making the pancakes, lightly buttering the pan and using all the batter. Brush the finished pancakes lightly with melted butter. Cover the pan lightly with foil and keep warm in the oven.

My favorite service for these pancakes is "from the grid-dle onto the plate," but one can shingle the pancakes on a round or rectangular platter. Dust the tops with con-fectioners' sugar, fill a sauceboat with the Banana-Stud-ded Maple Syrup and let your guests drench their own pancakes with the sauce. Peel the whole bananas halfway down and open each peel to form 2–3-inch leaves. Place the whole walnuts on the banana leaves, and arrange the bananas in front of the pancakes.

The Inventive Chef

WARM FRUIT SAUCES SUCH AS STRAWBERRY
(PAGE 274) OR APRICOT (PAGE 253), ADD TO
THE GLORIOUS TASTE OF THE BANANA
PANCAKES. TRY SUBSTITUTING WELL-DRAINED
CRUSHED PINEAPPLE FOR THE BANANAS.

Banana-Studded Maple Syrup

MAKES 4 CUPS

4 tablespoons cornstarch
2 cups pineapple juice
2 cups maple syrup
1/2 teaspoon almond extract
2 large bananas, peeled and finely diced

1. Dissolve the cornstarch by whisking it into the pineapple juice until well combined and lump-free.

2. In a small saucepan, heat the maple syrup, cornstarch–pineapple juice mixture, and the almond extract over medium heat, stirring occasionally, until the syrup comes to a boil. Allow it to boil for 1 minute or until syrup has thickened. Remove it from the heat.

3. Cool the syrup for 2 minutes, then stir in the bananas.

ON THE SIDE

Turkey Sausage, Savory Vegetables, and Melted Jarlsberg

MAKES 8 SERVINGS

SPECIAL COOKWARE
2 1/2–3-quart oven-to-table casserole

1 1/2 pounds turkey sausage (thin breakfast links, available in the meat department of most markets)
4 tablespoons salted butter
1 large fennel bulb, trimmed of green, core removed, and finely chopped
1 medium onion, peeled and finely chopped
1 pound wild or domestic mushrooms, washed, stemmed, and cut into 1/2-inch dice
8 plum tomatoes, diced large
1/2 cup dry white wine
2 teaspoons finely chopped fresh sage
3/4 teaspoon salt, or to taste
1/2 teaspoon freshly ground black pepper, or to taste
1 1/2 cups finely grated Jarlsberg or Swiss cheese

1 bunch flat-leaf parsley
1 cup fresh cranberries

1. Preheat the broiler. Cut the turkey sausages in half lengthwise, then cut each half into 1-inch pieces. Place the sausage pieces on a baking sheet and broil them about 5 inches from the heat, turning once, until they are golden brown on both sides, about 2 minutes on each side. Drain and discard any accumulated fat and reserve the sausage at room temperature.

2. Heat the butter in a large skillet over medium heat and sauté the fennel until it is golden, about 8–10 minutes. Add the onion, mushrooms, tomatoes, and wine and sauté for 5 minutes more. Add the sage and season with the salt and pepper.

3. Preheat the oven to 350°.

4. Blend the sausage and the vegetables together in a 2¹⁄₂–3-quart oven-to-table casserole. Sprinkle the top of the casserole with the cheese and bake for 15 minutes, until the cheese has melted and is a light golden brown.

FINISHING TOUCHES AND
TABLE PRESENTATION

Place the casserole on a 12-inch platter next to the Banana-Walnut and Brown Sugar Pancakes. Arrange a bouquet of parsley in front of the casserole. Loosely scatter the cranberries among the parsley.

The Inventive Chef

THIS CASSEROLE BECOMES A HEARTY ENTRÉE WHEN YOU ADD 1 POUND OF PEELED DICED POTATOES. JUST SAUTÉ THE POTATOES IN BUTTER UNTIL THEY ARE GOLDEN, SEASON THEM WITH SALT AND PEPPER, AND ADD THEM TO THE VEGETABLES BEFORE BAKING.

ON THE SIDE

Pineapple and Orange Mosaic with Strawberry Puree and Toasted Coconut

MAKES 8 SERVINGS

¹⁄₂ cup flaked coconut
1 quart fresh strawberries, washed and hulled, or two
*   12-ounce bags individually quick-frozen strawberries,*
*   semi-thawed*
1 tablespoon fresh lime juice
3 tablespoons superfine sugar
¹⁄₄ cup brandy or Grand Marnier
2 pineapples, peeled, eyes removed, cored, and sliced in
*   ¹⁄₈-inch rounds*
5 oranges, peeled, pith removed, and sliced in ¹⁄₈-inch
*   rounds*

GARNISH

1 bunch fresh mint sprigs

1. Preheat the oven to 350°.

2. Spread the coconut on a baking sheet and place it in the oven for about 10 minutes, or until golden. Stir the coconut twice while it bakes so it browns evenly.

3. Place the strawberries in the bowl of a food processor, fitted with the knife blade and process to obtain a thick puree. Pass the puree through a fine mesh strainer to remove the seeds. Pour the puree into a small bowl and blend in the lime juice, sugar, and liqueur.

FINISHING TOUCHES AND TABLE PRESENTATION

Arrange the pineapple slices in concentric circles on a decorative large round platter. Arrange the orange slices over the pineapple. Drizzle some of the strawberry puree over the fruit. Sprinkle the toasted coconut over the fruit, and garnish the platter with the mint leaves. Serve the remaining sauce in a glass bowl.

The Inventive Chef

I LIKE TO ADD RASPBERRIES AND BLUEBERRIES TO THE FRUIT IN THE SUMMER. IN FALL AND WINTER, I CUT PITTED PLUMS AND APRICOTS INTO QUARTERS AND ARRANGE THEM OVER THE PINEAPPLE-ORANGE MIX.

ON THE SIDE

Smoked Bacon, Vegetable, and Cheddar Egg Custard

MAKES 8 SERVINGS

SPECIAL COOKWARE
4-quart oven-to-table-casserole

1/2 pound hickory-smoked bacon, diced into 1-inch pieces
8 scallions, white and green parts, peeled and finely chopped
2 medium (about 8 ounces each) zucchini, washed and sliced into 1/8-inch rounds
10 ounces fresh spinach, stemmed, washed, dried and coarsely chopped
2 large ripe tomatoes, cut into 1/8-inch rounds
1 1/4 teaspoons salt
3/4 teaspoon freshly ground pepper, or to taste
12 large eggs, well-beaten
3 cups half-and-half
1/4 cup drained and chopped canned mild green chilies
1 teaspoon Dijon mustard
1 1/2 cups grated sharp Cheddar
2 teaspoons finely chopped fresh cilantro

GARNISH
1/2 bunch cilantro
1/2 pint cherry tomatoes

1. Preheat the oven to 350°.

2. Cook the bacon in a large skillet over medium heat until it is brown and crisp. Remove the bacon with a slotted spoon and set it aside to drain on paper towels.

3. In the same skillet, sauté the scallions and zucchini in the bacon drippings over medium heat until they have wilted, about 3–4 minutes.

4. Add the chopped spinach and the tomatoes and cook an additional 2 minutes, or until the spinach has wilted and the tomatoes have softened. Season with ¹/₂ teaspoon of the salt and ¹/₄ teaspoon of the pepper, or to taste. Remove from the heat and strain the vegetables in a colander to remove any excess liquid. Set aside.

5. In a large bowl, beat the eggs with the half-and-half. Add the chilies, Dijon mustard, Cheddar, cilantro, reserved vegetables, and reserved bacon. Season the egg mixture with the remaining ³/₄ teaspoon salt and ¹/₂ teaspoon pepper and pour it into a 4-quart oven-to-table casserole. Bake the custard for 45 minutes, until a knife inserted in the center comes out clean.

FINISHING TOUCHES AND TABLE PRESENTATION

Place the custard on a 14-inch platter and set it on the brunch table. Place the cilantro loosely in front of the casserole with the cherry tomatoes nestled among the leaves.

The Inventive Chef

NOW IS CERTAINLY THE TIME TO BE CREATIVE AND DESIGN YOUR OWN VEGETABLE-EGG CUSTARD. YELLOW SQUASH, RED AND YELLOW BELL PEPPERS, AND A LITTLE GARLIC ADD SAVORY TASTE TWISTS AND CHANGES IN TEXTURE.

ON THE SIDE

Tart Rhubarb and Apple Sauce

MAKES 8 SERVINGS

SPECIAL COOKWARE
Food mill

3 pounds McIntosh or Cortland apples (5 or 6 apples), unpeeled
¹/₄ cup fresh lemon juice
1 teaspoon ground cinnamon
1 pound fresh rhubarb, all green leaves removed, or 1 pound frozen
Juice of 1 large or 2 medium oranges (about ¹/₂ cup)
¹/₂ teaspoon ground cloves
³/₄ cup brown sugar, firmly packed
1 pint strawberries, washed, stemmed, and halved

1. Wash, core, and quarter the apples. *(Do not peel them. The skin adds color and texture to the sauce.)* Place the apple quarters, lemon juice, ¹/₂ cup of water, and the cinnamon in a large saucepan and cook, covered, over medium-low heat for 30 minutes, or until the apples are completely soft. Stir the apples a few times as they cook.

2. While the apples are cooking, if using fresh rhubarb, cut off the tough ends of the stalks and scrape the strings with a vegetable peeler. Cut the rhubarb into 1-inch pieces and place it in a saucepan with the orange juice and cloves. If using frozen rhubarb, place it in the saucepan without defrosting it. Cook, uncovered, over medium heat until the rhubarb has become a thick puree, about 12–15 minutes. *(The* *rhubarb will still be chunky.*) If the rhubarb gets too dry while cooking, add additional orange juice or a little water, but use as little liquid as necessary to prevent rhubarb from sticking to the pan.

3. When the apples have finished cooking, puree them through a food mill or in a food processor fitted with the knife blade and return them to the saucepan. Blend the apples into the rhubarb in the saucepan. Add the brown sugar and strawberries and cook over low heat for about 2–3 minutes, stirring often. Add more sugar for a sweeter taste, if desired. Cool the sauce to room temperature and refrigerate it, covered.

FINISHING TOUCHES AND TABLE PRESENTATION

Serve the sauce from a cut-glass or white pottery bowl. The rosy color of the sauce shows off brilliantly. Warm or chilled, it's delicious.

The Inventive Chef

I LOVE TO SERVE THIS SAUCE WITH ABIGAIL'S SECRET BRISKET OF BEEF (PAGE 223), ROAST CHICKEN, AND ALL LEFT-OVER COLD MEATS. THE SAUCE TRAVELS WELL FOR PICNICS AND IS PERFECT WARM, AT ROOM TEMPERATURE, OR CHILLED.

THE GRAND FINALE

Citrus Poppy-Seed Pound Cake

MAKES 8 GENEROUS SERVINGS

SPECIAL COOKWARE
10–12-inch tube pan

THE CAKE
1 1/2 tablespoons unsalted butter for greasing
1 1/2 cups plus 2 tablespoons unsalted butter, softened or at room temperature
1 1/2 cups sugar
6 eggs
1 tablespoon pure vanilla extract
2 1/2 tablespoons freshly grated lemon zest (from about 6 large lemons)
1/4 cup poppy seeds
1/2 cup whole milk
3 cups sifted all-purpose flour
1 1/2 teaspoons baking powder

THE LEMON SYRUP
2/3 cup sugar
1/2 cup fresh lemon juice
3 tablespoons brandy or orange liqueur, such as Cointreau or triple sec

GARNISH
14 small lemon leaves

1. Preheat the oven to 350°. Butter and flour a 10-inch tube pan.

2. In the bowl of an electric mixer fitted with the paddle attachment, beat the butter with the sugar until light and fluffy. Beat in the eggs one at a time. Add the vanilla, lemon zest, and poppy seeds. Gradually beat in the milk and mix at low speed until well combined.

3. Sift the flour with the baking powder into a separate bowl.

4. With the mixer set on slow speed, gradually add the sifted dry ingredients to the batter and beat until just combined, scraping down the sides of the bowl with a rubber spatula.

5. Spoon the batter into the prepared tube pan and bake for 45–55 minutes, until a cake tester inserted in the center comes out clean.

6. Cool the cake in the pan for 5 minutes, then invert it onto a wire rack placed on a large round plate.

7. While the cake is cooling, prepare the lemon syrup. In a medium saucepan over medium heat, stir the sugar and lemon juice together until the sugar is fully dissolved. Simmer for 1 1/2 minutes, until the glaze reaches a light syrupy consistency. Remove from the heat and gently stir in the liqueur.

8. Pierce the top and sides of the cake with a cake tester or wooden skewer. Pour the warm syrup over the top of the cake and brush it over the sides. Any syrup that runs off the cake will be caught on the plate. Transfer the cake to a round serving platter.

FINISHING TOUCHES AND
TABLE PRESENTATION

Arrange small lemon leaves around the edge of the cake—the beautiful simplicity of the cake needs no further garnish.

The Inventive Chef

SERVE WARM TART RHUBARB AND APPLE SAUCE WITH THE CAKE. THE TASTE CONTRASTS ARE PALATE-TINGLING.

KITCHEN SCHEDULE

3 DAYS AHEAD OF THE PARTY

GRAND FINALE Cake — Prepare through step 6; cool, cover, and freeze.
Prepare the glaze but do not glaze the cake; cool, cover, and refrigerate.

2 DAYS BEFORE THE PARTY

MAIN EVENT Pancakes — Chop walnuts; set aside covered at room temperature.
Prepare step 2; set aside covered at room temperature.

Syrup — Prepare through step 3; store covered in refrigerator. Do not add the bananas.

TOQUE 1 Turkey Sausage — Prepare through step 2; cool; store sausage and vegetables separately, covered, in refrigerator.
Grate cheese; store covered in refrigerator.

Fruit — Prepare steps 1–3; store toasted coconut covered at room temperature; Store strawberry puree covered in refrigerator.
Prepare pineapple and oranges; store separately, covered, in refrigerator.

TOQUE 2 Custard — Drain and chop chilies and grate Cheddar; store separately, covered, in refrigerator.
Prepare step 2; cool; store covered in refrigerator.
Prepare steps 3–4; cool; store covered in refrigerator.

Sauce — Prepare through step 3; cool; store covered in refrigerator.

GRAND FINALE Cake — Prepare and bake cake and glaze, if not done before; cool; store separately, covered, in refrigerator. If frozen, defrost in refrigerator.

Strategic Maneuvers: — Fill creamers; cover and store in refrigerator.
Fill sugar bowl.
Set table.
Check ice and beverages.
Set up coffee and tea service.
Check garnishes for each recipe.
Locate and label all serving dishes, bowls, and utensils.

THE MORNING OF THE PARTY

Plug in coffee. (Expect more coffee drinkers at this hour, so make plenty.)
Preheat oven to 200°.

MAIN EVENT Pancakes — Prepare through step 4.
Syrup — Reheat and add the bananas; keep warm in double boiler.

TOQUE 1 Turkey Sausage — Finish recipe through step 4; keep warm in oven if serving within the hour.

Fruit — Arrange pineapple and oranges and set aside at room temperature. Put strawberry puree in glass bowl (save some for dressing fruit) and set aside in the refrigerator.

TOQUE 2	Custard	Prepare step 5; keep warm in oven if serving within the hour.
GRAND FINALE	Sauce	Place in serving dish and set aside at room temperature.
	Cake	Warm lemon syrup on stovetop and cake in oven. Brush and pour warm syrup over cake and arrange on serving platter.

up griddle to cook pancakes in front of guests.
Spoon berry puree over fruit.
Plug in coffee.

15 MINUTES BEFORE BRUNCH:

Cook pancakes as in steps 5–6; keep warm on baking sheet in oven or set

BRUNCH SERVICE:

Bring out food.

AFTER SERVICE:

Unplug coffee.
Turn off oven.

Father Knows Best: A Slightly Formal Brunch

THE MAIN EVENT:

Baked Acorn Squash and Savory Ham

THE OPENING ACT:

Smoked Salmon with Chive Butter

ON THE SIDE:

Maple Syrup–Sweetened Grits

◆

Asparagus with Lemon Butter (page 84)

THE OPENING ACT:

Chilled Fruit Soup with Melon and Strawberries

ON THE SIDE:

Wild Rice and Zucchini Fritters

◆

Basil-Scented Apples of Love (page 107)

THE GRAND FINALE:

Cranberry Tartlets

BEVERAGE RECOMMENDATIONS:

Bloody Marys (page 356)
"Bay Mist" Riesling, J. Lohr

FATHER IS A BIT FROM THE OLD SCHOOL: MANNERS ARE STILL quite important to him. You knew when you invited Mother and him to a Father's Day brunch that he would arrive wearing a jacket and tie, at eleven on the dot. And you didn't need her to remind you that he likes to eat "at table"—none of this shuffling down a line of casseroles or sitting with a plate on his knees. Not that he's a stick-in-the-mud: He just appreciates a well-prepared dish (even something as simple as grits) and a nicely presented plate. Fancies himself something of a gourmand, in fact, and likes to try a new flavor every now and then. He's been in a garrulous mood since he sampled your tangy Bloody Mary; and certainly he's going to be pleased with the first-course fruit soup, elegantly garnished with a mint leaf tucked into a floating slice of lime.

It can be a great pleasure to serve brunch in the ordered and well-mannered fashion of a formal dinner. It slows things down so that you can really appreciate the great tastes before you. This is certainly a menu deserving of such attention.

The Main Event, stuffed acorn squash, is a wonderful combination of savory and sweet, soft and chewy textures. After baking the squash with a brown-sugar butter, you fill it with an intriguing mix of sautéed mushrooms, ham, and ripe pear, all seasoned with fresh chives and the subtle herb savory. Baked again under a layer of Gruyère, this is a sublime way to start the day.

But for this menu, I actually start brunch with a plated first course. The one-toque Opening Act is a wonderful mini-smorgasbord of melting Norwegian salmon slices and triangles of pumpernickel bread with garnishes of mustard-dill butter, capers, and radicchio. Commence the two-toque menu with a brilliant fruit soup, composed of pureed cantaloupe, strawberries, and poached ap-

ples with white wine, orange, and ginger nuances. And it has a fabulous garnish!

Side dishes complement the lovely boat of squash with ham filling. For the one-toque menu, there's a nice North-South quality to my Maple Syrup–Sweetened Grits. The corn sweetness of this filling breakfast grain is enhanced with butter, maple syrup, golden raisins, and a hint of spice. Asparagus spears in a sauce of lemon and mustard provide a tangy and pretty contrast.

On the two-toque menu, Wild Rice and Zucchini Fritters are delightfully crispy and savory with shallots and scallions, bits of dried apricot, and fresh rosemary. The beautiful plate is completed with quickly sautéed tomatoes—"apples of love"—in a rich, basil-scented sauce.

A sit-down brunch needs a grand ending, and the finale here is a pleasingly simple tartlet with brandy-soaked cranberries, dried cherries, apricots, and raisins enclosed in a flaky puff-pastry envelope. A golden poached apricot and a crown of crème fraîche or Calvados Whipped Cream make this a gorgeous ending to a perfectly lovely meal.

S E T T I N G   T H E   S T A G E

Why not? Set a beautiful formal table with your best china and silver. Wipe the water stains off the crystal; do this the night before brunch and see how magnificent your best stuff looks in the sunlight. Use table-linen colors that say, "Good morning."

It's peak rose season around Father's Day, so indulge in a mass of flowers, either a single color or a vibrant mix. If it's a warm June day, open the windows and let the floral perfumes mingle with the great aromas of your food.

THE MAIN EVENT

Baked Acorn Squash and Savory Ham

MAKES 8 SERVINGS

5 tablespoons salted butter

3 tablespoons light brown sugar

4 medium acorn squash (about 13 ounces each), halved lengthwise and seeded

1 medium onion, peeled and finely chopped

3 cups cleaned and quartered mushrooms, domestic or wild

1 cup cooked diced ham

2 ripe pears, Bartlett or Bosc, unpeeled, cored, and cut into 1/2-inch dice

2 teaspoons finely chopped fresh chives

1 teaspoon finely chopped fresh savory

1/2 teaspoon salt, or to taste

1/4 teaspoon freshly ground black pepper, or to taste

1/2 cup finely grated Gruyère

1. Preheat the oven to 350°.

2. Heat 3 tablespoons of the butter in a small saucepan over medium heat until melted and bubbly. Remove from the heat and stir in the brown sugar until it has dissolved.

3. Level the bottoms of each squash half with a sharp knife and place on a large baking pan. Brush the insides and tops of the squash generously with the brown-sugar butter, and bake the squash for 30–35 minutes, until tender when pierced with a fork.

4. While the squash are baking, heat the remaining 2 tablespoons of butter in a large skillet and sauté the onion over medium-high heat until it is translucent, about 3 minutes. Add the mushrooms and cook, stirring, for 2 minutes more. The mushrooms will still be crisp to the bite.

5. Add the ham, pears, chives, and savory to the skillet, and cook over medium heat for 1 minute, stirring frequently, to blend all the flavors. Season with the salt and pepper.

6. Remove the squash from the oven and fill the center of each squash half with the ham mixture. Sprinkle the top of each half with 1 tablespoon of the Gruyère, and put the baking pan back in the oven. Bake the squash for about 15 minutes, until the ham filling is heated through and the cheese has melted.

ONE-TOQUE: Place the squash at 12 o'clock on a dinner-size plate. Arrange the grits at 9 o'clock and the asparagus from 6 o'clock to 3 o'clock with the tips pointing toward the squash.

TWO-TOQUE: Place the squash at 12 o'clock on a dinner-size plate. Arrange the fritters loosely at 9 o'clock. Place a bed of arugula between 6 o'clock and 3 o'clock. Place the tomatoes and garnish over the arugula.

THE OPENING ACT

Smoked Salmon with Chive Butter

MAKES 8 SERVINGS

8 tablespoons sweet butter, at room temperature
1 tablespoon finely chopped fresh chives
$1/2$ teaspoon Dijon mustard
2 teaspoons finely chopped fresh dill
1 teaspoon fresh lemon juice
1 pinch salt
1 pinch ground white pepper

16 slices (1–1$1/2$ ounces each) smoked Norwegian salmon
8 large radicchio leaves
2 tablespoons drained capers
16 fresh dill sprigs
24 thin slices whole-grain or pumpernickel bread, cut into thirds lengthwise
2 large lemons, quartered

1. In a small mixing bowl, blend the butter with the chives, mustard, dill, lemon juice, salt, and pepper, and set aside.

FINISHING TOUCHES AND
TABLE PRESENTATION

Arrange 2 slices of salmon horizontally over the center of each 8- or 9-inch plate. Fill the center of each radicchio leaf with one mounded tablespoon of the reserved herbed butter and place on the plate at 9 o'clock. Create a circle of capers around the butter inside the leaf and garnish with sprigs of dill. Place 3 overlapping triangles of bread at 5 o'clock on each plate. Place a lemon wedge in front of the radicchio leaf.

The Inventive Chef

ADD 8 TABLESPOONS OF WHIPPED CREAM
CHEESE, 3 TEASPOONS OF FINELY MINCED RED
ONION, AND 3 TEASPOONS OF RED-SALMON ROE
TO THE GARNISHES ON THE PLATE. INCREASE
THE BREAD PORTION AND CREATE A FINE
LUNCHEON APPETIZER.

Maple Syrup-Sweetened Grits

MAKES 8 SERVINGS

4 1/2 cups whole milk or half-and-half
1 1/2 cups quick grits
4 tablespoons unsalted butter, softened
1/2 cup maple syrup
1/2 cup golden raisins
1/2 teaspoon ground cinnamon
1/8 teaspoon ground cloves
1 pinch salt

GARNISH
1/4 cup maple syrup

1. Bring the milk or half-and-half to a boil in a large saucepan. Reduce the heat to medium-low and slowly stir in the grits. Cook grits for about 5 minutes, stirring often.

2. When the grits have thickened and are soft, add the butter, maple syrup, raisins, cinnamon, cloves, and salt. *(The grits can be held for 30 minutes in the top of a double boiler over simmering water. Stir in an additional 1/2 cup of warm milk if they become too thick.)*

Chilled Fruit Soup with Melon and Strawberries

MAKES 8 SERVINGS

SPECIAL COOKWARE
Large (6-quart) stockpot

6 large McIntosh or Granny Smith apples, peeled, cored, and chopped large
3/4 cup sugar
1 cinnamon stick
Peel of 1 lemon, cut into very thin 1/2-inch-long strips
1 large ripe cantaloupe, peeled, seeded, and coarsely cut up
1 pint strawberries, washed and hulled
3/4 cup fresh orange juice
1/3 cup dry white wine
1/2 teaspoon powdered ginger
1/2 tablespoon fresh lime juice
1 pinch salt

GARNISH
8 lime slices, seeded, about 1/8-inch thick
8 small mint sprigs with 1/4-inch stems

1. Bring 3 1/2 cups of water to a simmer in a large stockpot over moderate heat. Add the apples, sugar, cinnamon stick, and lemon peel. Simmer uncovered for 20 minutes, until the apples are very soft.

2. While the apples are cooking, place the cantaloupe, in batches, into the bowl of a food processor fitted with the knife blade, and process until the melon is entirely pureed. Pour the puree into a large bowl and refrigerate until needed.

3. Place the strawberries into the food processor bowl and puree. Add the strawberry puree to the bowl with the melon puree and return it to the refrigerator.

4. Remove the cinnamon stick from the pot with the cooked apples and add the orange juice, white wine, and ginger. Cook over medium heat about 2 minutes, just to combine flavors. Remove the apples from the pot. Reserve the liquid. Using a bit of the liquid in the pot, puree the apples in batches in the food processor. Add the apple puree to the reserved berry-and-melon puree. Strain the pureed fruits through a colander back into the liquid in the stockpot. Stir in the lime juice and salt and chill for about 2 hours.

FINISHING TOUCHES AND
TABLE PRESENTATION

With a sharp paring knife, cut a small incision in the center of each lime round. Insert a mint sprig in each center. Ladle the soup into white or decorative soup bowls with underliners. Float a mint-studded lime garnish in the center of each bowl.

ON THE SIDE

Wild Rice and Zucchini Fritters

MAKES 8 SERVINGS

1 tablespoon olive oil
3 shallots, peeled and finely chopped

4 scallions, white and green parts, finely chopped
6 eggs, separated
3 medium zucchini, julienned $^1/_8$-inch wide by $2^1/_2$-inches long ◆
2 cups cooked wild rice ◆◆
$^1/_3$ cup finely chopped dried apricots
2 tablespoons minced flat-leaf parsley
2 teaspoons minced fresh rosemary
$^1/_8$ teaspoon cayenne pepper
$1^1/_4$ teaspoons plus 1 pinch salt
$^1/_2$ teaspoon freshly ground black pepper
$^3/_4$ cup all-purpose flour
$^3/_4$ cup unseasoned dry bread crumbs
$^3/_4$ cup vegetable oil, for frying

GARNISH
1 bunch finely chopped flat-leaf parsley
$^1/_2$ cup dried apricots

◆The zucchini can be julienned in the bowl of a food processor fitted with the julienne attachment or shredded on the coarse side of a box grater.

◆◆Wash $^2/_3$ cup wild rice and drain through a sieve. Stir the rice into $3^1/_4$ cups of boiling water. Add a pinch of salt. Cook without stirring, until tender, about 35–40 minutes.

1. Heat the olive oil in a small skillet. Add the shallots and scallions and sauté over medium-high heat until they are translucent, about 2 minutes. Set the skillet aside.

2. Combine egg yolks, zucchini, rice, apricots, sautéed shallots and scallions, the parsley, rosemary, cayenne, $1^1/_4$ teaspoon salt and $^1/_2$ teaspoon pepper in a bowl and blend well.

3. Gradually add the flour and bread crumbs, blending well to incorporate all ingredients.

4. Beat the egg whites in the bowl of an electric mixer with the whisk attachment. Add a pinch of salt and beat until they form stiff peaks. Stir $1/3$ of the egg whites into the fritter batter. Gently fold in the rest with a rubber spatula. *(To test the seasoning in the batter, fry a small fritter, check herbs and spices, and adjust to taste before forming the remaining fritters.)*

5. For easy handling, lightly flour the hands before forming the fritters. Form the batter into 16 3-inch-round fritters. Place them on a $15^1/2$-by-$10^1/2$-by-1-inch baking sheet and refrigerate covered for 1 hour or overnight.

6. Preheat the oven to 250°. Pour the oil into a large skillet to a depth of $1/4$ inch. Heat the oil until a drop of water pops up and sizzles when added to the pan. Fry the fritters, 3 or 4 at a time, turning occasionally, until they are golden brown on each side, about $1^1/2$ minutes. Drain the fritters on paper towels as they are finished and then transfer to a baking sheet. *(Do not crowd the baking sheet, or the fritters will steam and not crisp.)* Keep the fritters warm in the oven while you finish frying the rest of the batter. *(The fritters can be kept warm in the oven for 20 minutes before finishing touches and table presentation.)*

The Inventive Chef

MAKE THE FRITTERS SILVER-DOLLAR-SIZE AND SERVE THEM AS DELIGHTFUL HORS D'OUEVRE. OR ADD COOKED HAM OR CHICKEN TO THE BATTER AND SERVE THE FRITTERS, ACCOMPANIED BY A CRISP SALAD, AS A LIGHT ENTRÉE.

Cranberry Tartlets

MAKES 8 TARTLETS

2 sheets of frozen puff pastry◆
1 cinnamon stick
2 whole cloves
1 vanilla bean split in half lengthwise
$1/8$ teaspoon ground nutmeg
12 black peppercorns
Zest of 1 lemon
3 cups port wine
$1/2$ cup sugar
$3/4$ pound cranberries, fresh or frozen
$1/2$ cup dried apricots, medium dice, plus 8 dried apricots left whole
$1/2$ cup raisins
1 cup dried cherries
4 ounces Mascarpone cheese
2 tablespoons honey
$1/2$ cup sugar for rolling pastry

◆Available in freezer cases of gourmet food stores and some supermarkets.

GARNISH
$1/2$ cup crème fraîche or Calvados Whipped Cream (page 228)
$1/4$ cup sifted confectioners' sugar
8 large lemon leaves
$1/2$ cup dried cranberries

1. Preheat the oven to 375°.
2. Defrost the puff pastry in the refrigerator (about 3 hours).
3. In a piece of washed cheesecloth, wrap the cinnamon stick, cloves, vanilla bean, nutmeg,

peppercorns, and lemon zest and tie securely with a piece of string. This is a spiced sachet.

4. In a saucepan, bring the port wine, $1/2$ cup of sugar, and sachet of spices to a boil. Simmer for 5 minutes.

5. Add the cranberries, apricots, raisins, and cherries and cook at a slow simmer for 8 minutes. Remove from the heat and strain the fruit, discarding the spices and liquids. Spread the fruit on a baking sheet or platter to cool off and stop the cooking.

6. In a small bowl with a rubber spatula, combine the Mascarpone cheese and honey until well blended. Set aside.

7. Over a flat surface, sprinkle some of the sugar reserved for rolling the pastry. Place a puff pastry sheet on top, sprinkle some sugar on top of the pastry, and, with a rolling pin, slightly stretch the pastry sheet both ways. Cut into quarters and place on an ungreased baking sheet. Repeat with the remaining sheet of pastry.

8. Put 1 tablespoon of the cheese mixture in the center of each square and put $1/4$ cup of the cooled fruit on top, placing one whole apricot on the very top. Fold the corners of each square toward the center, pinching the sides together to enclose the filling but leaving the top open so that you can still see the whole apricot.

9. Bake the tartlets for 25 minutes, or until puffed and golden brown. Peek in the oven after 15 minutes. If any of the folded edges of the pastry open during baking, fold them back toward the center of the tart while the pastry is still warm and semipliable. Transfer the pastry to a cooling rack with a metal spatula.

FINISHING TOUCHES AND
TABLE PRESENTATION

Place the warm tartlets on an 8- or 9-inch dessert plate. Top each pastry with a dollop of crème fraîche or Calvados Whipped Cream (page 228). Lightly dust the tartlets with sifted confectioners' sugar. Slip a lemon leaf under each tart and place a teaspoon of dried cranberries in the center of the lemon leaf.

KITCHEN SCHEDULE

2 OR 3 DAYS BEFORE THE PARTY

MAIN EVENT   Squash   Prepare brown-sugar butter as in step 2; store covered in refrigerator.

Grate Gruyère; store covered in refrigerator.

TOQUE 1   Salmon   Prepare chive butter as in step 1; store covered in refrigerator.

TOQUE 2   Chilled Soup   Prepare all the fruit; store separately, covered, in refrigerator.

THE DAY BEFORE THE PARTY

MAIN EVENT   Squash   Halve, seed, and bake squash as in steps 1 and 3; cool; store covered in refrigerator.

Prepare stuffing as in steps 4–5; cool; store covered in refrigerator.

TOQUE 1   Salmon   Prepare lemons; store covered in refrigerator.

   Asparagus   Peel asparagus and prepare as in step 1; dry and store covered in refrigerator.

TOQUE 2   Chilled Soup   Prepare through step 4; store covered in refrigerator.

Prepare garnish; store covered in refrigerator.

   Fritters   Sauté shallots and scallions as in step 1; cool; store covered in refrigerator.

Separate eggs; prepare zucchini, wild rice, apricots, parsley, and rosemary; store separately, covered, in refrigerator.

Measure flour and bread crumbs; set aside at room temperature.

   Tomatoes   Prepare basil puree as in step 1; store covered in refrigerator.

Slice and julienne mozzarella; place in separated strips on a covered plate in refrigerator.

Wash and dry arugula; store in plastic bag in refrigerator.

GRAND FINALE: Tartlets   Prepare steps 2–8; store covered in refrigerator.

Strategic Maneuvers: Fill creamer; cover and store in refrigerator.

Fill sugar bowl.

Set table.

Check ice and beverages.

Set up coffee and tea service.

Check garnishes for each recipe.

Locate and label all serving dishes, bowls, and utensils.

THE MORNING OF THE PARTY

GRAND FINALE: Tartlets   Preheat oven to 375°. Bake tartlets and cool.

1 1/2 HOURS BEFORE BRUNCH:

MAIN EVENT   Squash   Bring squash and filling to room temperature. Fill squash. Lower oven to 250°.

GRAND FINALE   Tartlets   Whip cream; store covered in refrigerator.

Set up dessert plates with lemon leaves and cranberries.

TOQUE 1	Salmon	Arrange plates as directed, cover well, set aside at room temperature.
	Grits	Prepare through step 2 and keep warm in top of double boiler.
	Asparagus	Prepare lemon butter as in step 2; set aside at room temperature.
TOQUE 2	Tomatoes	Slice tomatoes; store covered in refrigerator.

30 MINUTES BEFORE BRUNCH:

		Plug in coffee.
TOQUE 1	Asparagus	Sauté as in step 3.
TOQUE 2	Fritters	Prepare steps 2–6; keep warm in low oven.
	Chilled Soup	Fill soup bowls, check seasonings, and garnish.
	Squash	Bake as in step 6. Reduce oven temperature to 250° and keep warm.

JUST BEFORE BRUNCH:

| TOQUE 2 | Tomatoes | Complete recipe. Place salmon or soup on table. |

BEFORE MAIN EVENT:

Arrange Main Event plates.
Place tartlets in 250° oven to rewarm.
Clear first course and serve Main Event.

DESSERT SERVICE:

Prepare as in finishing touches.
Serve tarts with crème fraîche or Calvados Whipped Cream (page 228).

AFTER SERVICE:

Turn off oven.
Unplug coffee.

The Energy and Informality of Hors d'Oeuvre Parties

When you want to entertain a good-size crowd (without going crazy) this is a terrific kind of party both to cook and to host. First, you get to create an entire menu's worth of wonderful canapés: gorgeous and dainty savories and sweets arranged in tempting displays. (Try to resist popping too many in your mouth!) Then you get to enjoy the happy hustle and bustle of your guests—whether family, friends, colleagues, or customers—having a great time and a great meal. They'll be eating, greeting one another, eating, talking, eating, drinking—and licking their fingers (discreetly, of course).

I've had a great time creating the two hors d'oeuvre parties in this chapter, and you will want to try them both:

• The heart of your St. Patrick's Day party stays in Ireland with dainty corned beef and soda bread sandwiches, but it takes a tasty international tour with curried chicken scones, lamb kabobs, tortilla-wrapped salmon, drunken shrimp, and other miniature masterpieces.

• At the grand opening of your new office, show off your good business sense and sophisticated taste with gingered beef kabobs, cherry tomatoes stuffed with crabmeat, sun-dried tomato *palmiers,* dainty custard pies with broccoli and mushrooms—and luscious bites of raspberry cheesecake.

These occasions are, of course, streamlined variations of buffets, but unlike regular buffet menus, you don't have to provide table or seating spots for everybody: It's entirely finger service. Each menu item, including dessert, can be eaten out of hand by your guests, most of whom will choose to stand while they savor and socialize; no need for rental chairs or stacks of plates. (You will, however, need to provide adequate stemware and cups for beverages, and lots of cocktail napkins!)

There's a streamlined quality to the flow of hors d'oeuvre parties, too. The whole show is presented at one time—no opening act, and no clearing the buffet for dessert. When you set up your buffet table, leave space for trays of miniature desserts. After the party has been going for an hour or so, and the first guests have had their fill of savories, put out the sweets. Your guests will come and go during the party, so keep all the trays of food attractively full for the enjoyment of late arrivals.

As in other buffet meals, the more dishes you make, the greater the merriment—and with finger foods as good as these, you will have to make plenty! Follow the kitchen schedules to efficiently produce the dishes on each menu. They are written to generously serve 16 guests, but are easily expandable if you are having a larger event—just proportionally increase each recipe. Or you can choose to add another hors d'oeuvre choice or two—there are 20 great ones in this chapter!

Your cooking will be completed, but as host you will be occupied during the party with keeping the buffet well stocked. All of the dishes on these menus are delicious when served at room temperature, so keep your back-up food in the kitchen, arranged on trays and garnished, ready to be presented. (You will need *lots* of trays and platters for this kind of party.) If you are serving foods that must be kept warm at the table, you can rent chafing dishes.

A final word: Because smooth service of both food and drink is such an important part of this party format, make sure you set up your buffet and bar tables with easy access. And if you have an especially large number of people, you will certainly want to consider hiring some serving and bar helpers to keep things moving. And since I *guarantee* that your guests will be crowding the buffet for extra bites of every hors d'oeuvre, you might relieve the crush by circulating through the room with trays of delicacies. It's a good opportunity for you to visit, and to gather kudos on your cooking, too!

MENU 1

St. Patrick's Day
Dinner by the Bite

THE MAIN EVENT:

A Wee Bit of Corned Beef and Cabbage
on Caraway-Studded Irish Soda Bread

ON THE SIDE

Drunken Shrimp with Cilantro and Tequila

◆

Tortilla Wraps with Smoked Salmon and Asparagus

◆

Zucchini and Spinach-Tortellini Skewers

◆

Pungent Meatballs Glazed in Green

ON THE SIDE

Green Pepper Scones with Curry-Rubbed Chicken

◆

Mussels with Parsley and Horseradish Mayonnaise

◆

Lamb, Carrot, and Potato Kabobs

◆

Pecan-Studded Cheddar Wafers

THE GRAND FINALE:

White and Dark Chocolate–Dipped Strawberries

BEVERAGE RECOMMENDATIONS:
Full Bar (see Chapter 14)

O N ST. PATRICK'S DAY, EVERYONE WANTS TO BE IRISH, AND THE cosmopolitan crowd at your party will take the holiday to heart. The room is alight with kelly green bow ties and emerald-sequined cocktail dresses. On this day, too, every hors d'oeuvre wants to be Irish—not only the leprechaun-sized corned beef canapés, but even the green-speckled Drunken Shrimp with Cilantro and Tequila and the Green Pepper Scones with Curry-Rubbed Chicken seem to have lilting Gaelic accent.

It certainly doesn't have to be St. Patrick's Day for you to enjoy the wee corned beef and cabbage sandwiches that are the Main Event on this menu of colorful, tempting, and rapidly disappearing hors d'oeuvre. The recipes that follow will delight a fast-talking, fast-eating crowd of 16 at any occasion (and you can easily multiply the formulas to meet your entertaining needs).

The corned beef canapés start with home-baked Irish soda bread generously flavored with caraway as a base for tender slices of corned beef brisket. The chopped cabbage and carrots that you cooked along with the beef make a marvelous sandwich spread. Top the canapés with a dab of Dijon mustard–sour cream and a cornichon.

There's a world of other flavors (and green garnishes) to please your guests as well. The one-toque menu includes drunken shrimp infused with a marinade of tequila, cilantro, ginger, chili powder, and a half dozen other bold seasonings. The tortilla wraps are bite-size rolls of herbed cheese, smoked salmon, and asparagus in a flour tortilla. Spinach tortellini and wedges of crisp-cooked zucchini are marinated in fragrant herbs and vinegars and served on skewers.

Finally, savory meatballs with garlic, ginger, tomato paste, and mustard are fried in sesame oil and glazed with a terrific blend of mint jelly and soy sauce.

The two-toque menu is also savory, gorgeous, and green-flecked. Tender scones with bits of sautéed green bell pepper are topped with a chunky and tangy mix of chicken breast and apple in a spicy curry sauce. Mussels are steamed with wine and aromatic vegetables, then beautifully arranged on the half shell with a tangy homemade horseradish mayonnaise. The meat and vegetables for the Lamb, Carrot, and Potato Kabobs gain sensational flavor from a tangy yogurt marinade. Then they are broiled (or grill them if you can!) until crisp on the outside and still tender inside. This menu is completed with Pecan-Studded Cheddar Wafers—easy-to-make-and-bake savory crackers topped with fennel seeds, pecans, and Parmigiano.

The simple and sublime ending for this meal—which never really ends until everyone decides to leave—is an array of fresh strawberries dipped in the finest-quality white and dark chocolates, gloriously arrayed on lemon leaves.

The gaiety (and perhaps the greenery) of your party crowd will fill your home with all the atmosphere you need. See the individual recipes for beautiful presentation suggestions.

Everything and anything goes on St. Patrick's Day. Check all the cupboards and drawers for green linens, crockery, glass bowls, or hidden gifts (green, of course) you never really liked. Use them wherever and whenever the spirit takes you.

THE MAIN EVENT

A Wee Bit of Corned Beef and Cabbage on Caraway-Studded Irish Soda Bread

MAKES 32 SANDWICHES

4 1/2-pound corned brisket of beef
8 whole cloves
1 large onion, peeled and quartered
2 large carrots, peeled and quartered
2 ribs celery with leaves, quartered
12 whole black peppercorns, crushed with the bottom of a heavy pan or meat pounder
1/4 teaspoon mustard seeds, crushed
2 bay leaves

8 sprigs fresh flat-leaf parsley
1 small (1–1 1/2 pounds) green cabbage, tough outer leaves removed, cored, and cut into quarters
1/2 cup plus 2 tablespoons Dijon mustard
2 tablespoons sour cream
Caraway-Stuedded Irish Soda Bread (recipe follows)

GARNISH

8 cornichons, cut lengthwise into 4 slices each.

1. Place the corned beef in a 6-quart or larger stockpot or kettle with water to cover. Poke the cloves into the onion sections and add them to the kettle along with the carrots, celery, peppercorns, mustard seeds, bay leaves, and parsley. Bring the corned beef to a boil over high heat, then reduce the heat and simmer, partially covered, until the beef is fork-tender, about 2 1/2–3 hours.

2. Remove the corned beef and reserve the cooking liquid. Let the beef cool to room temperature, lightly covered.

3. Add the wedges of cabbage to the corned beef cooking broth and simmer it over medium heat, uncovered, until tender, about 15–20 minutes. Remove the cabbage and half of the carrots and cool to room temperature. In the bowl of a food processor fitted with the cutting blade, pulse the cabbage together with the carrot pieces several times until you have a coarse but spreadable texture. Reserve this cabbage spread until needed for service. (*Refrigerate this spread if preparing ahead. If the corned beef and cabbage are prepared the day before, save the broth, covered, in the refrigerator, and use it for reheating the meat.*)

4. In a small bowl, whisk 2 tablespoons of the Dijon mustard with the sour cream until well blended. Refrigerate, covered, until needed for service.

Carve the corned beef into ¹/₈-inch slices, then cut each slice to fit the soda bread. Spread each piece of soda bread with a thin coat of the remaining ¹/₂ cup of Dijon mustard followed by a spread of the cabbage and a slice of corned beef. Finish the "sandwich" with a small dab of the sour-cream mustard placed in the center of the beef. Set a cornichon slice over the top. Arrange the corned beef sandwiches on a large tray lined with emerald green napkins.

Caraway-Studded Irish Soda Bread

MAKES 32 SLICES

1 tablespoon vegetable shortening
6 cups all-purpose flour
1 teaspoon caraway seeds
1¹/₂ teaspoons salt
1¹/₂ teaspoons baking soda
12 tablespoons salted butter, chilled and cut into
    small cubes
1 tablespoon Dijon mustard
2¹/₄ cups buttermilk

1. Preheat the oven to 425°. Grease two 13-by-18-inch baking sheets and set aside.
2. Place the flour, caraway seeds, salt, and baking soda in a large mixing bowl. Add the butter, and using your fingers or a pastry blender, combine until the mixture resembles small peas.

3. Mix the mustard and buttermilk gradually into the flour mixture. Knead the dough gently, flouring your hands as needed, and gather it into a ball. Cut the ball in half, forming each half into a 6-inch, somewhat flat, circle. With a sharp knife, cut the figure X 2 inches long and ¹/₂ inch deep in the center of each bread, extending the cut to the sides of the bread.
4. Place the bread rounds on the 2 greased baking sheets. Bake for about 45 minutes, until the breads are golden brown. Cool the breads on a wire rack.

Cut the cooled breads into quarters down the cross marks. Cut each quarter into at least four ¹/₄-inch slices. Don't worry, some of the bread will inevitably crumble, but you'll have plenty to work with.

ON THE SIDE

Drunken Shrimp with Cilantro and Tequila

MAKES 16 SERVINGS

THE MARINADE
2 tablespoons tequila
1 tablespoon finely chopped fresh cilantro
¹/₂ cup vegetable oil
2 cloves garlic, peeled and finely minced
2 teaspoons finely minced fresh ginger
2 tablespoons Dijon mustard

¹/₂ cup orange marmalade
¹/₄ teaspoon red pepper flakes
1 teaspoon ground cumin
¹/₂ teaspoon chili powder
2 tablespoons orange juice concentrate
Grated zest and juice of two limes (about 1¹/₂ tablespoons zest and ¹/₃ cup juice)

THE SHRIMP

32 large cooked shrimp (16–20 count), tails off, deveined◆

GARNISH

8–10 green kale leaves
32 long (about 4 inches) toothpicks

1. Mix all the ingredients for the marinade together in a noncorrosive bowl. Let the marinade rest for 3 hours or overnight, covered, in the refrigerator.
2. Two hours before the party, remove the marinade from the refrigerator and mix well. Add the shrimp, making sure they are all well covered with the marinade. Marinate the shrimp for 2 hours at room temperature.

◆Bring 3 quarts water to a boil over medium-high heat. Add the raw shrimp and simmer for about 3–4 minutes. Drain immediately and chill.

FINISHING TOUCHES AND
TABLE PRESENTATION

Remove the shrimp from the marinade with a slotted spoon and lay them on paper towels to remove any excess drippy marinade. Arrange the shrimp over a bed of green kale on a black lacquered or woven basket tray. Place the toothpicks to one side of the tray. Place a flat dish in front of the shrimp for the used toothpicks.

The Inventive Chef

DOUBLE THE RECIPE AND SERVE THE SHRIMP AS A FIRST COURSE WITH THE SOBA NOODLES (PAGE 189).

ON THE SIDE
*Tortilla Wraps
with Smoked Salmon
and Asparagus*

MAKES 16 SERVINGS

12 medium asparagus spears, tough stalk ends removed
9 ounces softened Boursin
2 teaspoons finely chopped fresh dill
Grated zest of one small lemon
2 teaspoons fresh lemon juice
7 ounces smoked salmon, cut in medium dice
6 (6-inch) flour tortillas

GARNISH

1 bag alfalfa sprouts, about 2 ounces

1. Using a vegetable peeler, peel the stems of the asparagus. Plunge the peeled asparagus into a pot of boiling water and cook for 2–3 minutes, until the asparagus are cooked but still crisp. Immediately place the asparagus in an ice-water bath to stop the cooking and set the bright green color. Strain, set aside, and dry on paper towels.

2. Mix together the cheese, dill, lemon zest and juice, and the smoked salmon in a bowl.

3. Place the tortillas on a work surface. Spread each one with about $1/3$ cup of the cheese mixture. Place two of the asparagus lengthwise on each tortilla and wrap them into tight rolls. Place the rolls on a baking sheet, cover with plastic wrap, and refrigerate for up to 2 hours.

4. Cut off and discard $1/2$ inch of each end of the tortillas. Cut each tortilla into 5 or 6 half-inch slices.

FINISHING TOUCHES AND TABLE PRESENTATION

Serve the salmon wraps at room temperature to ensure that the cheese is soft and creamy. Arrange the wraps, cut-side up, over a bed of alfalfa sprouts on a decorative tray. Top each wrap with a few alfalfa sprouts.

The Inventive Chef

THE TORTILLAS CAN BE WRAPPED AROUND MANY COMBINATIONS OF COOKED FILLINGS. CENTERPIECES FOR THE TORTILLAS CAN BE GRILLED CHICKEN WITH GINGER, SAUTÉED SHRIMP AND SCALLION, BARBECUED BEEF, OR GRILLED VEGETABLES WITH GOAT CHEESE. THEY ARE FUN TO CREATE, AND SERVING TWO OR THREE DIFFERENT FILLINGS WITH DIFFERENT HERBS AND SPICES IS AN INTERESTING TREAT.

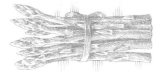

ON THE SIDE

Zucchini and Spinach-Tortellini Skewers

MAKES 16 SERVINGS

SPECIAL COOKWARE
32 (8–10-inch) wooden skewers, soaked in water, or metal skewers

THE MARINADE
4 cloves garlic, peeled and finely minced
2 tablespoons capers, drained and finely chopped
3 tablespoons finely chopped fresh basil
$1/4$ cup balsamic vinegar
$1/4$ cup red wine vinegar
$1 1/2$ cups olive oil
1 teaspoon salt or to taste
4 teaspoons freshly ground black pepper, or to taste
2 tablespoons finely chopped pimiento

THE SKEWERS
2 medium-large zucchini, washed, ends removed
64 cheese-filled green spinach tortellini, cooked al dente

GARNISH
2 large heads of radicchio, leaves separated
2 tablespoons finely chopped flat-leaf parsley

1. In the bowl of a food processor fitted with the cutting blade, combine all the marinade ingredients except the pimiento. Pulse several times to mix well, then add the pimiento and pulse twice to blend. Remove to a large, noncorrosive pottery, glass, or stainless steel bowl and reserve.

2. Slice the zucchini in half lengthwise. Then slice each piece crosswise into 8 semicircles.

3. Bring at least 3 cups of water to boil in a medium saucepan over high heat. Add the zucchini and cook for 1 minute, until the zucchini is crisp to the bite. Strain and shock the zucchini under cold running water. Drain it on paper towels.

4. Place the zucchini and tortellini in the marinade. Marinate at room temperature for 2 hours. Remove the zucchini and tortellini from the marinade. Thread and alternate 2 zucchini pieces, skin-side first, and 2 tortellini on each skewer, beginning and ending with the zucchini.

5. Arrange the skewers on baking sheets lined with foil. Brush each skewer well with the marinade, constantly mixing the ingredients in the bowl. *(Refrigerate the skewers, covered, if not using immediately. Bring to room temperature before serving.)*

FINISHING TOUCHES AND
TABLE PRESENTATION

Arrange a layer of radicchio leaves on a flat round or square woven basket or pottery tray. Arrange the skewers over the radicchio leaves in concentric circles. Dust the tops of the skewers with parsley.

The Inventive Chef

INTERSPERSE SKEWERS OF CRISPLY BLANCHED YELLOW AND RED BELL PEPPERS AND WHITE CHEESE-FILLED TORTELLINI WITH THE SKEWERS OF ZUCCHINI AND GREEN TORTELLINI FOR AN INTERESTING VARIETY.

ON THE SIDE

Pungent Meatballs Glazed in Green

MAKES ABOUT 60 MEATBALLS

1 medium onion, peeled and finely minced
2 tablespoons peanut or vegetable oil
2 large cloves garlic, peeled and finely minced
2 pounds ground beef round
1 tablespoon finely minced fresh ginger
2¹/₂ tablespoons dark soy sauce
1 tablespoon tomato paste
1 tablespoon Dijon mustard
¹/₄ cup finely minced flat-leaf parsley
¹/₄ cup unflavored dry bread crumbs
¹/₂ teaspoon salt
¹/₄ teaspoon freshly ground black pepper
2 tablespoons sesame oil
¹/₃ cup mint jelly

GARNISH
One 8–10-inch round bread, whole-grain or sourdough
  (purchased in bakeries)
12 stems mint leaves

1. Sauté the onion in the peanut oil in a large ovenproof skillet over medium-high heat for 3 minutes. Add the garlic and continue to sauté for 30 seconds. Remove from the heat and set aside to cool.

2. In a large bowl, combine the beef with the cooled onion and garlic, the ginger, 1¹/₂ tablespoons of the soy sauce, the tomato paste, mustard, parsley, bread crumbs, salt, and pepper, and mix well. Form the beef mixture into 1-inch balls.

3. Heat 1 tablespoon of the sesame oil over medium heat in the skillet used to sauté the onion. Sauté as many meatballs as will comfortably fit in the skillet, turning them gently with a small spoon until they have browned on all sides, about 4 minutes. Do not crowd the pan. Remove the browned meatballs to a paper towel–lined baking sheet and cook the remaining meatballs in the same manner, adding the second tablespoon of sesame oil only if the pan gets too dry. Once all the meatballs have been browned and drained on the paper towels, discard any excess oil in the skillet and wipe it clean.

4. Over medium heat, melt the mint jelly together with the remaining 1 tablespoon soy sauce in the skillet until well combined. Return all of the meatballs to the skillet and toss them gently to warm through and coat all sides with the mint glaze.

FINISHING TOUCHES AND TABLE PRESENTATION

Cut a six-inch-wide–by-6-inch-deep circle from the center of the bread, leaving a 1¹⁄₂-inch thickness on the bottom. Remove the top and fill the bread with the meatballs. Place the bread on a large platter. Garnish the platter with stems of mint leaves. Place toothpicks near the platter in an old-fashioned glass with a small dish alongside for the used toothpicks.

ON THE SIDE

Green Pepper Scones with Curry-Rubbed Chicken

MAKES ABOUT 2¹⁄₂ DOZEN

SPECIAL COOKWARE
Parchment paper
1¹⁄₂-inch biscuit cutter

1 tablespoon vegetable oil
2¹⁄₂ tablespoons olive oil
1 green bell pepper, seeded and finely chopped
1 medium onion, peeled and finely minced
1³⁄₄ cups all-purpose flour, plus extra for working the dough
1 tablespoon baking powder
¹⁄₄ teaspoon salt
6¹⁄₂ tablespoons butter, cut into ¹⁄₄-inch cubes
2 eggs
¹⁄₃ cup whole milk
Curry-Rubbed Chicken (recipe follows)

GARNISH
1 ripe mango, peeled, pitted, quartered lengthwise, and cut into 32 pieces
32 small mint leaves
12 mint stems

1. Preheat the oven to 450°. Line two baking sheets with parchment paper or, if the paper is unavailable, grease the baking sheets. Reserve two additional baking sheets and set aside.

2. In a medium skillet, heat the oil and sauté the green pepper and onion over medium-high heat for

5–6 minutes, until the onion is translucent and the green pepper is wilted. Use a spoon to transfer the onions and green pepper to paper towels to drain any excess oil, and cool to room temperature.

3. Place the flour, baking powder, salt, and butter in the bowl of an electric mixer fitted with the paddle attachment and blend until the butter is the size of small peas.

4. In another bowl, beat together the eggs and milk with a whisk until they are well blended. Mix the sautéed onion and green pepper into the beaten milk and eggs. Add this mixture all at once to the flour and blend on slow speed or with a wooden spoon just until smooth, about 1 minute. The dough should be sticky.

5. Turn the dough onto a *heavily* floured surface. Sprinkle the top of the dough with flour and knead it 6 times. Roll or pat the dough into a $1/2$-inch-thick circle. Cut the dough into circles with a $1\,1/2$-inch biscuit cutter. Re-form dough once only, to make more biscuits. *(Continually dip the biscuit cutter in the flour between cuts.)*

6. Arrange the scones 2 inches apart on the baking sheets. To protect the bottoms of the scones from becoming too brown before they are baked, place each baking sheet on top of an empty sheet before baking the scones for 10–12 minutes, until they are golden brown. Cool the scones on a wire rack.

FINISHING TOUCHES AND TABLE PRESENTATION

Cut each scone in half. Heap 1 tablespoon of chicken on each scone half. Top each scone half with a piece of mango and a small mint leaf. Arrange the scones in flat baskets over brightly colored cloth napkins, and highlight with the mint stems.

Curry-Rubbed Chicken

MAKES 16 SERVINGS

SPECIAL COOKWARE
Meat pounder

$1/2$ plus $1/8$ teaspoon ground turmeric
$1/2$ plus $1/8$ teaspoon powdered ginger
$1/2$ plus $1/8$ teaspoon ground cumin
$1/2$ teaspoon salt
$1/4$ teaspoon freshly ground black pepper
$1\,1/2$ pounds skinless and boneless chicken breasts
6 tablespoons butter
1 medium onion, peeled and cut into $1/4$-inch dice
2 large green apples, Granny Smith or greenings, unpeeled, cored, and finely diced
3 tablespoons apple juice
$2/3$ cup sour cream

1. Mix the $1/2$ teaspoons of turmeric, ginger, cumin, salt and pepper in a small bowl.

2. Pound the chicken breasts to a $1/4$-inch thickness with a meat pounder or the flat side of a large chef's knife. Pat the spices well onto all the surfaces of the chicken.

3. Heat 4 tablespoons of the butter in a large skillet and sauté the chicken breasts over medium heat until they are cooked through, about 3–4 minutes on each side. *(Do not crowd the pan.)* Remove the chicken to a cutting board and let cool for 10 minutes. Cut the breasts into $1/4$-inch dice. Set aside.

4. Add the remaining butter to the skillet and sauté the onion over medium heat for 3 minutes, until translucent. Add the apples and continue to sauté, stirring often, for $1\,1/2$ minutes more.

5. With the heat on high, return the chicken to the skillet. Add the apple juice and cook the mixture briskly for 30 seconds, continually shaking the pan.

6. Remove the pan from the heat, add the sour cream, and continue to blend and mix the chicken well with all the ingredients. Transfer the chicken to a bowl and blend it well with the remaining ¹/₈ teaspoons of turmeric, ginger, and cumin.

The Inventive Chef

SERVE THE CHICKEN OVER THE MINTED COUSCOUS WITH SAUTÉED EGGPLANT, ZUCCHINI, AND CURRANTS (PAGE 109), TOPPED WITH THE APPLES AND ONIONS.

ON THE SIDE

Mussels with Parsley and Horseradish Mayonnaise

MAKES 16 SERVINGS

2 quarts (about 2¹/₂ pounds) cultivated mussels♦
³/₄ cup dry white wine
1 large onion, peeled and finely minced
2 large cloves garlic, peeled and finely minced
4 sprigs flat-leaf parsley
2 egg yolks
2 teaspoons fresh lemon juice
1 tablespoon Dijon mustard
2 teaspoons well drained white horseradish
1 cup vegetable oil
¹/₄ cup finely minced curly parsley
¹/₂ teaspoon salt, or to taste
¹/₈ teaspoon cayenne pepper, or to taste

GARNISH
1 bunch curly parsley, long stems removed
Julienned zest of 1 lemon

1. Place the mussels in a large stockpot or saucepan with the white wine, onion, garlic, and parsley sprigs. Cover the stockpot tightly with a lid, and bring the mussels to a boil over high heat. Lower the heat to medium-high and steam the mussels about 5–6 minutes, or until almost all the mussels are open. Remove the lid; pour off the liquid, reserving ¹/₄ cup. Cool the mussels, uncovered, in the pan.
2. When the mussels have cooled, open the shells completely and gently remove the flesh from the connective muscle that holds the meat to the shell. Place the mussel in the clean shell half on a baking sheet. *(Discard any mussels that have not opened.)*
3. While the mussels are cooling, place the egg yolks, lemon juice, mustard, and horseradish in the bowl of a food processor fitted with the knife blade, and pulse to blend the ingredients. With the motor running, *slowly* add the cup of oil in a steady stream, until the mixture has thickened. *(If you add the oil too fast, the mayonnaise will not thicken.)* Transfer the mayonnaise to a bowl.
4. Blend the reserved ¹/₄ cup of cooled broth and the minced parsley with the mayonnaise and season with the salt and cayenne pepper.

♦ Cultivated mussels are *almost* sand-free. If there is a small beard clinging to the shell, be sure to remove it. Stir the mussels around in a sink filled with cold water and let them soak for 5 minutes to clean them. Discard any mussels that do not close on their own when you press the shells together gently.

Arrange the mussels on a large flat tray or a basket lined with curly parsley. Spoon ¹/₈ teaspoon of the mayonnaise onto each mussel. I like to highlight the mussels with the lemon zest.

ON THE SIDE

*Lamb, Carrot, and
Potato Kabobs*

MAKES 16 SERVINGS

SPECIAL COOKWARE
32 (6-inch) wooden skewers, soaked in water

2 tablespoons plus ¹/₄ cup peanut or vegetable oil
1 medium onion, peeled and finely minced
3 cloves garlic, peeled and finely minced
1¹/₄ cups plain yogurt
2 teaspoons ground cumin
1 teaspoon ground turmeric
1¹/₂ teaspoons powdered ginger
¹/₂ teaspoon dry mustard
1 teaspoon salt, plus additional to taste
¹/₂ teaspoon cayenne pepper
*1¹/₂ pounds boneless leg of lamb, fat removed, cut into 32
    1-inch cubes*
*14–18 baby carrots, peeled, cut into ¹/₂-inch pieces (at least
    32 pieces), and steamed crisp*
*8–10 small new potatoes, washed, unpeeled, cut into
    ¹/₂-inch quarters (at least 32 pieces), and steamed crisp*
Freshly ground black pepper to taste

GARNISH
1 bunch curly parsley
¹/₂ cup unsweetened flaked coconut

1. Heat 2 tablespoons of the oil in a skillet over medium heat and sauté the onion for 5–6 minutes, until it is soft and lightly golden brown. Set aside.
2. Blend together the garlic, yogurt, cumin, turmeric, ginger, mustard, salt, and cayenne in a large bowl with the reserved onions and blend well. Add the lamb, carrots, and potatoes, stir well to coat the meat and vegetables, and marinate, covered, in the refrigerator for 4 hours or overnight.
3. Bring the ingredients to room temperature and thread each skewer with a cube of lamb, one potato quarter, and one piece of carrot. Arrange the skewers on baking sheets.
4. Preheat the broiler, or even if it is March, brave the wind and fire up the charcoal grill if you prefer. Mop up any marinade that has accumulated between the skewers with paper towels. Brush the skewers with the remaining ¹/₄ cup of oil and sprinkle them with salt and pepper.
5. Broil the lamb kabobs 2 inches from the broiler or over charcoal for 2–3 minutes on each side. The lamb should be crisply brown on the outside and pink inside. Serve the kabobs warm.

Arrange the kabobs over *clean* outdoor grill racks. Place the racks on woven trays filled with curly parsley. The skewers can also be placed in concentric circles on clean hibachis filled with unlit coals. Dust the kabobs with the coconut.

Pecan-Studded Cheddar Wafers

MAKES ABOUT 3 ¹/₂ DOZEN

SPECIAL COOKWARE

1 ¹/₂-inch fluted cookie cutter

¹/₃ cup fennel seeds
¹/₂ cup coarsely chopped pecans
¹/₂ cup plus ¹/₃ cup freshly grated Parmigiano Reggiano
3 cups all-purpose flour
1 cup grated and firmly packed sharp, orange Cheddar
12 tablespoons chilled unsalted butter
3 eggs, well beaten
1 tablespoon Dijon mustard
¹/₂ teaspoon salt
¹/₈ teaspoon cayenne pepper
¹/₂ cup finely chopped fresh chives
2 teaspoons heavy cream

GARNISH

1 bunch fresh chives

1. In a small bowl, toss together the fennel seeds, pecans, and ¹/₂ cup of the Parmigiano Reggiano and set aside.

2. Preheat the oven to 375°.

3. Place the flour, Cheddar, and the remaining ¹/₃ cup of the Parmigiano Reggiano in the bowl of a food processor fitted with the knife blade and pulse twice to incorporate the flour and cheese.

4. Break or cut the chilled butter into small pieces. Add the butter to the flour and cheese through the feeding tube, pulsing often until the mixture resembles rough cornmeal.

5. Beat the eggs with the Dijon mustard, salt, and cayenne. Reserve and set aside 3 tablespoons of the egg mixture. Pulse the remaining egg into the flour and cheese until the mixture is a smooth dough, about 6 pulses. On the last pulse, add the chives to the batter. Remove the dough from the processor and gently gather it into a flattened ball. Chill the dough, well wrapped, in the refrigerator for 2 hours.

6. Roll the dough out into a ¹/₈-inch-thick circle on a lightly floured board. Cut the cheese wafers with a 1 ¹/₂-inch fluted cookie cutter. Place the wafers on an unbuttered baking sheet, allowing 1 inch between each wafer. Chill the leftover dough and reroll for additional wafers.

7. Brush the wafers with the reserved beaten egg mixed with the 2 teaspoons of heavy cream. Sprinkle some of the mixed fennel seeds, pecans, and Parmigiano Reggiano on top of each wafer and bake until golden brown, about 15–18 minutes. Transfer the wafers to wire racks to cool.

FINISHING TOUCHES AND
TABLE PRESENTATION

The wafers show splendidly served on a shiny silver surface. The bits of chive will subtly symbolize the green of St. Patrick's Day. Separate the long chive strands into bunches of 4 and thread them among the wafers.

304 ◆ *Invitation to Dinner*

The Inventive Chef

MONTEREY JACK AND ASIAGO ARE FINE
SUBSTITUTES FOR THE CHEDDAR. I LIKE TO
VARY THE FENNEL SEEDS WITH CARAWAY OR
POPPY SEEDS. THE WAFERS PERFECTLY
COMPLEMENT DISPLAYS OF FRESH FRUIT.

THE GRAND FINALE

White and Dark Chocolate-Dipped Strawberries

MAKES 32 CHOCOLATE-COVERED STRAWBERRIES

*8 ounces sweet or semisweet chocolate (preferably Callebaut
   or Valrohna) chopped fine*
8 ounces Callebaut or Valrohna white chocolate, chopped
   fine*
32 jumbo strawberries, preferably long-stemmed, cleaned**

GARNISH
20 medium lemon leaves

1. Warm the dark and white chocolates separately
over simmering water in the top of double boilers or
in metal or heat-proof glass bowls set over small
saucepans of simmering water.

*Because of butterfat content, the white chocolate–dipped strawberries
will work well only if you use the quality chocolate recommended here.*

***Brush any dirt from the strawberries with a pastry brush. Do not
wash the berries or they will not hold the chocolate.*

2. Stir the chocolates often until they are completely
melted. Remove the double boilers from the heat but
allow the chocolates to remain above the hot water.
3. Line two baking sheets with waxed or parchment
paper. Divide the strawberries into two batches.
Holding each one by the stem, dip 16 strawberries
into the dark chocolate, coating the bottom ⅔ of each
berry. Using the same method, coat the rest of the
fruit with the white chocolate.
4. As soon as each strawberry is coated with
chocolate, place it on the paper-lined baking sheet to
harden for about 30 minutes.

FINISHING TOUCHES AND
TABLE PRESENTATION

I like to use a silver tray for the strawberries. Alternate
the white and dark chocolate-covered berries and arrange
lemon leaves around the edge of the tray.

The Inventive Chef

DON'T STOP WITH STRAWBERRIES. DIP BANANA
SLICES, ORANGE SLICES, DRIED APRICOTS, AND
DRIED PEARS INTO THE CHOCOLATES. ARRANGE
THESE FRUITS WITH THE STRAWBERRIES AND
LUXURIATE IN GREAT SUBTLETIES OF TASTE
AND TEXTURE.

1 WEEK AHEAD

TOQUE 2	Cheese Wafers	Prepare through step 5; cover well and freeze.

2 OR 3 DAYS BEFORE THE PARTY

MAIN EVENT	Corned Beef	Prepare the onion, carrots, celery, and cabbage; store separately, covered, in refrigerator.
TOQUE 1	Shrimp	Prepare marinade as in step 1; store covered in refrigerator.
	Zucchini Skewers	Prepare marinade as in step 1; store covered in refrigerator.

THE DAY BEFORE THE PARTY

MAIN EVENT	Corned Beef	Prepare through step 4; slice when cool; store covered separately in refrigerator. *Don't forget to reserve and refrigerate the cooking stock.*
	Bread	Prepare through step 4; store covered in refrigerator.
TOQUE 1	Tortilla Wraps	Prepare through step 3; store covered in refrigerator.
	Zucchini Skewers	Prepare steps 2–4; store covered in refrigerator. Prepare radicchio and parsley garnish; store covered in refrigerator.
	Meatballs	Prepare through step 2; store covered in refrigerator. Set up cabbage and mint garnishes; store covered in refrigerator.
TOQUE 2	Scones	Prepare scones through step 5.
	Chicken	Prepare chicken through step 6;

		remove from skillet; cool; store covered in refrigerator. Prepare mango and mint garnishes; store separately, covered, in refrigerator.
	Mussels	Prepare curly parsley and lemon garnish; store separately, covered, in refrigerator.
	Lamb	Prepare through step 2; store covered in refrigerator. *(Think about how the cooking will be done: the broiler or the grill. If the grilling method is used, fill the grill with charcoal.)*
	Cheese Wafers	Place pastry in refrigerator to defrost overnight.
GRAND FINALE	Berries	Prepare through step 4; when the chocolate has hardened, place berries in refrigerator, lightly covered with foil.

Strategic Maneuvers:

Fill creamers; cover and store in refrigerator.
Fill sugar bowls.
Set table. Check table decor.
Check ice and beverages.
Set up lemon and lime wedges, cocktail olives, and onions for bar drinks, as needed.
Chill wine, if white.
Check garnishes for each recipe.
Locate and label all serving bowls, platters, and utensils.

◆ *Kitchen instructions are given for finishing the hors d'oeuvre through service presentation. If your refrigerator is too small to handle all the arranged food, place the finished hors d'oeuvre on baking sheets and arrange them on their serving vessels 30 minutes before your guests are scheduled to arrive.*

MAIN EVENT	Corned Beef	Reheat reserved stock; add beef and gently reheat until warmed through, about 30 minutes. Slice beef as directed in service instructions; cover well; set at room temperature. Set cabbage and mustard spreads at room temperature. Line service tray with green napkins. Slice cornichon garnish.
	Soda Bread	Slice bread; seal well under plastic wrap; set aside at room temperature.
TOQUE 1	Shrimp	Marinate shrimp as in step 2; arrange for service as directed and refrigerate lightly covered with foil.
	Tortilla Wraps	Prepare step 4 and arrange for service as in finishing touches; set aside at room temperature.
	Zucchini Skewers	Prepare step 5 and arrange for service as in finishing touches; refrigerate lightly covered.
	Meatballs	Prepare steps 3–4; set aside at room temperature; set up unfilled serving platter with decor.
TOQUE 2	Scones and Chicken	Prepare scones as in step 6; slice in half; cover well. Bring chicken to room temperature. Finish step 6. Arrange and garnish as in finishing touches.
	Mussels	Prepare through step 4 and arrange as in finishing touches; refrigerate lightly covered with foil.
	Lamb	Prepare steps 3–4; set aside at room temperature. Ready the grill if you choose to use it. Prepare coconut garnish.
	Cheese Wafers	Prepare steps 6–7 and arrange as in finishing touches; set aside at room temperature or place on food table.
GRAND FINALE	Berries	Arrange as in finishing touches; set in cool place, away from all heat, to keep chocolate set.

45 MINUTES BEFORE GUESTS ARRIVE:

MAIN EVENT	Corned Beef	Make open-faced sandwiches and arrange as directed in service instructions; place on food table lightly covered with foil.

35 MINUTES BEFORE GUESTS ARRIVE:

		Arrange all hors d'oeuvres on garnished platters if this has not been done.
TOQUE 1	Meatballs	Warm over low heat, stirring often.

20 MINUTES BEFORE GUESTS ARRIVE:

TOQUE 1:	Meatballs	Arrange as in finishing touches; cover lightly with foil; remove foil when guests arrive.
TOQUE 2	Lamb	Grill or broil as in step 5. Arrange for service; cover lightly with foil to keep warm.

GUESTS ARRIVE:

Arrange buffet table.
Uncover all foods 5 minutes
before invitation time.

**30 MINUTES AFTER FIRST GUESTS
ARRIVE:**

Place dipped strawberries on
food table.
Set out coffee and tea.

Small Delicacies for a Big Business Occasion

THE MAIN EVENTS:

Gingered Beef Satés
with Pineapple Chutney
Black-and-White Sesame Wontons

ON THE SIDE:

Cherry Tomatoes, Crabmeat, and Green Pepper

◆

Sun-dried Tomato Palmiers

◆

Parsley-Dusted Wild Mushroom–Stuffed Eggs

ON THE SIDE:

Shrimp, Red Onion, and Monterey Jack Quesadillas

◆

Prosciutto, Chicken, and Honey-Mustard Bundles

◆

Broccoli and Portobello Mushroom Custard Tart

THE GRAND FINALE:
Raspberry Cheesecake Squares

BEVERAGE RECOMMENDATIONS:
Full bar (see Chapter 14)
Carbernet Sauvignon, California, Louis M. Martini Winery

THE OPEN HOUSE AT YOUR NEW OFFICE ACCOMPLISHED EVERY-thing you wanted. How many people came? Thirty? Forty? It all seemed so easy: Clients, friends, and business colleagues were meeting and mingling, singing your praises and predicting great success. What an impression you made: Everyone was knocked out by your sophistication, good taste, artistic talent, and terrific sense of organization. And that was just about the food! Guests kept exclaiming over the skewers of sizzling spicy beef, the cherry tomatoes bursting with crabmeat, the wild-mushroom stuffed eggs, the dainty squares of raspberry cheesecake. And everyone made the same joke—that whenever you got bored selling real estate, you really should consider catering!

The delight of this hors d'oeuvre buffet—in addition to the range of great flavors—is how beautiful everything looks, with hardly any fuss. The Main Event is a trio of simple showpieces: sprinkle a mix of black and white sesame seeds on wonton-skin triangles, deep-fry them briefly, and you have a basketful of black, white, and golden crispy crackers. Weave spicy marinated strips of sirloin on wooden skewers, grill or broil until seared, and set the skewers in a basket lined with lemon leaves. Alongside you will place leafy pineapple halves heaped with chili-spiked fruit chutney and showered with shredded coconut.

The one-toque menu presents three more colorful creations. Fill scooped-out cherry tomatoes with a smooth and crunchy mix of crabmeat, cream cheese, green pepper, and red onion (with a zing of Tabasco and horseradish) and top each morsel with a pretty frond of dill. Sun-dried Tomato *Palmiers* are flaky puff pastry rounds swirled with a pesto, minced sun-dried tomatoes, and Fontina and Parmigiano cheeses. Finally, you will stuff hard-cooked egg halves with a rich blend of golden yolks, sautéed wild mushrooms and shallots, roasted garlic, and sour cream. They are gorgeous on a platter, dusted with parsley and topped with a slice of cornichon and a dice of pimiento.

On the two-toque menu, tortilla sandwiches are filled with spicy sautéed shrimp and Monterey Jack cheese, then baked. The savory, melting quesadillas are garnished with cilantro and lime slices. For the Prosciutto, Chicken, and Honey-Mustard Bundles, strips of prosciutto are wrapped around sautéed cubes of marinated chicken breast, piqued with mustard and tiny scoops of cantaloupe. A quiche-like broccoli and mushroom custard pie combines a cheesy pastry crust and a rich custard loaded with vegetables, baked in a sheet pan and simply cut into bite-size pieces.

The Grand Finale, Raspberry Cheesecake Squares, are also made in a sheet pan, starting with a delectable crumbly crust with brown sugar and walnuts. The crust is baked, coated with raspberry jam, and then baked again with a lush cream cheese filling.

I recommend this menu heartily for business entertaining and also encourage you to make imagi-
native table decorations that will cleverly remind
your guests of the business purpose underlying
your party. Since selling real estate is all about
good presentation, why not make a buffet centerpiece from a house model, with exterior shrub-
bery made from curly-leaf parsley and edible
flowers such as nasturtiums, pansies, or rose
petals? For an all-purpose office occasion, create
a humorous gift basket built from rolls of fax and
computer paper, and other staples of the office
diet, such as pencils, rulers, jotting pads, and
sticky notes!

Gingered Beef Satés with Pineapple Chutney

MAKES AT LEAST 32 KABOBS

SPECIAL COOKWARE
Meat pounder
32 (6-inch) wooden skewers, soaked in water

THE SATÉS
2¹/₂ pounds boneless beef sirloin, outer fat removed
2 cloves garlic, peeled and finely minced
1 medium onion, peeled and finely chopped
1 tablespoon finely minced fresh ginger
1 tablespoon finely minced fresh cilantro
3 tablespoons fresh lime juice
1 teaspoon ground turmeric
1 teaspoon ground cumin
¹/₂ teaspoon salt
2 tablespoons sugar
¹/₃ cup dark soy sauce (available in Asian food stores)◆
¹/₂ cup canned coconut milk, stirred well before measuring
¹/₂ cup peanut oil

◆Dark soy sauce has a musty flavor, with no noticeable taste of salt.

GARNISH
12–14 lemon leaves
Pineapple Chutney (recipe follows)
¹/₂ cup shredded unsweetened coconut

1. Slice the beef into at least 32 strips each ¹/₂–1-inch
wide when lying flat by 3 inches long (about 1 ounce
each). Lay the sliced beef flat on a cutting board and
cover it with a sheet or two of plastic wrap.
2. Whisk together the garlic, onion, ginger, cilantro,

lime juice, turmeric, cumin, salt, sugar, soy sauce, coconut milk, and oil in a large noncorrosive bowl, such as glass, pottery, or stainless steel. Put the beef in the bowl, covering all the strips well with the marinade, cover, and put it in the refrigerator to marinate for 3–5 hours.

3. While the satés are marinating, soak 32 wooden skewers in water to prevent them from burning while grilling or broiling.

4. Thread the strips of marinated beef on the skewers using a back-and-forth motion, and place them on a foil-lined baking sheet. Save the leftover marinade for rebrushing the satés before broiling. (*The satés can be refrigerated at this point.*)

5. Bring the satés to room temperature. Preheat the broiler. If they are being grilled, make certain the coals are gray before you begin. Brush the meat with the remaining marinade and grill them for $1^1/2$ minutes, on each side, until the beef is lightly browned. The satés can also be broiled on a rack placed 3 inches from the broiling element of your oven. (*The satés must be broiled under a preheated hot broiler about 2 inches from the heat.*)

FINISHING TOUCHES AND TABLE PRESENTATION

Arrange the satés in concentric circles in a large, round, shallow basket lined with lemon leaves.

Fill the pineapple shells with the chutney and dust the top with the shredded coconut. Your guests can dip the kabobs into the chutney.

The Inventive Chef

CHICKEN OR LAMB SATÉS WORK WELL WITH THE BEEF MARINADE. I WOULD SERVE THE PINEAPPLE CHUTNEY WITH LAMB BUT SUBSTITUTE 2 LARGE MANGOES IN THE CHUTNEY TO SERVE WITH THE CHICKEN SATÉS.

Pineapple Chutney

MAKES 3 CUPS

1 medium (about 2 pounds) ripe pineapple
$^1/2$ cup coarsely chopped red onion
$^1/4$ cup fresh cilantro
$^3/4$ cup golden raisins
1 tablespoon finely chopped fresh ginger
$^1/4$ teaspoon chili powder
$^1/4$ teaspoon salt
Juice of 2 limes
1 small red bell pepper, seeds and ribs removed
    and finely diced

1. Cut the pineapple in half lengthwise. Make sure to cut through the green fronds or leaves to make certain that there are leaves on each half shell.

2. With a sharp knife, cut around the inside edge, separating the fruit from the shell. Cut under the fruit to release the bottom. Remove the fruit and place the empty shells in the refrigerator, well covered, if preparing the day before. Coarsely chop the pineapple. Place the pineapple, red onion, cilantro, raisins, ginger, chili powder, salt, and lime juice in the bowl of a food processor fitted with the knife blade and process until the mixture is smooth, about $^1/2$–1 minute. Place the

---

chutney in a fine mesh strainer to drain all the excess juices. Transfer the drained chutney to a bowl and stir in the diced red pepper for color.

Black-and-White Sesame Wontons

MAKES 72–80 WONTONS

SPECIAL COOKWARE
Spray bottle or pastry brush
Deep-fat-frying thermometer

36–40 wonton skins
1/4 cup black sesame seeds
1/4 cup white sesame seeds
Salt
Peanut or vegetable oil, for frying

1. Cut each wonton into 2 triangles. Arrange the wontons on two baking sheets and spray a mist of water over the wontons with a spray bottle (or, if you don't have a spray bottle, brush the wonton skins lightly with a pastry brush dipped in water). Sprinkle the wontons with a coating of black and white sesame seeds and sprinkle them lightly with salt.
2. Pour 1 1/2 inches of oil into a 10–12-inch skillet. Heat the oil over medium heat until the temperature on a deep-fat-frying thermometer reaches about 280°. Fry the wontons in small batches, about 8–10 at a time. The wontons will take less than 15 seconds to brown lightly on one side. Flip them with tongs and brown on the second side. Remove the wontons from the pan to drain and cool on a baking sheet lined with paper towels. *(If the wontons fry too fast, they will turn an unattractive dark brown; too slow and they will get oily. Adjust the oil temperature so that your wontons are golden brown. Do not crowd the skillet.)*
3. Line an airtight container with paper towels. Fill the container with the cooled wontons and cover tightly, sealing the container. The wontons can be stored at room temperature for up to 1 week.

FINISHING TOUCHES AND TABLE PRESENTATION

Line a woven basket with emerald green napkins, creating a deep cushion for the wontons. Pile the wontons into the basket and watch them disappear as soon as the party begins. I like to double the recipe and enjoy nibbling on any leftovers my guests may have overlooked.

ON THE SIDE

Cherry Tomatoes, Crabmeat, and Green Pepper

MAKES 32 PIECES

32 cherry tomatoes, 1 1/2 inches in diameter
  (about 2 pints)
7 ounces fresh lump crabmeat or 1 (6 1/2 ounce) can
  crabmeat, picked through for shells and cartilage
1/2 teaspoon salt

5 ounces cream cheese, at room temperature
6 tablespoons finely minced green bell pepper
3 tablespoons peeled and finely minced red onion
1 teaspoon finely minced fresh dill
1/8 teaspoon Tabasco sauce
1 teaspoon fresh lemon juice
Finely minced zest of 1 lemon
1/2 teaspoon well-drained horseradish
32 small dill sprigs

GARNISH
1 bunch dill
12 cherry tomatoes with stems

1. With a sharp knife, cut a very thin slice from the bottom of each cherry tomato so it stands without tipping over. Cut a 1/8-inch slice from the top of each tomato, and using a small spoon, scoop out and discard the pulp, making certain you do not puncture the bottom of the tomatoes. Turn the tomatoes open-side down on a tray lined with paper towels to drain for 20 minutes.

2. In a large bowl, combine the crabmeat, salt, cream cheese, green pepper, red onion, minced dill, Tabasco, lemon juice and zest, and the horseradish. Blend the ingredients well.

3. Turn the cherry tomatoes, cut-side up and spoon (or use a pastry bag without a tip) to pipe the crabmeat mixture into the center of each tomato. Garnish each one with a small sprig of dill.

FINISHING TOUCHES AND
TABLE PRESENTATION

Arrange the tomatoes on a flat basket or black lacquered tray or silver platter. Arrange small bouquets of dill in

front of the platter and nestle whole cherry tomatoes with stems in the dill.

The Inventive Chef

CHOPPED COOKED SHRIMP IS AN EXCELLENT SUBSTITUTE FOR THE CRABMEAT AND BALANCES WELL WITH ALL THE OTHER INGREDIENTS IN THE RECIPE.

ON THE SIDE
Sun-dried Tomato Palmiers

MAKES ABOUT 44 *PALMIERS*

2 cloves garlic, peeled and finely minced
1/2 cup prepared pesto (available in the refrigerator cases of most markets)
17 1/4-ounce package or two sheets frozen puff pastry, defrosted
1 cup grated Fontina
1/4 cup finely grated Parmigiano Reggiano
1/2 cup finely minced sun-dried tomatoes, rehydrated in hot water for 5–8 minutes (if not packed in oil)
4 pinches freshly ground black pepper

1. Preheat the oven to 350°.

2. Stir the minced garlic into the prepared pesto.

3. Unfold the pastry sheets and on a lightly floured board roll them slightly with a rolling pin to make a rectangle that measures 11 by 12 inches. Cut each pastry sheet in half lengthwise.

4. Spread 1/4 of the pesto (2 tablespoons) over the entire surface of each of the four pastry sheets.

5. Combine the cheeses. Divide and sprinkle the cheeses and sun-dried tomatoes over the pesto on each pastry sheet. Season each with a pinch of pepper.

6. Tightly roll each sheet, starting at a long side, into a 1-inch-wide log. Using a sharp serrated knife, cut each log into about twenty-four ¹/₂-inch slices and place them cut-side-down on ungreased baking sheets 1¹/₂ inches apart. (*The* palmiers *may be baked right away or refrigerated for up to 2 days. The unbaked* palmiers *can be frozen, covered, for up to 2 weeks.*)

7. If frozen, defrost the *palmiers* in the refrigerator before baking. Bake the *palmiers* in the preheated oven for 10–15 minutes, until golden brown. Let them cool for 3 minutes on the baking sheets, then transfer them to cooling racks.

FINISHING TOUCHES AND TABLE PRESENTATION

Line different-shaped baskets or long silver bread trays with white cloth napkins. Arrange the *palmiers* in concentric circles or rows in the baskets or trays.

The Inventive Chef

SPRINKLE ¹/₃ CUP OF CHOPPED HAM OR CRUMBLED, CRISPLY COOKED BACON OVER THE PUFF PASTRY SHEETS WITH THE CHEESES AND SUN-DRIED TOMATO.

ON THE SIDE

Parsley-Dusted Wild Mushroom-Stuffed Eggs

MAKES 16 SERVINGS

16 eggs, at room temperature
4 large shallots, peeled and finely minced
4 tablespoons salted butter
1 pound wild mushrooms, such as shiitake or portobello, washed, stems removed, and finely diced
1 cup sour cream
¹/₄ cup (about 2 large heads) roasted garlic (page 87), mashed well
¹/₂ teaspoon salt, or to taste
¹/₄ teaspoon freshly ground black pepper, or to taste

GARNISH

3 heads Boston lettuce (about 32 leaves), separated into cups
¹/₄ cup finely chopped flat-leaf parsley
4 cornichons, sliced in half lengthwise, each half sliced into thin strips
32 small pieces pimiento

1. Place the eggs with water to cover in a large saucepan over medium-high heat. Bring the water just to a boil, then lower the heat and simmer, uncovered, for 12 minutes.

2. When the eggs are hard-cooked, place the saucepan under cold running water to cool the eggs.

3. Drain the eggs and gently roll them on the counter to facilitate peeling. Peel the eggshells and slice the eggs in half lengthwise; remove and set aside yolks.

Cut a thin slice of egg white from the bottom of each half to allow the eggs to stand firmly.

4. In a large skillet, sauté the shallots in the butter over medium heat until they are soft, about 2 minutes. Add the mushrooms and sauté for 4–6 minutes, or until the mushrooms are lightly browned. Set aside.

5. Place the egg yolks in the bowl of a food processor fitted with the knife blade and pulse until they resemble fine cornmeal.

6. Transfer the yolks to a bowl and blend well with the sour cream, roasted garlic, shallots, and mushrooms. Season with the salt and pepper. Heap the egg yolk mixture into the whites.

FINISHING TOUCHES AND
TABLE PRESENTATION

Arrange the smaller lettuce leaves on flat baskets. Set the stuffed eggs on the lettuce, dust the tops with the chopped parsley, and top each one with a slice of cornichon and a piece of pimiento for color. Serve chilled.

The Inventive Chef

RED CAVIAR, COOKED SHRIMP, SMOKED SALMON, AND ASPARAGUS ARE SOME OF THE DELICACIES THAT CAN BE ADDED TO THE YOLKS.

ON THE SIDE

Shrimp, Red Onion, and Monterey Jack Quesadillas

MAKES 32 QUESADILLAS

4 tablespoons olive oil
1/2 cup finely chopped red onion
2 cloves garlic, peeled and finely minced
1 pound large shrimp (21–25 count), washed, deveined, tails removed, coarsely chopped
1 1/2 cups coarsely grated Monterey Jack
1 tablespoon chili powder
1/2 teaspoon Tabasco sauce
1 tablespoon finely chopped fresh cilantro
1 tablespoon fresh lime juice
1/2 teaspoon salt, or to taste
8 (8-inch) flour tortillas

GARNISH
32 fresh cilantro leaves
2 medium limes, each cut into 8 wedges

1. Preheat the oven to 425°. Set aside 2 baking sheets. Do not grease.

2. Heat 2 tablespoons of the olive oil in a large skillet over medium heat and sauté the onion for 3 minutes. Add the garlic and continue to sauté for 1 minute more. Add the shrimp and sauté for 2 minutes, stirring briskly. *(The shrimp should be undercooked, as they will finish cooking in the oven.)* Set aside to cool.

3. In a medium bowl, combine the cooled shrimp

mixture with 1 cup of the cheese, the chili powder, Tabasco, cilantro, lime juice, and salt. Blend the ingredients well.

4. Brush one side of 4 tortillas lightly with most of the remaining olive oil. Place 2 of the tortillas, oil-side down, on each baking sheet. Divide and spread the shrimp mixture among the 4 tortillas leaving a $^3/_4$-inch border around the outer edge. Sprinkle 2 tablespoons of the remaining $^1/_2$ cup cheese over the entire surface of each tortilla and cover them with the remaining tortillas. Press the sandwiched tortillas gently together with your fingers and brush the tops lightly with olive oil.

5. Bake the quesadillas for 10–12 minutes, until the tortillas are lightly browned and crisped and the cheese has melted. If the edges pop up, just press them down. Let them rest for 3 minutes to allow the cheese to firm slightly before cutting each tortilla into 8–10 wedges.

FINISHING TOUCHES AND TABLE PRESENTATION

Arrange the quesadilla wedges on a flat basket or a terra-cotta tray lined with a Mexican printed napkin. Garnish each wedge with a cilantro leaf and tuck the lime wedges around the platter's edge. The quesadillas can be served hot or at room temperature.

The Inventive Chef

QUESADILLAS ARE VERY VERSATILE. JULIENNED RED OR YELLOW BELL PEPPERS, OTHER CHEESES (SUCH AS GOAT CHEESE OR THE MORE POWERFUL MONTEREY JACK WITH JALAPEÑO PEPPERS) CAN BE ADDED TO THE RECIPE.

ON THE SIDE

Prosciutto, Chicken, and Honey-Mustard Bundles

MAKES 32 BUNDLES

SPECIAL COOKWARE
Melon-ball scooper
32 toothpicks

1 small yellow onion, peeled and coarsely chopped
2 large cloves garlic, peeled and coarsely chopped
12 large leaves fresh basil
$^1/_2$ cup plus 1 tablespoon Dijon mustard
1 tablespoon fresh lemon juice
1 tablespoon balsamic vinegar
$^3/_4$ cup olive oil
2 pounds skinless and boneless chicken breasts cut into 32 or more 1-inch cubes
2 tablespoons honey
$^1/_2$ teaspoon ground oregano
3 tablespoons salted butter
$^1/_2$ teaspoon salt
$^1/_4$ teaspoon freshly ground black pepper
1 small ripe cantaloupe
32 thin slices prosciutto, outer fat removed, each slice cut into strips approximately 1$^1/_2$ inches wide by 5 inches long

GARNISH
1 bunch fresh basil
1 bunch fresh oregano

1. Combine the onion, garlic, basil, 1 tablespoon of the Dijon mustard, the lemon juice, balsamic vinegar, and olive oil in the bowl of a food processor fitted with the knife blade and blend until smooth. Place the marinade in a large nonreactive bowl, such as glass or stainless steel. Add the chicken, coat all the pieces well, and refrigerate, covered, for 2 hours.

2. Remove the chicken from the marinade and discard the marinade.

3. While the chicken is marinating, blend the remaining $1/2$ cup of Dijon mustard with the honey and oregano in a small bowl and set the mixture aside until ready to use.

4. Heat the butter in a large skillet over medium-high heat and sauté the chicken, in batches if necessary, stirring often, until the pieces are golden on all sides. Do not crowd the pan. Season with salt and pepper and lower the heat to medium. Continue to sauté for 3–5 minutes until the pieces are cooked through. Remove the chicken to a paper-towel-lined tray or platter and cool to room temperature.

5. While the chicken is cooling, cut the cantaloupe in half and discard the seeds. Using a small melon-ball scooper, scoop out thirty-two very tiny melon balls (about $1/4$-inch round). If you do not own a small melon baller, cut the melon into thirty-two $1/4$-inch cubes. Set aside until ready to assemble. Wrap any remaining melon with plastic and refrigerate it for healthy munchies.

6. Lay the slices of prosciutto on a work counter. Spread a thin layer, about $1/2$ teaspoon, of the honey mustard over the surface of each piece of ham.

7. Place one piece of chicken at one end of each prosciutto slice. Wrap the chicken in the prosciutto, rolling it away from you, using the entire slice. *(The honey mustard will hold the chicken and prosciutto together.)* Slide a toothpick into each bundle and skewer a piece of cantaloupe onto the end of the toothpick.

These bundles are a pop-in-your-mouth, irresistible savory hors d'oeuvre. I like to arrange them on colorful pottery trays garnished with the fresh basil and oregano. Don't forget a plate for the discarded toothpicks.

The Inventive Chef

CUT MANGOES, PAPAYAS, OR PINEAPPLE INTO $1/2$-INCH PIECES AND ROLL THEM WITH THE CHICKEN IN THE PROSCIUTTO.

ON THE SIDE

Broccoli and Portobello Mushroom Custard Tart

MAKES APPROXIMATELY 4 DOZEN LITTLE BITES

THE TART SHELL
3 cups all-purpose flour
$1/4$ teaspoon salt
$1/8$ teaspoon cayenne pepper
$3/4$ cup freshly grated Parmigiano Reggiano
$3/4$ cup unsalted butter, chilled and cut into rough pieces
$1/2$ cup cold water
3 cups dry beans or pie weights

THE VEGETABLE FILLING
5 tablespoons salted butter
1 medium Vidalia or yellow onion, peeled and finely chopped

$3/4$ pound portobello mushrooms, cleaned and cut into
  $1/4$-inch dice
1 large head broccoli florets, finely chopped
2 teaspoons salt
$1/4$ teaspoon freshly ground black pepper
2 cups heavy cream
6 eggs
1 teaspoon finely minced fresh rosemary
$1/4$ teaspoon cayenne pepper
$1/3$ cup freshly grated Parmigiano Reggiano
$2/3$ cup coarsely grated Swiss cheese
$1/2$ teaspoon paprika

GARNISH

8 small radicchio cups (about 1 small head)
16 broccoli florets, crisply blanched

1. Lightly grease a $15^{1}/2$-by-$10^{1}/2$-by-1-inch baking
sheet

2. Place the flour, salt, cayenne pepper, cheese, and
butter in the bowl of a food processor fitted with the
knife blade and process until the mixture has the
consistency of coarse cornmeal. Pulsing intermittently,
add the water through the feeding tube until the
dough comes together. Turn the dough out onto a
large sheet of plastic wrap and gently press it together
and flatten it. Wrap the dough and refrigerate it for at
least 45 minutes.

3. Preheat the oven to 450°.

4. Roll the dough out into a rectangle $1/4$ inch thick
by $16^{1}/2$ inches long by $11^{1}/2$ inches wide on a
lightly floured board. Lift the dough by gently folding
it around the rolling pin, and line the baking sheet
with the pastry, pressing the dough gently into the
pan. Fold the edges of the pastry under and mark
them by pressing the back of a fork against the sides
of the baking sheet.

5. Lightly prick the bottom of the pastry with a fork
and completely line the pastry with aluminum foil.
Spread the dry beans or pie weights evenly over the
foil and prebake the tart shell for 14–18 minutes.
Remove the foil and beans and cool the shell to room
temperature. Reduce oven to 350°.

6. While the shell is cooling, heat 3 tablespoons of
the butter in a large skillet over medium heat and sauté
the onions until they begin to soften, about 3 minutes.

7. Add the mushrooms and continue to sauté until
they are soft, about 4 minutes. Remove the
mushrooms and onions to a large bowl.

8. Heat the remaining 2 tablespoons of butter in the
same skillet and sauté the broccoli over medium-high
heat for 3–4 minutes, until the broccoli is tender but
still slightly crunchy to the bite. Add the broccoli to
the onions and mushrooms and season the vegetables
with 1 teaspoon of the salt and black pepper.

9. Whisk together the cream, eggs, rosemary, the
remaining 1 teaspoon of salt, and the cayenne pepper in
a large bowl until the custard mixture is well blended.

10. Spoon the vegetables into the prebaked shell. Top
with cheeses, pour the custard mixture evenly over the
top, and sprinkle the paprika lightly over the surface.
*(Since the edges of the tart shell will have already browned,
cover them with a collar of aluminum foil by carefully folding 1-
inch strips of foil over the edge of the crust to prevent it from
getting too dark.)* Bake the tart until the custard has set
and is lightly golden and puffed, about 25–30 minutes.

FINISHING TOUCHES AND
TABLE PRESENTATION

Cut the cooled tart into 1-by-$1^{1}/2$-inch pieces. Arrange
the pieces on white-napkin-lined baskets or trays. Divide

the broccoli florets among the radicchio cups. Arrange the radicchio cups among the tarts.

THE GRAND FINALE

Raspberry Cheesecake Squares

MAKES ABOUT 65 SQUARES

THE PASTRY

3 cups all-purpose flour
$^1/_2$ cup light brown sugar, packed
$^1/_2$ cup granulated sugar
$^1/_2$ pound unsalted butter, cut into $^1/_2$-inch dice
$1^1/_2$ cups walnuts

THE FILLING

$1^1/_2$ pounds cream cheese, at room temperature
$^3/_4$ cup plus 1 tablespoon sugar
3 large eggs
Zest and juice of one lime
$1^1/_2$ teaspoons pure vanilla extract
$^3/_4$ teaspoon almond extract
1 cup seedless raspberry jam

GARNISH

10 lemon leaves
1 pint fresh raspberries

1. Preheat the oven to 350°.
2. To make the pastry, put the flour, sugars, butter, and

walnuts in the bowl of a food processor fitted with the knife blade and pulse 8–10 times, until the ingredients resemble coarse cornmeal and remain crumbly. (*Do not overprocess.*) Set aside $1^1/_2$ cups of the crumbs to sprinkle over the cheese filling.

3. Place the remaining crumbs in the middle of a $15^1/_2$-by-$10^1/_2$-by-1-inch baking sheet. Press the mixture with your fingertips until it evenly covers the bottom of the baking sheet. Bake for 15 minutes. Set aside at room temperature while you make the filling.

4. Place the cream cheese and sugar in the bowl of an electric mixer and beat with the paddle attachment on medium speed until smooth and creamy, about 3 minutes. Beat in the eggs, zest and lime juice, and vanilla and almond extracts until the mixture is light and fluffy, about 2 minutes.

5. Spread the raspberry jam over the cooled pastry shell. Pour the cream-cheese filling evenly over the jam, and sprinkle with the $1^1/_2$ cups reserved pastry crumbs. Bake for 30–35 minutes. Cool the cheesecake to room temperature.

FINISHING TOUCHES AND
TABLE PRESENTATION

Cut the cake into $1^1/_2$-by-$1^1/_2$-inch squares. Arrange the squares on silver trays or in flat baskets, garnished with the lemon leaves and clusters of fresh raspberries.

KITCHEN SCHEDULE

1 WEEK AHEAD

TOQUE 1	*Palmiers*	Prepare through step 6; cover tightly and freeze.
TOQUE 2	Custard Tart	Prepare crust through step 5; cool; cover well with plastic wrap and freeze in baking sheet.
GRAND FINALE	Cheesecake	Prepare through step 5; wrap cooled, uncut cake and freeze.

2 OR 3 DAYS BEFORE THE PARTY

MAIN EVENT	Satés	Prepare marinade ingredients as in step 2; store covered in refrigerator.
	Wontons	Prepare recipe through step 3 and store as directed.
TOQUE 1	Eggs	Roast garlic; cool; store covered in refrigerator.

THE DAY BEFORE THE PARTY

MAIN EVENT	Satés	Bring marinade to room temperature. Prepare through step 4. Prepare coconut garnish. Set up grill if being used.
	Chutney	Prepare through step 2; store covered in refrigerator.
TOQUE 1	Cherry Tomatoes	Prepare tomatoes as in step 1; refrigerate on tray. Prepare filling as in step 2; store covered in refrigerator. Prepare dill garnish.

	Palmiers	Defrost overnight in refrigerator.
	Eggs	Prepare through step 4; store covered in refrigerator.
TOQUE 2	Bundles	Prepare chicken and melon through step 5; store covered, separately, in refrigerator. Prepare basil and oregano garnish.
	Custard Tart	Defrost crust at room temperature. Prepare filling and bake tart through step 11; cool; store covered in refrigerator. Prepare radicchio and broccoli garnishes; store covered in refrigerator.
GRAND FINALE	Cheesecake	Defrost overnight in refrigerator.
Strategic Maneuvers:		Fill creamers; cover and store in refrigerator. Fill sugar bowls. Set table. Check decor. Check ice and beverages. Set up lemon and lime wedges, cocktail olives, and onions for bar drinks, as needed. Chill wine, if white. Check garnishes for each recipe. Locate and label all serving bowls, platters, and utensils.

THE DAY OF THE PARTY♦

MAIN EVENT	Satés	Place kabobs at room temperature. Prepare chutney through step 2 and garnish with coconut. Line serving basket with lemon leaves.
	Wontons	Arrange for service as in finishing touches.
TOQUE 1	Cherry Tomatoes	Prepare step 3; arrange as in finishing touches.
	Palmiers	Bake as in step 7; cool and arrange for service as in finishing touches; set at room temperature.
	Eggs	Prepare step 6 and arrange as in finishing touches; refrigerate, lightly covered with waxed paper.
TOQUE 2	Quesadillas	Preheat oven to 450° and prepare through step 5; arrange as in finishing touches; set at room temperature.
	Bundles	Prepare steps 6–7 and arrange as in finishing touches; refrigerate, covered lightly with waxed paper.
	Custard Tart	Set at room temperature and arrange as in finishing touches.

GRAND FINALE	Cheesecake	Cut into squares and prepare as in finishing touches; set at room temperature.

35 MINUTES BEFORE GUESTS ARRIVE:

Arrange all hors d'oeuvre on garnished platters if this has not been done.

15 MINUTES BEFORE GUESTS ARRIVE:

Grill or broil beef satés as directed in step 5.
Arrange for service as in finishing touches and cover lightly with foil to keep warm. Remove foil as guests arrive.

GUESTS ARRIVE:

Set table with all foods.

30 MINUTES AFTER FIRST GUESTS ARRIVE:

Place cheesecake squares on food table.

♦Kitchen instructions are given for finishing the hors d'oeuvre through service presentation. If your refrigerator is too small to handle all the arranged food, place the finished hors d'oeuvre on baking sheets and arrange them on their serving vessels 20 minutes before your guests are scheduled to arrive.

The Luscious Indulgence of Dessert Parties

Caramel, cookies, crèmes, and cakes. Sundaes, parfaits, puddings, tarts, and tortes. Strawberry, coconut, lime, almond, pear, peach, praline, mango, hazelnut, lemon, cherry—and chocolate.

Just naming the multitudes of forms and flavors of my favorite desserts starts to put me in a good mood. And when you welcome guests to a lavish desserts-only buffet, you will discover that you don't need to serve a round of drinks to create a party atmosphere. Facing a display of sweet fantasias, your guests' fun begins before they've even taken one taste. Spontaneous grinning is a certainty on the two occasions I share in this chapter:

♦ Shower a bride-to-be with more than appliances: Treat her to a luscious caramel fruit fondue accompanied by an array of tarts, cakes, and cookies.

♦ A teen celebration is the coolest place to be when guests construct their own ice cream sundae extravaganzas—and load up on M&M cookie pops and peanut butter and jelly sandwich cookies, too.

Of course, just serving an abundance of sugary dishes does not make a wonderful party. Sweetness should be enjoyed in a range of intensities and flavors—and the textures of a dessert menu should be as contrasting and complementary as for other parts of a meal. My dessert menus always balance these sensual qualities, mixing sweet and tart, smooth and crunchy, adding a subtle spice or highlighting a big, bold taste—like chocolate!

The buffets in this chapter are especially exciting because they leave the balancing act up to each individual. Both the fondue party and the open ice cream bar are make-it-yourself activities filled with tactile and artistic pleasure. Everyone loves being a dessert chef, and guests of every age will try to outdo one another building utterly unique ice cream sundaes.

For the host, the dessert party is planned as a buffet (at an hour that minimally conflicts with "normal" eating habits). Depending on the number of guests, your table capacity, and the atmosphere you want to achieve, plan for lap service or preset tables. Beautiful presentation is a must, so arrange your platters artfully (see the tips on buffet setup on page 130) and make suitable decorations for the table.

Your guests will be occupied for a bit with the Main Event activities of dipping fondue and constructing ice cream sundaes, which can create a buffet-table bottle-neck, so make certain your other desserts are easily accessible to traffic. You will want to have beverage service available throughout the party, both hot and cold drinks that will cut through the sweetness—and enable your guests to head back to the dessert table for "just a tiny bit more."

Showering the Bride-to-Be with Sweet Sensations

THE MAIN EVENT:

Fresh Fruit Caramel Fondue

ON THE SIDE:

Coconut Lime Tart

◆

Goblets of Strawberries, Cream, and Praline Crunch

◆

Zebra Cake

◆

Hazelnut Biscotti

ON THE SIDE:

*Mocha Butter-Cream Layer Cake
with Coffee Whipped Cream Filling*

◆

Pear Clafouti

◆

*Blood Orange Crème Brûlée
(double recipe on page 89)*

◆

Toasted Hazelnut Cookie Cups

BEVERAGE RECOMMENDATIONS:
Champagne
Muscat Blanc, Robert Pecota Winery, "Sweet Andrea"

*I*F HER BEST FRIENDS COULD MELT TOGETHER ALL THEIR WISHES for the bride-to-be, the result would probably taste like the pot of creamy caramel you've made for her wedding shower. May her marriage be as sweet and tangy as chunks of mango and pineapple dipped in this fondue! But life, you know, does not always come smooth and warm, with touches of rum, orange, and vanilla—it comes in many shapes and textures. That's why someone has brought a coconut lime tart—and another friend has baked toasted hazelnut cookie cups and filled them with strawberries and cream. That is why you've built a towering Mocha Butter-Cream Layer Cake, too. And to make sure there are many more days like this one, you've deluged the bride with gifts: angel-cake pans, tart rings, chocolate molds, whisks and spatulas . . . and a fondue set.

For a young bride, an old friend (or a crowd of friends), for anyone with a sweet tooth and an appreciation of desserts, this party is an extraordinary delight. It can be a pleasure for the host, too, as so many elements can be prepared well in advance of the party (and it becomes even more convenient if you assign some of the recipes to "pastry chef" friends).

A sweet fondue with a variety of foods for dipping is always a conversational catalyst at a party, and the Main Event here will truly give everyone something to talk about. Quite simple to prepare, the caramel dipping sauce has a wonderful depth of flavor from vanilla, orange zest, and rum, and "marries" perfectly with the varied tastes and textures of all kinds of fruit morsels. Set up your fondue to maintain the sauce at a moderate temperature, about 120°, to successfully coat the fruit.

The fondue will be the focal point of your buffet, but there are wonderful accompaniments for guests to choose as well. The simple one-toque menu includes a terrifically "tart" coconut lime tart with a crunchy crust of flaked coconut and egg whites and a foolproof filling cooked on top of the stove. Homemade praline crunch, whipped cream, and fresh strawberries are easily assembled into a colorful parfait presentation in glass goblets. There's a delicious two-tone vanilla and chocolate Zebra Cake that requires no icing, and finally a fun-to-make batch of crispy Hazelnut Biscotti with a hint of hazelnut liqueur.

The two-toque menu requires only a bit more preparation time. For the mocha layer cake, two layers of simple cocoa almond torte are filled with coffee whipped cream and thickly frosted with a classic, smooth butter cream made with espresso and semisweet chocolate. I love clafouti, the rustic custardy tart classically made with cherries.

This version, with poached pears, is luscious. Small ramekins of creamy Blood Orange Crème Brûlée are topped with a crisp layer of caramelized sugar. Finally, it is fun to bake and shape the Toasted Hazelnut Cookie Cups—and fabulous to fill them with almost any kind of ice cream, sorbet, or flavored cream.

SETTING THE STAGE

The array of colorful desserts on your buffet will provide nearly all the visual excitement this party needs. A simple and appropriate centerpiece would of course be a bowl full of the same fruits—whole apples, bananas, mangoes, pears, pineapples, strawberries, and others—which are also presented in pieces for the fondue. You might even strew the fruits artfully right on the table, around and between the platters. Also, as many of these desserts are particularly lovely when garnished with small flower blossoms (see individual recipe presentations), you can build a floral theme with vases full of similar flowers.

Some of the basic rules of buffet presentation apply here. Variation in elevation of the dishes is important: Use cake stands of different heights or improvise pedestals for the cakes and tarts. Try to keep "traffic" flowing around both sides of the table: Set up your fondue fruits in two platters, with two dipping pots of hot caramel sauce located on either side. Make sure you have dessert plates, fondue forks or skewers, and napkins on both sides as well—and cake servers for all of the other desserts. (Of course, there will always be some drips with a fondue, so you should put plates under the fondue forks.)

If your event is a wedding shower or another party where presents are an important feature, use the excitement and beauty of the gaily wrapped packages as a decorative element. Leave a large area of the buffet table (or designate another centrally located table) just for gifts. As guests arrive, add their gifts to the growing pile, creating a mysterious and tempting treasure trove as a centerpiece. Just keep it well away from the caramel sauce!

THE MAIN EVENT

Fresh Fruit Caramel Fondue

MAKES 16 SERVINGS

SPECIAL COOKWARE
Large (at least 4-quart) heavy-bottomed saucepan
Dessert fondue or fondue pot♦
Fondue forks or wooden skewers

THE CARAMEL SAUCE
1/2 cup light corn syrup
4 cups sugar
1 pound unsalted butter
1 pint heavy cream
2 vanilla beans

♦A fondue pot is nice but not necessary for this dessert. You can simply place the fondue in a heatproof decorative bowl. If it gets too cold for dipping, heat the covered bowl over a pot of warm water until it is reheated.

Grated zest of 2 oranges

¹/₄ cup dark rum

THE FRUIT

³/₄ cup fresh orange juice

2 tablespoons Calvados or Grand Marnier liqueur

4 ripe bananas, cut on the bias into 8 pieces each

*3 large Granny Smith apples, washed, cored, and cut into
   16 slices each*

*4 Red Crimson pears, washed, cored, and cut into 8
   slices each*

*2 large ripe mangoes, peeled, pitted, and sliced into
   16 slices each*

*4 large peaches, peeled, pitted, and sliced into 16
   slices each*

*1 medium pineapple, peeled, eyes and core removed, halved
   lengthwise, and sliced into 16 spears, 8 per half*

1 bunch fresh mint

3 pints large strawberries with stems

GARNISH

14 large lemon leaves

1. To make the fondue, heat the corn syrup in a large heavy-bottomed saucepan over medium heat until it is warm, about 2 minutes. Slowly add the sugar and continue to cook the mixture, stirring with a wooden spoon, until the sugar caramelizes to a rich golden brown, about 15 minutes.

2. In a medium saucepan, heat the butter, cream, and vanilla beans over low heat, until the butter has melted.

3. Slowly add the butter and cream to the caramelized-sugar syrup and blend well. Make sure to do this slowly and stir constantly. The mixture will bubble up briskly as the ingredients blend.

4. Blend in the orange zest and rum, transfer the caramel sauce to the top of a double boiler, and keep it warm over low-simmering water, maintaining the fondue at 120°. *(If the fondue is too hot, it will not coat the fruit properly.)*

5. To prepare the fruit, combine the orange juice and liqueur in a large bowl.

6. Toss the bananas, apples, and pears separately with the orange juice mixture for about 1 minute, coating all the fruit. Drain well.

FINISHING TOUCHES AND
TABLE PRESENTATION

Fan slices of banana, apple, pear, mango, peach, and pineapple on an attractive dessert platter garnished with the fresh mint. Set the strawberries on a flat basket lined with lemon leaves. Fill a dessert fondue pot with the warm caramel syrup. Maintain the sauce at 120°. Arrange long fondue forks or 6-inch wooden skewers on the table. Let your guests enjoy choosing the fruits they like most.

ON THE SIDE

Coconut Lime Tart

MAKES 2 TARTS

SPECIAL COOKWARE

Two 9-inch round tart pans with removable bottoms

Parchment or waxed paper

THE COCONUT SHELL

2 tablespoons unsalted butter

*4 cups sweetened coconut flakes (available in food
   markets)*

¹/₄ cup all-purpose flour
1 teaspoon salt
4 large egg whites
²/₃ cup sugar

THE LIME FILLING
6 large eggs, lightly beaten
6 large eggs yolks, lightly beaten
1¹/₂ cups sugar
1 cup fresh lime juice (from about 6 limes)

GARNISH
1 cup coarsely grated semisweet chocolate

1. To make the shells, preheat the oven to 375°. Butter the bottom and sides of two 9-inch tart pans. Line the bottom of each pan with a round of buttered parchment paper, buttered side up.

2. Toss together the coconut, flour, and salt in a large bowl. In another large bowl, whisk together the egg whites and sugar until the mixture is foamy. Combine the coconut and egg-white mixtures until they are well blended.

3. With a rubber spatula, spread the bottom and sides of the tart pans with the coconut mixture. Bake the tarts for 20–25 minutes, or until the crusts are golden and firm.

4. Immediately loosen the sides of the tarts from the pans with a small knife. Remove the sides of the tart pans and let the crusts cool on a cooling rack to room temperature. When the crusts have cooled, remove the bottom of the tart pans and the parchment paper.

5. To make the filling, combine all the filling ingredients in the top of a large noncorrosive double boiler. Cook the mixture over simmering water until it becomes a thick custard, about 10–12 minutes.

6. Strain the custard into the coconut tart shells and

refrigerate until the custard sets, about 2 hours or overnight.

FINISHING TOUCHES AND
TABLE PRESENTATION

With a serrated knife, preslice each tart into 8–10 wedges, but do not separate the slices. Just before serving, sprinkle the grated chocolate over the top of each tart. Set the tarts on decorative cake stands or round cake platters.

ON THE SIDE

Goblets of Strawberries, Cream, and Praline Crunch

MAKES 16 SERVINGS

SPECIAL COOKWARE
Large heavy-bottomed saucepan
Sixteen 14–16-ounce brandy snifters

3 cups whole skinless almonds or slivered almonds
4 cups granulated sugar
2 cups heavy cream
2 teaspoons confectioners' sugar
2 teaspoons pure vanilla extract
Grated zest of two oranges
2¹/₂ quarts strawberries, washed, stemmed, and cut into
*   ¹/₄-inch rounds*

1. Preheat the oven to 350°.

2. Place the almonds on an ungreased baking sheet and toast them in the oven until they are golden brown, about 5–7 minutes. Set aside.

3. Melt the granulated sugar in 1 ¹/₃ cups of water in a large heavy-bottomed saucepan over medium heat. Stir gently just until the sugar is mixed with the water. Simmer the syrup until it becomes a golden brown, about 15–20 minutes. Add the toasted almonds, blend well, and immediately pour the caramelized almond praline onto a greased baking sheet. *(Plunge the pot into a waiting soak of warm soapy water to ensure easy cleanup.)*

4. When the praline is cool, break it into 1-inch chunks and place the chunks, in batches, in the bowl of a food processor fitted with the knife blade. Pulse the praline until it resembles rough cornmeal. Set aside at room temperature. *(Do not overprocess the praline to a powdery consistency for this recipe.)*

5. Whip the cream in the bowl of an electric mixer on medium speed until it begins to take shape. *(For the best results when whipping cream, chill the beaters in the refrigerator and make sure the cream is very cold.)* Add the confectioners' sugar, vanilla, and orange zest and continue to whip the cream until it stands in soft mounds. Fold the strawberries into the cream.

FINISHING TOUCHES AND
TABLE PRESENTATION

Spoon about ¹/₃ cup of the strawberry cream into each snifter and cover with ¹/₈ inch of praline crunch, then repeat for a second layer, ending with ¹/₄ inch of the praline crunch. Arrange the goblets on a large square or rectangular platter, preferably silver, and garnish the platter with fresh flowers.

The Inventive Chef

RASPBERRIES, BLUEBERRIES, OR BLACKBERRIES ARE FINE SUBSTITUTES FOR THE STRAWBERRIES. MIXED BERRIES ADD SPECIAL COLOR IN THE GOBLETS.

ON THE SIDE
Zebra Cake

MAKES ABOUT 14 SERVINGS

SPECIAL COOKWARE
10-inch tube pan

1 tablespoon vegetable shortening
1 ¹/₂ cups (about 10–12) egg whites
1 ¹/₄ teaspoons cream of tartar
1 ¹/₂ cups superfine sugar
1 cup sifted cake flour
1 teaspoon pure vanilla extract
Pinch of salt
²/₃ cup miniature chocolate chips
¹/₄ cup sifted cocoa powder

1. Preheat the oven to 350°.

2. Lightly grease the tube pan and set aside.

3. Beat the egg whites in the bowl of an electric mixer with the whip attachment on medium speed until they are frothy. Add the cream of tartar, increase the mixer speed to high, and slowly add the sugar. Whip the egg whites until they form stiff, moist peaks. There will still be beads of moisture in the whites.

4. Transfer ¹/₃ of the whipped egg whites to a second

bowl and set aside. With a rubber spatula, fold $^3/_4$ cup of the cake flour, the vanilla, salt, and chocolate chips into the bowl containing the $^2/_3$ of the whipped egg whites. Set aside.

5. Fold the remaining $^1/_4$ cup of cake flour and the cocoa powder gently into the reserved $^1/_3$ cup plain egg whites, making sure the dry ingredients are totally incorporated. (*To fold: Move the spatula with a continuous up-and-over motion down through the center of the batter and up over the sides.*)

6. Spoon $^1/_2$ of the chocolate-chip mixture into the cake pan and smooth the top with the spatula. Layer the cocoa mixture on top, and the remaining chocolate-chip mixture over that.

7. Bake the cake for 40–45 minutes, until a knife inserted into the center comes out clean. Invert the cake onto a cooling rack. When the cake is at room temperature, slide a knife between the cake and the pan and invert the cake onto a large round cake plate.

FINISHING TOUCHES AND
TABLE PRESENTATION

The cake looks regal on a cake stand. Preslice it into $^3/_4$-inch slices but do not separate the slices. Arrange small flowers, such as violets, around the bottom of the cake and the stand.

The Inventive Chef

SPLIT THE CAKE IN HALF AND FILL IT WITH WHIPPED CREAM AND BERRIES. WHAT A LUXURY!

ON THE SIDE
Hazelnut Biscotti
MAKES ABOUT 4 DOZEN BISCOTTI

SPECIAL COOKWARE
Parchment paper

$1^1/_4$ cups hazelnuts
$1^1/_2$ cups all-purpose flour
$1^1/_2$ teaspoons baking powder
$^1/_4$ teaspoon salt
5 tablespoons unsalted butter
6 tablespoons granulated sugar
Zest of 2 oranges
1 egg
1 teaspoon almond extract
1 teaspoon pure vanilla extract
1 tablespoon orange juice

1. Preheat oven to 350°.

2. Place hazelnuts on a baking sheet and bake in the oven for 5–8 minutes, until they are golden brown. Reserve 8–10 for garnish. Chop the rest coarsely and set aside.

3. Sift together flour, baking powder, and salt. Set aside.

4. Cut butter into 1-inch pieces, and in an electric mixer with the paddle attachment, at medium speed, beat butter, sugar, and orange zest for about 6 minutes, or until light and fluffy. Occasionally scrape the sides of the bowl with a rubber spatula.

5. Add egg and mix to incorporate.

6. Add almond and vanilla extracts along with orange juice, and mix to incorporate.

7. Add flour mixture along with hazelnuts; and mix to combine.

8. On a lightly floured board, divide the dough in half. Roll each half into a log about 12 inches long. Place logs on a parchment-lined baking sheet and bake until golden brown, about 30 minutes. Let cool about 20 minutes.

9. Remove the logs to a cutting board and slice them into $^3/_4$-inch diagonal pieces. Lay the biscotti slices on their sides on the cookie sheet and bake the slices again until firm, about 15 minutes.

FINISHING TOUCHES AND TABLE PRESENTATION

Arrange the biscotti in baskets or on decorated pottery dishes. Scatter the reserved toasted whole hazelnuts over the biscotti.

The Inventive Chef

CURRANTS, PISTACHIOS, DRIED CRANBERRIES, AND CHOPPED DRIED APRICOTS CAN BE ADDED TO THE BISCOTTI DOUGH BEFORE BAKING.

ON THE SIDE

Mocha Butter-Cream Layer Cake with Coffee Whipped Cream Filling

MAKES 16–20 SERVINGS

SPECIAL COOKWARE
Three 8-inch round layer-cake pans

1 tablespoon unsalted butter
6 ounces unsweetened chocolate
2$^2/_3$ cups sugar
2$^1/_4$ cups sifted all-purpose flour
1$^1/_8$ teaspoons baking soda
$^3/_4$ teaspoon salt
2 tablespoons instant espresso, dissolved in 1 cup plus
    2 tablespoons boiling water
$^3/_4$ cup sour cream
$^3/_4$ cup vegetable oil
2 teaspoons pure vanilla extract
3 large eggs
Coffee Whipped Cream, for filling (recipe follows)
Mocha Butter Cream, for frosting (page 333)

1. Preheat the oven to 350°.
2. Lightly grease three 8-inch round layer-cake pans.
3. Melt the chocolate in the top of a double boiler over gently simmering water. Turn off the heat and let the chocolate remain on the stove.
4. Mix together the sugar, flour, baking soda, and salt into a large bowl and set aside.
5. In the bowl of an electric mixer fitted with the paddle attachment, blend the dissolved espresso, sour

cream, vegetable oil, and vanilla extract on low speed until well combined.

6. Slowly add the dry ingredients to the espresso mixture and continue to beat until well blended. Scrape down the sides of the bowl.

7. Add the eggs one at a time on medium-low speed, blending until the batter is smooth, and scraping down the sides of the bowl as necessary.

8. Slowly add the reserved melted chocolate and mix until incorporated.

9. Divide the batter among the three cake pans and bake for 35–40 minutes, or until a cake tester comes out clean. Cool the cake layers for 5 minutes, then invert them onto cooling racks.

10. To make two 3-layer cakes, slice each cake round in half horizontally so that you have 6 layers. Place a bottom cake layer onto each of the two decorative platters and spread a 1-inch layer of Coffee Whipped Cream over each bottom layer. Place a second cake layer over the whipped cream and repeat the layering process using another 1 inch of Coffee Whipped Cream and a final layer of cake.

11. Frost the top and sides of the two cakes with a generous amount of Mocha Butter Cream.

FINISHING TOUCHES AND
TABLE PRESENTATION

Preslice each cake into about 1-inch slices, but do not separate the slices. Set each cake on a 12–14-inch round decorative serving platter. Arrange fresh flowers, such as violets or small rosebuds, around the edge of the platters.

Coffee Whipped Cream

4 1/2 cups heavy or whipping cream
3 1/2 tablespoons instant espresso crystals
1 1/4 cups confectioners' sugar

1. Using the whip attachment, beat the cream in the bowl of an electric mixer until it stands in soft peaks.
2. Add the espresso crystals, then gradually add the confectioners' sugar while continuing to whip the cream until it holds its shape. Cover and refrigerate until needed.

Mocha Butter Cream

MAKES ABOUT 4 1/2 CUPS

SPECIAL COOKWARE
Instant candy thermometer

6 ounces semisweet chocolate
1 1/4 cups sugar
12 egg yolks
1/2 cup brewed espresso at room temperature
2 1/2 cups unsalted butter at room temperature, cut into rough pieces

1. Melt the chocolate in a small saucepan over medium heat. Set aside to cool.
2. Bring the sugar and 3/4 cup of water to a boil in a large heavy-bottomed saucepan. While the sugar-water is heating, place the egg yolks in the large bowl of an electric mixer and beat on high speed with the whip attachment until they are thickened and a light lemony color.

3. When the temperature of the sugar-water reaches 234° on an instant candy thermometer, remove the pan from the heat, and with the mixer on low speed, in small batches add this syrup alternately with the espresso to the egg yolks in a very slow steady stream. *(Warning: If you add the syrup too fast, the eggs will scramble.)* Beat the mixture until it has completely cooled.

4. With the mixer still on low speed, gradually beat in the softened butter and the chocolate until the cream is smooth. If the cream separates, beat it for 2–3 minutes more. If you still feel the cream is not silky smooth, add more softened butter, 1 tablespoon at a time. Store the butter cream in the refrigerator for 2–3 days.

ON THE SIDE

Pear Clafouti

MAKES 16 SERVINGS

SPECIAL COOKWARE
*Two 10-inch tart pans with removable bottoms or two
   ovenproof 10-inch pottery cake pans*
Dry beans or baking weights

THE TART SHELL
2 cups all-purpose flour
2 cups whole-wheat flour
^{1}/$_2$ teaspoon salt
^{1}/$_4$ cup light brown sugar, firmly packed
1^1/$_2$ cups unsalted butter, well chilled, cut into small pieces
4 egg yolks
4–6 tablespoons ice water

THE PEARS
2^1/$_4$ cups sugar
*6 large ripe pears, Anjou or Comice (about 3 pounds),
   peeled, cored, and cut into ^{1}/$_2$-inch cubes*
*2 large red Anjou or Comice pears, washed, unpeeled,
   cored, and cut into ^{1}/$_8$-inch slices*
6 large eggs
1^1/$_2$ cups heavy cream
^{3}/$_4$ cup whole milk
1 tablespoon pure vanilla extract

GARNISH
^{1}/$_2$ cup confectioners' sugar

1. To make the tart shells, place 1 cup each of the all-purpose and whole-wheat flours, ^{1}/$_4$ teaspoon of the salt, and 2 tablespoons of the light brown sugar into the bowl of a food processor with the cutting blade. Add 12 tablespoons of butter to the bowl and pulse the dough for 30 seconds. Add 2 of the egg yolks and 2–3 tablespoons of the ice water and pulse until the pastry pulls away from the sides of the bowl, about 30 seconds.

2. Form the dough into a flattened round, cover it with plastic wrap, and refrigerate it for at least 1 hour.

3. Repeat steps 1 and 2, using the remaining ingredients, to make the second crust.

4. Preheat the oven to 425°.

5. Roll each ball into a 12-inch circle and fit the circles into two 10-inch tart pans. Gently press the edges of the dough against the sides of the pans.

6. Lay a piece of foil over each of the crusts to cover completely. Add the dry beans or pie weights to each of the pans to weight the foil. Place the tart shells on a baking pan and bake for 20 minutes. Remove the foil and beans and continue to bake the shells for 4 minutes longer. Set them aside at room temperature.

(If the edges of the pie crusts brown before the rest of the crust, carefully cover the edges with a foil collar as directed on page 319.)

7. Reduce the oven to 375° and make the filling.

8. In a large saucepan, bring 3 cups of water and 2 cups of the sugar to a boil over high heat. Boil the syrup for 4 minutes. Place the cubed pears in the simmering syrup and cook for 5 minutes, or until they are tender but still crisp to the bite. Remove the pears to a small bowl with a slotted spoon and cool to room temperature. Reserve the poaching liquid in the saucepan.

9. While the cubed pears cool, prepare the pear slices. Return the poaching liquid to a simmer on medium heat and add the sliced pears. Simmer for 2 minutes, until the slices are softened but still crisp to the bite. Strain the sliced pears from the liquid and set them aside to cool on a plate. Reserve $1/3$ cup of the poaching liquid and either discard the remaining liquid or refrigerate it, covered for future poaching.

10. In a large bowl, whisk together the remaining $1/4$ cup of sugar, the reserved $1/3$ cup of poaching liquid, the eggs, heavy cream, milk, and vanilla extract. Add the cubed pears, blend well, and pour half the mixture into each of the prepared tart shells. Fan half the reserved pear slices in a decorative round on top of each of the tarts.

11. Bake the clafoutis for about 40–50 minutes, until a knife inserted in the center comes out clean and the tops are a light golden brown. Cool the tarts for 10 minutes on cake racks, then remove the bottoms. *(If using the pottery tart pans, this will not be necessary.)*

FINISHING TOUCHES AND
TABLE PRESENTATION

Cut each tart into 8 wedges with a serrated knife, but do not separate the wedges. Set each tart on a 12–14-

inch round colorful platter. Dust the tops of the clafoutis with confectioners' sugar.

The Inventive Chef

INDULGE YOURSELF BY TOPPING THE CLAFOUTIS WITH ICE CREAM, WHIPPED CREAM, OR HUGE DOLLOPS OF SWEETENED CRÈME FRAÎCHE. VARY THE CLAFOUTIS WITH SEASONAL FRESH OR POACHED FRUIT.

ON THE SIDE

*Toasted Hazelnut
Cookie Cups*

MAKES 16 SERVINGS

SPECIAL COOKWARE
Four 6-ounce custard cups

16 tablespoons unsalted butter, at room temperature
1 1/2 cups sugar
2 tablespoons Frangelico liqueur
1 teaspoon salt
2/3 cup all-purpose flour
1/2 cup hazelnuts, toasted and finely ground (page 331)◆

GARNISH
16 mint sprigs

1. Preheat the oven to 350°. Grease two 15 1/2-by-

◆Grind hazelnuts in a food processor fitted with knife blade.

$10^{1}/_{2}$-by-1-inch baking sheets with 1 tablespoon of the butter.

2. Place the remaining butter, sugar, liqueur, and salt in the bowl of an electric mixer and beat on medium speed using the paddle attachment for 2 minutes. Scrape down the sides of the bowl with a rubber spatula and continue beating for 1 minute more.

3. Reduce the speed to low and add the flour. Beat until the flour is incorporated, about 1 minute. Add the toasted hazelnuts and beat for 30 seconds.

4. Place four 6-ounce custard cups on the counter. Using 1 teaspoon of batter for each cookie, put 2 teaspoons of batter onto one of the baking sheets with about 6 inches of space between them. *(The cookies will spread as they bake.)* Repeat with the second baking sheet.

5. Bake the cookies for 10 minutes, until they are bubbly and golden brown around the edges. Remove from the oven and allow the cookies to cool briefly on the baking sheets, just until you can handle them. While the cookies are still warm and pliable, fit a cookie into each of the custard cups. If the cookie cups become too stiff to mold, return them to the oven for 20 seconds. While the cookies cool, continue to prepare the pans with additional batter and bake until all the batter has been used.

6. As soon as the cups have hardened, about 2–3 minutes, remove them from the ramekins and cool them on a cake rack. Once the cups are cool and formed, they can be stored in a covered plastic container for 2–3 days at room temperature.

Arrange the cups in concentric circles on 12–16-inch platters. Fill the cups with ice cream, strawberries and cream (page 329), or fresh fruit sorbets. Place the mint sprigs between the cups.

The Inventive Chef

ARE THE CUPS FRAGILE? OF COURSE THEY ARE. IN CASE THEY BREAK, CHANGE THE GAME PLAN. BREAK THE COOKIES INTO COARSE PIECES, FILL GOBLETS WITH ICE CREAM, CUT FRESH FRUIT, AND TOP WITH THE CRUMBLED COOKIE CUPS. PASSION FRUIT, RASPBERRY, AND LEMON SORBETS TASTE AND LOOK WONDERFUL IN THE COOKIE CUPS. PLAN ON PURCHASING 4 OUNCES OF SORBET FOR EACH CUP.

KITCHEN SCHEDULE

2 OR 3 DAYS BEFORE THE PARTY

MAIN EVENT	Fondue	Prepare caramel sauce through step 4; store covered in refrigerator.
TOQUE 1	Biscotti	Prepare through step 5; freeze or store in airtight container at room temperature.
TOQUE 2	Cookie Cups	Prepare through step 6; store in covered container at room temperature.

THE DAY BEFORE THE PARTY

MAIN EVENT	Fondue	Buy fruit.
TOQUE 1	Tart	Prepare shells through step 4; store covered in refrigerator.
	Strawberries	Prepare Praline crunch through step 4; set aside at room temperature.
	Zebra Cake	Prepare through step 7; store covered in refrigerator.
TOQUE 2	Layer Cake	Prepare the cakes through step 9; store covered in refrigerator. Prepare butter cream through step 3; store covered in refrigerator.
	Clafouti	Prepare ingredients; store covered in refrigerator.
	Crème Brûlée	Prepare through step 6; store covered in refrigerator.
Strategic Maneuvers:		Fill creamers; cover and store in refrigerator. Fill sugar bowls. Set up buffet table and fondue paraphernalia. Check ice and beverages. Set up coffee and tea service.

Chill wine if white.
Check garnishes for each recipe.
Locate and label all serving bowls, platters, and utensils.

THE DAY OF THE PARTY

MAIN EVENT	Fondue	Cut fruit, prepare through step 2, and arrange as in finishing touches; store covered in refrigerator. Place caramel in top of double boiler for reheating.
TOQUE 1	Tart	Prepare filling through step 6; cut as in finishing touches but do not separate pieces; store covered in refrigerator.
	Strawberries	Wash, stem, and cut berries. Whip the cream as in step 5; fill goblets with berries and cream as in finishing touches; do not top with final layer of praline; store covered in refrigerator.
	Zebra Cake	Cut and garnish cakes as in finishing touches; set on table.
	Biscotti	If frozen, defrost biscotti. Arrange as in finishing touches and set on table.
TOQUE 2	Layer Cake	Prepare whipped cream through step 2. Put butter cream at room temperature. Prepare steps 10–11 of layer cake.
	Clafouti	Prepare through step 7; cool, cut, and garnish; set on table.

| Crème Brûlée | Caramelize tops as in step 7; garnish as in finishing touches and set on table. |
| Cookie Cups | Arrange as in finishing touches. |

Place all desserts on the buffet. Light candles and smile.

30 MINUTES BEFORE GUESTS ARRIVE:

MAIN EVENT	Fondue	Warm caramel for fondue.
TOQUE 1	Tart	Separate pieces and garnish as in finishing touches.
TOQUE 2	Layer Cake	Separate pieces and arrange as in finishing touches. Precut all cakes and tarts if not already done.

DESSERT SERVICE:

Top strawberries with last layer of praline.
Invite guests.
Serve coffee.

AFTER SERVICE:

Unplug coffee.

The Team Takes Over the Ice Cream Counter

THE MAIN EVENTS:

The Irresistible Ice Cream Bar

◆

Confetti Pretzels

ON THE SIDE:

M&M Melt-in-Your-Mouth Cookie Pops

◆

Peanut Butter and Jelly Crunchy Cookie Sandwiches

◆

Goblets of Strawberries, Cream, and
Praline Crunch (page 329)

ON THE SIDE:

Double-Chocolate Stuffed Sugar Cookie Sandwiches

◆

Tangy Lemon Tart (double recipe on page 110)

◆

Jelly Bean Bars

BEVERAGE RECOMMENDATIONS:
Strawberry Citrus Punch (page 354)
Soft drinks: Cola, root beer, lemon-lime soda, juices

FTER EVERY GAME, WIN OR LOSE, YOU TOOK YOUR DAUGH-ter's lacrosse team out for ice cream cones. Strict training rules in effect: one cone per girl, one scoop per cone, *no* toppings. "If you win the championship," you told them, "you can have all the toppings you want." Well, today they enjoy the taste of victory. The ice cream bar you have created for them is a fantasyland of flavors: baskets of chocolate-dipped sugar cones, mounds of multicolored ice cream scoops, billowing bowls of whipped cream, glistening fudge sauce, dish after dish of crumbled candies, cookies, and sprinkles. The display stretches to the ends of the buffet: pretzels coated with marshmallow, M&M cookie pops, jelly bean bars, and bags of jelly beans. And in the middle of the table is the sweetest sight of all: the championship trophy.

The competition for teens (or any other winner lucky enough to come to my Irresistible Ice Cream Bar party) doesn't necessarily end before this fun-filled feast. Seeing who can create the biggest, most gorgeous and complicated ice cream cone *ever* is certainly part of the pleasure of this party.

The ice cream bar fixings are all prepared ahead of time: cones, creams, candies, and sprinkles can be set out quickly whenever the party is about to start. The ice cream balls, all ready on trays in the freezer, will have just enough time to soften to the perfect consistency. A fun accompaniment to the cones are Confetti Pretzels, coated with chocolate and a host of toppings.

There are plenty of added attractions for teens' bottomless appetites. M&M candies make colorful polka dots in clever cookie pops and there will be many takers for Peanut Butter and Jelly Crunchy Cookie Sandwiches, too. Pretty glasses

layered with strawberry cream and praline complete the one-toque array of desserts.

For two-toque, I share a wonderful recipe for delicious Double-Chocolate Stuffed Sugar Cookie Sandwiches, extravagantly displayed on a bed of chocolate chips. Delightful Jelly Bean Bars are served with gift bags of small jelly beans. And the Tangy Lemon Tart, with its medley of citrus flavors and sprinkling of toasted coconut, provides a pleasing contrast to the rich textures of the other desserts.

SETTING THE STAGE

The colors and shapes of these sweet treats are so bright and appealing that they are almost enough decoration in themselves. See the individual recipes for presentation suggestions.

The Irresistible Ice Cream Bar

MAKES 16 GENEROUS SERVINGS

SPECIAL COOKWARE

4-ounce ice cream scoop

THE ICE CREAM

2 quarts chocolate–chocolate chip ice cream
   (or teen's pick)
2 quarts cookies-and-cream ice cream (or teen's pick)
2 quarts strawberry ice cream (or teen's pick)

THE CHOCOLATE-DIPPED CONES

1/2 pound semisweet chocolate, melted
24 sugar cones

THE FIXINGS

4 cups whipped cream (page 329 & 30; omit orange zest)
4 cups chocolate sauce (recipe follows)
2 cups toasted coconut (page 110)
2 cups of each of the following toppings: M&M's; Reese's
   Pieces; Heath Bar Crunch; crushed Oreos
2 cups rainbow sprinkles
4 cups small jelly beans

GARNISH

2 pounds assorted candy to cover buffet table

Chocolate Sauce

MAKES 4 CUPS OF SAUCE

1 pound German sweet cooking chocolate, coarsely chopped
2 cups whole milk
1 cup heavy cream
2 teaspoons pure vanilla extract

Simmer the chocolate and milk in a small saucepan for 15 minutes, until the chocolate has melted and the mixture is smooth. Still cooking gently, stir in the cream and vanilla extract and blend well. Do not let the mixture boil.

THE ICE CREAM

Scoop the ice cream with a 4-ounce scoop into balls. Place the balls on baking sheets lined with parchment paper or plastic wrap, cover the ice cream well with plastic, and freeze. (The portion amounts for this recipe are generous.)

CHOCOLATE-DIPPED CONES

1. Melt the semisweet chocolate over medium heat in the top of a double boiler. Remove from the heat and brush a 1 1/2-inch border of chocolate on the outside top of 16 cones (leave the rest of the cones for plain-cone lovers).

2. To set "or dry" the chocolate on the cones: Poke holes in the bottom of an egg carton and stand the cones straight, with their tips in the cups, until the chocolate dries, about 10 minutes. Store the cones at room temperature.

PREPARE THE FIXINGS

1. Keep the chocolate sauce warm over simmering water.

2. Store the whipped cream covered in the refrigerator.

3. Store the toasted coconut covered at room temperature.

FINISHING TOUCHES AND
TABLE PRESENTATION

Heap the three kinds of pre-scooped ice cream in three separate 3–4 quart bowls at least 6 inches deep with serving spoons, 15 minutes before you open the ice cream bar. Place sixteen 6-ounce dessert dishes, fruit bowls, or banana-split boats in front of the ice cream, with serving spoons. Arrange the empty cones in a wicker basket. Put some of the fixings in bowls with classic teaspoons. Place other toppings, such as the M&M's, in different-shaped candy jars of varying heights. Don't be surprised when the guests stop using the spoons and comfortably resort to pouring the fixin's in an avalanche of toppings over the ice cream. Scatter loose candy over the dessert table.

ONE-TOQUE: Place the ice cream at the beginning of the buffet. This is a truly casual celebration—a line at a busy buffet is expected and fun! Place the M&M pops and cookies next to the ice creams, followed by the peanut butter and jelly cookies. Set the goblets with strawberries and cream on silver platters with 16

dessert spoons. Place the Confetti Pretzels at the end of the buffet.

TWO-TOQUE: Place the Double-Chocolate Stuffed Sugar Cookie Sandwiches next to the ice cream, followed by the Jelly Bean Bars. Finish the fun with the Tangy Lemon Tarts surrounded by dessert forks and two cake servers. Place the Confetti Pretzels at the end of the buffet.

The Inventive Chef

ONCE THE CONES ARE DIPPED IN THE CHOCOLATE, WHILE THE CHOCOLATE IS STILL WET, ROLL A FEW CONES IN THE CRUMBLED CANDY, A FEW IN TOASTED COCONUT, AND SOME IN THE RAINBOW SPRINKLES. IT'S A GOOD IDEA TO LEAVE SOME CONES PLAIN FOR THOSE WHO WANT THE UNADULTERATED TASTE OF PURE ICE CREAM. IF YOU HAVE INVITED CARAMEL LOVERS, THE CARAMEL FONDUE (PAGE 327) MAKES A WONDERFUL ICE CREAM TOPPING.

THE MAIN EVENT

Confetti Pretzels

MAKES 36 CONFETTI PRETZELS,
ABOUT 2 PER PERSON

3 cups semisweet chocolate chips
2 (10-ounce) bags pretzel rods (approximately 36 pieces)

ASSORTED TOPPINGS
1/2 cup rainbow or chocolate sprinkles
1 cup mini marshmallows, halved

1 cup graham cracker bits
1 cup Rice Krispies
1/2 cup crushed toffee bits
1 cup mixed nuts (walnuts, pecans, and peanuts), coarsely
   chopped
1 cup butterscotch, white, or milk-chocolate chips

1. Melt the semisweet chocolate chips in the top of a
double boiler over simmering water.
2. Dip a pretzel stick into the melted chocolate to
come halfway up the stick. Place the toppings on
pieces of foil or wax paper. Roll the chocolate-covered
end of the stick into any mixture of toppings while
the chocolate is still soft. *(Be creative. Anything goes.)*
3. Place each coated pretzel on a baking sheet lined
with wax paper or aluminum foil as it is finished.
4. Chill the pretzels in the refrigerator for 30
minutes to set and harden the chocolate.

FINISHING TOUCHES AND TABLE PRESENTATION

Stack the pretzels in a rectangular basket with 2-inch
sides, the dipped ends pointing up.

The Inventive Chef

SINCE THIS IS A "TEENAGERS' PARTY," HAVE
THE "TEEN HOSTS" PREPARE THE CONFETTI
PRETZELS FOR THEIR FRIENDS.

ON THE SIDE

M & M Melt-in-Your-Mouth Cookie Pops

MAKES 20-24 LARGE COOKIES

1 tablespoon vegetable shortening
2 1/4 cups all-purpose flour
1 teaspoon baking soda
Pinch of salt
1/2 pound unsalted butter, at room temperature
2/3 cup granulated sugar
2/3 cup light brown sugar, firmly packed
2 teaspoons pure vanilla extract
2 large eggs
2 1/2 cups M&M chocolate candies
20-24 popsicle sticks or tongue depressors, about 4-5
   inches long (popsicle sticks can be found in large
   supermarkets; tongue depressors in the drugstore)

GARNISH
4 cups M&M's

1. Preheat the oven to 375°. Lightly grease 2 baking
sheets.
2. In a small bowl, combine the flour, baking soda,
and salt, and set aside.
3. In the bowl of an electric mixer fitted with the
paddle attachment, combine the butter, granulated and
brown sugars, and the vanilla. Beat the mixture on
high speed until it is light and creamy, about 2
minutes. Add the eggs and blend well.
4. Decrease the speed of the mixer to low and slowly
beat in the reserved dry ingredients until the batter is
well blended. Stir in the M&M's by hand.

5. Drop the batter in generous balls, about 3 tablespoons each, onto the baking sheets. Allow 4 inches between each cookie. Insert a popsicle stick into each ball of dough, making sure that the top of the stick is firmly embedded in the center.

6. Bake the cookies for 10 minutes. Check the cookies halfway through the baking process to ensure that the sticks have remained well embedded. If they have popped up, just give them a push down again. Remove the cookies from the oven and cool on the baking sheets for 3 minutes. Carefully remove the cookies with a metal spatula to a wire rack to finish cooling.

7. Repeat this process until all the batter has been used.

FINISHING TOUCHES AND TABLE PRESENTATION

Buy a 24-by-24-inch piece of Styrofoam and cover it with foil. Stick the pops into the foil. Sprinkle the surface of the foil with heaps of M&M's.

The Inventive Chef

REESE'S PIECES AND HEATH BAR CRUNCH MAKE FUN ADDITIONS OR SUBSTITUTIONS FOR THE M&M'S. DON'T STEP ON THE SCALE FOR TWO WEEKS!

ON THE SIDE

Peanut Butter and Jelly Crunchy Cookie Sandwiches

MAKES ABOUT 24 LARGE COOKIE SANDWICHES

3 1/2 cups all-purpose flour
1 1/2 cups granulated sugar
1 cup light brown sugar, firmly packed
2 teaspoons baking soda
2 teaspoons pure vanilla extract
1/2 pound unsalted butter, at room temperature
1 cup chunky peanut butter
2 eggs
1/4 cup whole milk
1 1/2 cups strawberry jelly

1. Preheat the oven to 375°.

2. Combine the flour, 1 cup of the granulated sugar, the brown sugar, baking soda, vanilla, butter, peanut butter, eggs, and milk in the bowl of an electric mixer fitted with the paddle attachment. Combine the ingredients on low speed until they are well blended, about 2–3 minutes.

3. Spread the remaining 1/2 cup of granulated sugar on a piece of foil. Form the cookie dough into 48 balls, using a 1-tablespoon measure. Coat the dough on all sides with the sugar.

4. Place the sugared balls on ungreased cookie sheets, 3 inches apart. Bake the cookies for 12 minutes, or until they look just crisp and not doughy. Continue to form and bake the cookies until all the batter has been used.

5. Remove the cookies from the oven and cool them on a wire rack. When the cookies have cooled, spread half the cookies with 1 tablespoon of strawberry jelly. Place the remaining cookies over the jelly, pressing the two cookies gently together, to form sandwiches.

FINISHING TOUCHES AND TABLE PRESENTATION

I like to gild the lily and place a jar of peanut butter, a jar of jelly, and a spreading knife around a large 14-inch platter or basket heaped with the cookies.

The Inventive Chef

I SPREAD PEANUT BUTTER WITH THE JELLY INSIDE THE COOKIES FOR MY HUSBAND. TRY IT—IT'S ADDICTIVE!

ON THE SIDE

Double-Chocolate Stuffed Sugar Cookie Sandwiches

MAKES ABOUT 36 SANDWICHES

3 1/4 cups all-purpose flour
2 1/2 teaspoons baking powder
1/4 teaspoon salt
12 tablespoons sweet butter, at room temperature
1 1/2 cups sugar
1 teaspoon banana extract
1 teaspoon pure vanilla extract
2 eggs
1 1/2 tablespoons heavy cream or whole milk

1 generous cup white chocolate chips
1 generous cup semisweet chocolate chips

GARNISH
1 cup semisweet chocolate chips
1 cup white chocolate chips

1. Preheat the oven to 350°.
2. Sift the flour together with the baking powder and salt. Set aside in a small bowl.
3. Cream the butter and sugar with the banana and vanilla extracts in the bowl of an electric mixer with the paddle attachment on medium speed until light and fluffy, about 2–3 minutes. Beat in the eggs, one at a time, along with small amounts of heavy cream.
4. Turn the mixer speed to low and gradually add the dry ingredients, beating until well blended. Divide the dough in half.
5. Place each half in the center of a piece of plastic wrap. Roll each half into a log 9 inches long by 2 inches wide. Refrigerate the dough until it is firm enough to slice, about 1 1/2–2 hours.
6. Cut each log into about three dozen 1/4-inch-thick circles. Place the circles, 2 inches apart, on ungreased baking sheets and bake for 8–12 minutes, until they are lightly golden.
7. While the cookies are still hot, flip half of them onto a clean baking sheet with a wide metal spatula, the underside facing up. Cover the surface of half the flipped cookies with a generous tablespoon each of white chocolate chips, and the other half with the semisweet chocolate chips. Be sure to spread the chips evenly over the entire surface of the cookies. (*The heat from the cookies will melt the chocolate.*)
8. Top the chocolate-covered cookies with the remaining plain cookies and press down gently to form

the sandwiches. *(If the chocolate does not melt completely, return the cookie sandwiches to a 250° oven for 2–3 minutes.)*

FINISHING TOUCHES AND TABLE PRESENTATION

Spread a layer of chocolate chips inside a 12–14-inch basket and arrange the cookies over the chips. What could be more outrageous?

> ## The Inventive Chef
>
> FOR AN AMUSING PRESENTATION, SPRINKLE THE INSIDE OF EACH COOKIE SANDWICH WITH BOTH WHITE AND DARK CHOCOLATE FOR A "WHITE-AND-DARK-CHOCOLATE COOKIE TREAT."

ON THE SIDE
Jelly Bean Bars

MAKES 16 BARS

SPECIAL COOKWARE
8-inch square baking pan

1 teaspoon unsalted butter
1 1/2 cups all-purpose flour
1 cup light brown sugar, firmly packed
1/2 cup granulated sugar
1 1/2 teaspoons baking powder
1/8 teaspoon salt
2 eggs
10 tablespoons melted unsalted butter, cooled to room temperature
2 teaspoons pure vanilla extract
1/2 cup small jelly beans

GARNISH
1 pound jelly beans
Small plastic bags and ties

1. Preheat the oven to 350°. Grease an 8-inch square pan with butter.
2. Blend together the flour, sugars, baking powder, and salt in a bowl. *(Make sure the brown sugar is free of lumps.)*
3. In another bowl, beat the eggs with a whisk until they are well blended. Gently whisk in the melted butter and vanilla.
4. Slowly pour the wet ingredients into the flour mixture, stirring until the batter is well blended. Mix the jelly beans into the batter, distributing them evenly, and pour the batter into the prepared pan.
5. Bake the cookies until the tops are golden, or a knife inserted in the center comes out clean, about 35–40 minutes. *(If sugar or a little moisture clings to the cake tester, don't be concerned; it is just from the melting jelly beans.)* Place the cake pan on a cooling rack for 45–60 minutes before cutting the cookies into sixteen 2-by-2-inch squares.

FINISHING TOUCHES AND TABLE PRESENTATION

Set the cookies on a tray. Fill the plastic bags with the loose jelly beans. Tie the bags into little bundles. Intersperse the bundles between the cookies on the tray.

> ## The Inventive Chef
>
> ADD 1/4 CUP SEMISWEET CHOCOLATE CHIPS TO THE JELLY BEANS IN THE BATTER FOR A LITTLE MORE SUGAR.

KITCHEN SCHEDULE

1 WEEK AHEAD

MAIN EVENT	Ice Cream Bar	Scoop ice cream and freeze as instructed.
		Buy candy fixings; set aside.
TOQUE 1	M&M Pops	Prepare through step 7; cool; freeze. Cover with waxed paper.
	PB&J Cookies	Prepare through step 4; cool; freeze.
	Strawberries	Prepare praline crunch through step 4; set aside at room temperature.
TOQUE 2	Chocolate Cookies	Prepare through step 8; cool; freeze.
	Bars	Prepare through step 5; cool; wrap in plastic wrap and freeze. Set up jelly bean bags for garnish as in finishing touches.

THE DAY BEFORE THE PARTY

MAIN EVENT	Ice Cream Bar	Prepare chocolate-dipped cones through step 2; store covered at room temperature.
		Prepare chocolate sauce; store covered in refrigerator.
		Prepare coconut; store covered at room temperature.
		Arrange all candy fixings.
	Pretzels	Prepare through step 4; Store covered at room temperature.
TOQUE 1	Strawberries	Cut and refrigerate.
TOQUE 2	Tart	Prepare and bake shell. Make custard, cool, and fill tart. Store covered in refrigerator.
Strategic Maneuvers:		Fill creamers. Cover. Store in refrigerator.
		Set up buffet table and decor; scatter top of table with candy.
		Check ice and beverages.

THE DAY OF THE PARTY

MAIN EVENT	Ice Cream Bar	Whip cream; place cream and coconut in bowls.
		Set chocolate sauce in top of double boiler for reheating.
		Arrange cones and candy as in finishing touches and bring to table.
	Pretzels	Arrange as in finishing touches and bring to table.
TOQUE 1	M&M Pops	Defrost and arrange as in finishing touches.
	PB&J Cookies	Defrost. Prepare step 5 and arrange as in finishing touches.
	Strawberries	Wash, stem, and cut berries. Whip the cream as in step 5; fill goblets with berries and cream as in finishing touches; do not top with final layer of praline; store covered in refrigerator.
TOQUE 2	Chocolate Cookies	Defrost. Arrange as in finishing touches.
	Bars	Defrost. Arrange as in finishing touches.

30 MINUTES BEFORE GUESTS ARRIVE:

Place ice cream in bowls and refrigerate.

15 MINUTES BEFORE GUESTS ARRIVE:

Top strawberries with final layer of praline.
Put out all remaining foods.

Basics of Beverage Service (And a Few Delicious Drinks)

There are literally dozens of delicious party beverages and drinks—alcoholic and nonalcoholic, hot and cold, plain and fancy. Sometimes I serve hot rum toddies, at other times I make minted ice tea; some occasions are perfect for hot chocolate and Bailey's Irish Cream, other events just call out for martinis and glasses of straw-berry-citrus punch.

The important thing is to choose beverages that fit the occasion, complement the meal, and are in tune with the season. For a leisurely Saturday-night dinner with friends, a cocktail hour with mixed drinks and hors d'oeuvre provides a sophisticated start to the evening. If this is a family party with children, you may choose to serve wine only, as opposed to mixed drinks. If the party is by the pool on a hot summer afternoon, you may want to offer cold beer only.

Throughout the menus in this book, I have made suggestions for beverages that will enhance the mood *and* the food of your party. In this chapter, I want to share a few tips on beverage service, based on my professional experience. These will be especially useful for large events, but are worth considering even when you are en-tertaining just a few people. I also share recipes for a few

of my favorite beverages. (The recipes are for 8 servings, but they can be easily multiplied to serve larger groups.)

THE BAR AND BASIC EQUIPMENT

Your "bar" can be any surface that will hold the neces-sities to make and serve the drinks. Possibilities include sideboards, tea carts, desks, workbenches, bridge tables, folding tables—or you might have a built-in bar in your home already.

The capacity you need will vary with the number of guests. For a party of 8 people, a bar surface of 2 feet by 3 feet (a total of 6 square feet) will be adequate. For a party of 16, a surface of 8 square feet would suffice—the additional space will be used for extra glasses. Also, remember that you don't have to put everything on the bar at once. Backup bottles can be kept hidden under the table; wine can be chilled in an ice chest under the table. Try and have everything you might need under the table or ready nearby so you don't have to stop and run in the middle of the party.

Locating the Bar

Have you noticed that people have a tendency to get their drink and then stay and talk at the bar? In the catering business, we are very aware of this habit, and we are careful to locate the bar so that it doesn't clog up the movement of the party. In your home, it is very important that the bar be set up away from the guests' entrance, that it not be in a hallway or corridor, nor in any location that blocks access to the kitchen or other party areas.

Try to place the bar in the back of the main entertaining room. If possible, allow room for you to stand behind it (as a bartender would) both to serve guests and to provide access to the backup supplies stored under the table.

Note that there's spillage and wear and tear on a bar surface. If you are using a piece of furniture with a surface that is not treated, be sure to cover it with a folded or draped tablecloth or a protective glass top.

Bar Equipment

Here's a list of the equipment you'll need to properly serve drinks:

1. Ice bucket: It is okay to substitute a glass bowl, but then keep the main ice supply in a chest below the bar and put just a small amount in the bowl at the last minute.

2. Ice tongs: I personally prefer using my hands—but it depends on how well you know the guests.

3. Corkscrew, for wine.

4. Bottle opener, for mixers and soft drinks.

5. Paring or fruit knife.

6. Cocktail napkins.

7. Small towel.

8. Small sponge.

9. Small dish for bottle caps, etc.

10. Small wastebasket (if possible hidden under the bar or nearby out of sight).

11. Glasses:

Quantity: 2 or 3 per guest, plus a reasonable number of extras.

Kinds: Champagne must be served in flutes. Otherwise, it is perfectly appropriate, as well as practical, to serve all *other* drinks in stemmed wine glasses. This makes for a simpler and neater bar setup and fewer total glasses. If you don't have enough stem glasses, it might be a good investment to buy some inexpensive ones. Many restaurant-supply houses will sell directly to the consumer, or sometimes have retail hours.

Setting Up the Bar in Advance

To be a guest and not a bartender, try to do as much as possible before the guests come:

1. Open a number of wine bottles in advance. For white wine, put the cork back; for red wine, you may want to let it breathe or decant it. Chill white wine in refrigerator or ice chest. Separate the dinner wine from the bar wine.

2. Cut lemon peels and lime and lemon wedges. Place in small dishes or glasses.

3. Wipe and set out glasses.

4. Place some glasses for vodka and beer in freezer; place bottle of vodka in freezer.

5. Set liquor and mixers on bar and backup supplies below bar.

6. Put out all miscellaneous items (cocktail napkins, etc.).

TIPS FOR MIXING AND SERVING ALCOHOLIC DRINKS

• *The key to an enjoyable mixed drink is the amount of ice used.* All drinks requiring ice should have the glass $^2/_3$ full with ice before the drink is poured. A small amount of ice melts too quickly, leaving you with a warm, diluted drink. A full glass of ice keeps the ice cubes whole and the drink fresh.

• Mixing drinks: First add the ice to $^2/_3$ full, then the alcohol to about $^1/_3$ up the ice. Do not measure—it is gauche and time-consuming. Finally add the mixers to fill up the glass up to $^3/_4$ inch below the top.

• On the rocks: The drink is poured to the top of the ice and nothing is added unless a splash of water or soda is requested, or appropriate bar fruit.

• In all cases, serve the drink with a cocktail napkin under it, or encourage your guests to take a cocktail napkin by having them at the ready.

TIPS FOR SERVING WINE

• When serving wine at the bar, pour it into a stemmed glass, $^1/_3$–$^1/_2$ full.

• When serving wine at the dinner table, you can do one of the following: pour the wine as the host; ask a guest to "do the honors"; put bottles on the table (on a wine holder or a dish) so guests will pour for themselves.

• If you are serving more than one kind of wine, place one bottle of each kind.

• When pouring champagne, pour slowly into a flute and fill it almost to the top.

• When serving cordials, pour a very small amount into a brandy snifter, special cordial glass, or a stemmed glass. Cordials are to be sipped slowly.

A FEW WORDS OF CAUTION TO THE HOST

It is your moral (and in many instances legal) responsibility to not serve any guests who appear to have had too much alcohol. In addition to not serving more, you should be sure they are not driving! This is sometimes difficult, but a responsibility you cannot avoid.

GUIDE TO SUGGESTED LIQUOR, WINE, AND BEVERAGE QUANTITIES

There are no absolute rules as to how much liquor, wine, and other beverages you will need for an event. Variables such as time of year, nature of occasion, age of guests, and personal habits all affect quantities consumed. It is always safer to over-buy than to under-buy, especially as most liquor stores will accept unopened returns if requested in advance.

Also, as you budget your event, remember that the true cost is what you consume or waste, not what is left over for another time. If you pay eighteen dollars for a bottle of vodka and have $^{2}/_{3}$ left over, it has cost you only six dollars; the other twelve dollars is in your inventory. Mixed drinks generally are no more expensive than wine and beer, because people generally consume fewer mixed drinks.

The following guidelines are designed to cover all needs for a cocktail hour with a full choice of spirits and wines, wines served with dinner, and even after-dinner cordials.

SUGGESTED QUANTITIES FOR ONE-HOUR OPEN BAR BEFORE DINNER

LIQUOR

(EACH LITER BOTTLE SERVES 16 GENEROUS DRINKS)

Item	Number of Guests	Estimated Quantity Needed
Scotch	up to 24	1 liter
Vodka	up to 16♦	1 liter
Gin	up to 32	1 liter
Bourbon	up to 48	1 liter
Blended Whiskey	up to 48	1 liter
Dark rum (not necessary)	up to 48♦	1 liter
Dry vermouth (for martinis)	up to 50	1 (375 milliliter) bottle

♦ Quantities for vodka and rum will increase if you serve Bloody Marys at brunch or rum punch at a summer party.

BAR WINES

(EACH STANDARD 750 MILLILITER BOTTLE SERVES 6 GLASSES)

WITH OTHER ALCOHOLIC BEVERAGES

Item	No. Guests	Est. Quantity
White	up to 6	1 bottle
Red	up to 12	1 bottle
Champagne	up to 6	1 bottle
Beer	up to 24	1 six-pack♦

WITH NO OTHER ALCOHOLIC BEVERAGES

Item	No. Guests	Est. Quantity
White	up to 3	1 bottle
Red	up to 3	1 bottle
Champagne	up to 3	1 bottle
Beer	up to 12	1 six pack♦

♦Double for a younger group

SUGGESTED QUANTITIES FOR DINNER WINES, CHAMPAGNE, AND DESSERT WINE

Wine

Let the experts at your wine and liquor store help you choose wines to enhance your menu. Bring your menu to the store, with an estimate of the number of guests, and your plans for beverage service. Remember, you can choose to serve one wine for the entire meal or a different wine with each course.

Item	When Serving	No. Guests	Est. Quantity
White, Red Rosé or champagne	1 wine only	every 2 guests	1 (750 milliliter) bottle
	2 wines	every 3 guests	1 (750 milliliter) bottle of each
	3 wines	every 4 guests	1 (750 milliliter) bottle of each
Dessert wine		every 6 guests	1 bottle

After-Dinner Cordials

♦ After-dinner cordials are a sophisticated way to continue a relaxed evening. It is a nice change of pace to leave the dining-room table and to serve the cordials in another room.

♦ You do not need a wide choice of cordials, and never more than one bottle of each unless you are having over one hundred guests.

♦ Suggest you choose one bottle from three of the following categories:

brandy; fruit liqueur; anisette; coffee liqueur (such as Kahlúa); Irish cream; Crème de Menthe.

Again, your wine merchant can make suggestions in various price ranges.

QUANTITY GUIDE TO NONALCOHOLIC BEVERAGES, BAR FRUITS, AND ICE

Soft drinks, fruit juices, fruit garnishes, and plenty of ice are essential items for any large party.

Soft Drinks

I suggest buying small bottles or cans, which, while more expensive, will avoid waste and store more easily than large bottles.

Item	No. Guests	Est. Quantity
Tonic water	up to 8	1 six-pack
Club soda	up to 8	3 12-ounce bottles/cans
Sparkling water	up to 8	3 12-ounce bottles/cans
Cola	up to 8	3 12-ounce bottles/cans
Diet cola	up to 8	3 12-ounce bottles/cans
Ginger ale	up to 8	3 12-ounce bottles/cans
Diet ginger ale	up to 8	3 12-ounce bottles/cans

Fruit Juices

These are generally purchased in cans or jars. They will look more attractive if you transfer them to pitchers. However, if you display juices in pitchers, you will use more because they are more appealing, and the power of suggestion is at work.

(CHOOSE TWO FROM THE FOLLOWING LIST)

Item	Special Purpose	No. of Guests	Est. Quantity
Orange	Mixed with vodka, gin, or rum	8	2 gallons
Grapefruit	Mixed with vodka, gin, or rum	8	2 gallons
Cranberry	Mixed with vodka or gin	8	2 gallons
Pineapple	Mixed with rum	8	2 gallons
Tomato	Bloody Marys	8	2 gallons

Fruits

Item	Special Purpose	No. Guests	Est. Quantity
Lemon wedges	Mixed drinks	8	3 large lemons
Lemon peel or	On the rocks	8	1 large lemon
Lime wedges	Mixed drinks	8	3 large limes
Lime peel	On the rocks	8	1 large lime
Olives	Martinis	8	1 small jar green olives
Cherries	Politically incorrect because of red dye used		

Ice

- As mentioned before, ice for the drinks and ice for chilling white wine (if the refrigerator is full) are both essential.

- Quantities vary depending on climate and drink usage as well as refrigerator chilling capacity.

- Safe rule: 2–3 pounds per person for all purposes. You can make ice in advance and store it in your freezer or buy commercially produced ice.

Strawberry Citrus Punch

SERVES 8

1¹/2 cups sliced, sweetened frozen strawberries with their
   syrup, defrosted
1¹/2 cups frozen lemonade concentrate, defrosted
¹/4 cup fresh lime juice
5 cups ginger ale, chilled

1. In a punch bowl or a large pitcher, stir to combine the strawberries with their syrup, the lemonade concentrate, and the lime juice.
2. Just before service, add the ginger ale and mix well.

GARNISH FOR INDIVIDUAL SERVINGS

8 beautiful, medium-size strawberries, washed and left
   whole
8 (¹/4-inch) lemon rounds, seeds removed

1. With a sharp knife, make a ¹/2-inch incision in the bottom of each strawberry and a ¹/4-inch cut into each lemon round. Secure a strawberry and a slice of lemon on the rim of each glass by fitting the small cut in the fruits over the rim of the glass.

GARNISH FOR PUNCH BOWL

SPECIAL COOKWARE

1 ring mold (at least 8-cup size)

4 large strawberries, washed and sliced in half lengthwise
4 (¹/4-inch) lemon rounds, seeds removed
6–8 cups ginger ale

1. Lay the strawberries and lemon rounds decoratively around the bottom of the ring mold. Gently pour about 2 cups of ginger ale into the mold so that the fruits are just barely floating. Place the mold into the freezer, being careful not to disturb the fruits. When the ginger ale has frozen, top it with the remaining ginger ale and return to the freezer until frozen solid.
2. To unmold the ring: Invert the mold under hot running water and catch the ice mold on a tray. Float the ice as a pretty and practical garnish in your punch bowl. The mold will help keep your punch cold without making it watery.

Margaritas with a Hint of Cranberry

SERVES 8

1 1/2 cups (12 ounces) tequila
1 3/4 cups (14 ounces) sour mix
1/2 cup (4 ounces) triple sec or Curaçao
1/2 cup (4 ounces) fresh lime juice
1/2 cup (4 ounces) cranberry juice

GARNISH
1 lime cut into 8 slices

1. In a 2-quart pitcher, combine the tequila, sour mix, triple sec, lime juice, and cranberry juice; stir to blend. Serve chilled, in glasses filled with ice, garnished with a perfect slice of lime.

The Inventive Chef

TO SERVE WITH SALT: RUN A WEDGE OF LIME AROUND THE RIM OF THE GLASS. FROST THE RIM BY TURNING THE GLASS UPSIDE DOWN INTO A PLATE OF SALT BEFORE FILLING IT WITH ICE AND THE MARGARITA.

Mint Juleps

SERVES 8

1 cup sugar
1/2 cup water

2 cups (16 ounces) bourbon
1/2 cup finely chopped fresh mint

1. Make a sugar syrup by combining the sugar and water in a small saucepan over medium heat. Simmer for 5–7 minutes, stirring occasionally, until the mixture is a syrupy consistency. Cool and refrigerate, covered, for at least 1 hour.
2. In a pitcher, combine the bourbon, 1/2 cup of the chilled sugar syrup and the mint leaves. Stir to mix and cover with plastic wrap. Allow the mint to steep 30–60 minutes (depending on how strong a mint taste you like) before straining it out of the drink by passing it through a fine mesh strainer.
3. Serve the juleps over crushed ice or on the rocks, and garnish each glass with a sprig of mint.

The Inventive Chef

UNUSED SUGAR SYRUP CAN BE STORED IN REFRIGERATOR FOR LATER USE.

Champagne Punch for a Festive Occasion

MAKES OVER 2 1/2 QUARTS, TO SERVE 8

1/2 cup triple sec or Curaçao
1/2 cup Chambord or black raspberry liqueur
1 cup chilled unsweetened pineapple juice
1 cup chilled white grape juice
3 cups chilled ginger ale
1 chilled (750 milliliter) bottle dry champagne

1 ring mold, 8-cup size
1 pint fresh raspberries or blackberries
4 pineapple circles
6–8 cups ginger ale

1. In a punch bowl, combine the triple sec, Chambord, and pineapple and white grape juices. Just before service, add the ginger ale and champagne.
2. Garnish with an ice ring mold (page 354), substituting raspberries or blackberries and fresh pineapple circles for the strawberries and lemons.
3. Be sure to have a second bottle of chilled champagne on hand. As the punch sits, more bubbly should be added.

Bellinis

SERVES 8

10 fresh ripe peaches, peeled, pitted, and sliced, or 1 1/2 pounds (3 cups) canned sliced peaches without their syrup
5 ounces chilled peach schnapps
1 bottle chilled brut champagne, 750 milliliters

GARNISH
8 peach slices
8 mint sprigs

1. Place the peaches and peach schnapps into a blender and puree until smooth. This mixture can either be covered and refrigerated for up to 1 1/2 hours or mixed into drinks right away.

2. At time of service, gently blend the champagne with the peach puree. Serve in champagne flutes.
3. Place 1 slice of fresh ripe peach and a small mint sprig on the rim of each glass.

Bloody Marys

SERVES 8

1–1 1/4 cups (8–10 ounces) chilled vodka (depending on taste)
3 cups (24 ounces) chilled tomato juice
3/8 cup (3 ounces) fresh lemon juice
1/4 cup (2 ounces) fresh lime juice
1/2 teaspoon Tabasco sauce
1/2 teaspoon Worcestershire sauce
1/4 teaspoon salt
1/4 teaspoon pepper
1 teaspoon horseradish, squeezed dry

GARNISH
8 slices lime, 1/4-inch thick, cut to fit over the rim of the glass
8 slices lemon, 1/4-inch thick, cut to fit over the rim of the glass

1. In a large pitcher, combine the vodka, tomato juice, the lemon and lime juices, the Tabasco and Worcestershire sauces, the salt, pepper, and horseradish. Stir to mix.
2. Serve over rocks or chilled straight up in large wineglasses, garnished with slices of lime and lemon.

Sunrise Mimosas

SERVES 8

1 1/2 cups (12 ounces) fresh orange juice, chilled
2 cups (16 ounces) apricot nectar, chilled
3 tablespoons (1 1/2 ounces) apricot brandy, chilled
1 bottle champagne, chilled, 750 milliliters

GARNISH

1/2 cup fresh orange juice
8 small dried apricots
8 small fresh mint sprigs

1. In a large pitcher, stir together the orange juice, apricot nectar, and brandy. Either cover with plastic wrap and store in refrigerator for up to 2 hours or use immediately.

2. At time of service, pour the juice mixture into 8 large chilled wineglasses. Fill each glass with the champagne and stir gently.

3. To prepare the garnish, bring the 1/2 cup of orange juice to a boil in a small saucepan and remove from the heat. Place the dried apricots in the hot orange juice to soak for 5–8 minutes. Drain well. Make a small slit in each apricot and slide one onto the rim of each glass, accompanied by a sprig of fresh mint.

Peach Sangria

SERVES 8

6 ripe peaches, peeled, pitted, and coarsely chopped
3 tablespoons sugar, or to taste
4 ounces peach schnapps

750 milliliter white wine, such as Soave
2 oranges thinly sliced (about 1/8 inch), seeds removed
2 lemons, thinly sliced (about 1/8 inch), seeds removed
2 limes, thinly sliced (about 1/8 inch), seeds removed
2 quarts club soda, chilled

1. Puree the peaches with the sugar and peach schnapps in a blender.

2. In one extra-large (1 1/2-gallon) or in two large (3-quart) pitchers, combine the peach puree with the wine and the orange, lemon, and lime slices. Cover and refrigerate at least overnight or for up to 2 days.

3. When ready to serve, gently stir the chilled club soda into the sangria and set out highball glasses.

Vodka Martinis, Very Dry

SERVES 8

2 tablespoons coarsely grated fresh horseradish
12 ounces plain or peppered vodka, chilled in freezer
1 ounce dry vermouth

GARNISH

8 pitted green cocktail olives

1. Fill a cocktail shaker, with a strainer attachment, with ice cubes.

2. Place the horseradish, vodka, and vermouth in the shaker. Stir until the vodka is chilled, about 30–45 seconds.

3. Strain the martini into 8 chilled martini glasses and place an olive in each glass.

Garnishes

My golden rule for garnishes is that they "reflect the ingredients" in the recipes they adorn. If fresh rosemary is used in a lamb recipe, for example, garnish the lamb with sprigs of fresh rosemary. Buffet enhancements, such as whole bulbs of roasted garlic nestled into bouquets of fresh basil for the Italian buffet, should dramatize the theme of the menu. Whole and sliced broiled turkey sausages with red and yellow bell peppers, some whole and some opened to show the beauty of the inside of a pepper, mirror the flavors of a merry buffet. The Blood Orange Crème Brûlée (page 89), is garnished on the underliner plate with sections of blood orange. Use your imagination when designing the decor of the table and plate, but make sure the garnish is an integral part of the food.

FRUITS AND NUTS

Lemon wedges: for fish, shellfish, and roast chicken.
Dried apricots: for cheese hors d'oeuvre.
Stemmed or large strawberries: for dessert buffets.
Fresh figs, cut in half: to decorate baked fruits.
Papaya, open with seeds: to decorate Asian buffets with other fruits such as pineapple halves, litchi nuts, and mandarin oranges.

VEGETABLES AND HERBS

Garlic braids (available in specialty gourmet shops): perfect for an Italian buffet.
Fresh vegetables, whole and halved: to decorate all buffets.
Fern tops of fennel bulbs.
Fresh basil.
Fresh curly or flat-leaf parsley.
Fresh rosemary.
Fresh tarragon.
Fresh dill.
Fresh mint.

ASIAN THEMES

Bamboo steamers.
Fans.
Chopsticks.
Sake cups.
Tins of tea.
Kumquats, fresh.

SEAFOOD THEMES

Steamed and whole shellfish (crabs, clams, lobsters, shrimp in shell, langoustines), placed over seaweed (available at specialty fish stores).

Seashells (find them on the beach or ask the fishmonger).

Lemons, quartered and whole.

Oysterette soda crackers, in baskets.

Fishnetting, placed over the tablecloth.

MEDITERRANEAN

Bowls of **black and green olives.**

Bowls of **feta cheese.**

Whole tomatoes with stems.

Sun-dried tomatoes.

Red, orange, and yellow bell peppers.

Grape leaves in jars (available in supermarkets or specialty food stores).

Fresh pastas set in different-shaped containers.

Whole breads of different grains and sizes.

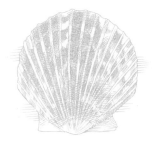

Kitchen Equipment

COOKWARE

6-inch skillet or sauté pan
8–10-inch skillet or sauté pan
12-inch skillet or sauté pan
14–16-inch skillet or sauté pan
1–2-quart heavy-bottomed saucepan with lid
$2^1/_2$–$3^1/_2$-quart heavy-bottomed saucepan with lid
4–6-quart heavy-bottomed saucepan with lid
8–10-quart stockpot with lid
2-quart oven-to-table flameproof casserole or Dutch oven with lid
3–4-quart oven-to-table flameproof casserole with lid
$4^1/_2$–6-quart oven-to-table flameproof casserole with lid
6–8-quart oven-to-table flameproof casserole with lid
10–12-inch wok
2-quart or larger stainless steel double boiler•
2 large roasting pans (at least 14 by 10 by 2 inches)
1 extra-large roasting pan ($16^1/_2$ by 11 by $2^1/_2$ inches)

•A note on double boilers: This size double boiler is indispensable for melting chocolate and heating delicate sauces. When it is necessary to use a double boiler to reheat larger amounts of already-prepared foods and you do not own one, "nest" a saucepan of food within a larger saucepan filled with a few inches of simmering water. This method will allow the food to heat gently without burning.

BAKEWARE

2 (2–3 quart) soufflé dishes
12-cup nonstick muffin tin
Nonstick loaf pan ($8^1/_2$ by 4 by $2^1/_2$ inches)
2–4 baking sheets with sides (at least $15^1/_2$ by $10^1/_2$ by 1 inch)
2–3 (8–9-inch) round cake pans
9–10-inch springform pan
2 (9–10-inch) tart or quiche pans with removable bottoms
9-inch pie plate
9–10-inch tube pan with or without a removable bottom (angel food cake pan)
8 (6–8-ounce) ceramic heatproof ramekins (custard cups)
2 (2–3-quart) oven-to-table baking dishes
Set of graduated mixing bowls:
      1–2 quarts
      3–5 quarts
      6–8 quarts
      10 quarts
Assorted metal cooling racks
Large decorative oven-to-table baking dish (12 by 9 by 2 inches)

KNIVES

3 1/2–4 1/2-inch paring or utility knife
8-inch carving knife
8–12-inch chef's knife
8–10-inch serrated bread knife
Electric knife sharpener or sharpening steel

APPLIANCES

Electric mixer with two bowls, paddle, and whip attachments
Food processor with cutting-blade and grating-disk attachments
Gas or charcoal grill
Handheld immersion blender
Blender
Coffeemaker

KITCHEN GADGETRY

Apple corer
Basting syringe
Berry huller
Biscuit cutters (fluted and smooth-edged), 1 1/2–4 inches
Bottle opener
Butcher's twine
Candy thermometer
Can opener
Colander
Corkscrew
Cutting board(s)
Deep-fat-frying thermometer
Flour sifter
Food mill
Funnel
Garlic press
Hand-grater with coarse and fine sides

Hand-juicer
Ice cream scoop (4 ounces)
Kitchen scissors
Kitchen timer
Ladle (6–8 ounces)
Lobster cracker
Measuring cups (graduated, for dry ingredients)
Measuring cups, glass or plastic (graduated, for liquid ingredients)
Meat fork (long, two-pronged)
Meat thermometer
Mesh strainer(s) (fine)
Metal tongs
Oven thermometer
Pastry bag with assorted tips
Pastry blender
Pastry brush(es)
Pastry or bench scraper
Pepper mill
Potato ricer
Rolling pin
Salad spinner
Spatula (flat metal)
Spatula (offset metal)
Spatula (rubber)
Spray bottle
Spreader knife (flat, small)
Squeeze bottle
Vegetable brush
Vegetable peeler
Vegetable steamer basket
Wire whisk (medium)
Wooden spoons

Not to mention . . . paper towels, plastic wrap, aluminum foil, parchment paper and waxed paper, garbage bags, plastic storage bags with ties, 6–8-inch wooden skewers, assorted toothpicks, cheesecloth.

Table Settings

INITIAL TABLE SETTING ◆

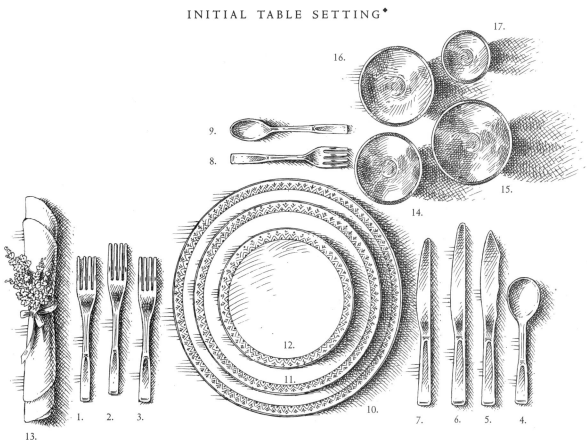

Flatware

1. Fish fork
2. Dinner fork
3. Salad fork
4. Soup spoon
5. Fish knife
6. Dinner knife
7. Salad knife
8. Dessert fork
9. Dessert spoon

Dishes

10. Charger or set plate
11. 8–9-inch soup underliner or fish plate or salad plate
12. Soup plate
13. Napkin (tied with fresh herbs), to the left of fish fork

Glasses

14. Water glass
15. White wine glass
16. Red wine glass
17. Champagne flute

◆Omitted from initial table setting: plates for subsequent courses (dinner plate, dessert plate, cup and saucer).

INDEX

Peanut Butter and Jelly Crunchy Cookie
    Sandwiches, 344–45
Pear Clafouti, 334–35
Pear Custard with Apricot Sauce, 252
Praline Cheesecake with an Oatmeal
    Crust, 141–42
Raspberry Cheesecake Squares, 320
Rice Pudding with Sambuca-Drenched
    Raisins, 167–68
Sour Cherry Cake with Black Cherry
    Ice Cream, 54–55
Spiced Fruit Crumble, 64–65
Tangy Lemon Tart, 110–11
Toasted Hazelnut Cookie Cups, 335–
    36
White and Dark Chocolate-Dipped
    Strawberries, 305
Zebra Cake, 330–31
Dinners, buffet, 14–15, 129–85
    Asian, 171–82
    brunch, 17, 19
    centerpieces for, 130, 159, 173
    costs, 15
    dessert, 18
    dinnerware for, 159
    formal, 20
    Italian, 157–69
    lap-service, 19, 20, 173
    linens for, 27
    menus, 129–85
    planning, 130–31
    seated, 20, 80
Dinners, casual, 14, 35–78
    centerpieces for, 38, 47, 59, 69
    dinnerware for, 38, 47, 60
    family, 14, 16, 19, 219–55
    finishing touches, 40, 41, 43
    linens for, 38
    menus, 35–78
    number of guests, 14, 19–21
Dinners, family-style, 14, 16, 19, 219–55
    centerpieces for, 232–33
    Italian, 232–42
    menus, 219–55
Dinners, formal, 14, 79–127
    announcing, 25–26
    centerpieces for, 82–83, 94, 106, 115,
        116
    dinnerware for, 82
    glassware for, 27
    linens for, 27, 82
    menus, 79–127, 219–55

number of guests, 14, 19–21
    seating, 80
Double-Chocolate Stuffed Sugar Cookie
    Sandwiches, 345–46
Dressings
    Arugula, Lemon, and Garlic Vinaigrette,
        138–39
    Calvados Mustard Vinaigrette, 72
    Lemon-Lime Vinaigrette, 202
    Mint Vinaigrette, 264
    Oven-Roasted Garlic-Basil Vinaigrette, 87
    Sour Cream, 61
Dried Cran-apple Chutney, 246
Drunken Shrimp with Cilantro and Tequila,
    296–97
Duck
    Cherry-Glazed Duck Breasts with Tart
        Mango Chutney, 70
    cracklings, 71

Eggplant
    Eggplant and Whit Bean "Lasagna,"
        165–66
    Marinated Eggplant, Red Peppers, Spiced
        Olives, and Feta Cheese, 137
    Minted Couscous with Sautéed Eggplant,
        Zucchini, and Currants, 109–10
    Pasta Caprese, 161–62
    Roasted Red Pepper and Eggplant Soup,
        118
Eggs
    Herbed Sausage Frittata, 261–62
    Parsley-Dusted Wild Mushroom-Stuffed
        Eggs, 315–16
    Smoked Bacon, Vegetable, and Cheddar
        Egg Custard, 275–76
Endive, Watercress, Baby Carrot, and Spiced
    Raisin Salad, 263
Endive with Roasted Asparagus, Ribbons of
    Cantaloupe, 86
Entertaining
    brunches, 257–90
    budgets, 21
    business, 22, 309–22
    casual dinners, 35–78
    date and time, 24–25
    decorations for, 28
    dessert parties, 323–47
    family-style dinners, 219–55
    flow in, 10, 26
    formal dinners, 79–127
    formats, 13–18

game plans for, 12, 13, 16, 23–31
    holiday, 16, 259–69
    hors d'oeuvre parties, 291–322
    invitations, 25–26
    menu design, 26
    preparation for, 10
    principles of, 9–12
    purpose of, 22
    room preparation, 28
    shopping for, 29
    site capacity, 19–21
    spirit of, 9, 10
    timing, 18
Entrees
    Abigail's Top Secret Brisket of Beef,
        223–24
    Baked Acorn Squash and Savory Ham,
        283–84
    Banana-Walnut and Brown Sugar
        Pancakes with Banana-Studded Maple
        Syrup, 272
    Black-and-White Sesame Wontons, 313
    Cajun-Rubbed Grilled Shrimp and Sea
        Scallops, 210–11
    Cherry-Glazed Duck Breasts with Tart
        Mango Chutney, 70
    Citrus-Scented Broiled Salmon, 135
    Cranberry-Glazed Cornish Hen, 95–96
    Exotically Spiced Moroccan Lamb, 106–7
    Fried Malaysian Chicken, 174–75
    Gingered Beef Kabobs with Pineapple
        Chutney, 311–12
    Grilled New York Strip Steaks, Sautéed
        Onions, and Champagne, 198
    Grilled Swordfish and Red Onion-Raisin
        Marmalade, 188
    Herbed Sausage Frittata, 261–62
    Lemon-Roasted Chicken, 48
    Lobster Corn Pudding, 147–48
    Mushroom-Studded Panfried "Ham"
        Burgers, 148–49
    Osso Buco Braised in Red Wine with
        Thyme, 39
    Oven-Roasted Tuscan Tuna with Chunky
        Tomato Sauce, 233
    Peach-Glazed Skewered Chicken, 149–
        50
    Rib Roast of Beef, 83
    Roasted Breast of Veal, 134–35
    Rock Cornish Hens, Pancetta, and
        Mushrooms, 160–61
    Spicy Barbecued Spareribs, 209–10